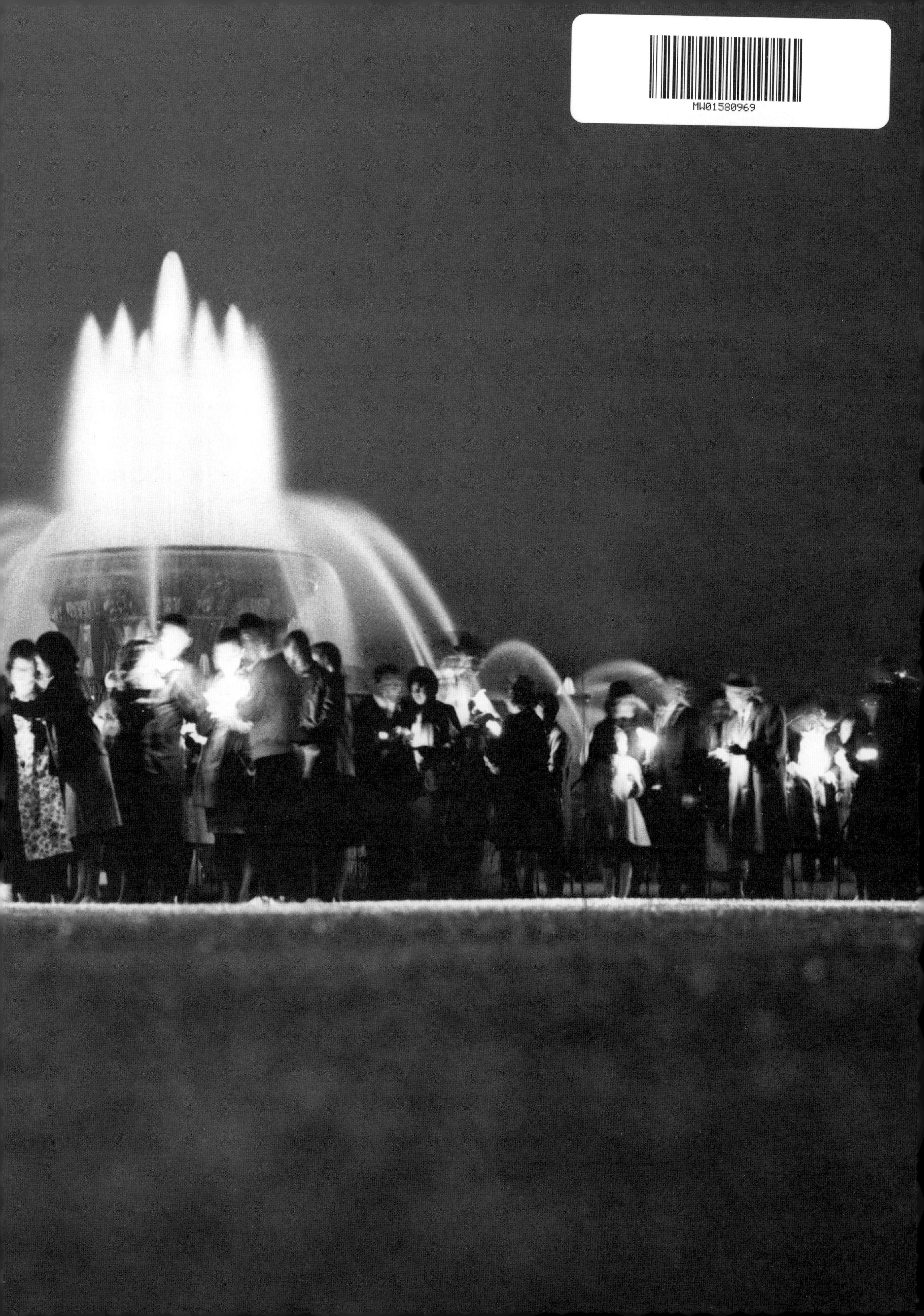

CHICAGO EXPOSED

CHICAGO EXPOSED

DEFINING MOMENTS FROM THE CHICAGO SUN-TIMES PHOTO ARCHIVE

Edited by Richard Cahan and Michael Williams
Introduction by Lee Bey
Foreword by John Russick

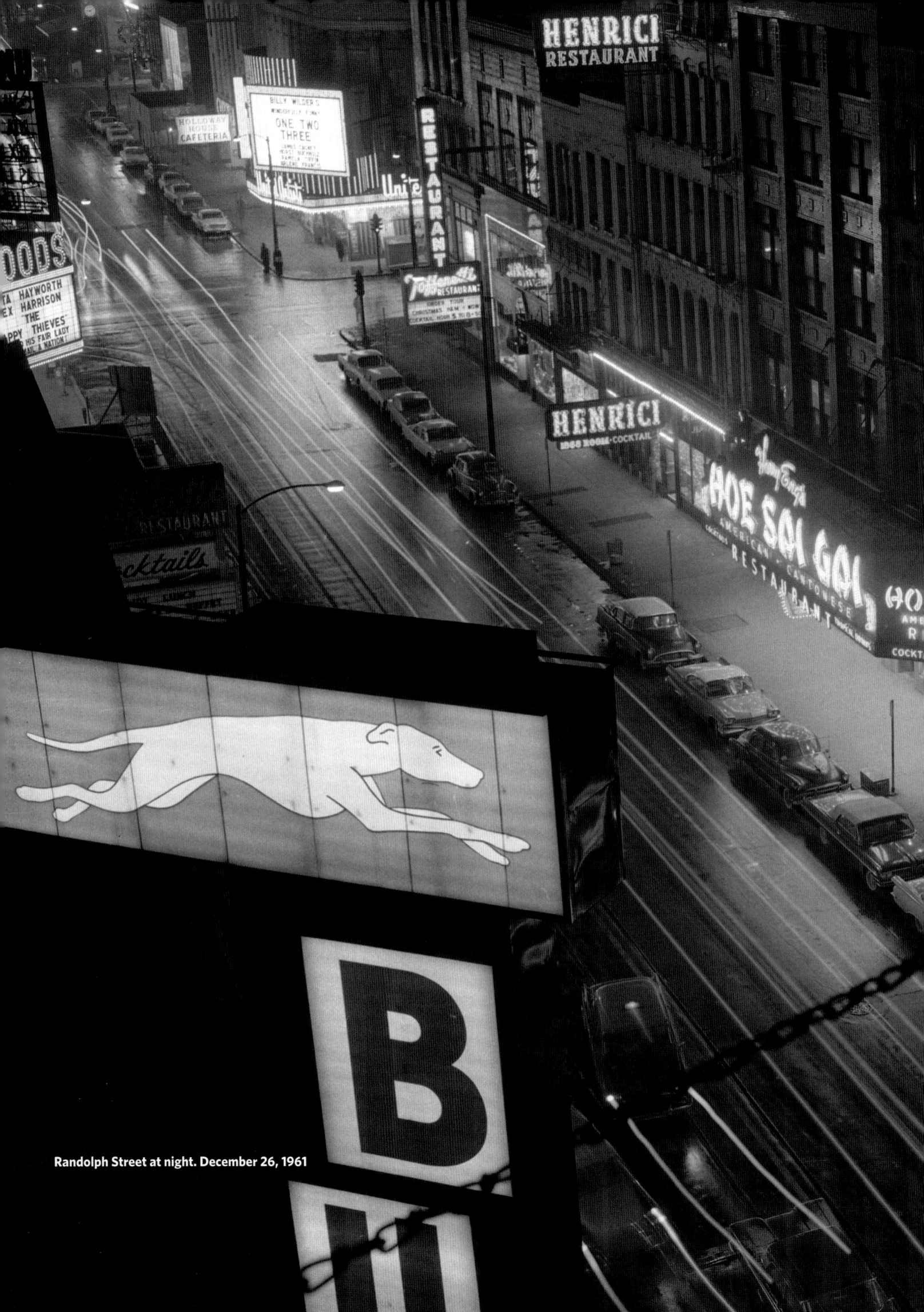

Randolph Street at night. December 26, 1961

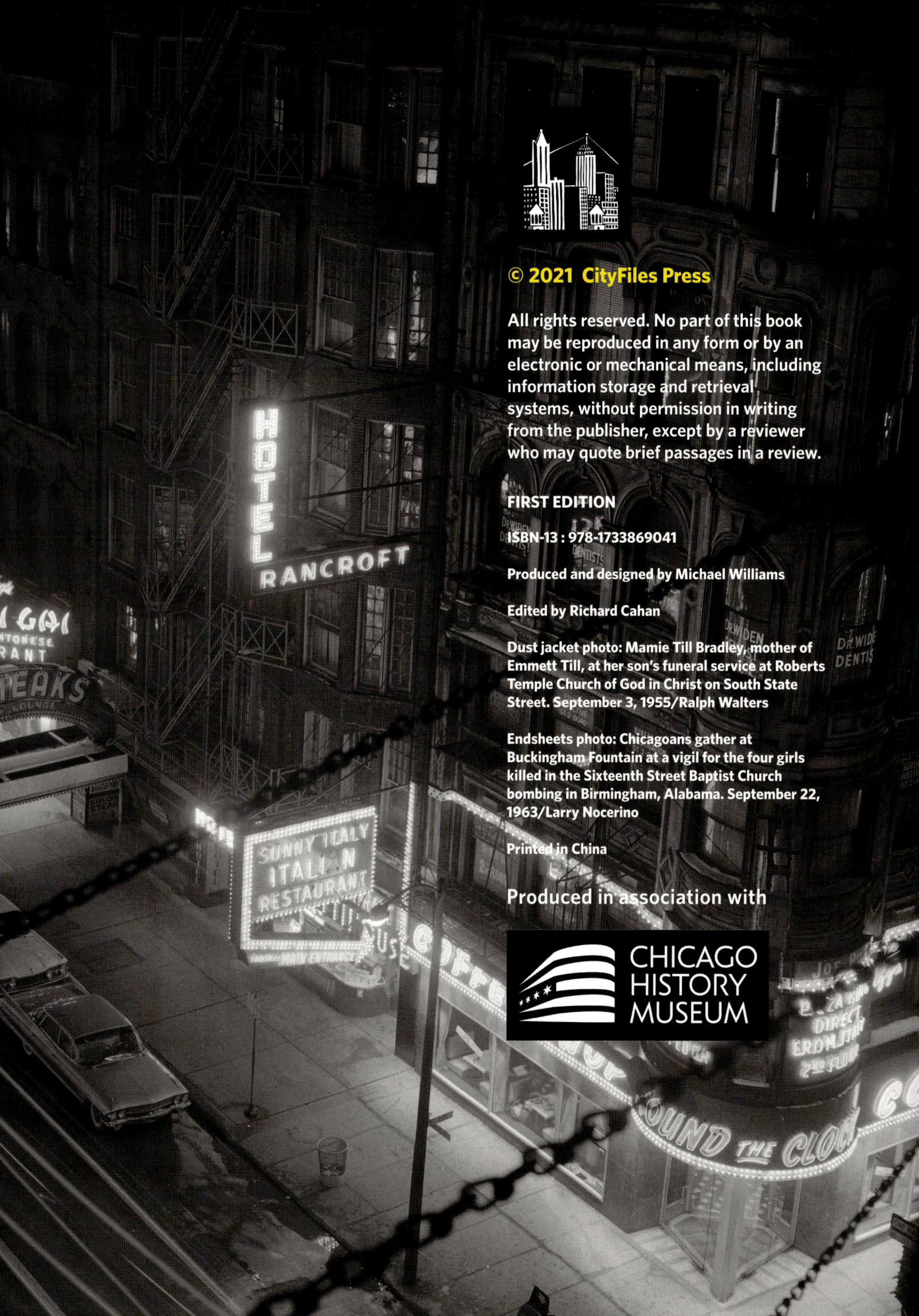

© 2021 CityFiles Press

All rights reserved. No part of this book may be reproduced in any form or by an electronic or mechanical means, including information storage and retrieval systems, without permission in writing from the publisher, except by a reviewer who may quote brief passages in a review.

FIRST EDITION

ISBN-13 : 978-1733869041

Produced and designed by Michael Williams

Edited by Richard Cahan

Dust jacket photo: Mamie Till Bradley, mother of Emmett Till, at her son's funeral service at Roberts Temple Church of God in Christ on South State Street. September 3, 1955/Ralph Walters

Endsheets photo: Chicagoans gather at Buckingham Fountain at a vigil for the four girls killed in the Sixteenth Street Baptist Church bombing in Birmingham, Alabama. September 22, 1963/Larry Nocerino

Printed in China

Produced in association with

CHICAGO HISTORY MUSEUM

CONTENTS

- **9**   **FOREWORD:** John Russick
- **11**   **INTRODUCTION:** Lee Bey
- **15**   **THE PICTURE NEWSPAPER:** Richard Cahan and Michael Williams

- **18**   **PART 1:** Hard Times

- **54**   **PART 2:** Coming Storm

- **106**   **PART 3:** Shocking News

- **146**   **PART 4:** These Days

- **160**   **CREDITS**

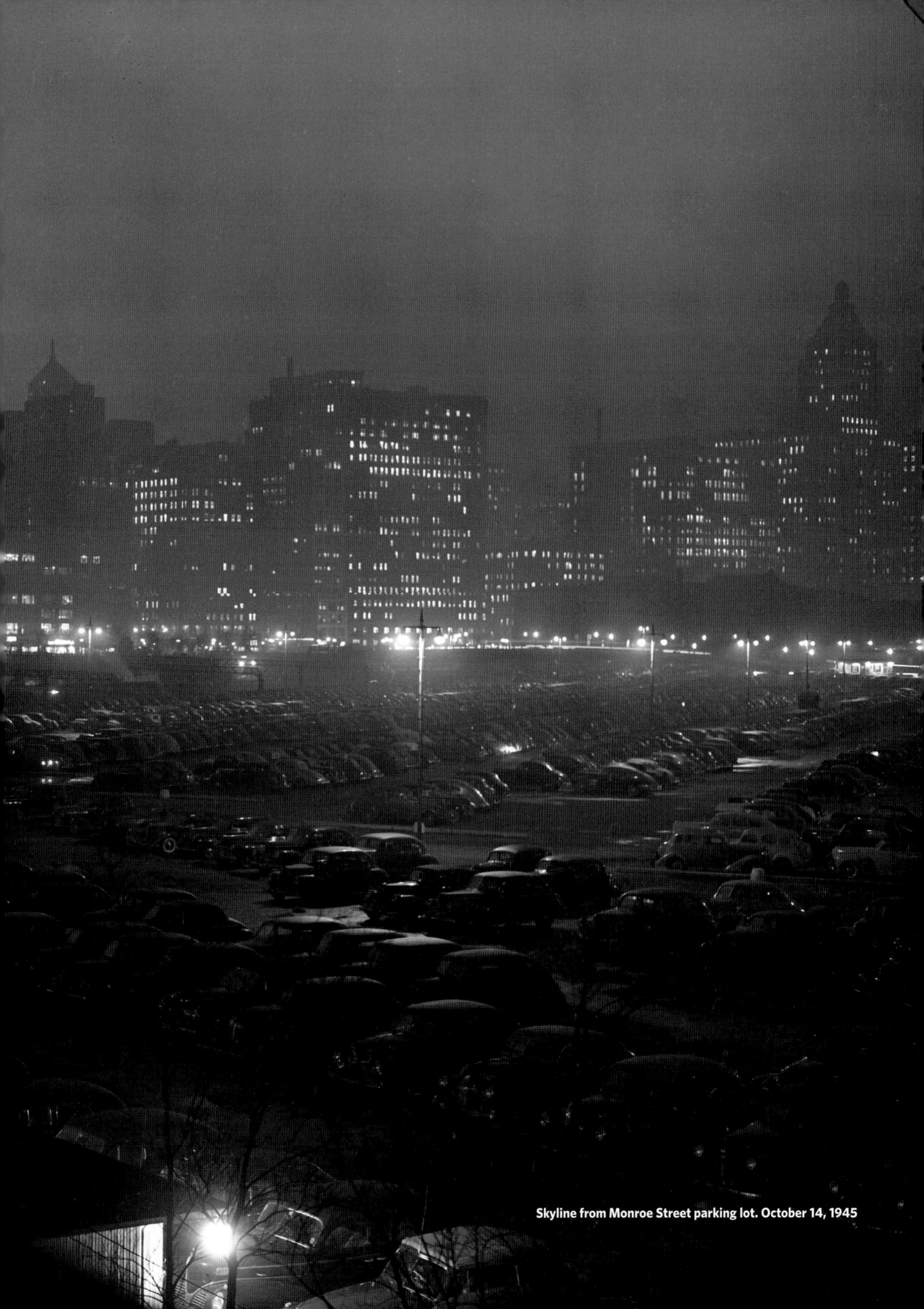

Skyline from Monroe Street parking lot. October 14, 1945

Michigan Avenue on a rainy night. January 13, 1960

FOREWORD
John Russick

In 1839, just two years after the city of Chicago was incorporated, French artist Louis Daguerre set the history of photography in motion when he invented a way to capture and save an image on a silver surface. Until Daguerreotypes, visual documentation was almost entirely in the form of works of artistic interpretation, maps, drawings, paintings, and prints produced by trained artists.

Photography changed how we see the world and the way we share it with others. It offered an original and objective visual record, and over time became increasingly available to people with little or no formal training. Today, the camera continues to shape our lives and the way we understand the past.

Chicago, from its start, was an attractive subject. It offered a landscape that was regularly being made and remade. The city's growth—advanced by the flood of newcomers looking for opportunity and flush with money, ambition, or both—reflected the rise of the United States. The new nation was on the move west, and Chicago was the place to be for people and enterprises that would shape the American story.

Perhaps no other city has more of its photographic history captured under one roof. The Chicago History Museum's holdings include approximately 8 million images—dating back to photographs that show the frontier town before the Great Chicago Fire of 1871. This massive number is due in large part to the recent acquisition of a collection of roughly 5 million Chicago Sun-Times photographs.

This remarkable group of photos was nearly lost. After being sold in 2009, it ended up jammed into plastic bins in a storage locker about 100 miles west of Chicago. In 2018, the museum acquired the photos and partnered with the Chicago Sun-Times to preserve, digitize, and make them available.

The quality of these images reminds us that photography is still a fine art. Composition, use of color, shadow, reflection, and movement all demonstrate that these pictures are not simply a batch of Chicago moments. The photos are both art and evidence. They show the breathtaking spectrum of the city and its people. And they serve as a record of our collective creativity, determination, joy, and heartbreak.

After more than two decades with the Chicago History Museum, I've seen how the institution has defined and redefined itself—much like our famous namesake. Throughout, we have sought to be a valued repository for records that trace the history of this amazing city.

Unfortunately, the impulses that drove our collecting efforts often left critical people, places, and events out of the record. Because the newspaper's photographers worked the entire city, capturing the daily life of people who were often just a footnote in the museum's archive, their work helps us rectify some of these omissions. This book and the efforts to digitize the acquired images taken by Sun-Times photographers are a part of our ongoing commitment to tell a more inclusive story of Chicago.

At the Chicago History Museum, all our best work is the result of teams of dedicated people with the vision to recognize opportunities and the drive to realize dreams. This project could not have been advanced without the extraordinary efforts of Gary T. Johnson, Russell L. Lewis Jr., Angela Hoover, Julie Wroblewski, and Hannah Zuber. And today, the work continues under the leadership of the museum's new president Donald Lassere.

The Chicago History Museum has not acted alone. Our partners at the Chicago Sun-Times worked closely to make its photographic legacy available through the museum's digital resource portals. Without the enthusiasm, encouragement, and collaborative spirit of the Chicago Sun-Times this collection would not be available to the public. We thank Leo Bauby, who acquired the collection and then approached the museum so that it could be preserved. We are also grateful to the TAWANI Foundation, the Gaylord and Dorothy Donnelley Foundation, and Bon and Holly French for their support of the acquisition and cataloging of the Sun-Times photography collection.

Support for *Chicago Exposed* was generously provided by the Gaylord and Dorothy Donnelley Foundation.

—John Russick is senior vice president of the Chicago History Museum.

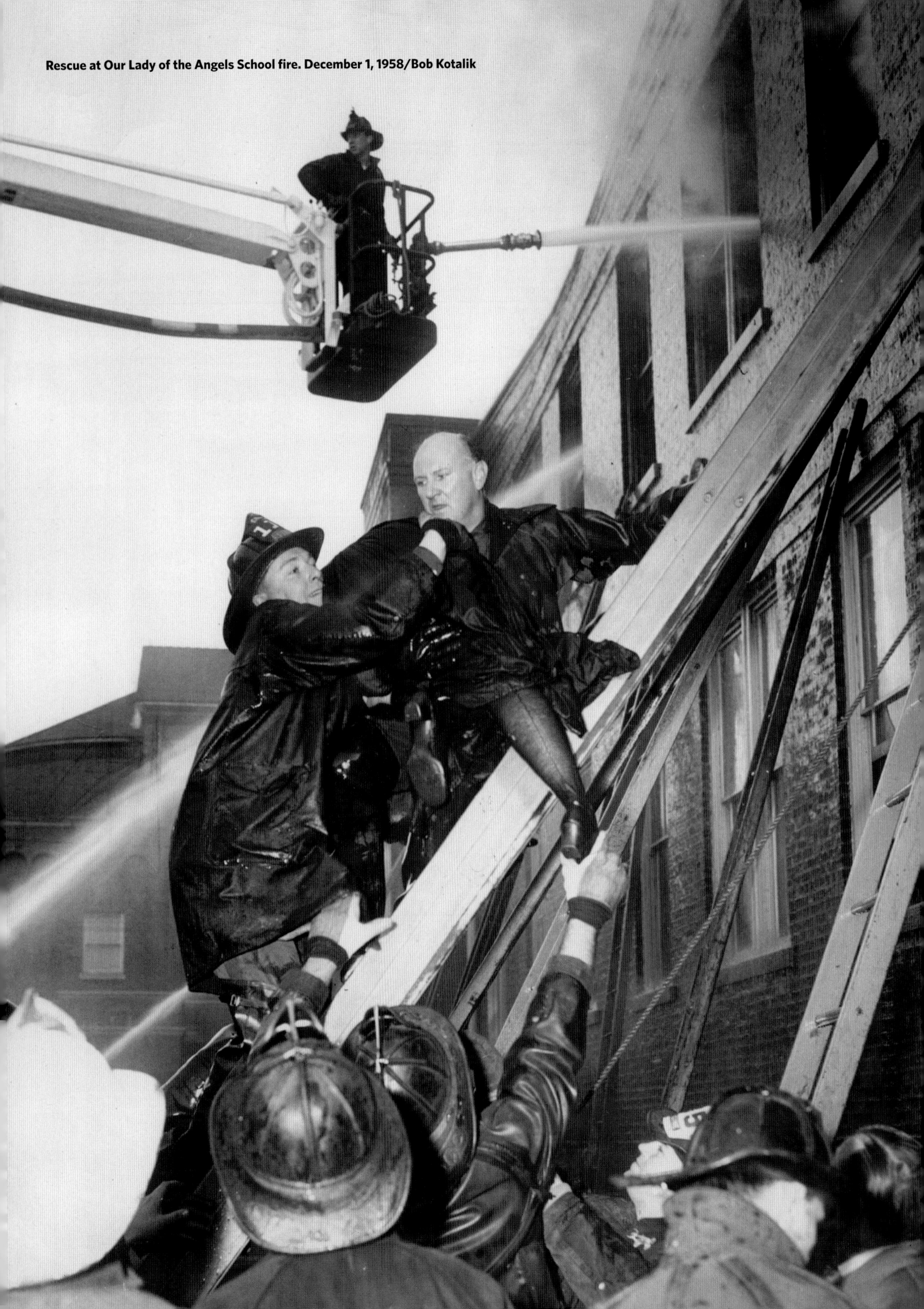
Rescue at Our Lady of the Angels School fire. December 1, 1958/Bob Kotalik

INTRODUCTION
Lee Bey

This book's first photograph—the opening shot—is a stunner. An evocative nighttime image of Randolph Street's old restaurant row. The photo looks like a scene snatched from a long-lost Chicago film noir.

Lighted and neon signs break the downtown darkness. Toffenetti restaurant, near Dearborn Street. Famous Henrici's. Hoe Sai Gai, with its marquee of faux Chinese script slashing the night like scimitars. Next door: Sunny Italy, boasting "The Finest Italian Food in Town." And: Round the Clock, a 24-hour coffee shop at Randolph and Clark.

To shoot the photo from atop the Greyhound Bus Terminal was a master stroke. The station was across the street from the restaurants; the sign bearing the bus company's galloping mascot is in the foreground. The angle, against the darkened street, gives the image a dreamlike yet melancholy feel of an era that was about to come to an end.

In fact, that's exactly what happened. The photograph was taken December 26, 1961, and within eighteen months the entire block was razed and hauled away to make room for what is now the Richard J. Daley Center.

But before the bulldozers rolled down Randolph, an unnamed Chicago Sun-Times photographer was there.

What could have been a routine assignment became art—brought to Sun-Times readers for pocket change. And it happened virtually every day, with every edition, through the work of photographers who were the best in the business.

Borrie Kantor. Dave Mann. Jack Dykinga. Howard D. Simmons. Al Podgorski. Ashlee Rezin Garcia. The list goes on. These professionals captured this tough, brawling, proud and oft-troubled city, and did so with style, truth, urgency, and beauty.

And to think that much of this work—including the marvelous restaurant row image—was headed to oblivion just a few years ago. Following a blunder by the newspaper's previous owner, the photo negatives for 5 million images from the 1940s through the early 2000s ingloriously wound up in Dixon, Illinois.

They were rescued by the Chicago History Museum.

I've been excited about this trove of photos ever since. I've spent more late nights than I dare admit looking through the thousands of Chicago Sun-Times Collection images now online.

In one dramatic photo, Bob Kotalik captures two firefighters—tension etched across their faces—urgently carrying a nun down a ladder during the catastrophic Our Lady of the Angels School fire of 1958. It's a heart-stopping image. We don't know if she lived or was among the 95 students and nuns who perished.

Almost thirty years after that fire, Sun-Times photographers captured the euphoria at a downtown parade honoring the newly crowned Super Bowl XX champs, the Chicago Bears. Revelers are frolicking on packed LaSalle Street, which was carpeted in ankle-deep ticker tape. People climb traffic lights to get a better view. Shirtless men defy 8 degree weather and a −29 windchill.

It's as if parade-goers somehow knew they were attending a once-in-a-lifetime event. And the Bears have done their best to keep it that way.

BLACK CHICAGO IS WELL represented. Sun-Times photographers captured newsworthy images of the peril and pain sometimes found on the city's South and West sides. Photos of Mamie Till, ripped by anguish as she viewed the tortured body of her son, Emmett—lynched by Southern racists in 1955—are as searing now as they were nearly 70 years ago.

But the Sun-Times also produced remarkable images that captured the spirit and humanity of the Black community. For instance, there is a 1974 photo essay on East 47th Street in the predominantly Black neighborhood of Grand Boulevard. Communities like these are easy pickings for grim, voyeuristic photography that does little but showcase tired stereotypes about poor and working-class Black neighborhoods.

Sun-Times photographers found laughing children and an Afro'd young mom posing with her bright-eyed toddler. There's a fashionably dressed Mack in a wide-brimmed hat—even in black-and-white you can still tell he's colorfully attired—proudly posing next to his tricked-out Cadillac Eldorado.

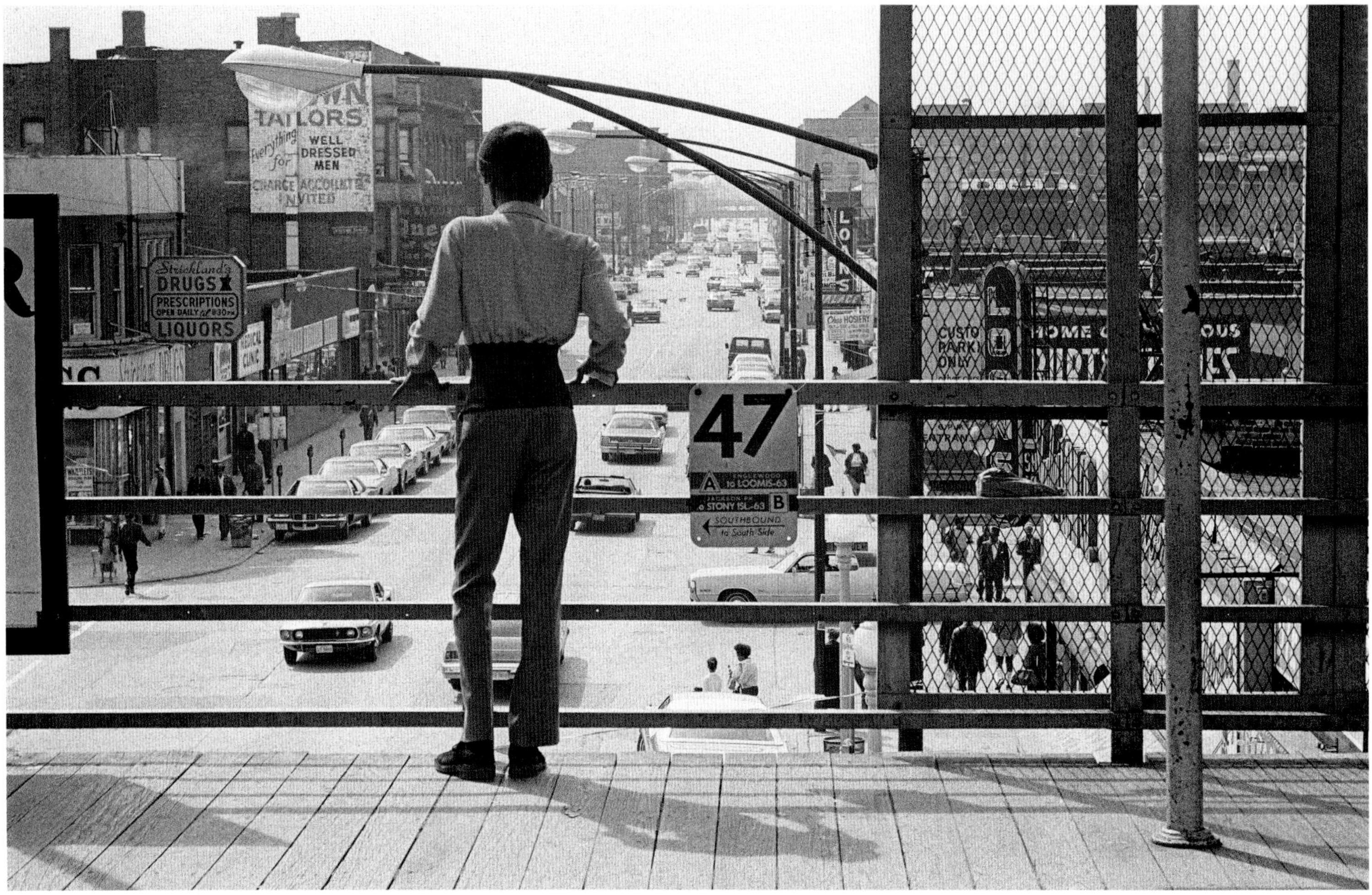

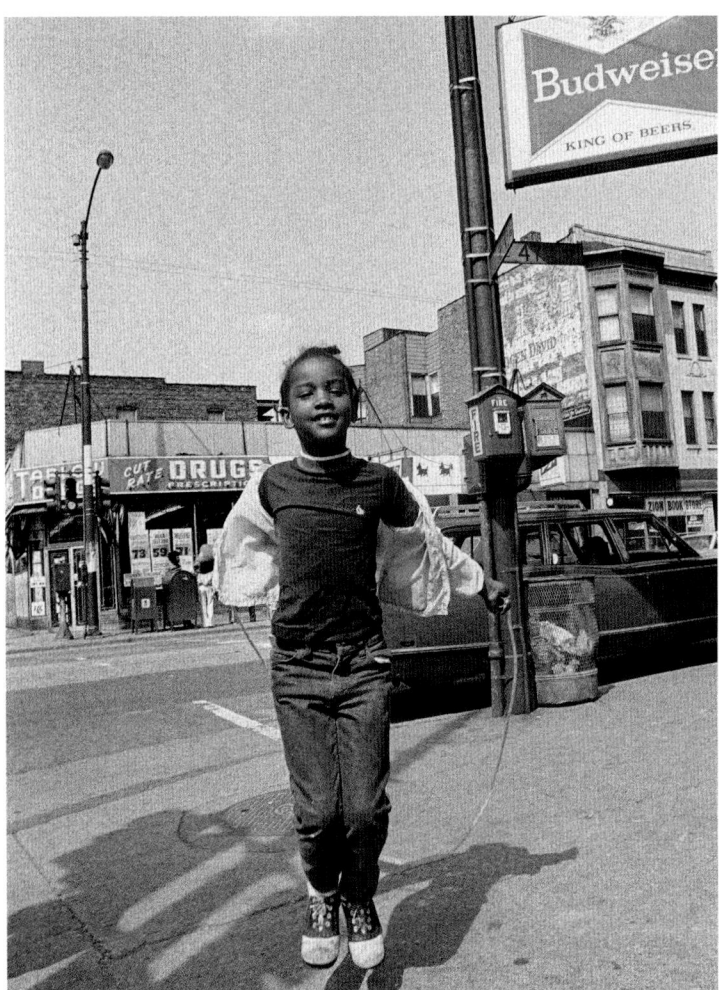
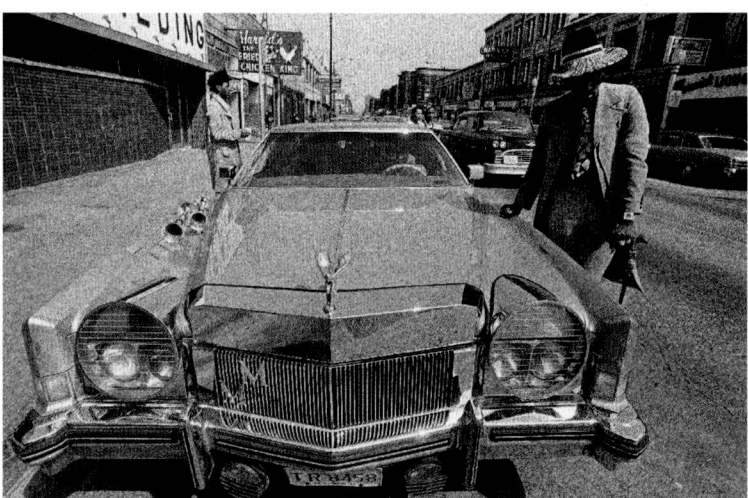
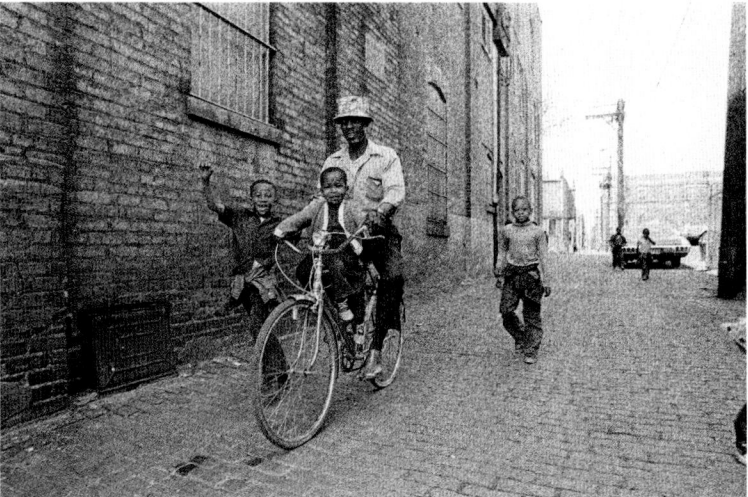

Street scenes along East 47th Street. April 10, 1974/Howard D. Simmons

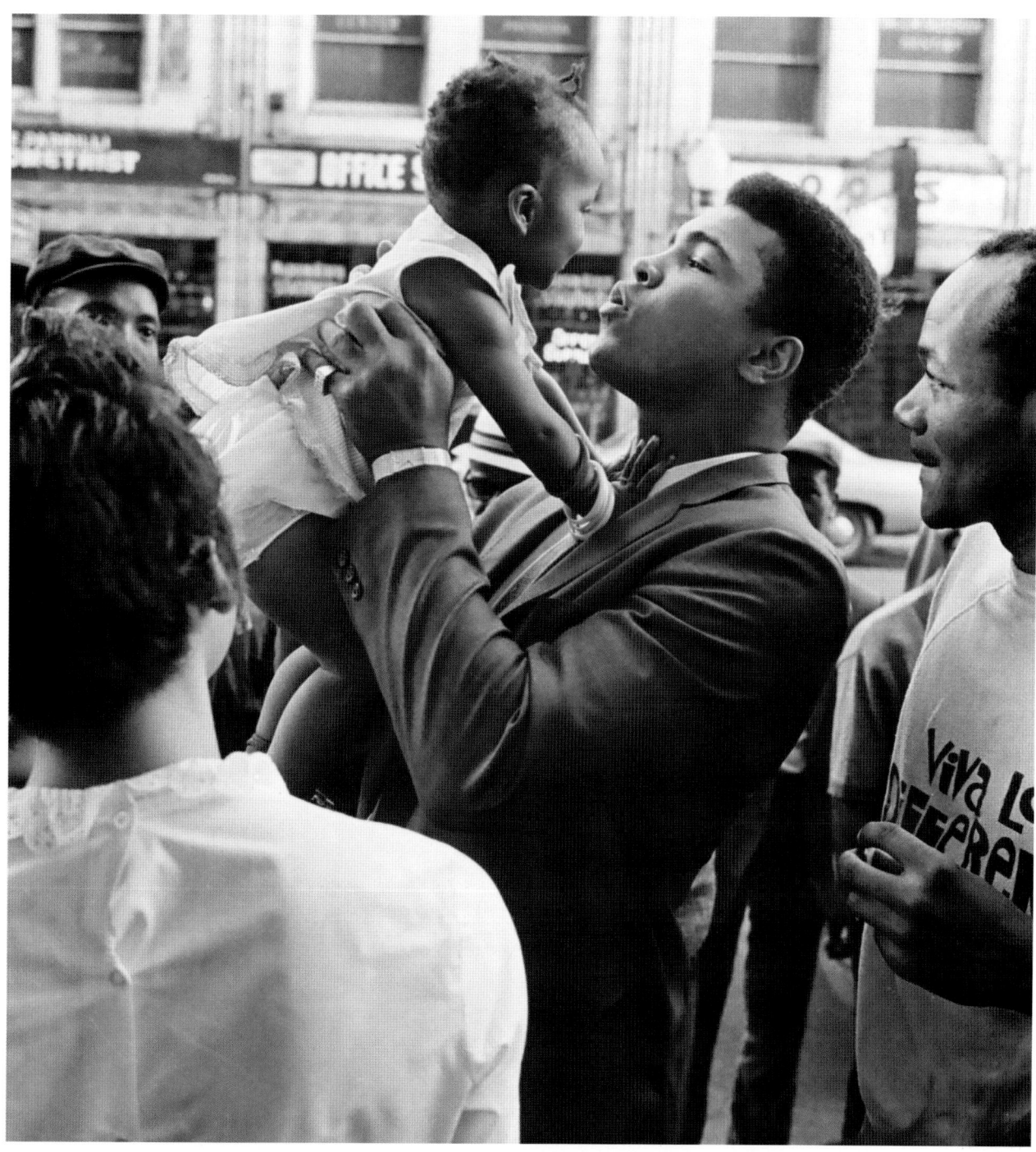

Muhammad Ali at the Senate Theatre, 3128 West Madison. July 24, 1967/Clarence Peters

Browsing the collection, I found myself amused by a sequence of 1967 photos showing Muhammad Ali holding up and playing with a baby outside the old Senate Theatre on West Madison Street.

Just three months earlier, Ali was stripped of his heavyweight title for refusing induction into the US Army. But here, on the West Side, just before attending a donation drive at the theater to help hungry Mississippi families, Ali is surrounded by admirers—not to mention that beautiful baby, who'd be a woman in her 50s now—and greeted like the champion he is.

Much of the documentation of Chicago's Black neighborhoods was done by a talented group of African-American photographers who knew and respected the communities they covered.

And the respect and admiration were returned. Countless times as a young reporter in the 1990s, I'd hit the streets with photographers John H. White, Bob Black, or Brian Jackson. They were greeted like celebrities. Indeed, when I told my mother about my first day at the Sun-Times back in 1992, her first question was: "Did you meet John White yet?"

I did. And now you can, too, along with scores of other Sun-Times photographers—artists, really—through the powerful work in this book.

—Sun-Times editorial writer Lee Bey is author of *Southern Exposure: The Overlooked Architecture of Chicago's South Side.* **He worked at the Sun-Times from 1992 to 2001 as a reporter and architectural critic and rejoined the paper in 2019.**

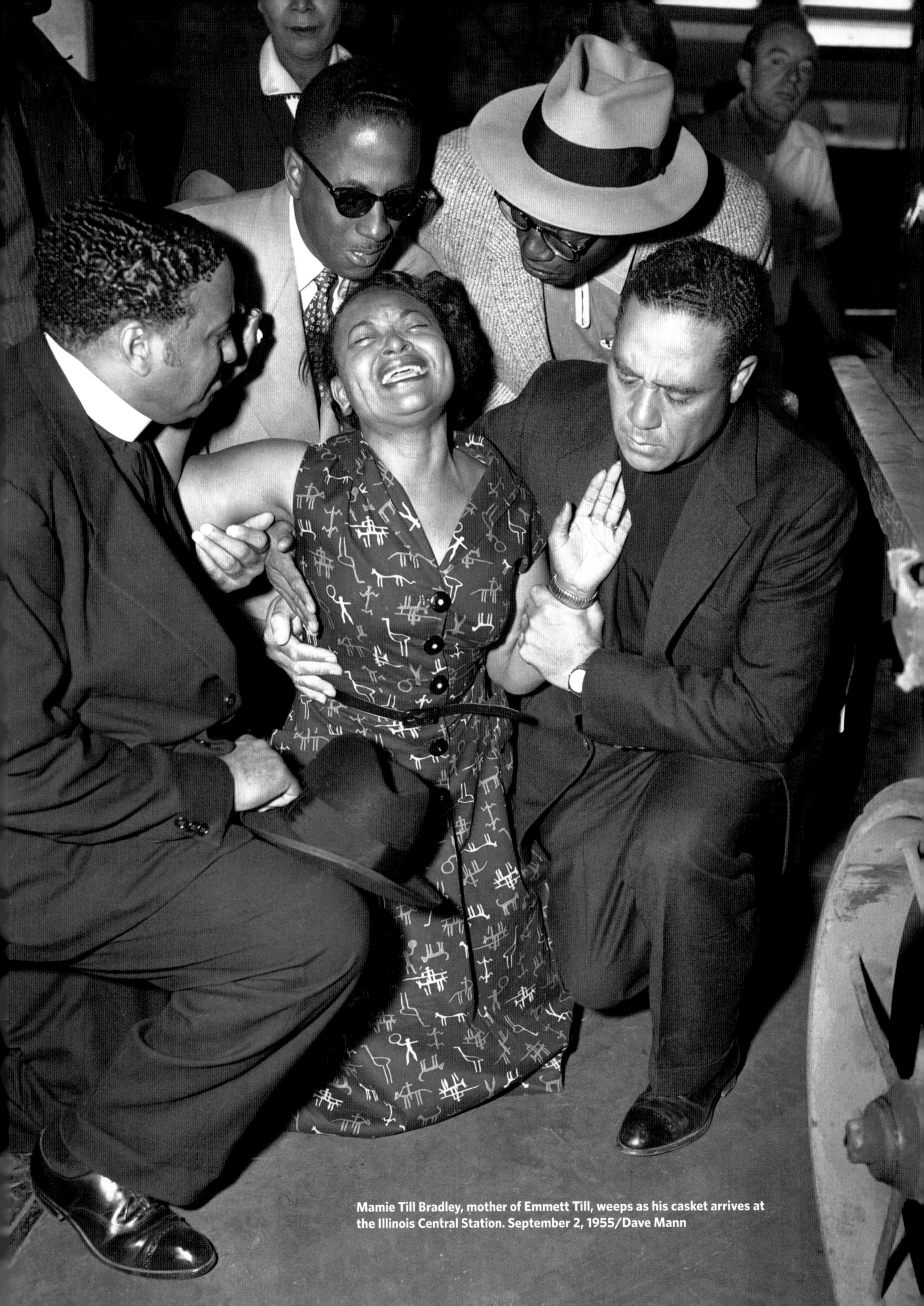
Mamie Till Bradley, mother of Emmett Till, weeps as his casket arrives at the Illinois Central Station. September 2, 1955/Dave Mann

THE PICTURE NEWSPAPER

Richard Cahan and Michael Williams

Mamie Till arrived at Chicago's Central Station to greet the *Panama Limited* train, up from Mississippi with a simple pine box containing her 14-year-old son, Emmett. Mrs. Till, in a wheelchair due to her grief, rose and sprinted across three sets of tracks toward the baggage car as the train pulled to a stop. She fell to her knees as her son's coffin was carefully rolled down an incline toward the platform.

"My darling, my darling. I would have gone through a world of time to get to you," she cried as her son's body was wheeled toward a hearse.

Later that day, Mamie Till saw what had been done to her son when he travelled to Mississippi on a summer trip to visit her relatives. Emmett Till had been beaten and shot. Most of his teeth were missing. His body had been found in the Tallahatchie River, weighed down by iron and barbed wire. When the coffin was opened at the funeral home, and—at last—she saw the condition of her son, Mamie Till announced that she wanted an open casket at her son's funeral the next day.

"Let the people see what they did to my boy."

Chicago Sun-Times photographer Dave Mann was waiting at Central Station when Till's remains returned to Chicago. His colleague Ralph Walters was sent to Till's funeral that next day. Walters' photograph of Mamie Till, then known as Mamie Till Bradley and later as Mamie Till-Mobley, in the first row of a South Side church graces the cover of this book. The two photos are part of a collection of 5 million images that have recently been acquired by the Chicago History Museum.

CHICAGO EXPOSED IS THE FIRST book based on the museum's Chicago Sun-Times Photograph Collection. Every picture in it, of course, is from the past, but this is a book for today. It examines issues that have challenged and haunted Chicago for decades—war, race, political power, crime and incarceration, urban decay, and urban progress. It looks at these photos with a fresh eye and attempts to better understand—in pictures and words—how we came to be Chicago.

Some of the pictures are familiar—the best of blockbuster photojournalism. And some have never been seen. Many are disturbing—revealing a side of Chicago that many might hope would remain unseen. We believe that each photo helps tell the story of contemporary Chicago, its accomplishments but also its capacity for indifference and hate. The time to see these photographs is now.

This is a book of photography, a celebration of 1/60th of a second. But the images selected are often quite different from what fills the front pages of a daily newspaper. Photojournalism is all about instant decisions and deadlines. Now we have a chance to reconsider what was taken, reframe what was left behind on the light table, and reflect on defining moments in Chicago history.

The Sun-Times Photograph Collection comprises work by the staffs of four metropolitan newspapers—the Chicago Sun-Times, Chicago Daily Times, Chicago Sun, and Chicago Daily News.

The Sun-Times was established in 1948 by the merger of the Times and the Sun. The Times, known originally as the Daily Illustrated Times, was Chicago's first tabloid newspaper when it debuted in 1929. Its owner, Samuel Thomason, promised "concise stories and plenty of pictures." Packed with crime news, sex scandals, journalism crusades, and big, bold photographs, the Times' logo brandished a Speed Graphic, the press camera of the era, and the words "Chicago's Picture Newspaper."

The Sun was created more than a decade later by Marshall Field III, grandson of the founder of the Marshall Field department store. He introduced the Sun, a big broadsheet newspaper, to counter the Chicago Tribune and usher in a liberal voice that would rally for the United States' entry into World War II. Three days after the Sun's first edition in December 1941, Japanese warplanes attacked Pearl Harbor. The paper's *raison d'être* was over, but the Sun pressed on.

Photography was essential to the Sun. The paper employed at least 25 photographers—including two women. The rest of the staff were all White males. (It wasn't until 1964, when John Tweedle was hired at the Daily News, that a Black photographer worked full-time on any Chicago metropolitan daily.)

Field purchased the Daily Times two years

after the war and converted the Sun to a tabloid so both papers could be printed on the Times' presses. A few months later, in January 1948, he merged the two newspapers to create a "'round the clock" Sun & Times. Its nameplate soon changed to the Sun-Times. Like the Daily Times, the new Sun-Times was called "The Picture Newspaper."

In 1959, three years after Field died, his Field Enterprises acquired the afternoon Daily News. The Sun-Times and Daily News shared a darkroom and photo studio as well as a photo library, a morgue of thousands of photographic prints. The Daily News closed in 1978. Many—but not all—of the photographers from the Daily News and Sun-Times were kept on staff, creating an all-star team.

The newspaper's photo archive was carefully stored by the Sun-Times until 2009, when it was sold to the Rogers Photo Archive, a commercial photo-sales company in North Little Rock, Arkansas, for close to $1 million. Owner John Rogers promised to digitize each of the 5 million prints and photo negatives and return the digital files with complete searchable captions, keywords, dates, and byline information. The Sun-Times retained the copyright of the images. Under the deal, Rogers could sell the physical prints and negatives.

But Rogers, whose reputation at the time was solid, digitized only a fraction of the material: most of the prints and a small portion of the negatives. His company, which also bought the archives of more than a dozen other newspapers and collectors, went bankrupt. His assets were seized and auctioned. Most of the Sun-Times material ended up in Memphis at Historic Images, a separate photo-sales company, and was later sold to a private dealer in Dixon, Illinois. The Chicago History Museum purchased that collection in 2018 after it worked out an agreement with the owners of the Sun-Times. This book contains images shot as recently as 2020 due to the partnership between the paper and museum.

The museum's Sun-Times Photograph Collection includes about 2.5 million images that were digitized by Rogers' company from the Sun-Times morgue and about 2.5 million medium- and small-format negatives that Rogers had not yet processed.

THE PHOTOGRAPHERS WHO TOOK those 5 million pictures in the Sun-Times collection did not give much thought to history. Mostly they thought about the next day.

"We wanted to make the best images for tomorrow's paper," said Jon Sall (Sun-Times, 1989–2013). "Images that showed what was happening as succinctly as possible. We wanted to catch the important moment."

That was the mission of every photographer on the paper, Sall said. They knew their work would be looked at by hundreds of thousands of Chicagoans every day—over breakfast, on the L, or at work. Their pictures might make people laugh or make them cry. But surely, their work helped Chicagoans understand their lives and times.

"We were a force," said Amanda Alcock (Sun-Times, 1984–93).

The job brought responsibility. "We saw things that other people never got a chance to see," said Bob Ringham (Sun-Times, 1984–97). Staff photographers knew they had special access recording the city on film. "I don't think I saw it as a responsibility as much as a gift, an honor," said Alcock. "I wanted to get deeper, stay longer. I always wanted more."

The Sun-Times photo staff ranged from a dozen to twenty photographers during its first 55 years. The Tribune's photo staff was twice as large. "We had to be more versatile, take on more assignments," said Nancy Stuenkel (Sun-Times, 1978–2014). But the paper's tabloid size lent itself to photos. Sun-Times pictures popped. They appeared bigger and more significant than in the broadsheet Tribune.

The job was a joy. "I never once got up in the morning and thought, 'Oh hell, I have to go to work,'" recalls photographer Bob Kotalik (Sun-Times, 1947–90), whose newspaper career actually dated back to the early 1940s when he helped care for the pigeons that carried sports film from Wrigley Field back to the Sun's offices. "I never knew what I was going to do. I could be with the president or Marilyn Monroe."

But of course, the job also came with challenges.

"The weather beat me up," said Ringham. "You have to overdress in the winter and our fingers got cold." And it wasn't just winter, said Pablo Martínez Monsiváis (Sun-Times, 1993–98). "There was a yin and yang to Chicago seasons, from crazy cold to crazy hot."

And the job came with hurdles that reporters did not encounter.

"Photographers should win awards for getting an assignment and getting back," said John H. White (Daily News and Sun-Times, 1969–2013). "A reporter can do an interview over the phone and arrive late on the scene and still get the facts in time for deadline. Photographers have only one chance to get the best picture. And then it's over, so you'd better be on time."

Sun-Times photographers were given assignments, often over the phone or via a two-way radio. "We are working guys, not artists," said Jack Lenahan (Sun-Times, 1949–92). "We never came back until we got the shot." Once back, they processed their film and worked with picture editors, who would pare down their dozens of negatives to a couple to consider for the paper. Prints from those negatives were made in the darkroom and handed to page editors, who decided on what shot or shots were used.

Editing became easier in the late 1990s when Sun-Times photographers were issued digital cameras. Photographers switched to all digital early in the 2000s. Several pictures from the digital age are included here. Perhaps one day they will be added to the museum's Sun-Times collection.

The low point in the storied tradition of Sun-Times photography came in 2013, the day that nearly every photographer on the Sun-Times and its suburban papers was laid off by Wrapports, a company headed by Michael Ferro Jr. that had purchased the Sun-Times two years earlier. Twenty-eight photographers and picture editors lost their jobs in what the owners announced was "part of a multimedia staffing restructure." The Sun-Times planned to rely on reporters with cell phone cameras for still images and videos.

But under terms of a new labor agreement, four of the photographers were rehired in 2014. And in 2017, new owners acquired the Sun-Times. At least six other photographers have been hired since 2013.

PHOTOGRAPHS DRIVE THIS BOOK, but each one is enhanced by a short essay from someone intimately connected to the image.

We started with keystone pictures: the egging of 1940 presidential candidate Wendell Willkie, the 1955 funeral of Emmett Till, the 1966 Marquette Park stoning of Dr. Martin Luther King Jr., and the turmoil surrounding the 1968 Democratic National Convention. We looked at disasters and tragedies, both local and national: airplane and L crashes as well as Chicago's reaction to the assassinations of President John F. Kennedy, Robert F. Kennedy, King, and Fred Hampton.

We gathered a rogue's gallery of criminals—William Heirens, Richard Speck, and John Wayne Gacy—as well as photos that take a closer look at incarceration, from the jailing of *Call Northside 777*'s Joseph W. Majczek to Gary Dotson and inmates freed during the innocence movement.

After selecting the pictures, we sought out people who could help us better understand the meaning behind each one. Our primary sources were the photographers themselves. Richard Derk remembered the day he encountered John Wayne Gacy. Jim Frost explained how he shot the Sun-Times's sweeping undercover Mirage investigation. And Kevin Horan took us on a flight over O'Hare Airport in search of the remains of American Airlines Flight 191.

Then we sought out the subjects of the photos. We tracked down Larry Moisan Sr., who remembered the 1968 bonfire rally he attended to protest school busing, and we found excerpts from Michele McBride's memoir about living through the 1958 Our Lady of the Angels School fire.

We also relied on experts. Helen Shiller wrote about Uptown; William Singer about Richard J. Daley; and Jamie Kalven about the murder of Laquan McDonald. Steve Lasker helped us understand how 1950s photographers—whom he still calls friends—worked in the days of fedoras and flash bulbs. Rosemary L. Bray told us about growing up Black during the turbulent 1960s. And Owen Keehnen recalls the 1990s, a turning point in the AIDS epidemic when he and fellow LGBTQIA+ comrades and supporters took to the streets.

We purposely gave our contributors few instructions, sending only a photograph and asking them to respond. Sometimes their reply was literal. Blaire Topash-Caldwell, a Native American scholar, explained the regalia worn by the Indigenous people who greeted the first freighter to sail through the Saint Lawrence Seaway. Lillian Williams used photographs to riff on her search for Black identity in the 1970s.

This is the first look at a collection that will take decades to comprehend. It's a collection that we hope will expand as other photographers and organizations add to it. The significance of each photograph will morph as the city evolves.

"I never thought of myself as an historian," said Phil Velasquez (Sun-Times, 1981—1997), but I witnessed a lot of history." He and other newspaper photographers say they now more fully appreciate the historical and artistic value of their work.

On the day the Sun was first published in 1941, owner Marshall Field III declared, "Well, Chicago, here it is."

Eighty years later, we take another look.

—Richard Cahan is a former picture editor at the Chicago Sun-Times. He and Michael Williams are the authors of two books about the Sun-Times— *Real Chicago* **and** *Real Chicago Sports* **and more than a dozen award-winning books.**

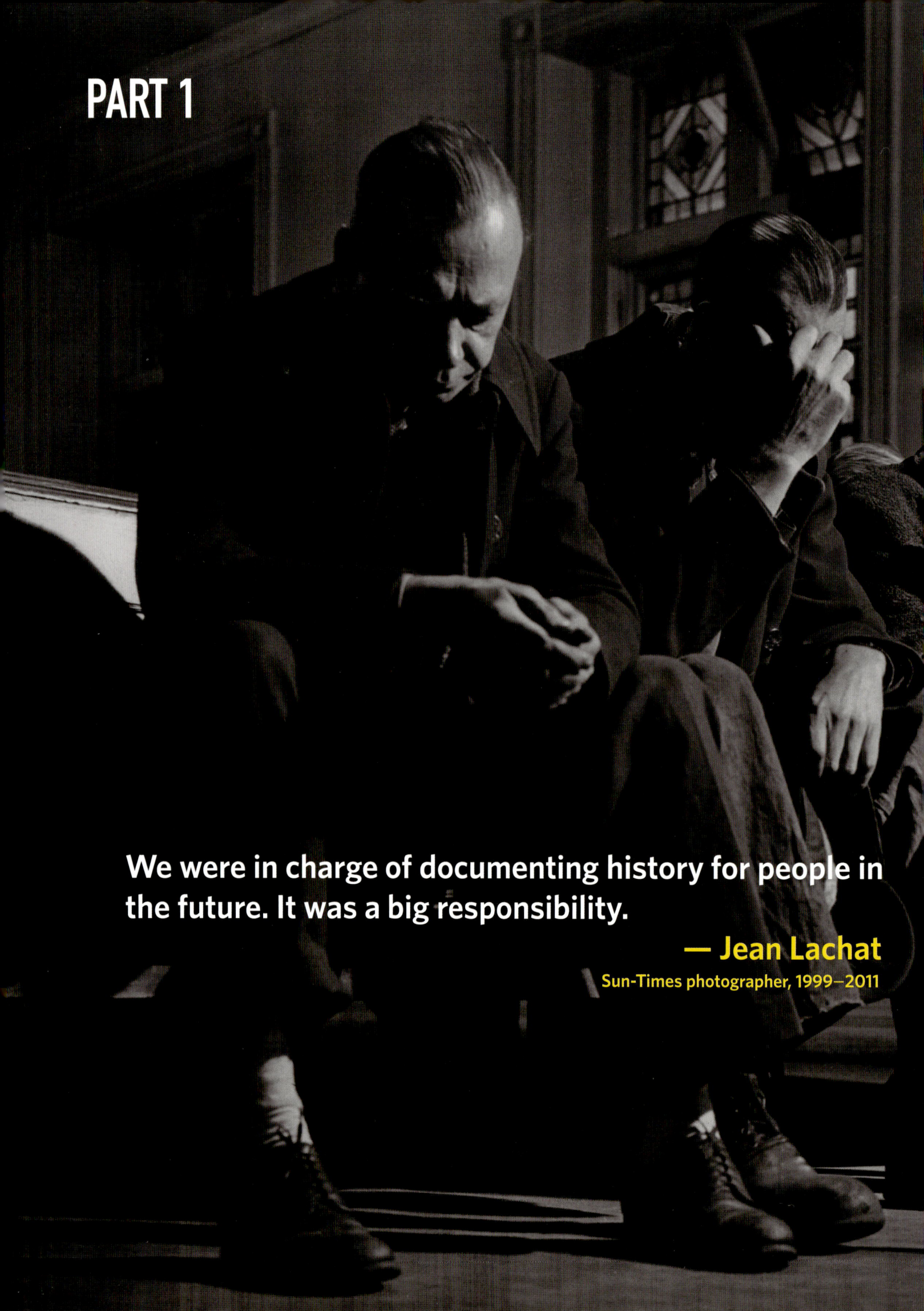

PART 1

We were in charge of documenting history for people in the future. It was a big responsibility.

— **Jean Lachat**
Sun-Times photographer, 1999—2011

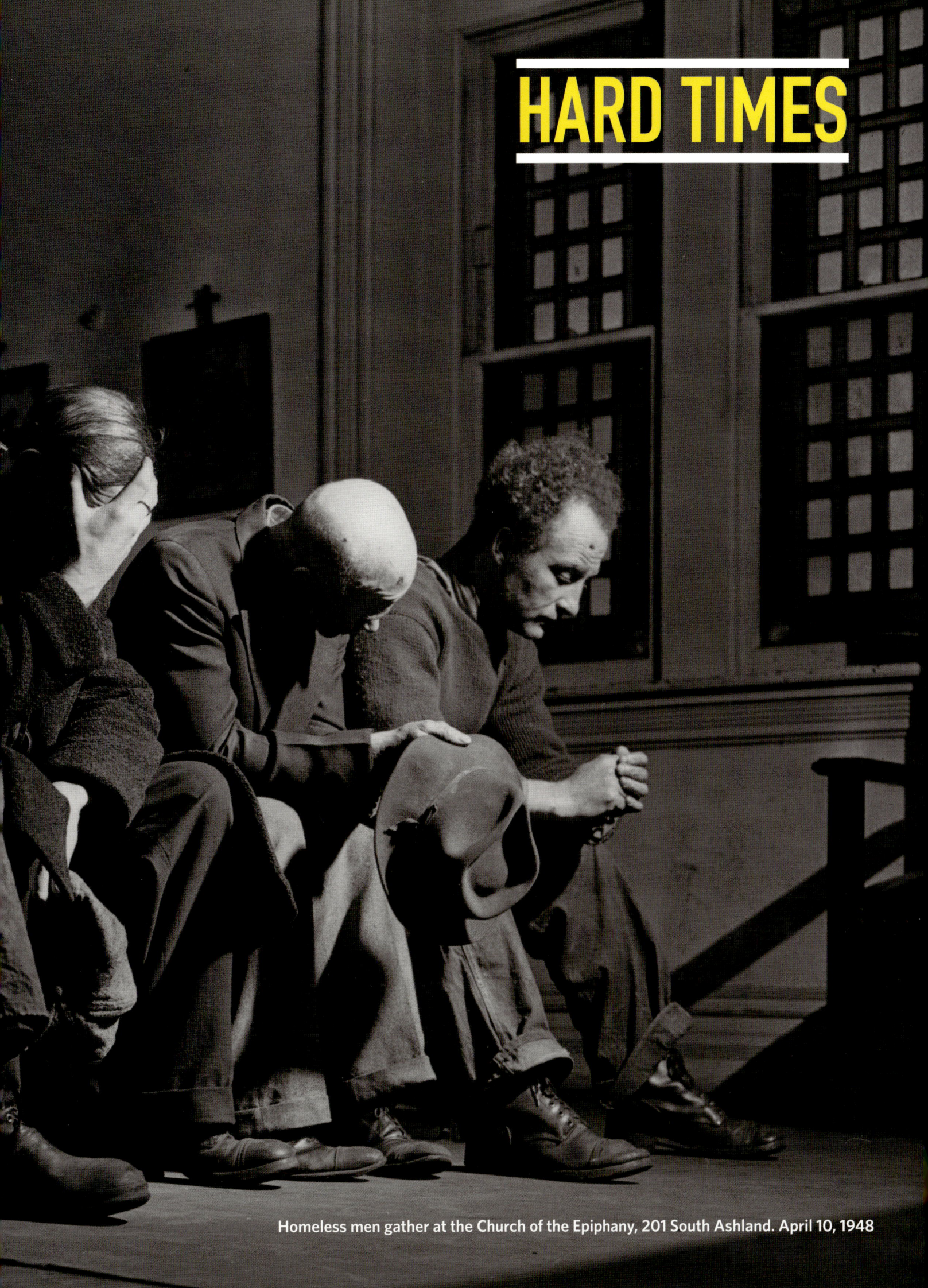

HARD TIMES

Homeless men gather at the Church of the Epiphany, 201 South Ashland. April 10, 1948

'IT SHOULDN'T HAPPEN HERE'

This photo—showing presidential candidate Wendell Willkie after being struck in the face by an egg—was shot by Borrie Kanter, my grandfather.

It is one of the most famous photographs in the Sun-Times Collection. At the time, my grandfather was working for the Chicago Daily Times, the city's first tabloid paper. The Times merged with the Chicago Sun in 1948, and the Chicago Sun-Times was born.

The photograph was taken in the LaSalle Street Station about two weeks before the 1940 presidential election. The Times ran the picture on page one with the headline: "It shouldn't happen here." Just a few days earlier, the paper wrote about a similar event. "Such incidents as the throwing of eggs and tomatoes at Mr. Willkie by overzealous onlookers are disgusting."

My grandfather was a vibrant, fun, and spunky man. It's no wonder that he was such a terrific newspaper photographer. As you can see, he knew just how to work in a crowd.

Like a lot of press photographers, he knew and befriended people from all walks of life—politicians to socialites to mobsters. An old photo shows Borrie Kanter as a man of the time—in a pinstripe suit with his hair parted down the middle.

I knew my grandfather as a loving family man who retired to California and lived to be 101. He never gave up his love of Chicago or its sports teams. He was proud of his famous pictures and humble, too. I recently learned that this photo was exhibited in 1949 at New York's prestigious Museum of Modern Art in an exhibit about photojournalism called *The Exact Instant*. I'm not sure if my grandfather ever knew that. He certainly never mentioned it.

We are proud that his work, and its impact, lives on.
—*Laora Fishman is a certified personal trainer and athlete who resides in Barbados.*

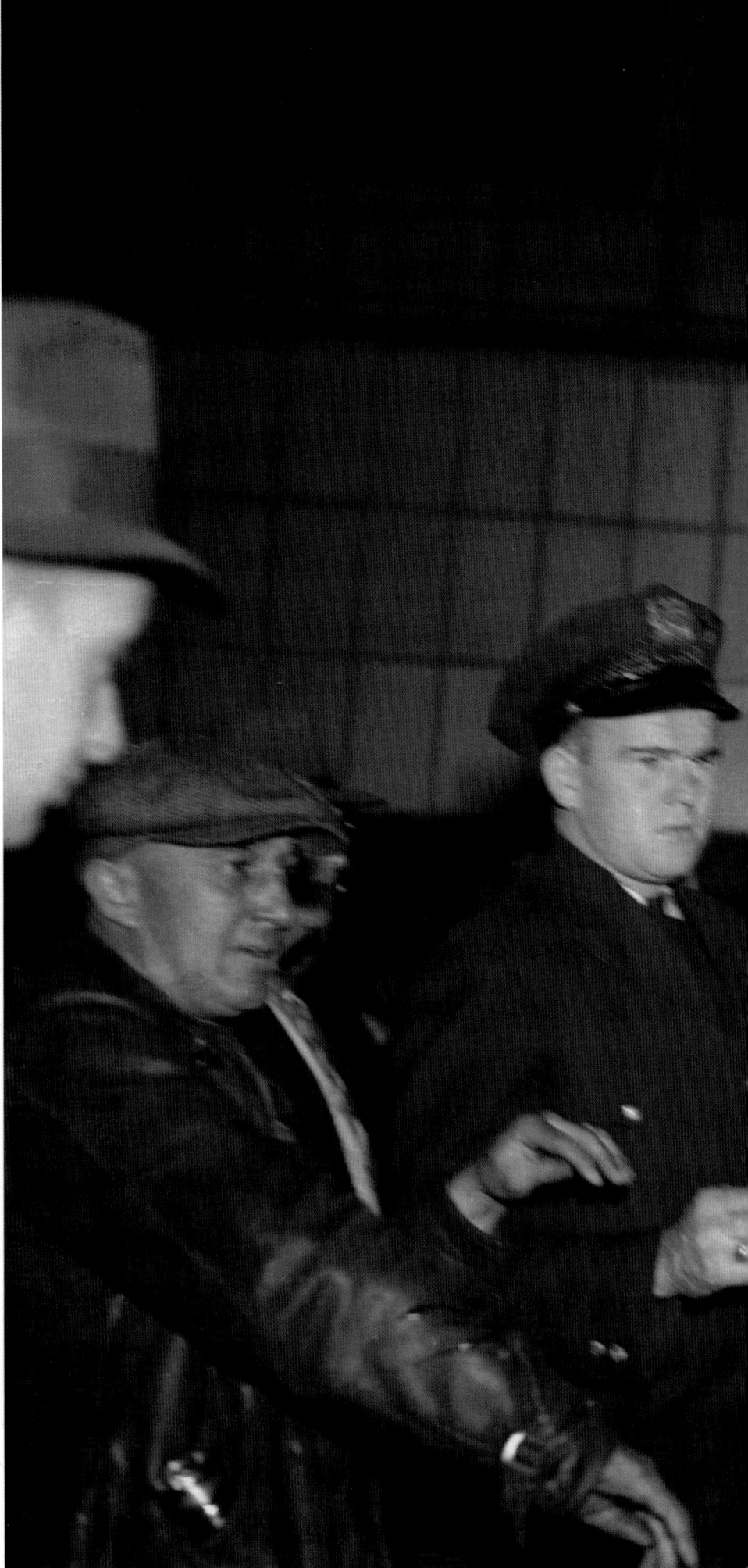

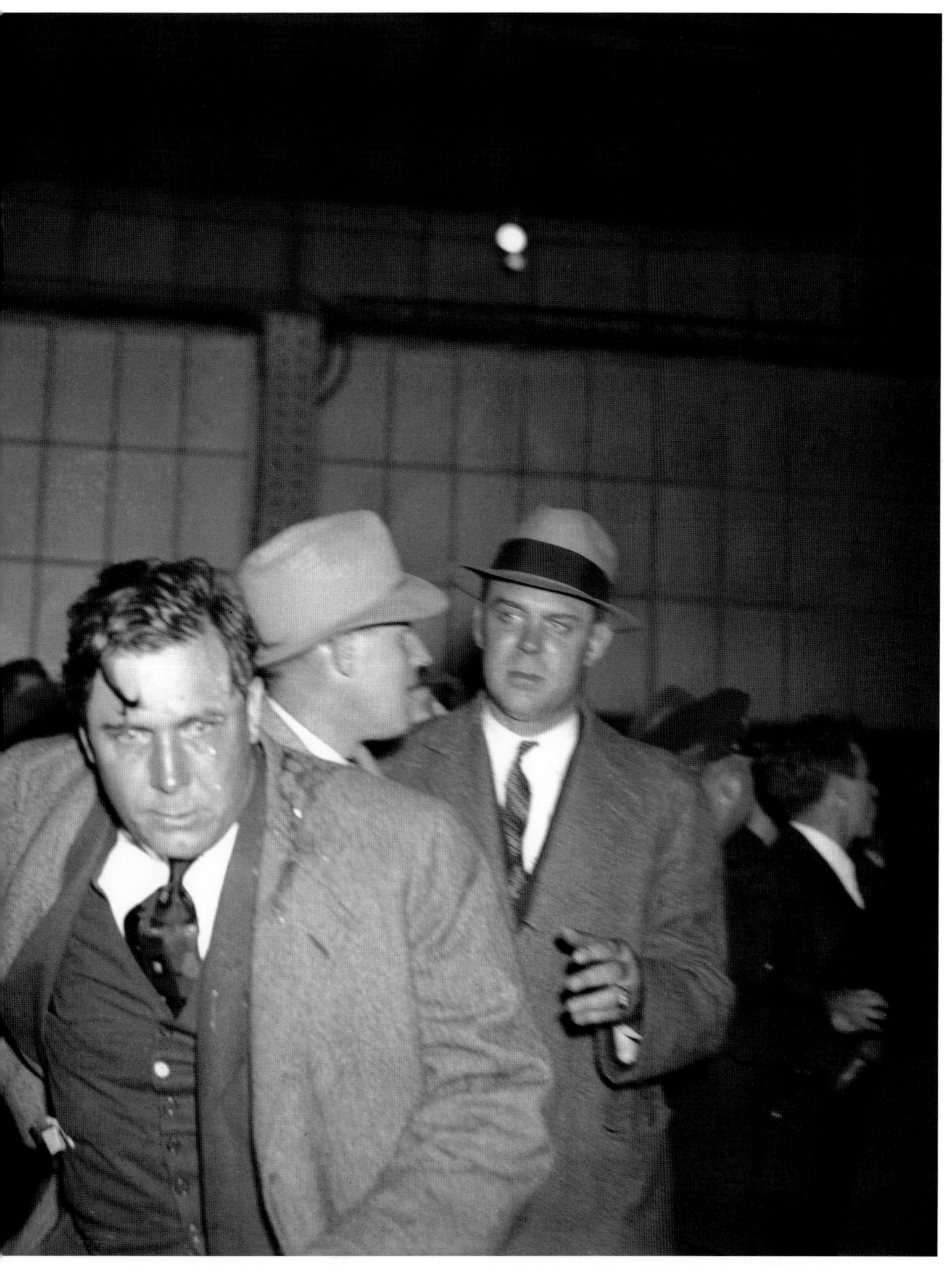
REPUBLICAN WENDELL WILLKIE IS STRUCK BY AN EGG WHILE CAMPAIGNING IN CHICAGO. OCTOBER 22, 1941/BORRIE KANTER

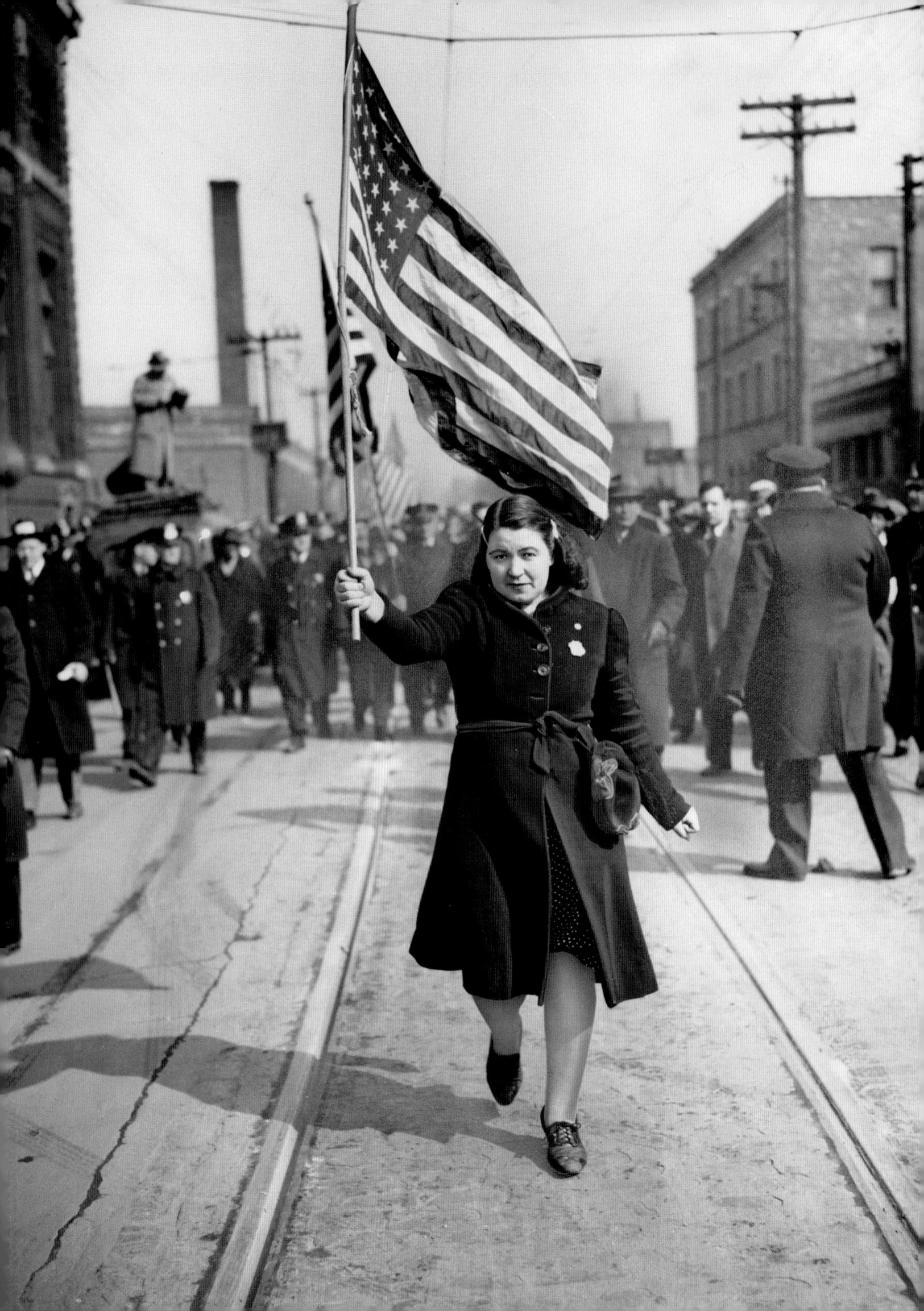

TO SERVE AND PROTECT?

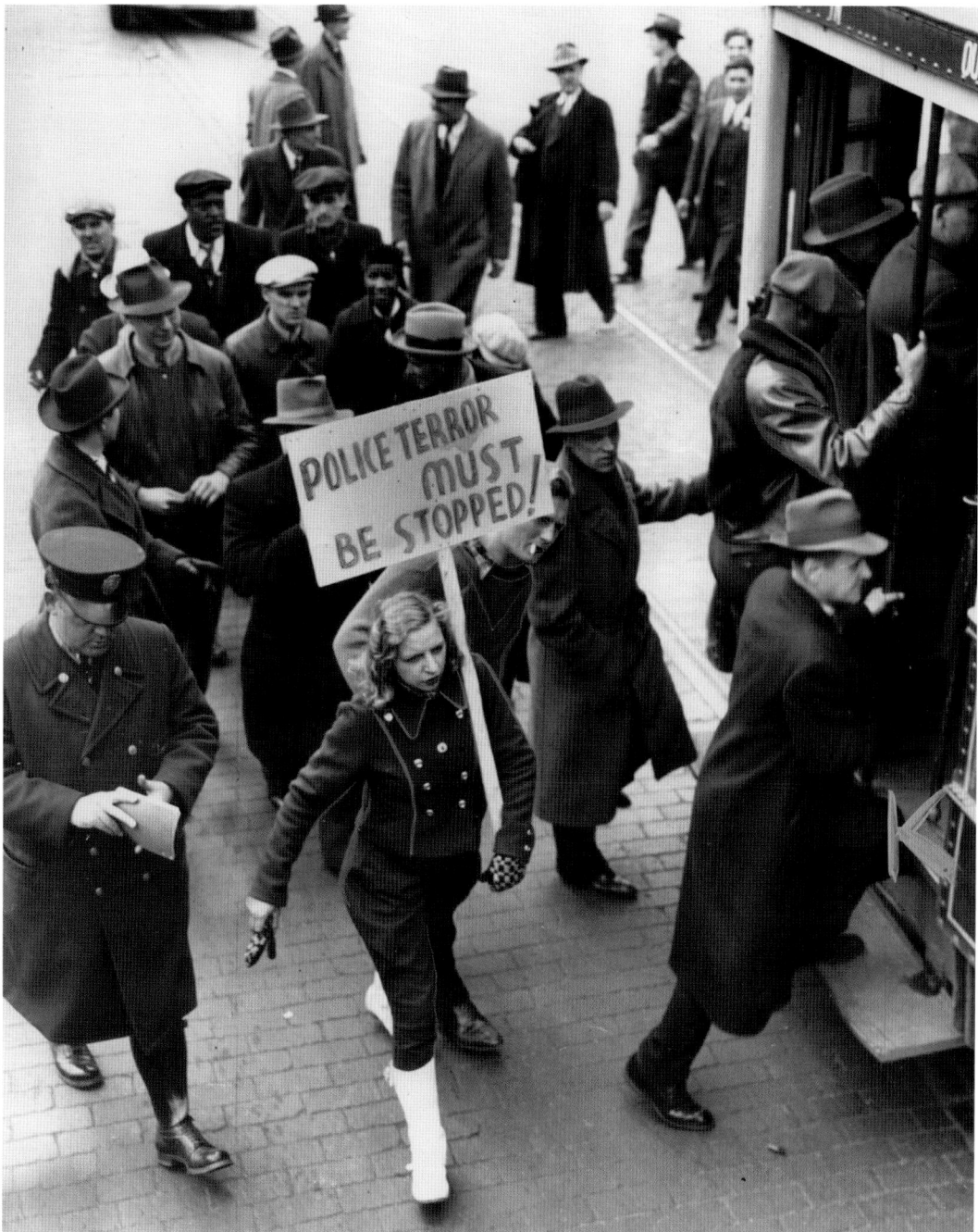

MCCORMICK WORKS STRIKE. POLICE WERE CALLED TO OPEN THE FACTORY. MARCH 25, 1941

Chicago was once synonymous with industry.

"City of the big shoulders," it was called, in recognition of the many thousands who labored in stock yards, steel mills, and factories large and small. As workers challenged employers to improve wages and conditions, Chicago also became the epicenter of American unionism.

Those challenges could spark conflict—frequently violent—between organized workers and employers. And the city's police department could be counted on to serve and protect the powerful instead of the working people of Chicago.

In late February 1941, McCormick Works, a factory on Chicago's Southwest Side that produced agricultural equipment, was shut down when its 7,000 employees went out on strike. The massive plant was the cradle of corporate behemoth International Harvester, controlled by Chicago's elite McCormick family. The McCormicks had a longstanding reputation for anti-unionism. In 1886, a clash between strikers and police in front of McCormick Works left several workers dead. That prompted the protest rally where the infamous Haymarket bombing took place.

It thus came as no surprise to labor advocates in 1941 when Harvester President Fowler McCormick decided to break the strike rather than negotiate with—or even recognize—the union. He announced that McCormick Works would reopen on March 24, encouraging employees to cross the union's picket lines.

On that day, Chicago law enforcement provided the muscle the company required. Half the entire police force was deployed to push pickets back from the plant gates and ensure safe passage for strikebreakers. The following morning, as these photos show, union supporters attempted to march toward McCormick Works bearing American flags to assert their right to assemble and organize. Police officers kept them far from the plant, beating some and arresting many others.

By the end of March, union leaders called off the strike.

Yet the McCormicks would not remain triumphant. In June 1941, workers at McCormick Works, along with several other Harvester plants, voted for the Farm Equipment Workers union to represent them in government-supervised elections. That meant Fowler McCormick would be obligated to recognize and negotiate with a labor union.

—Drawn from The Long Deep Grudge: A Story of Big Capital, Radical Labor, and Class War in the American Heartland by Toni Gilpin.

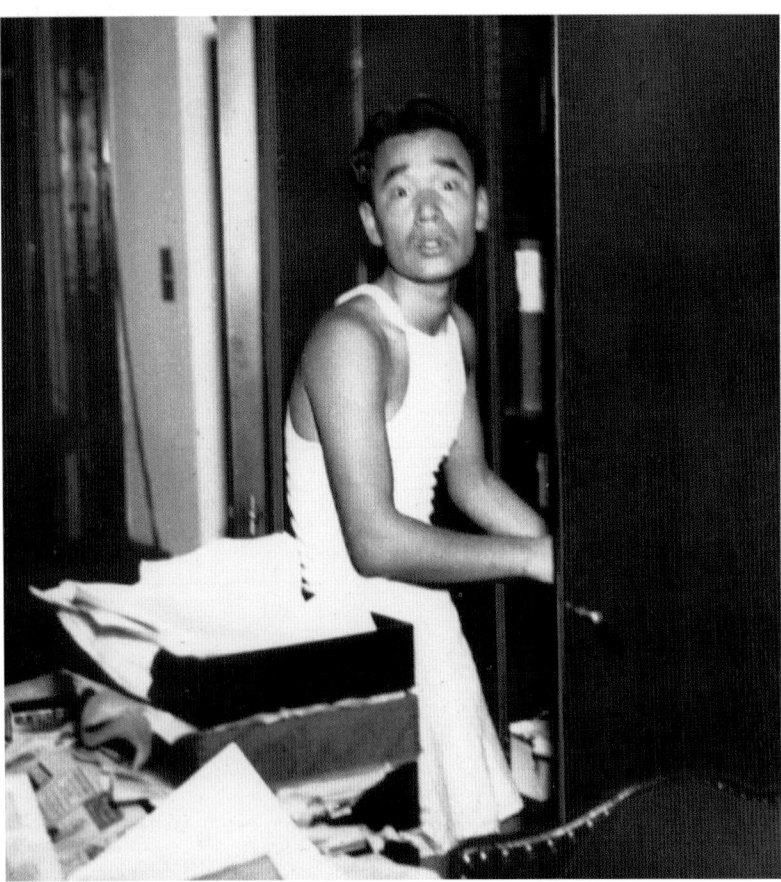

"CAUGHT WITH HONORABLE PANTS DOWN." DECEMBER 7, 1941/GEORGE KOTALIK

OFF TO WAR

Japan's December 7, 1941, raid on Pearl Harbor plunged the United States into World War II—and caused a scramble at the Japanese consulate in Chicago.

Moments after reports of the surprise attack, Chicago Daily Times photographer George Kotalik rushed to the Japanese consulate, only to be stopped by guards. After sneaking around them, the photographer spotted a diplomat—in his underwear—hastily burning documents.

"Hey," Kotalik yelled. When the agent looked up, Kotalik snapped the picture. It was an award-winner. The Times called the photo "Caught with honorable pants down."

Even before the attack, Chicagoans were preparing for war. In March 1941, Grace Huillier and Eleanor Rockwood bid farewell to their soldier boyfriends at Chicago's Dearborn Station. A photographer recorded their names on a caption card and scribbled down the names of the beaus. Rockwood was there to see off Sergeant Bob Grens. By 1945, when Grens was discharged, he and Rookwood were married.

The war took place far from Chicago, but it transformed life here. By one estimate, the typical street block contributed seven people to the military. Lake Michigan became a place for Navy fliers to practice takeoffs and landings on passenger steamers converted into makeshift aircraft carriers.

But Chicago's biggest contribution was top secret: the first controlled nuclear chain reaction, which took place under the University of Chicago football stands on December 2, 1942. Less than three years later, the Nuclear Age dawned.

—*Mark Jacob, former Sun-Times Sunday editor, is coauthor of* Aftershock: The Human Toll of War.

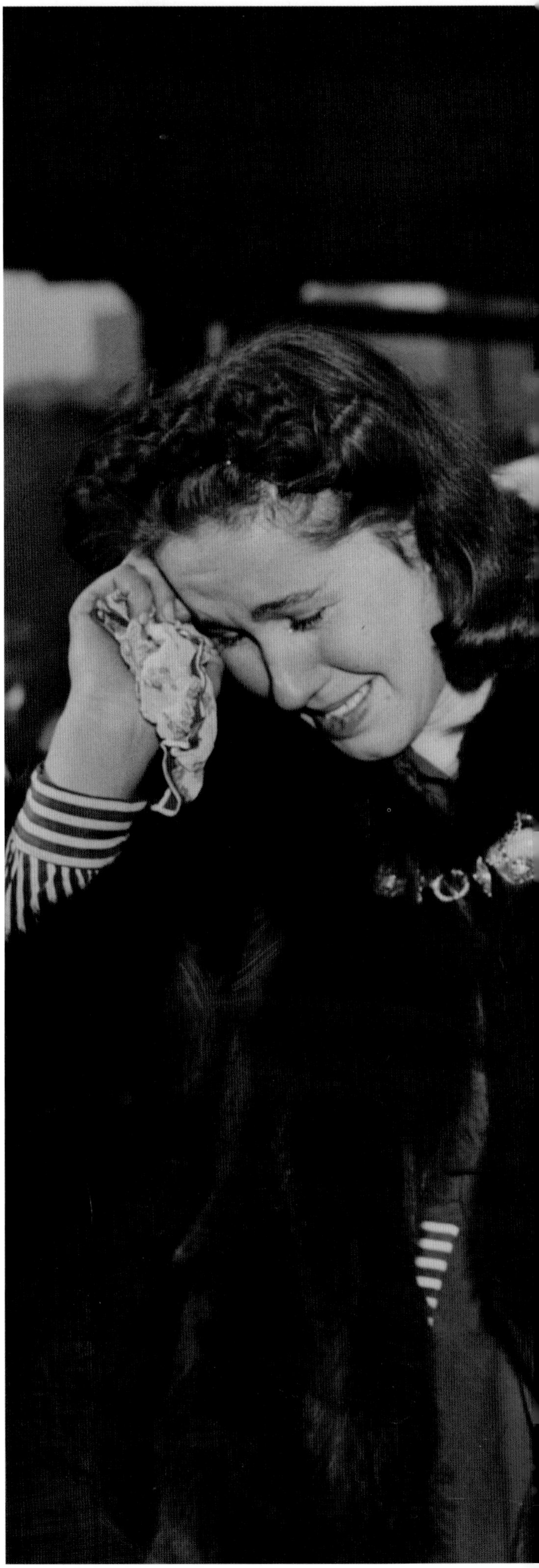

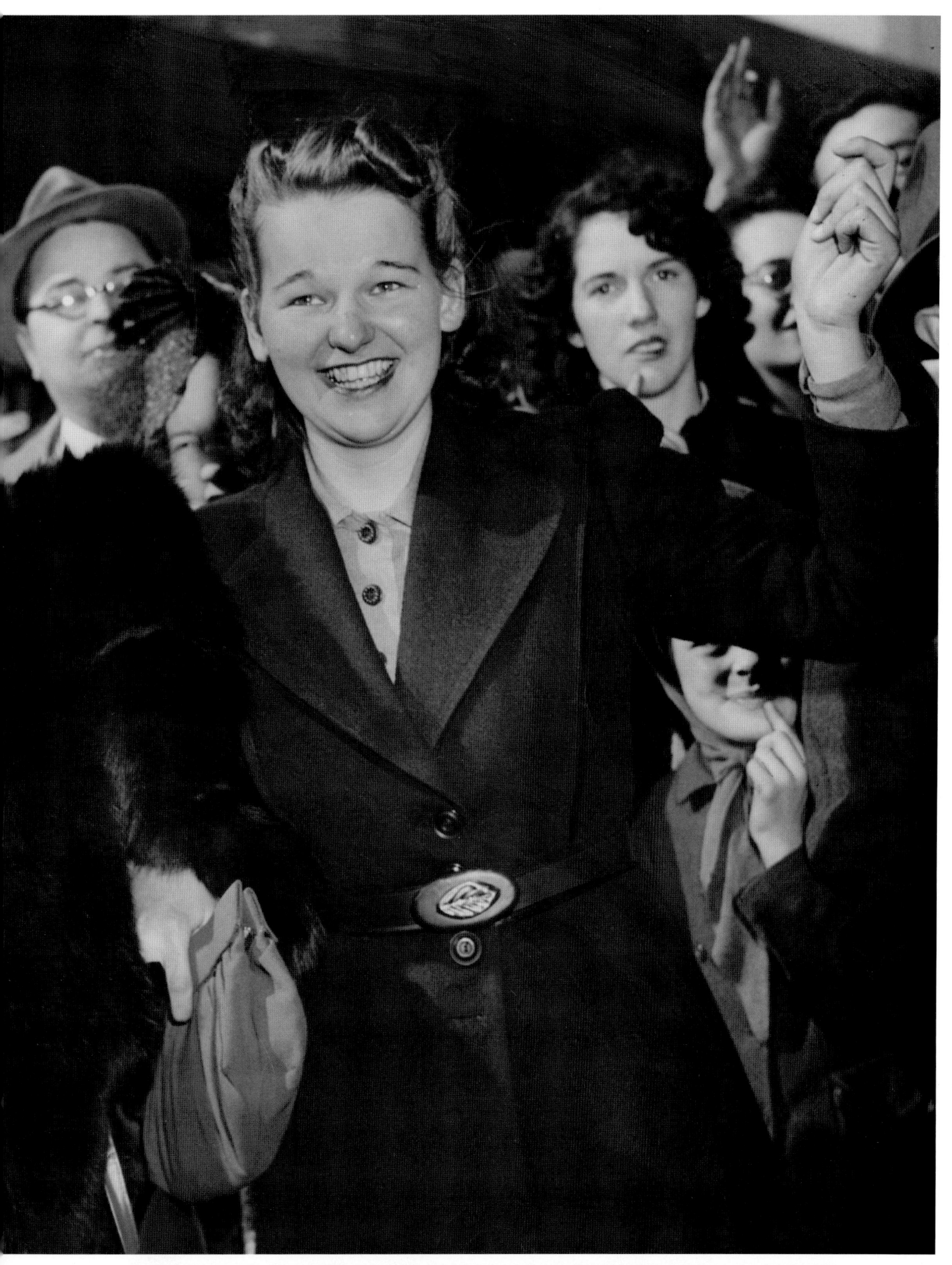
GRACE HUILLIER (LEFT) AND ELEANOR ROCKWOOD SEE OFF THE 132ND INFANTRY REGIMENT. MARCH 24, 1941/DAVE MANN

VICTORY ABROAD, VICTORY AT HOME

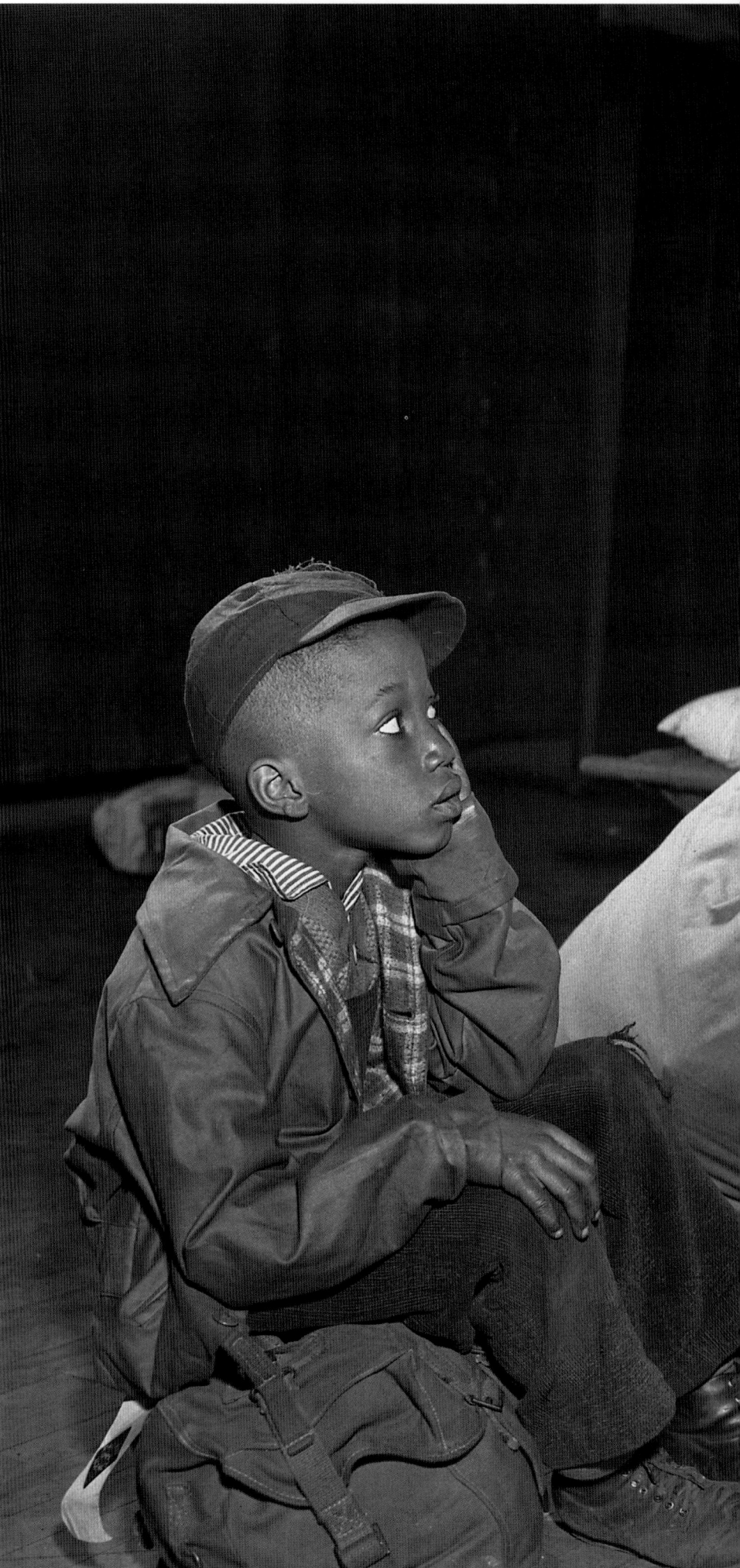

African Americans have always answered the call to serve in times of war. President Lincoln made it possible for Blacks to join the military near the end of the Civil War. However, for many African Americans, military service has come with mixed emotions. The willingness to fight for and represent a country that struggles to represent them is a dichotomy of being Black in America.

This reality of being treated as second-class citizens continued into World War II and helped spark the "Double V" (victory abroad, victory at home) campaign for African Americans. As America spoke of eliminating tyranny and the threat of fascism abroad, it upheld Jim Crow segregation laws and ignored racial violence against African Americans at home. The campaign's demands to end racial discrimination in the early 1940s was at the dawn of the civil rights movement.

In Chicago, the number of African-American residents swelled during the war years because of the Great Migration. As Blacks moved from the South seeking jobs and a better life, the city's military recruitment centers filled with African-American volunteers and draftees.

This image is a bit of a mystery. Most photographs in the Sun-Times collection arrived with caption information. This one did not, but that doesn't take away from its pictorial significance. According to his unit insignia, the soldier is a member of the 555th Parachute Infantry Battalion. Nicknamed the "Triple Nickles," the all-Black airborne battalion was activated in 1943 but did not serve overseas during the war. After the war, many of its members served in the 82d Airborne Division, the US Army's first racially integrated combat unit.

Now that the photograph is being published, perhaps the mystery can be solved.
—*Charles E. Bethea is the Andrew W. Mellon director of collections and curatorial affairs at the Chicago History Museum.*

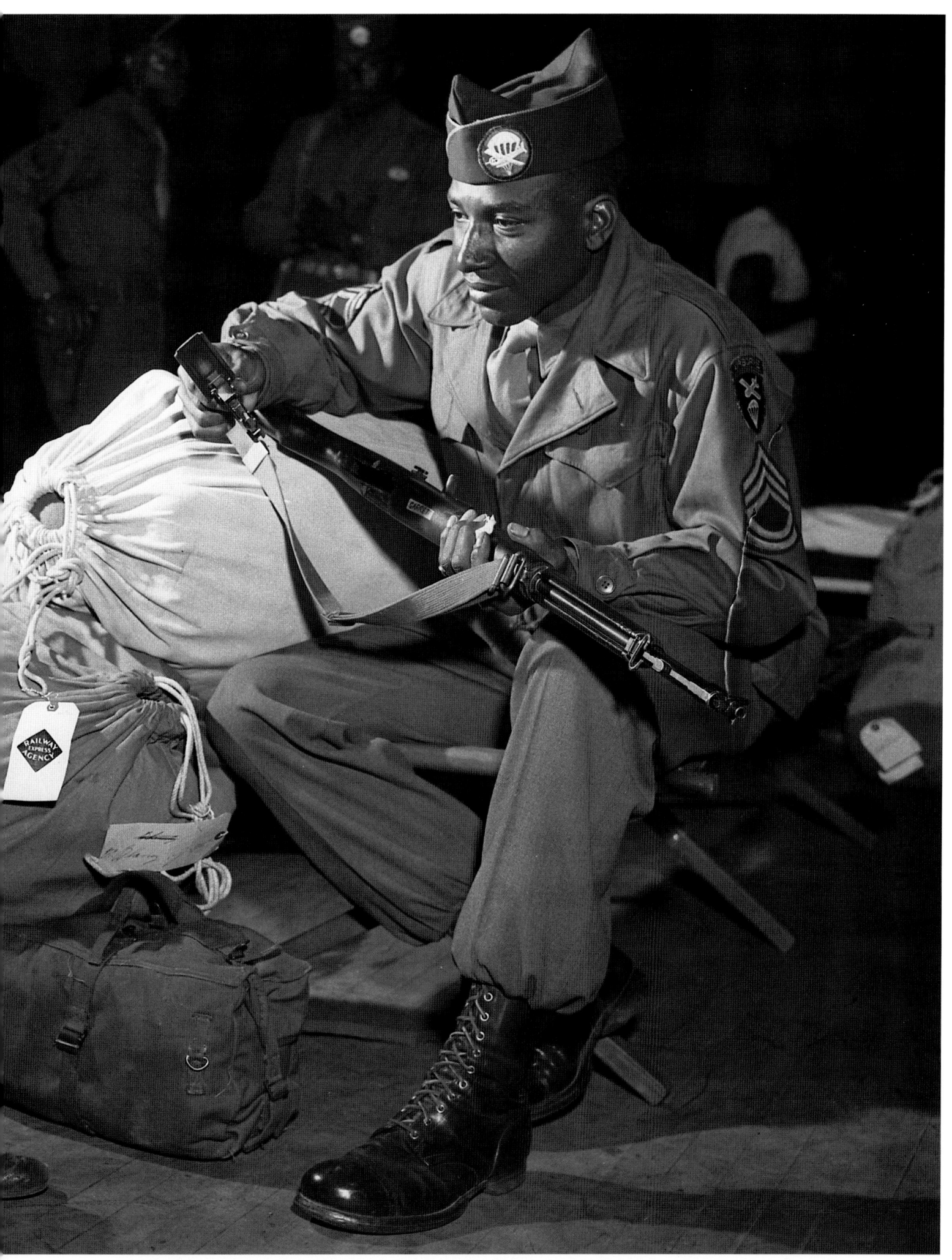
DUFFLE BAGS PACKED AND UNIFORM READY, A SOLDIER SPENDS HIS FINAL MOMENTS WITH A YOUNG BOY. 1946/RALPH FROST

WE HAD TO BE GOOD SOLDIERS

When we got into World War II, many of the Blacks of draft age were already married and had children, so were not going to be selected. So the Black men from Chicago who went into the army were mostly single. Besides those Black men like me who were drafted, there were many who volunteered, including a good many of my friends. Some of them were in the acclaimed Tuskegee Airmen. They were loyal Americans, and they also wanted to learn to fly, to become officers, to win recognition for Black Americans. This was not the first such instance in our history. We decided we had to be good soldiers. We had to come out with an honorable discharge and take whatever assignments we had seriously and become good soldiers.

We moved on to New Jersey, to the base camp of departure for overseas. We shipped out and went the roundabout way to the British Isles, touching land in Scotland, and finally winding up in Wales, where we continued our training. The local people where we were in Wales had never seen any Blacks; they thought that we had just stayed out in the sun too long. But some of them had been informed by the White soldiers that we were like dogs and had tails, and that we were not quite human. So they were curious about us. They came to find that we were very human; the young ladies in particular found that out rather quickly.

I was about 26 years old by this time, going on 27. I was a man. We were getting ready to come home. The war was over. Some young White soldiers were assigned to our ship. They had just arrived in France, and yet they were given the opportunity to board that ship. We Black troops were taken off and reassigned.

A young White soldier said to me, "You mean to tell me you are going to let them take you off that ship?" And it was amazing to me for him to say that. You gonna let them do that to you? An expression of fairness. Was it amazing that a White person could see the injustice? Or that he would have the nerve to criticize me for going along with it? Anyway, I should have said, "Oh, no, I wouldn't let that happen." But in my shame, I said to him, "See, you don't understand. You are not a Negro."
—Timuel D. Black Jr. remembers World War II in his memoir, Sacred Ground.

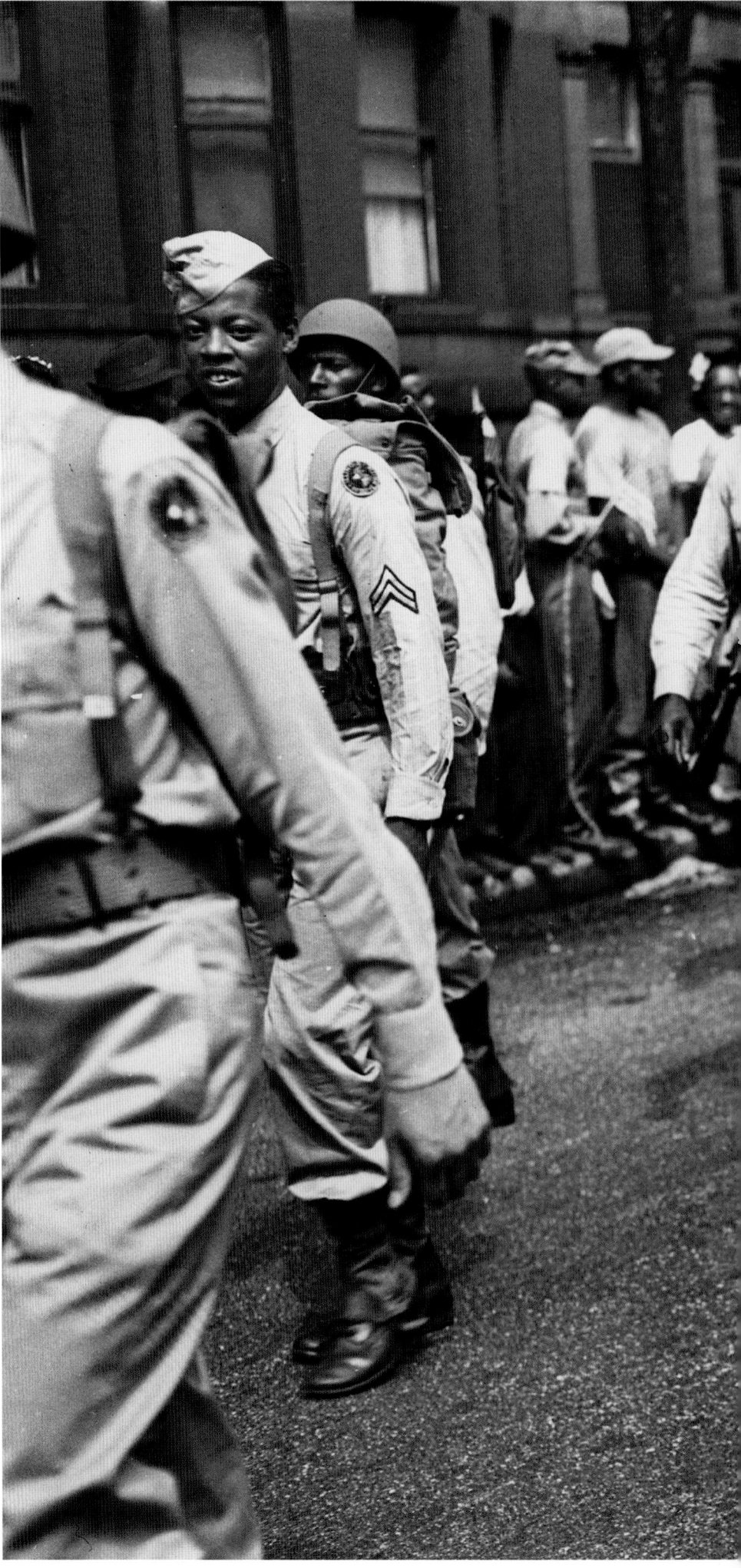

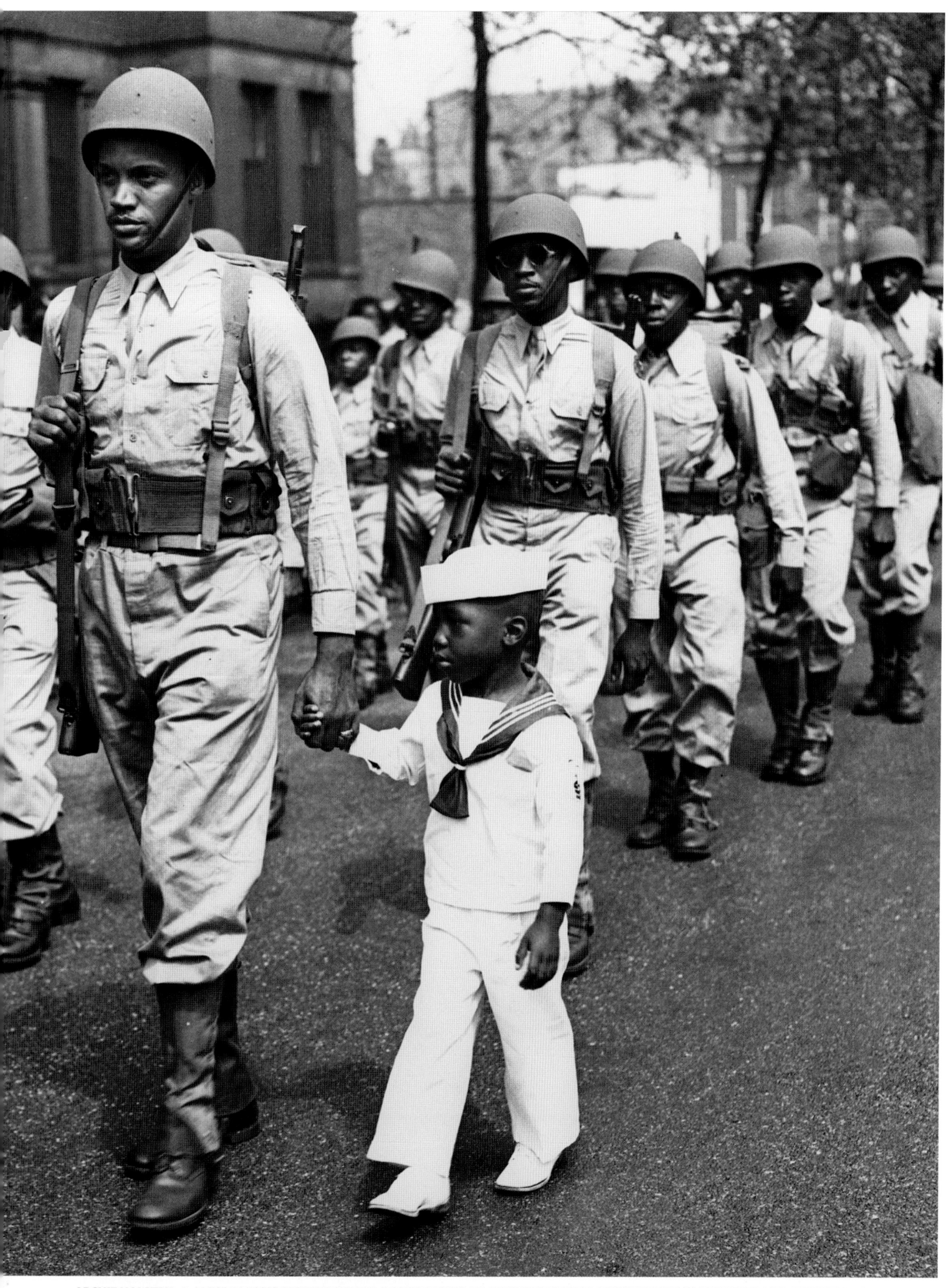
ARCHIE HALSTEN, 4, JOINS ILLINOIS RESERVE MILITIA DOWN MICHIGAN AVENUE IN HONOR OF RETURNING BLACK VETERANS. AUGUST 11, 1945

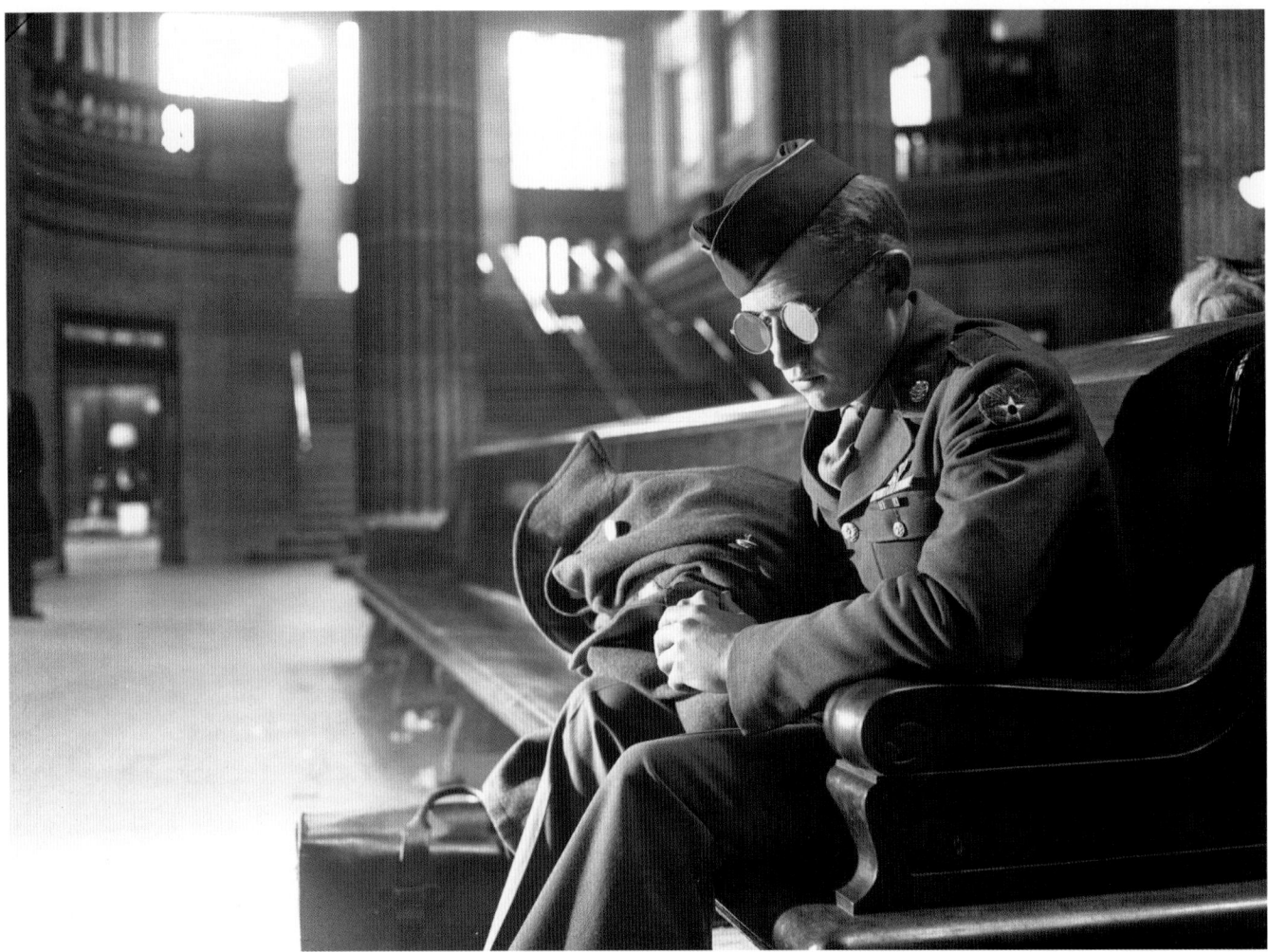

WORLD WAR II TABLEAUX: A SOLDIER AT UNION STATION. BILL STURM OPPOSITE: LOOP V-J CELEBRATION. AUGUST 14, 1945/BILL BENDER

HOME FROM GOD KNOWS WHERE

All boozy smiles and Gene Krupa tom-toms, here's post-war Chicago on the make, celebrating in bow ties and bobby socks. The war had poured enough money into the city to finally float it out of the Depression and point it towards a brand-new world; this V-E Day party in many ways didn't stop for the next fifteen years. There'd be jobs and smokestacks for all, experiments and exuberance that would change the arts, technology, and industry forever.

But Chicago was this soldier, too. Silent, stunned, home from God knows where, witness to unimaginable things maybe in Hiroshima, in Dachau, or from the edge of his foxhole. What he wanted now was to be alone after the years of desire and fear so he could get on with his life. He's scared of what he's learned. He's exhausted by death. Some 75 million people had died worldwide over the preceding six years, out of 2.5 billion; scale that to today and it would be around 225 million dead. In six years. Forgive him if he doesn't look as optimistic as the partiers.

This had been a "good war" for most Chicagoans, left safe and sound and well fed. But with so many immigrants who still had ties to Europe, that breathtaking loss was felt in uncountable, visceral ways.

My introduction to the concept of "concentration camp" came when I was five or six, rooting around in an old sideboard in our basement where I found pamphlets hidden there by, I'm guessing, my grandfather. I couldn't read Polish, but the detailed drawings introduced me to existential evil way too early.

My father, who'd grown up speaking only Polish, raised my sister and me to run from the Old World that had authored that horror and into the colorblind meritocracy that triumphant America supposedly offered. Others around us hunkered down in their little villages on the big grid of Chicago and prepared to repel any and all invaders. I could never stop wondering which people in that pamphlet were my relatives.

So Chicago moved ahead, balanced on this knife-edge of industry, technology, creativity, and renewal on one side, and our own fears on the other. Fear of not getting what we had coming. Fear of losing what we had. The ride ahead would not be smooth.

—*Thomas Dyja is the author of* The Third Coast: When Chicago Built the American Dream *and* New York, New York, New York: Four Decades of Success, Excess, and Transformation.

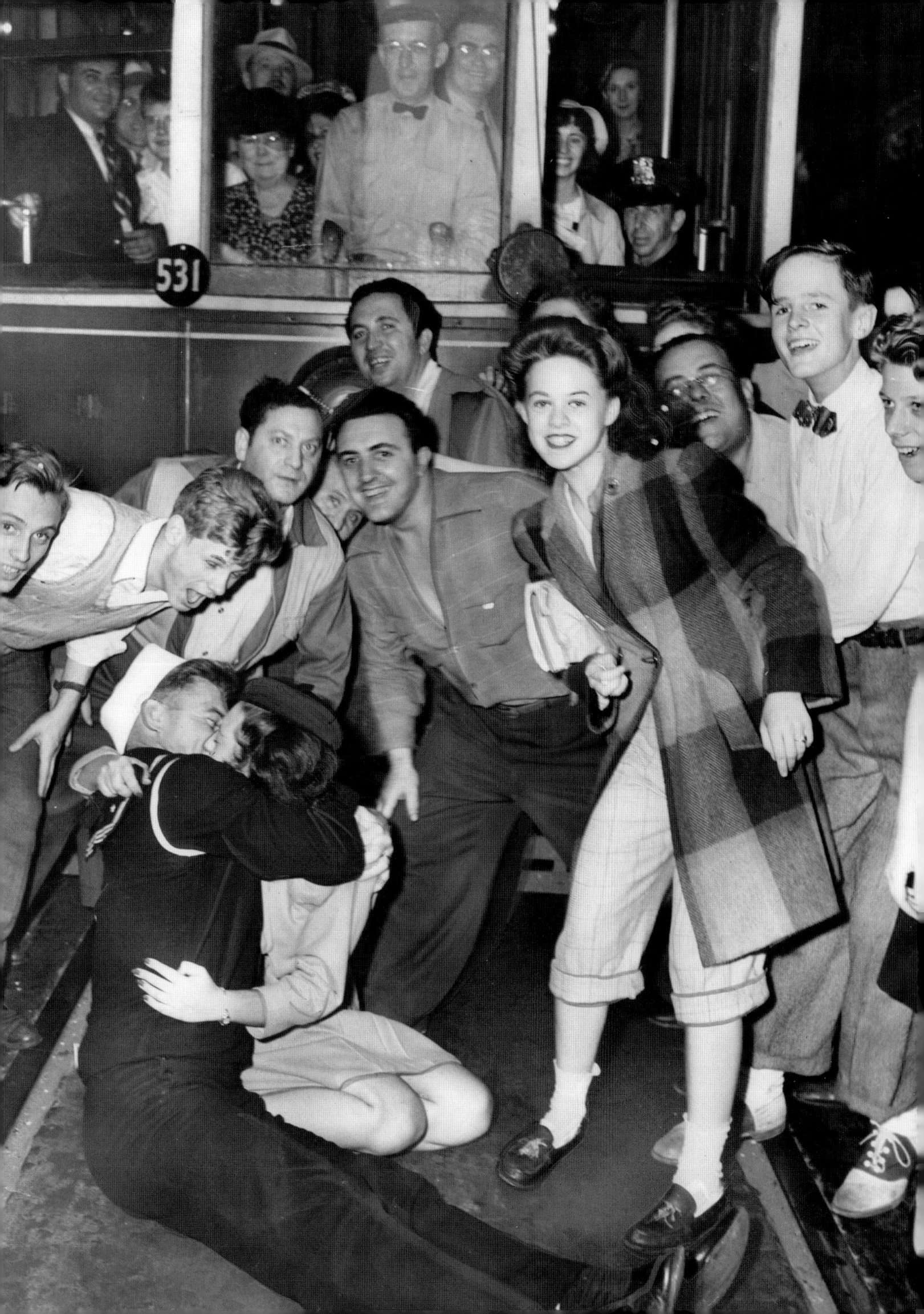

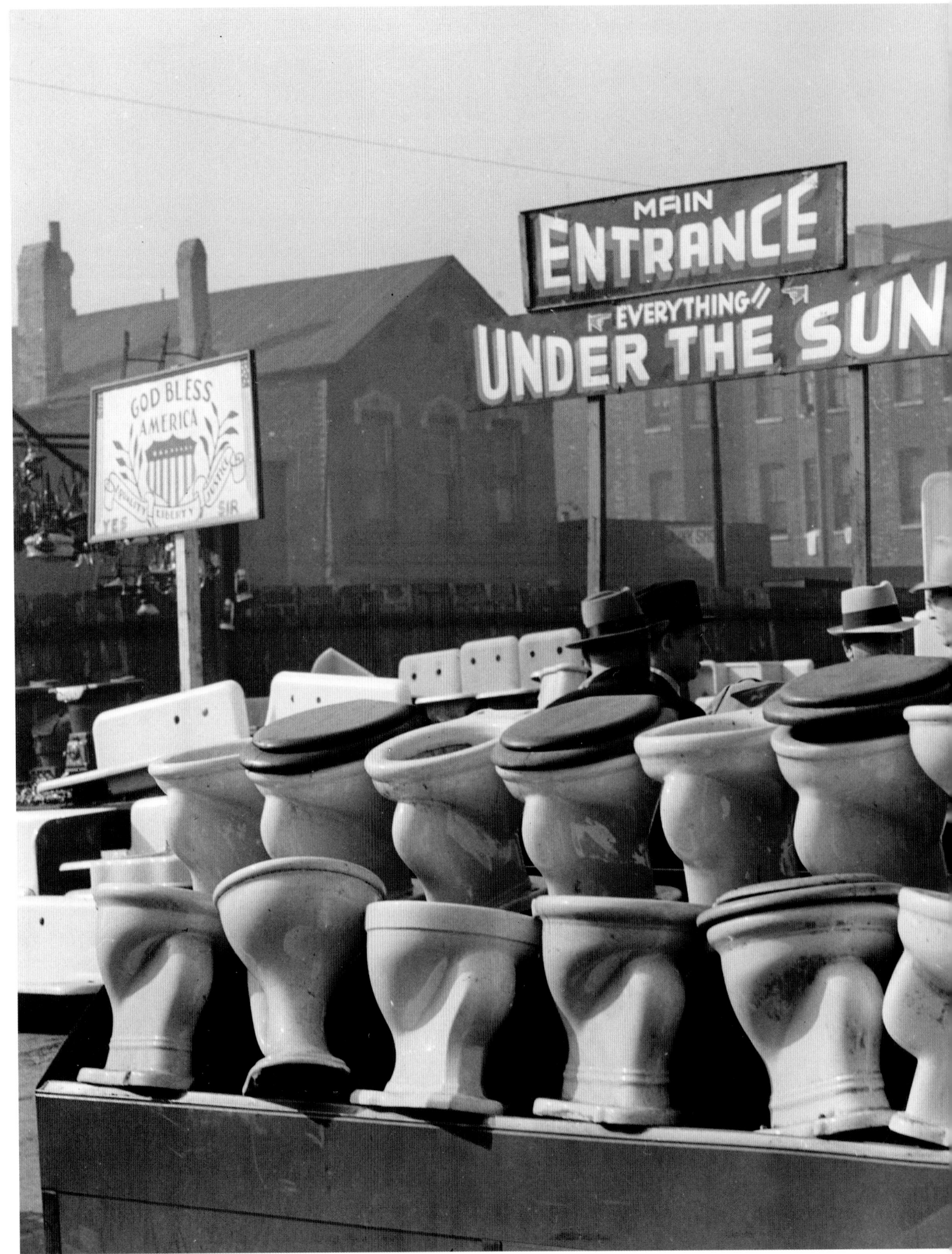

CHICAGO'S MAXWELL STREET REMAINED CONSTANT FOR DECADES IN A CHANGING WORLD. OCTOBER 24, 1942/RUSSELL V. HAMM

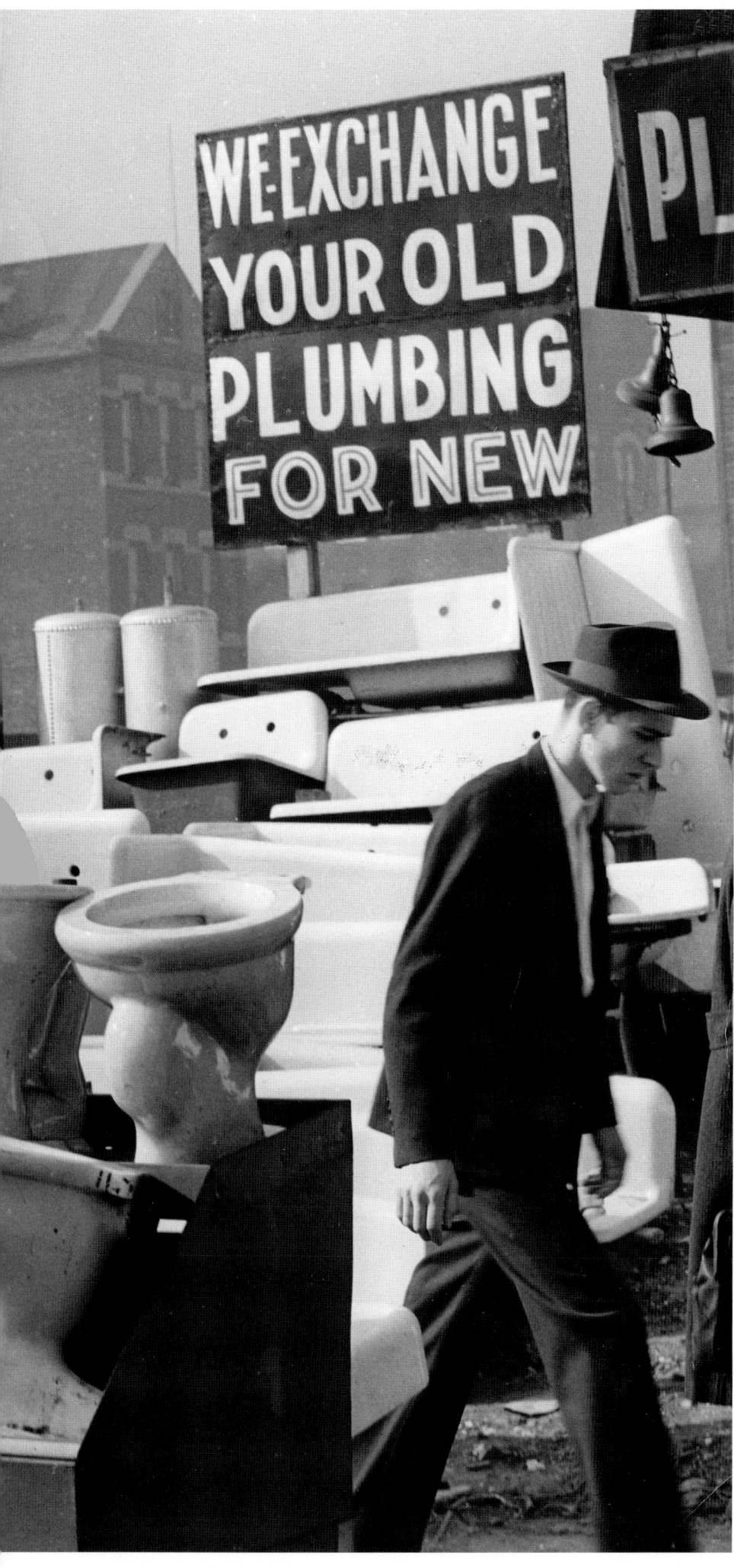

FREE MARKET ECONOMY

Used toilets, stacked and ready for resale. So Maxwell Street.

Ah, old Maxwell Street, sadly gone, was a wild, messy, sprawling, relentlessly capitalist, open-air market packed every Sunday with shoppers and gawkers, hawkers, and thieves.

Card tables, makeshift tables of plywood or planks on milk crates or concrete blocks or sawhorses. Tables crammed with TVs, car radios, computer monitors, stereos, tools, and gear. And stuff.

Boxes of vinyl, comic books, videotapes, CDs, DVDs, BVDs, and hubcaps AWOL from BMWs and VWs. Suit coats, swimsuits, pant suits, zoot suits, bib zoots, house paint, art supplies, old 8-mm home movies, dining room sets, wrench sets, socks, produce, paperback novels, old magazines, Underwood typewriters, Epson printers, reams of printer paper, fountain pens, knick-knacks, paddywacks, dog bones, *tchotchkes*, toothbrushes and, of course, used toilets.

The spirit of the free-wheeling, free market hung over the place like the heavy smell of fried onions from Jim's Original red hots. I bought my 16-mm Eclair movie camera on Maxwell Street. It was my camera right up to the moment it was swiped from the trunk of my car, while I was wandering around Maxwell with friends.

When we came back the trunk was popped, and the camera gone. On a whim I asked some kids playing nearby if they would help me get my camera back. They told me to wait—and walked away. They returned a short time later—to tell me the price would be $100. We came up with $80. They took the money and told us we could find the camera hidden by the basement back door behind a nearby building.

Sure enough, that's where we found it.
—Tom Palazzolo
is an experimental filmmaker and photographer who directed a documentary and cowrote a book about Maxwell Street.

CALL NORTHSIDE 777

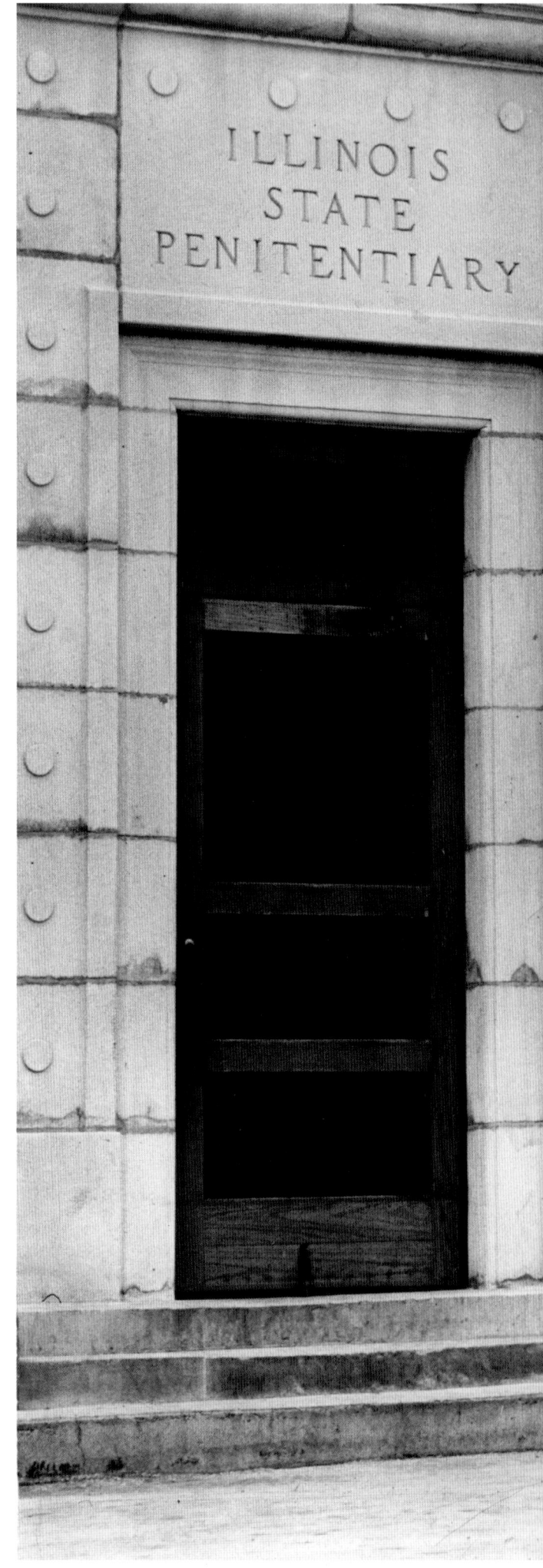

A chance meeting with retired Chicago newspaperman Jack McPhaul several months before his death in 1983 aroused my curiosity about the story that inspired the 1948 film noir classic *Call Northside 777*. That's the film in which Jimmy Stewart played a composite character based on McPhaul and fellow newsman James P. McGuire.

Their involvement in the story began on October 10, 1944, when a classified ad appeared in the paper they worked for, the Chicago Times (forerunner of the Sun-Times): "Five Thousand Dollars reward for killers of Officer Lundy on December 9, 1932. Call GRO-1758, 12-7 p.m."

The ad was placed by Tillie Majczek. In 1933, her son Joseph W. Majczek, 24, and his friend Theodore Marcinkiewicz, 26, were convicted of murdering Chicago Police officer William D. Lundy in a speakeasy near the Union Stock Yards. They were sentenced to 99-year prison terms. Tillie, believing her son was innocent, scrubbed floors on her hands and knees at Commonwealth Edison's downtown headquarters for eleven years to save the reward money.

McPhaul and McGuire were skeptical of the claim of innocence. "I wrote a story making Tillie the heroine, tossed in a couple of lines from Kipling's 'Mother of Mine,' and figured that was it," McPhaul told me. But he and McGuire were spurred to investigate after reading 30 pages of "facts" prepared by Joe Majczek in prison.

Within days, McPhaul and McGuire found evidence of perjury by the prosecution's star witness, Vera Walush, proprietor of the speakeasy where the murder occurred. She confided to friends that she falsely identified Majczek and Marcinkiewicz because State's Attorney Thomas J. Courtney threatened to have her arrested for violating the Prohibition Act if she didn't. (At the trial, Courtney called the speakeasy "a delicatessen.")

Based on eight stories by the Times reporters, Governor Dwight Green pardoned Majczek in 1945. The Illinois General Assembly awarded him $24,000 for the dozen years he languished behind bars. He went on to a successful insurance sales career in Chicago. Marcinkiewicz was exonerated and released from prison in 1950. The General Assembly awarded him $35,000 for his seventeen years of wrongful imprisonment. He changed his name to Marcin and moved to Los Angeles, where he became a beer delivery truck driver.

In researching the case, I was struck by a number of things, among them: Joe Majczek was at least as good looking as Richard Conte, the star who played him in the movie. Hollywood presented the story reasonably accurately—with the exception of changing GRO (for Grovehill) 1758 to something with (pardon the pun) a better ring. And, sadly, newspapering isn't what it once was.

—*Rob Warden worked for the Chicago Daily News from 1965 to 1978. He later served as executive director of the Center on Wrongful Convictions at Northwestern University School of Law.*

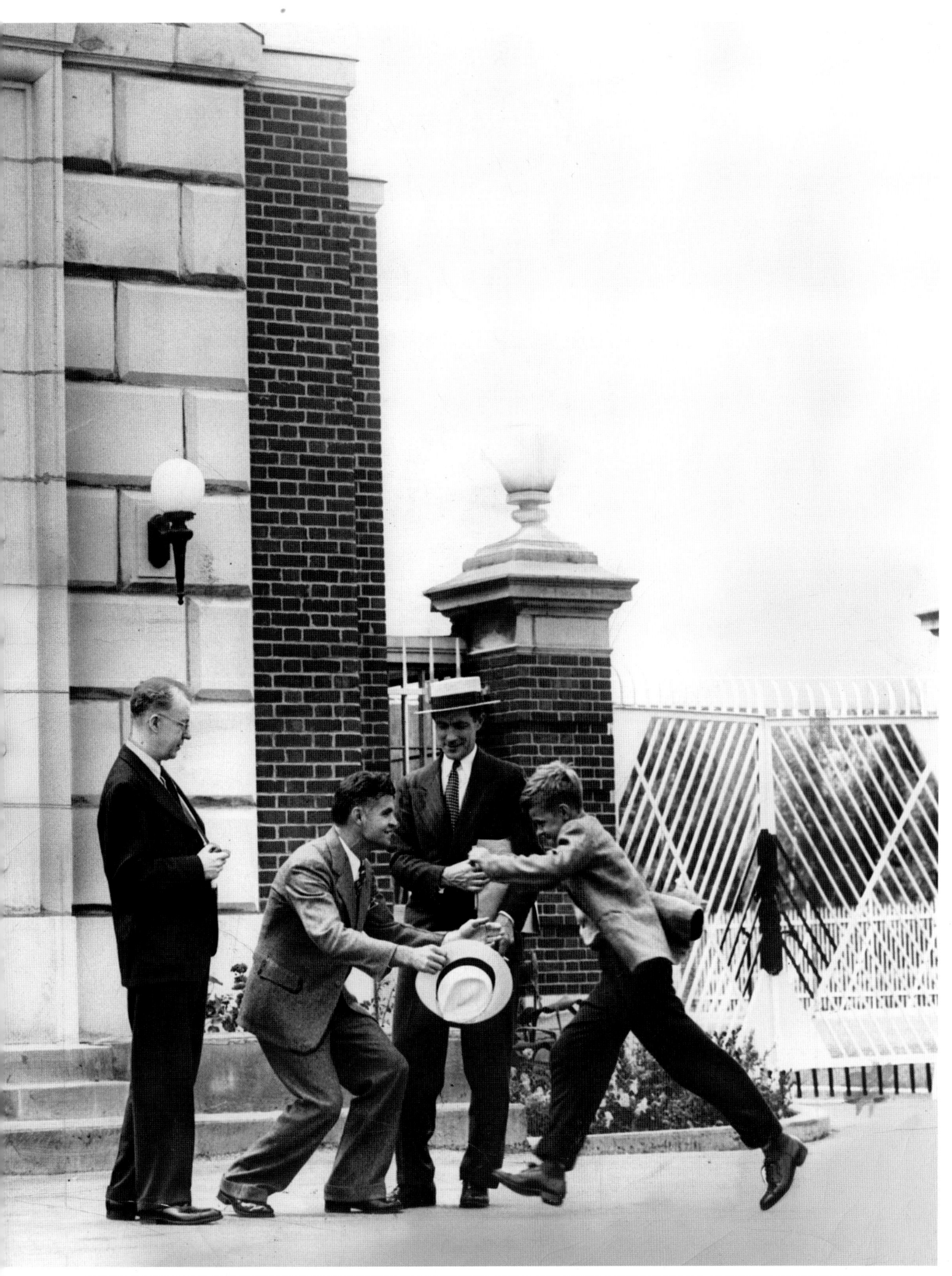
JOSEPH W. MAJCZEK GREETS HIS SON AS REPORTERS JACK MCPHAUL (LEFT) AND JAMES MCGUIRE WATCH. AUGUST 15, 1945/BILL PAUER

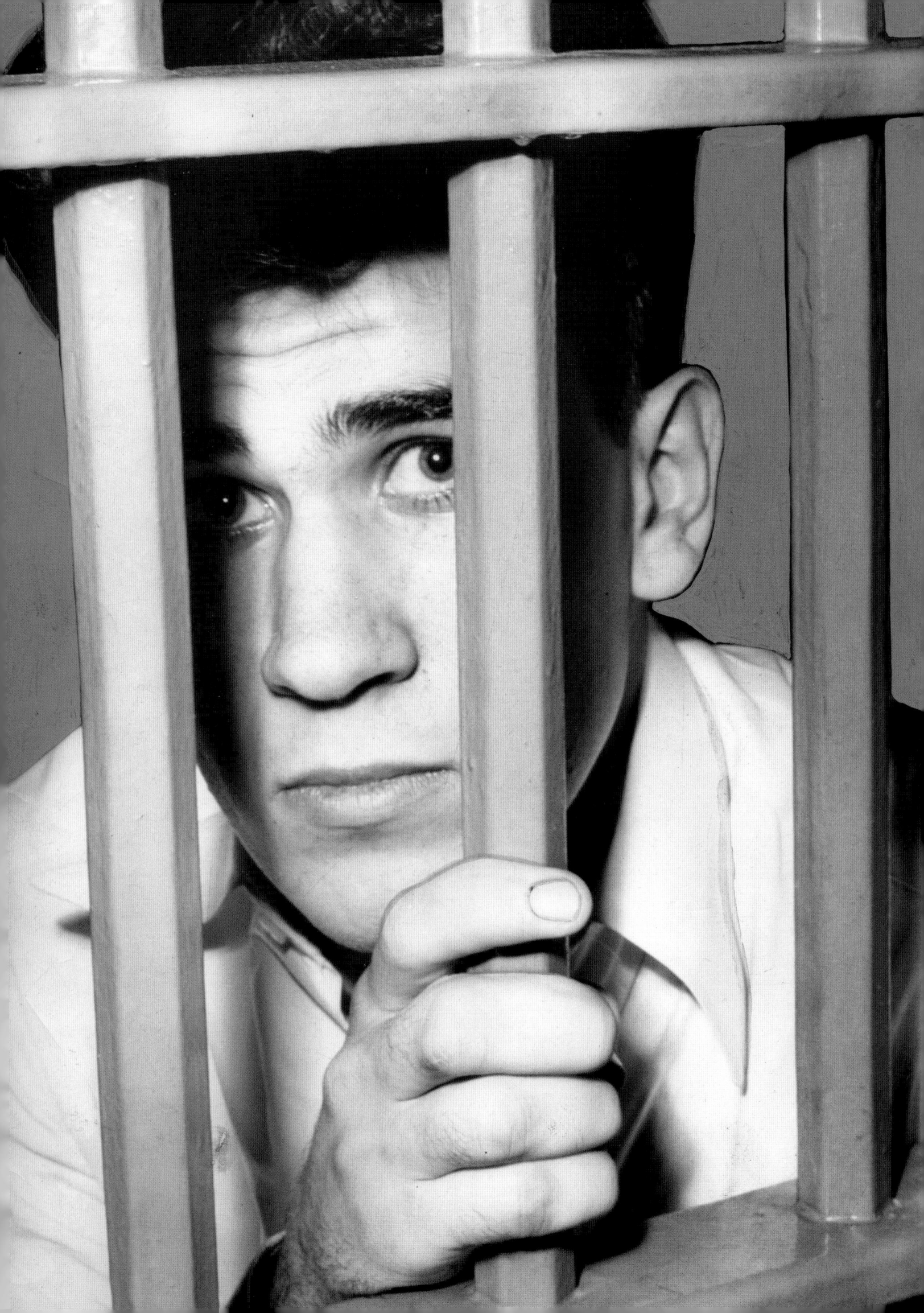

THE MAN BEHIND BARS

In the early morning hours of January 7, 1946, James Degnan looked in on his six-year-old daughter, Suzanne. The girl was not in her bed—the adjoining window had been thrown open. Suzanne had been abducted.

Police discovered a ladder lying near the garage and an oil-stained ransom note demanding $20,000 in small bills. Later that day, the kidnapper phoned to arrange a meeting to present a sample of the girl's hair and a pajama fragment as proof of the abduction. Degnan pleaded for his daughter's safe return, but detectives soon made a grisly discovery. They found Suzanne's severed head in a catch basin several blocks from the Degnans' Rogers Park home.

Mayor Edward Kelly reassured residents that the fiend would be identified and brought to justice. Autopsy surgeons determined the killing happened between 12:30 and 1 a.m. Traces of coal dust suggested that the murder occurred in a basement, leading to the arrest of two elderly janitors, Hector Verburgh and Desere Smet. The men were brutally interrogated. Verburgh eventually won a $15,000 settlement against seventeen of Chicago's "toughest cops."

With valuable assistance from Chicago Daily News staff artist Frank San Hamel, who deciphered faint impressions of handwriting on the ransom note, police traced its origin to the University of Chicago.

Five months later, detectives seized seventeen-year-old William George Heirens after the U of C student fired shots at them during a failed North Side burglary. Heirens' arrest record, which dated back to 1942, included 24 residential burglaries.

His fingerprints had some similarity to the print found on the ransom note. Under intense "third-degree" questioning that critics later decried as brutal and coerced, Heirens confessed to Suzanne's murder. Incriminating items recovered from his dormitory room linked Heirens to two earlier North Side slayings. Detectives later found a discarded hunting knife, believed to be in Heirens' possession, near the Granville Avenue L train station.

Heirens agreed to plead guilty and was sentenced to three life terms in 1946. Though his defenders long contended he was not guilty of the Degnan murder, Heirens remained incarcerated until his death in 2012. At the time, he was the longest-serving Illinois Department of Corrections inmate.
—*Richard C. Lindberg is the author of twenty published books relating to Chicago history, true crime, politics, and sports.*

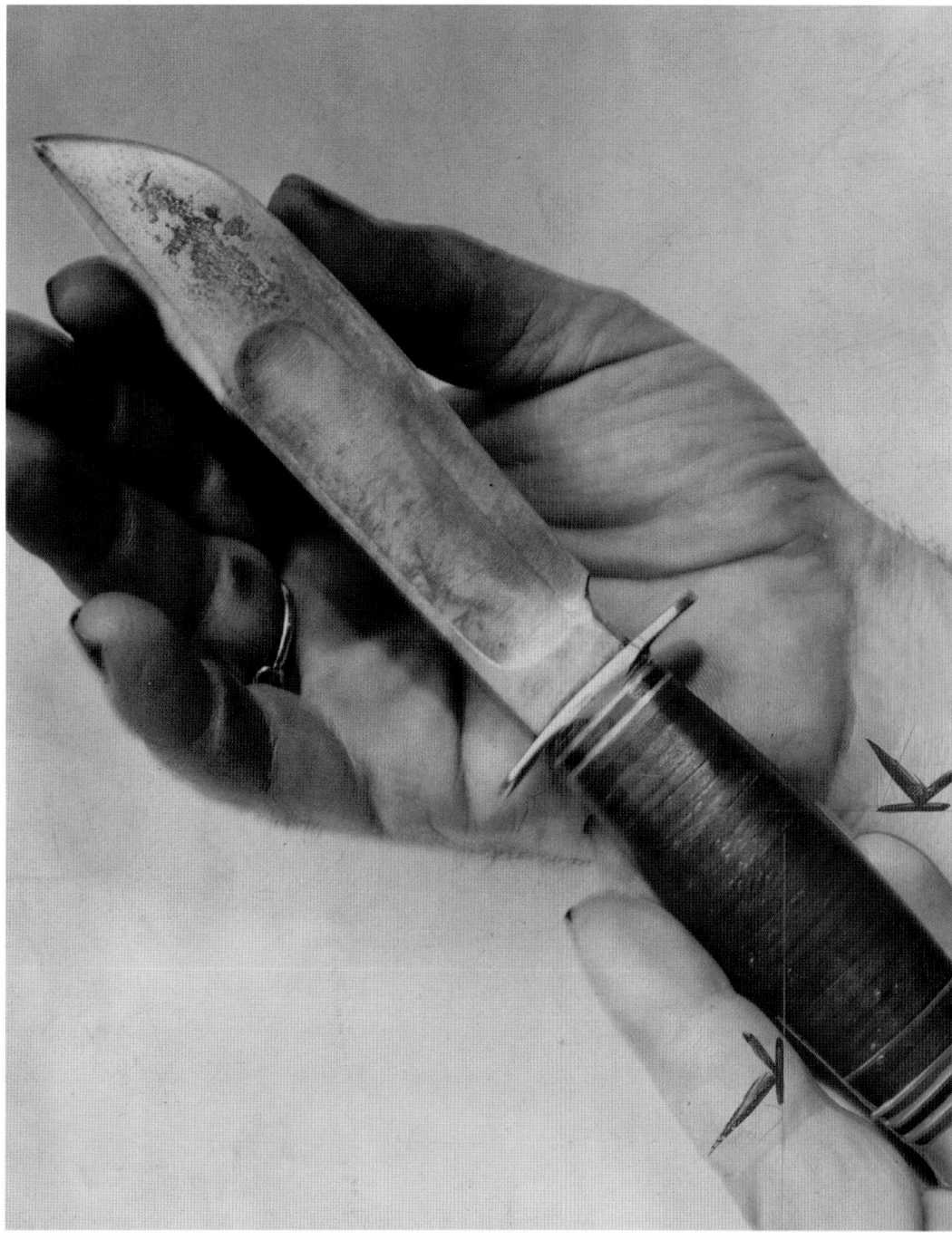

POSSIBLE MURDER WEAPON. OPPOSITE: WILLIAM HEIRENS AT COOK COUNTY JAIL. JULY 12, 1946

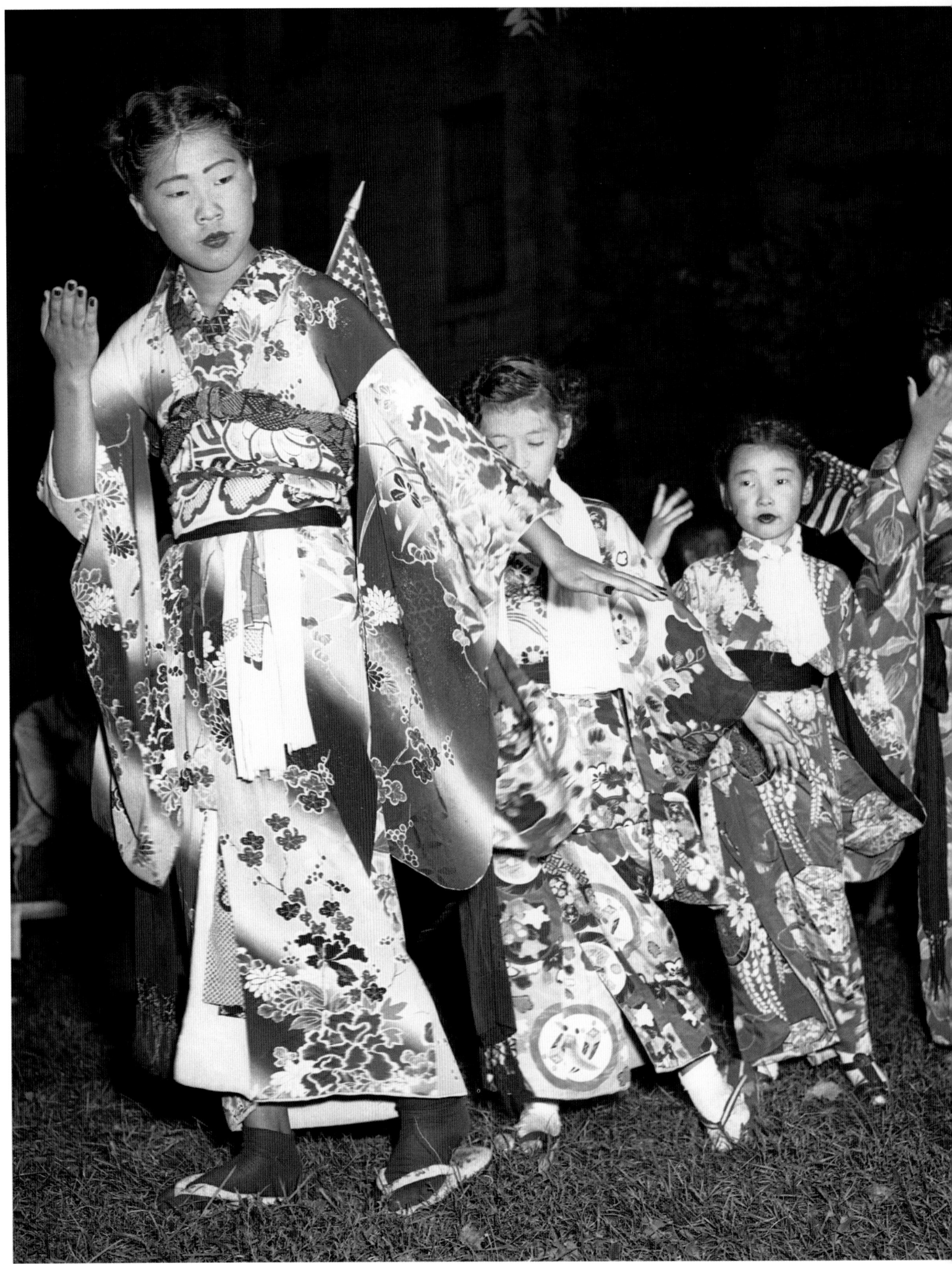

RITUAL DANCE HONORING WAR DEAD. JAPANESE-AMERICAN RESETTLERS ESTABLISHED A THRIVING ETHNIC COMMUNITY. AUGUST 24, 1947

LEAVING THE CAMPS, FINDING A HOME

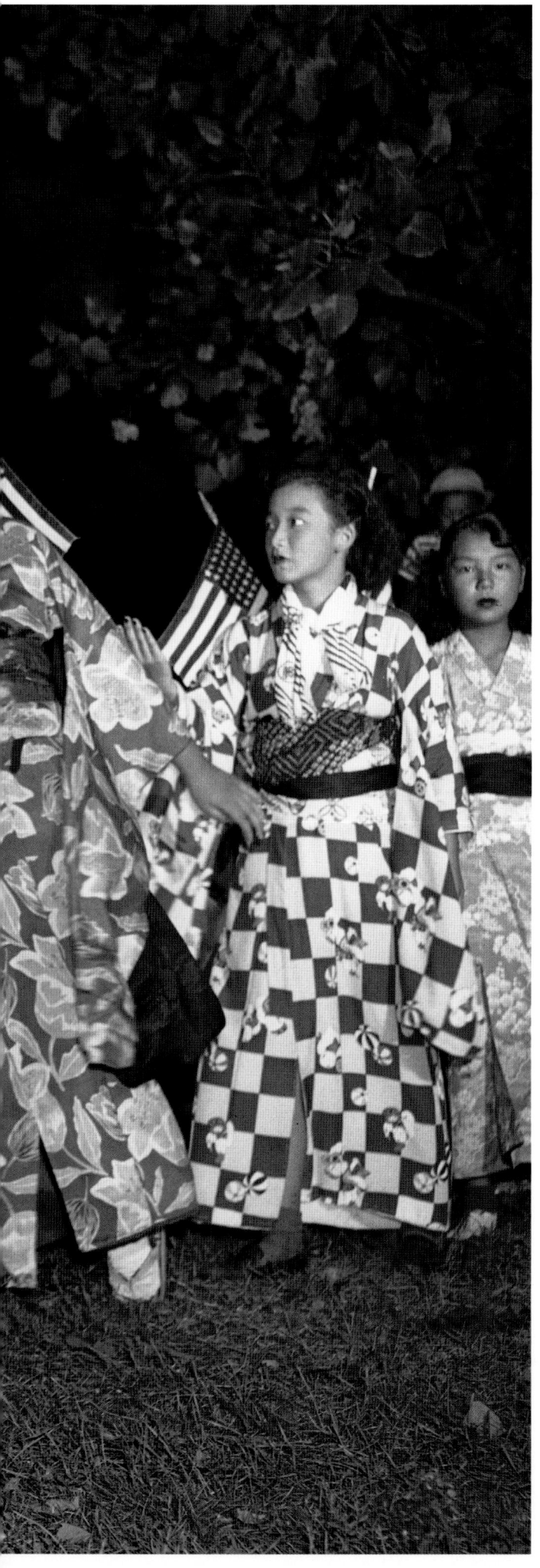

The explosion of Chicago's Japanese-American population from just under 400 on the eve of World War II to more than 20,000 by 1946 reflects an extraordinary moment in Japanese-American history.

Chicago's prewar Japanese community differed markedly from its Pacific Coast contemporaries. Unlike those settlements, agricultural laborers did not predominate in Chicago. Small business owners, service workers, and students comprised the local population.

Residentially, they scattered throughout the city rather than concentrating in a "Little Tokyo." Japanese Americans in Chicago did not encounter the tremendous levels of discrimination that their western counterparts faced. And the city itself was never subject to President Franklin Delano Roosevelt's Executive Order 9066, which authorized the incarceration of more than 110,000 Japanese Americans, most of whom were US citizens, in ten concentration camps in the West.

Select Japanese Americans in these camps were allowed to move East, or "resettle," starting in 1943. Chicago offered plentiful employment prospects. Defense-related industries, especially, sought laborers, and resettlers eagerly applied for positions in munitions factories. Others took service, clerical, or light-manufacturing jobs. And many gravitated towards companies willing to take Japanese Americans en masse, including Curtiss Candy, McClurg Publishing, Stevens Hotel, and Edgewater Beach Hotel. (Many employers preferred hiring Japanese Americans as an alternative to hiring African Americans.)

The War Relocation Authority, the federal agency in charge of Japanese Americans removed from their homes, emphasized that resettlers from the camps should "avoid segregation *at all costs*" and "spread out thinly," joining *"Hakujin* [White]" groups, churches, clubs, and professional associations. A number of resettlers to Chicago took this advice to heart.

But most tested the WRA's guidelines. Preoccupied with day-to-day survival issues during the early years of resettlement, lonely Japanese Americans readily sought each other out for companionship. Resettlers were hesitant about interacting with Whites, a nervousness that stemmed from their tenuous status in a society still at war with Japan and a painful awareness about the race riots sweeping the country during the war.

Racial discrimination made life in Chicago a challenge. Though restrictive covenants were not aimed at Japanese, finding satisfactory housing was the single most difficult task for resettlers.

For the most part, they were only able to rent apartments and homes in restricted areas (understood as zones of transition or buffer regions between Whites and Blacks) on the city's Near North Side and in Hyde Park-Kenwood on the city's South Side. In addition to housing, Japanese Americans—like the city's other racial minorities, especially African Americans—encountered racism in the workplace and other public spaces, including dance halls, hospitals, and even cemeteries.

—*Ellen Wu is associate history professor at Indiana University. Adapted from the Densho Encyclopedia.*

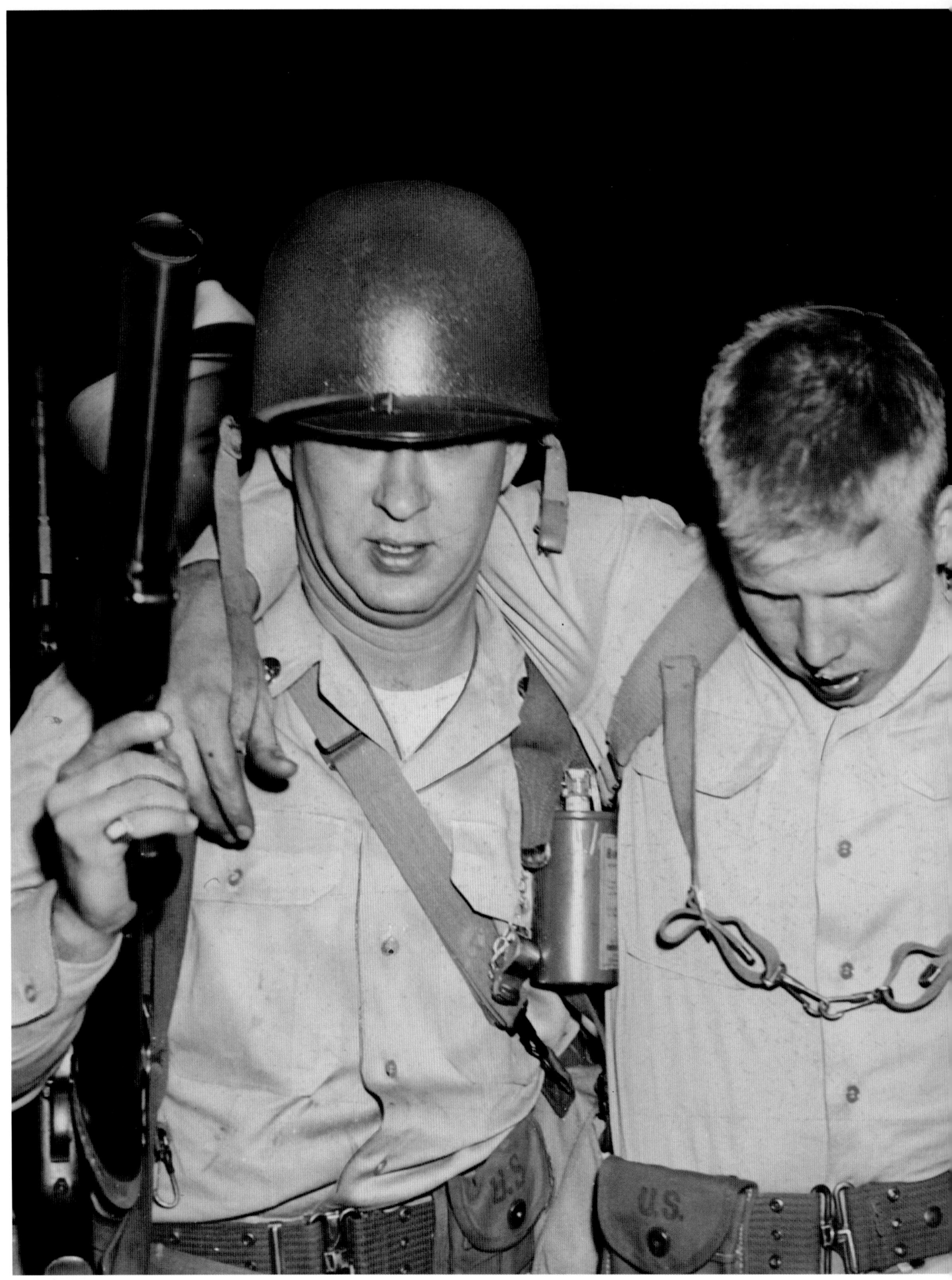
NATIONAL GUARDSMAN ROBERT ANDERSON IS LED AWAY AFTER HE WAS HIT IN THE MOUTH WITH A STONE. JULY 12, 1951/RUSSELL DALEY

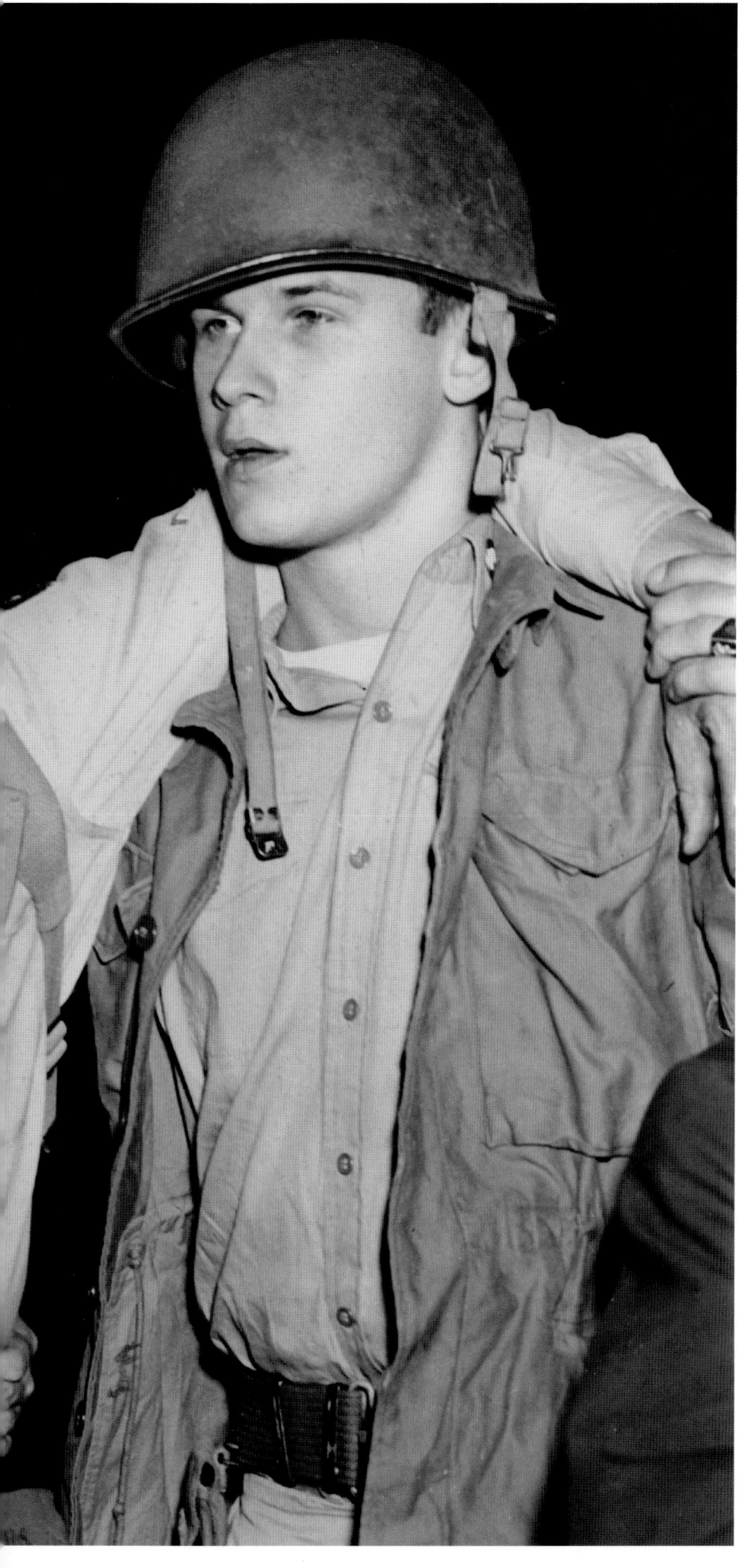

A WHITE CROWD'S HATRED

During the summer of 1951, five hundred weary Illinois National Guardsmen battled a mob of White youth and adults in suburban Cicero. They'd been ordered to protect the African-American family of Johnetta and Harvey E. Clark Jr. A war veteran, Harvey Clark had returned home with the hope of living in a neighborhood of his family's choice. He chose this community on Chicago's western border instead of the segregated, overcrowded South and West sides of Chicago.

Cicero's police chief Erwin Konovsky barred the Clarks from their newly rented apartment and threatened to shoot Mr. Clark. When Cicero officials refused to protect the family the Illinois Guard was deployed.

Clark obtained a federal injunction mandating protection, with the help of the Chicago branch of the National Association for the Advancement of Colored People. But the family's second attempt to move in was met by an even larger and more determined mob.

Cicero police offered token resistance. The crowd's hatred was satisfied only when the Clarks' apartment and several others were burned and gutted.

Cook County state's attorney John S. Boyle acted in the same spirit as his predecessor in the Chicago Race Riot of 1919 by pushing a Cook County grand jury to indict victims of the disturbance—such as the Clarks and their attorneys. A federal grand jury later investigated the riots and the conduct of the Cook County grand jury. The Clarks were never able to move to Cicero, marking Cicero as a triumph for injustice.

In later years, I met and talked to one of the guardsmen, who told me they had been authorized to use bayonets and tear gas to try to control the rioters, but no bullets.

—*Christopher Robert Reed, professor emeritus of history at Roosevelt University, is the author of* The Rise of Chicago's Black Metropolis 1920–1929.

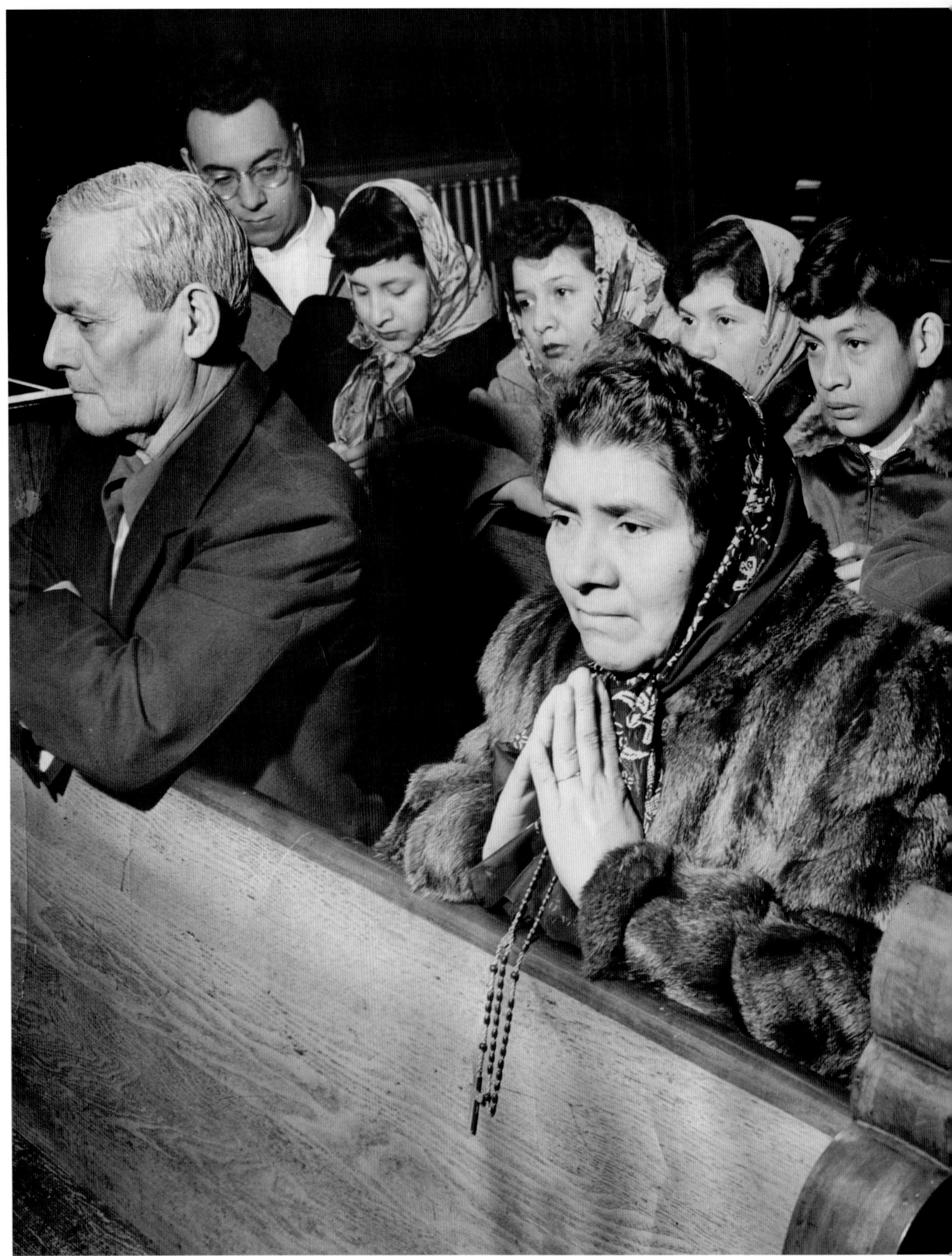

FAMILY OF LOUIS AGUIÑAGA, CAPTURED IN THE KOREAN WAR, PRAY FOR THEIR 23-YEAR-OLD SON. HE WAS LATER RELEASED. JANUARY 6, 1952

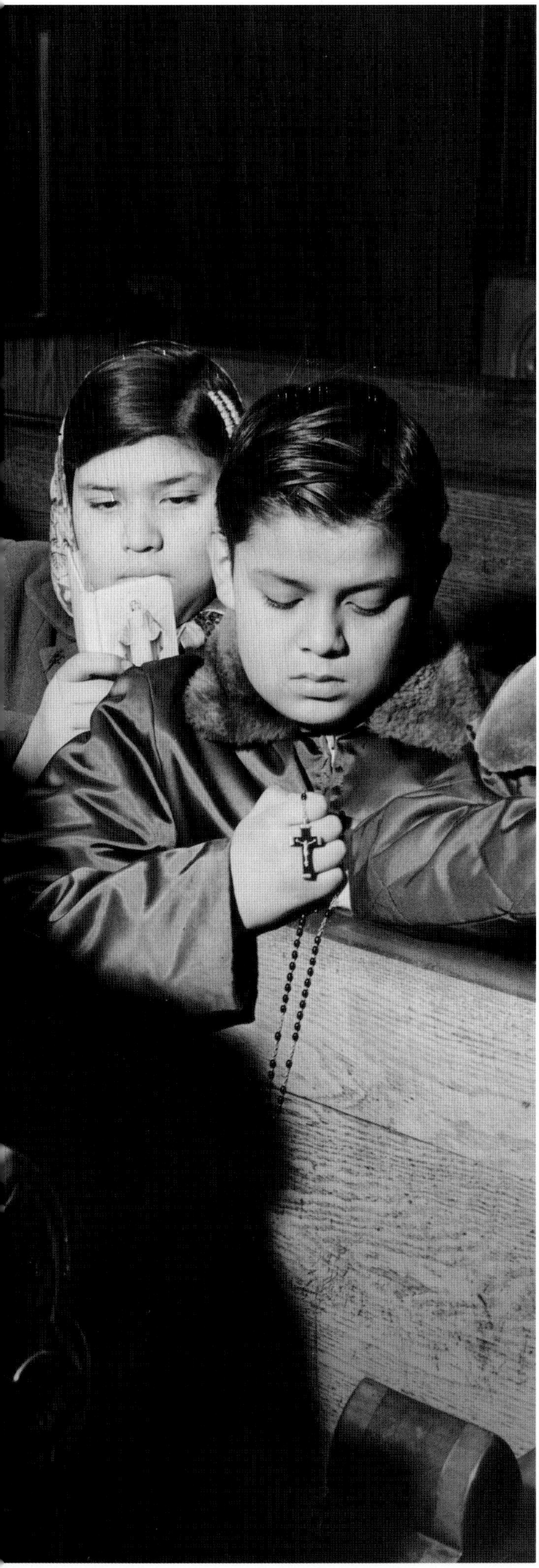

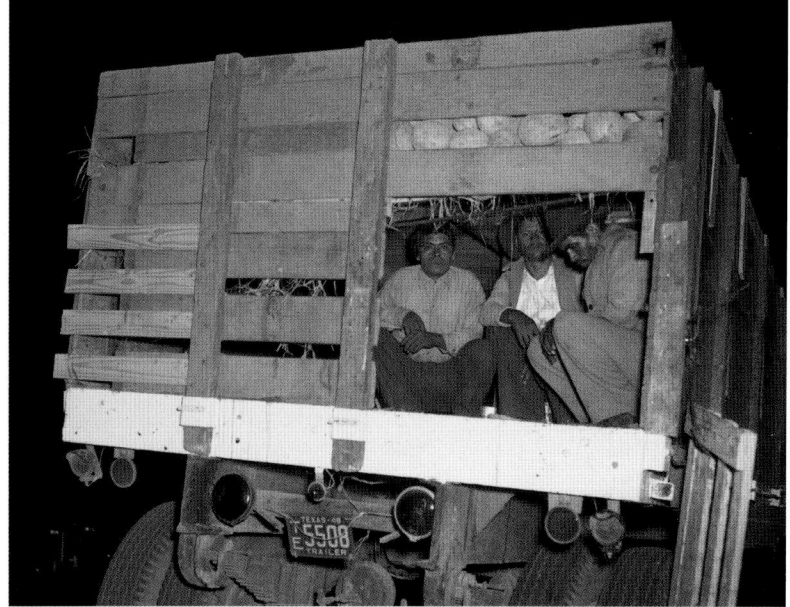

MEXICAN MEN SHOW HOW THEY WERE SMUGGLED FROM TEXAS. JUNE 12, 1948

THE LONG ROAD HOME

Two such distinct photographs, yet each carries the shared weight of personal and community memory.

My grandfather, Don Lucio, could tell you about the struggles and desperation that would drive men to be smuggled north in the back of a truck under a canopy of lettuce. It was the late 1940s. Don Lucio was a steelworker, butcher, and raconteur. He told me stories about fleeing dangers of the Mexican Revolution and crisscrossing this country in search of work. The fruit of his labor was a two-flat he bought in South Deering, a block from the Wisconsin Steel works. Mexican immigrant *colonias* or communities grew in nearby neighborhoods like South Chicago, in Back of the Yards close to the Stock Yards, and near the rail yards around Hull-House on the near West Side.

Our family home was in the middle of a multiethnic, multilingual working-class district. I was too young to understand its tensions—or its importance.

The photograph here of the Aguiñaga family made me wonder. How many hours did I spend kneeling in pews saying the rosary? I always hoped that Doña Chencha was leading prayer; her rapid-fire Spanish meant we finished much faster than in English. I couldn't even begin to guess how many prayers were launched from Saint Kevin Catholic Church on Torrence Avenue by Mexican families for sons and daughters at war.

Our neighborhood came alive as veterans returning from World War II and Korea found jobs, married, started families, and joined friends in organizations like the American Legion, VFW, League of United Latin American Citizens, and the Mexican Community Committee of South Chicago. There was always something to do: Friday fish fries, sports, dances, and parish celebrations.

I grew up where lives were forged by the whistles of shift changes, the bells of moving bridges, and the sound of steel being made. This was South Deering, a small American town on the Far South Side of Chicago.
—*Rita Arias Jirasek is the co-author of* Mexican Chicago.

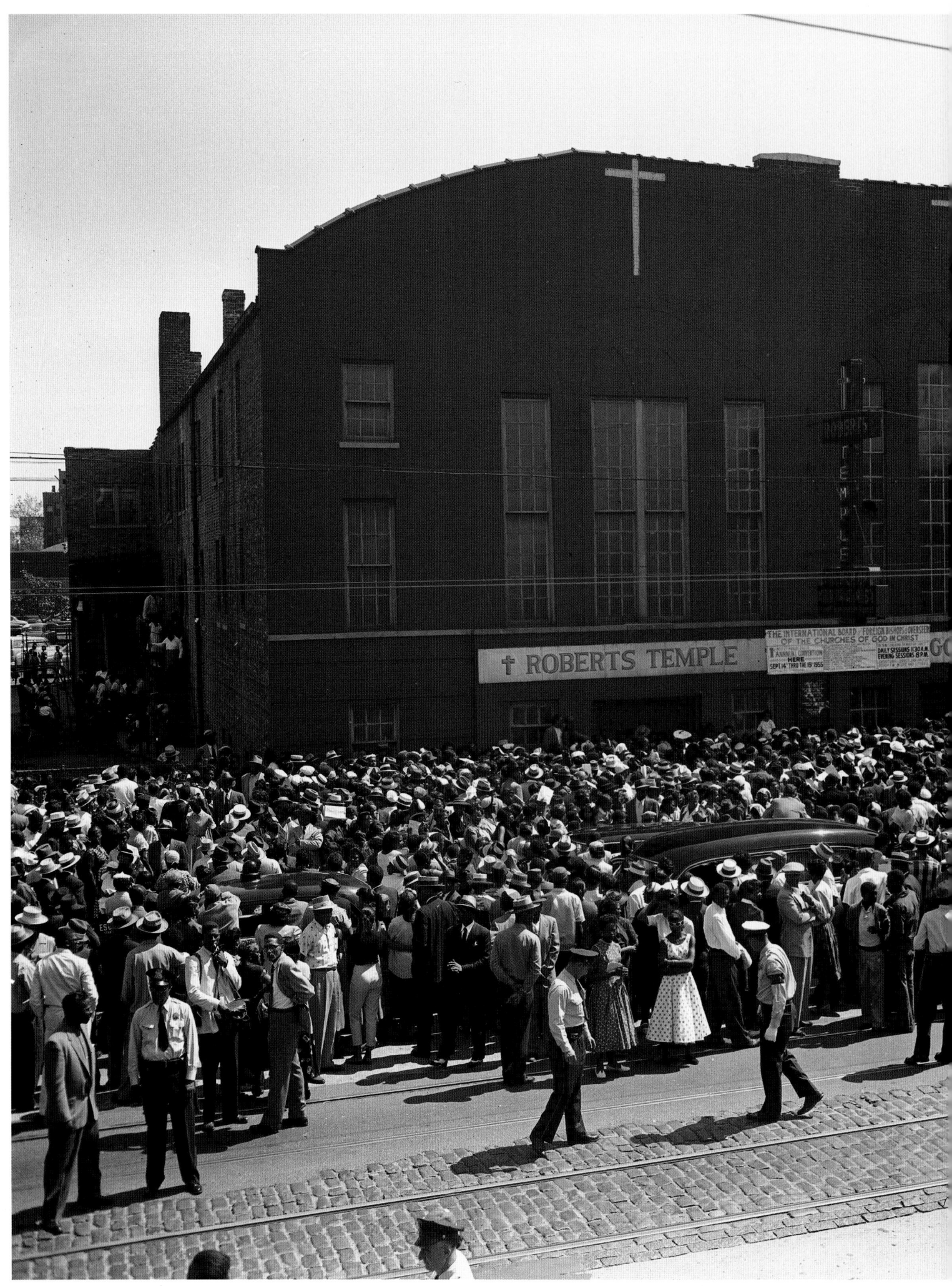

CROWDS ARRIVE AT THE ROBERTS TEMPLE CHURCH OF GOD IN CHRIST AS EMMETT TILL'S CASKET DEPARTS FOR BURIAL. SEPTEMBER 6, 1955/RALPH WALTERS

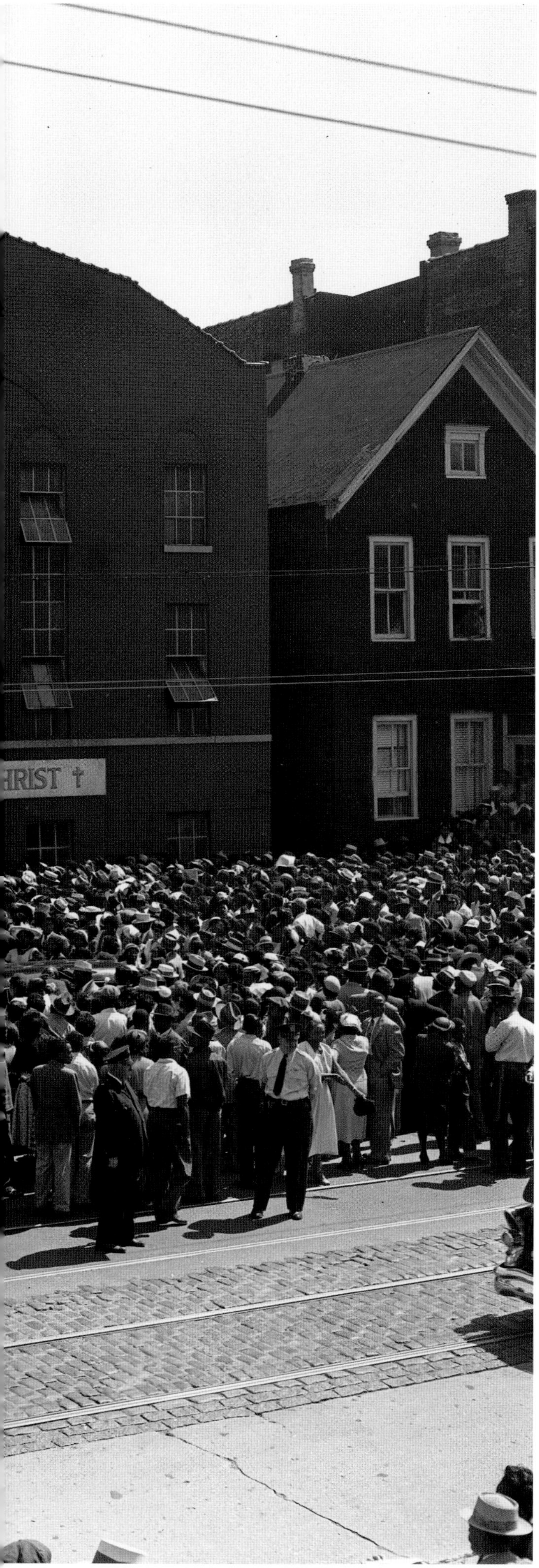

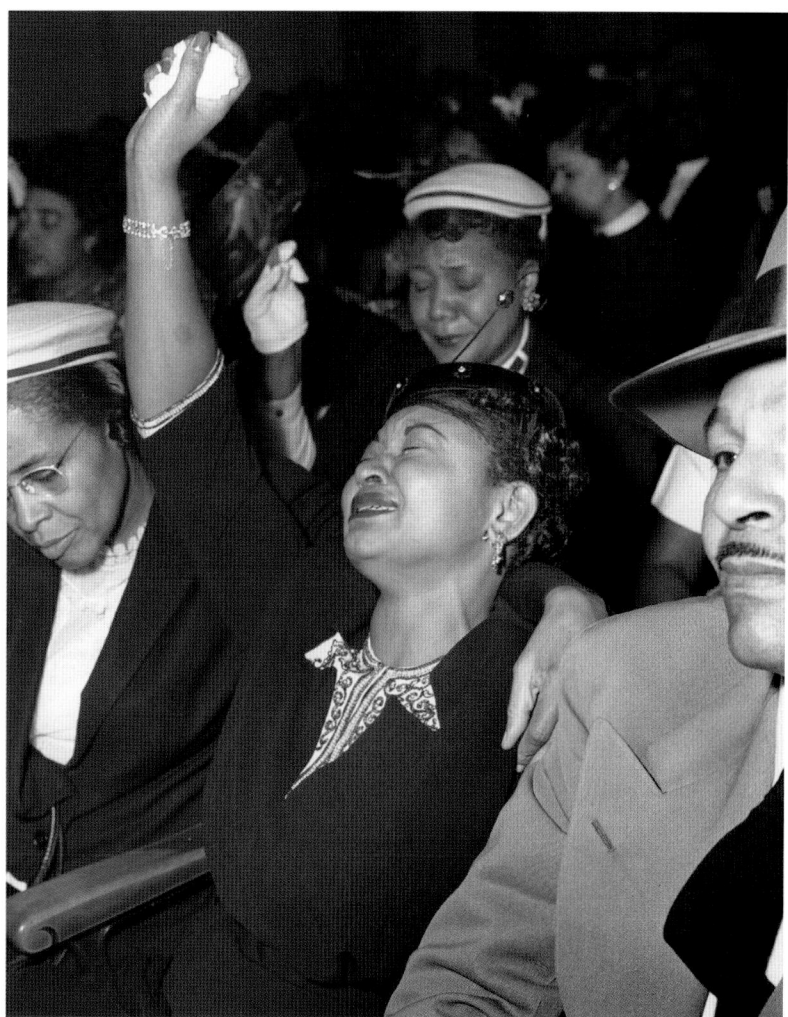

MAMIE TILL GRIEVES FOR HER SON, EMMETT. SEPTEMBER 3, 1955/RALPH WALTERS

A MOTHER'S AGONY

It was late on Friday when I viewed the body. Funeral home director A.A. Rayner did some work to prepare Emmett for the public viewing, despite our talk. Looking back on it now, I think he probably felt he had to do something.

Emmett was in such bad shape when we got him back. Monstrous condition. But Mr. Rayner did what he could. That tongue had been recovered, I guess, and put somewhere. The mouth was closed now. And you could see on the side of Emmett's head that some coarse thread had been used to sew the pieces back together. I guess it was like that on the right side, too, but I couldn't see that. The eye that had been dangling, that was removed, too, and the eyelid closed, like on the other side, where no eye was left.

I told Mr. Rayner he had done a beautiful job. You would have to have seen Emmett when I first saw him to really appreciate what Mr. Rayner had done before my son's body was viewed by the public and photographed for public view.

What I had seen was so much worse than what other people would ever see. And what tens of thousands of people filing past Emmett would see would make men cry and women cry out.
—*Mamie Till-Mobley, mother of Emmett Till, in her memoir,* Death of Innocence: The Story of the Hate Crime That Changed America, *coauthored with Christopher Benson.*

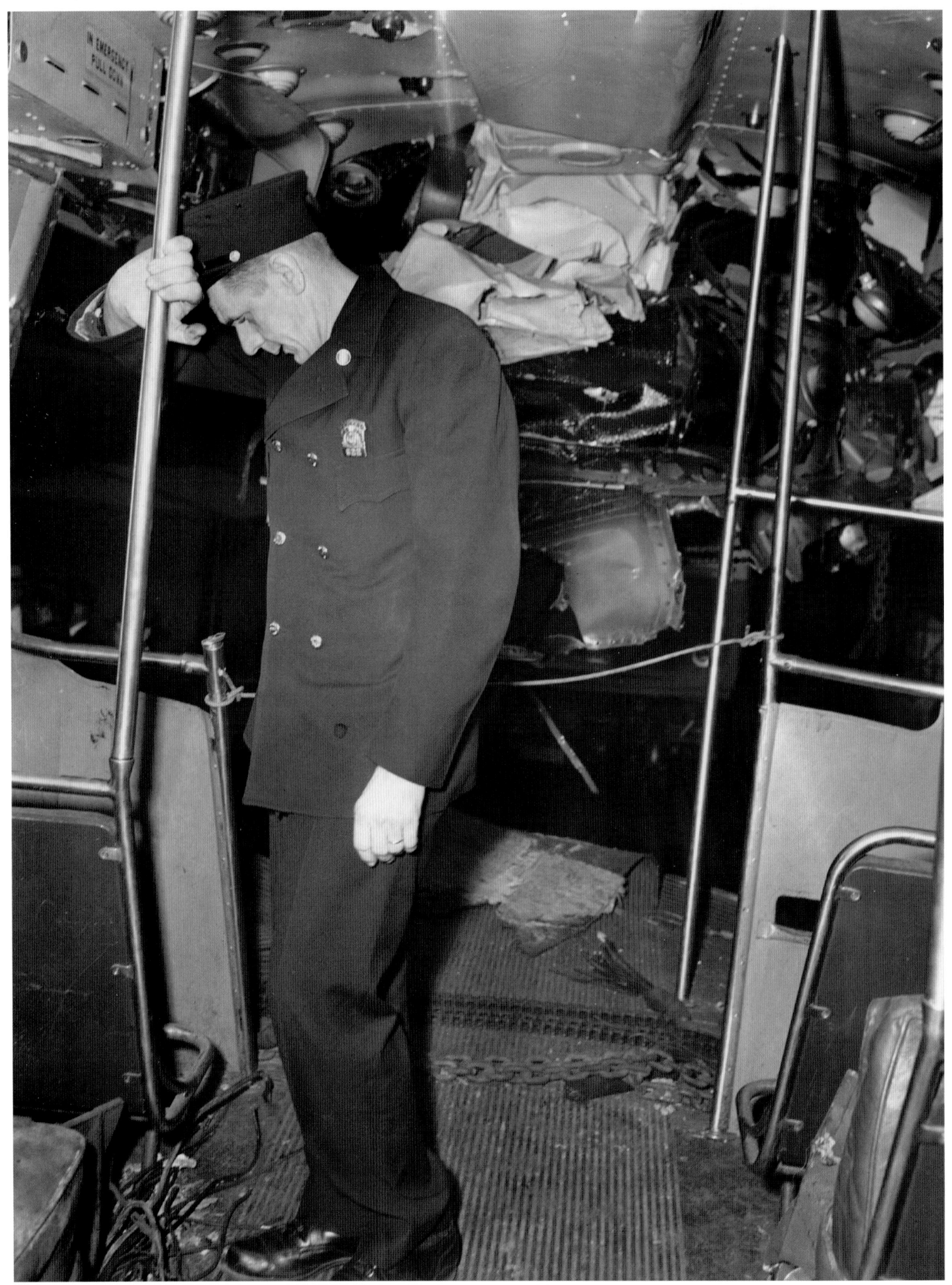

ELLWOOD STRAUSS HANGS HIS HEAD ON THE SAME L TRAIN THAT HIS WIFE WAS KILLED. NOVEMBER 14, 1956/LARRY NOCERINO

SPOT NEWS IN THE CITY

The 1950s was a heyday for newspaper photographers. At the time, five daily papers—Chicago Sun-Times, Daily News, Tribune, American, and Daily Defender—were going strong. And the new TV channels like Channel 5 were experimenting with still photographs on newscasts.

These two photographs, taken by two guys I remember well from the Sun-Times, show exactly how we worked.

The large one, by Larry Nocerino, was taken on a routine assignment. An L train crashed at the Wilson Avenue Station, and Nocerino was sent to a coroner's jury investigation. A firefighter named Ellwood Strauss was one of the first to arrive at the crash site, but he did not know his wife was trapped in the wreckage. This photograph was taken a few days later, when Strauss went back and entered the train where his wife had been killed. This is a searing photo.

In those days, we used Speed Graphic press cameras that produced negatives 4x5 inches large. That made for remarkable detail, but you had to get close. Zoom lenses hadn't been invented. And because you only had enough film for a couple of shots, you had to think about every frame.

Look at how well Nocerino used the flash, which in those days was basically a bulb and chrome reflector. Lighting a scene was essential because we did not have fast film. Look at the details in the fireman's face and the wreckage around him. He is holding onto a pole bent in the accident.

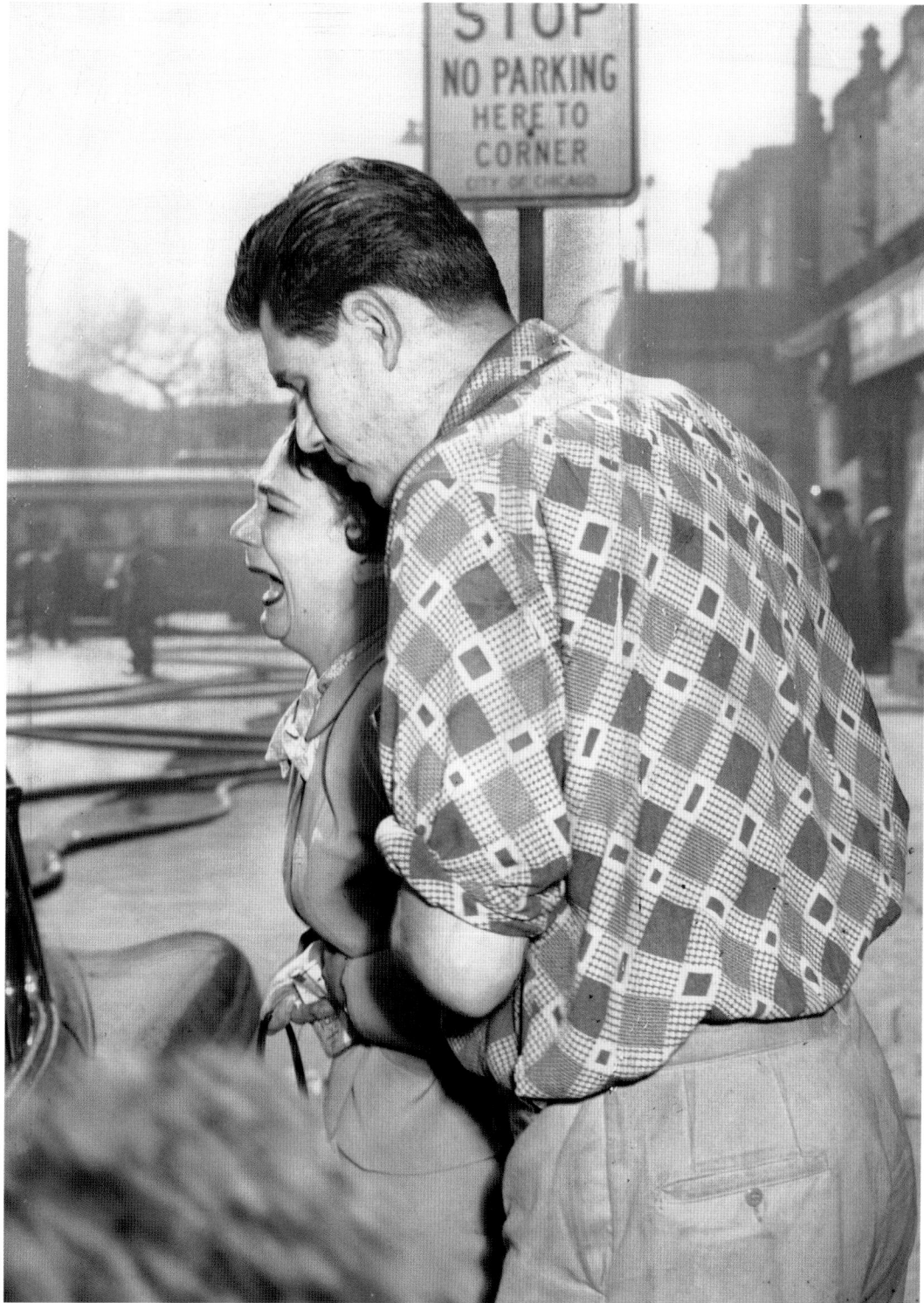

BEATRICE THOMAS FEARS FOR HER HUSBAND AFTER AN EXPLOSION. MAY 7, 1956/RALPH WALTERS

The other photo, taken by Ralph Walters, shows a distraught woman arriving at a factory explosion. She has a look of horror because she thinks her husband is still inside. She later learned he was safe.

We often used flash even outside so we could highlight fine points. We had to frame the picture, focus, set the shutter and aperture.

Most press photographers were artists. Our equipment was big and bulky. I'm paying for it now with my back, but I don't care. Where could you get a better education?
—Steve Lasker photographed the Green Hornet streetcar disaster in 1950 and the Our Lady of the Angels School fire in 1958. He worked for the Chicago Herald-American and American through the 1950s before switching to TV news.

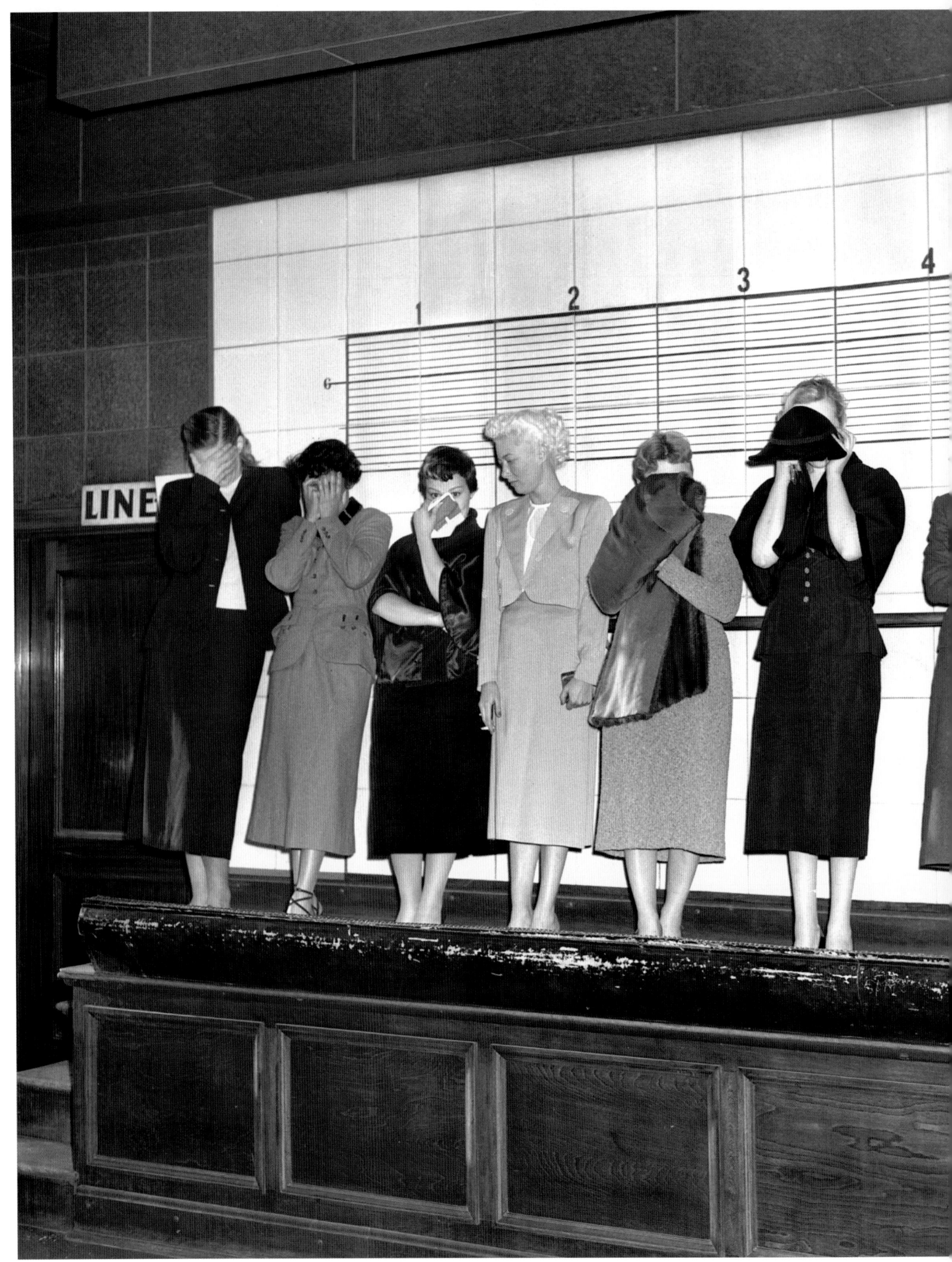
WOMEN ARE LINED UP FOLLOWING A PROSTITUTION RAID AT 64 EAST WALTON. SEPTEMBER 9, 1953/BILL KNEFFEL

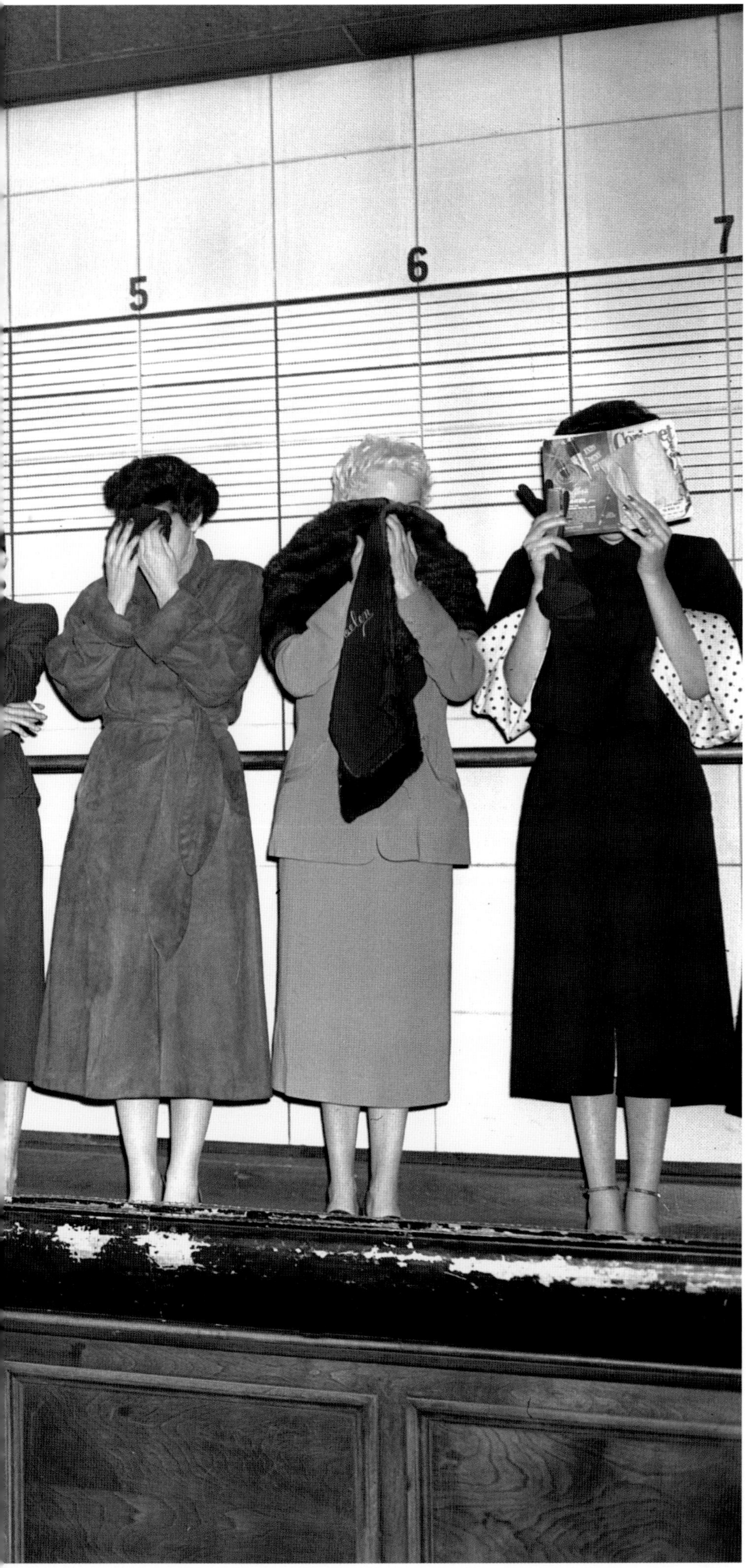

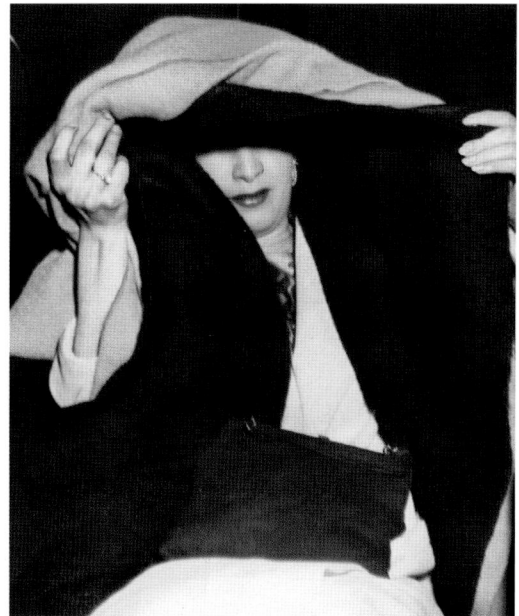

VICE-RAID SUSPECT. NOVEMBER 5, 1959

THE 'EASY WAY'

They were wives who had overspent and couldn't account to their husbands. They were women under the gun of a loan shark who threatened to take away furniture or a fur coat. They were divorcées desperate to provide schooling and keep for one or two children. They were wives who lost money at poker and couldn't get more from their husbands. They were women whose darling sons or daughters would lose their graduation from some school or college if they did not have the money for expenses and tuition.

One woman on the street was 58, no less. She had been a schoolteacher. Her husband was a druggist from whom she was divorced. She came to Chicago to find work, to add income to alimony she had been receiving. The Depression threw her out of work. The ex-husband failed in business. At 58 she was forced to a life she had dreaded. None of us girls ever had a notion that we would be in the racket. We read about such things, just as we read about the "Snake Pit." It is something that only happens to others. It can't happen to us.

Like other girls, I would read about this or that girl taking the "easy way." I now wonder if those writers were in their right mind.
—*Adapted from Camille DeRose's memoir* The Camille DeRose Story.

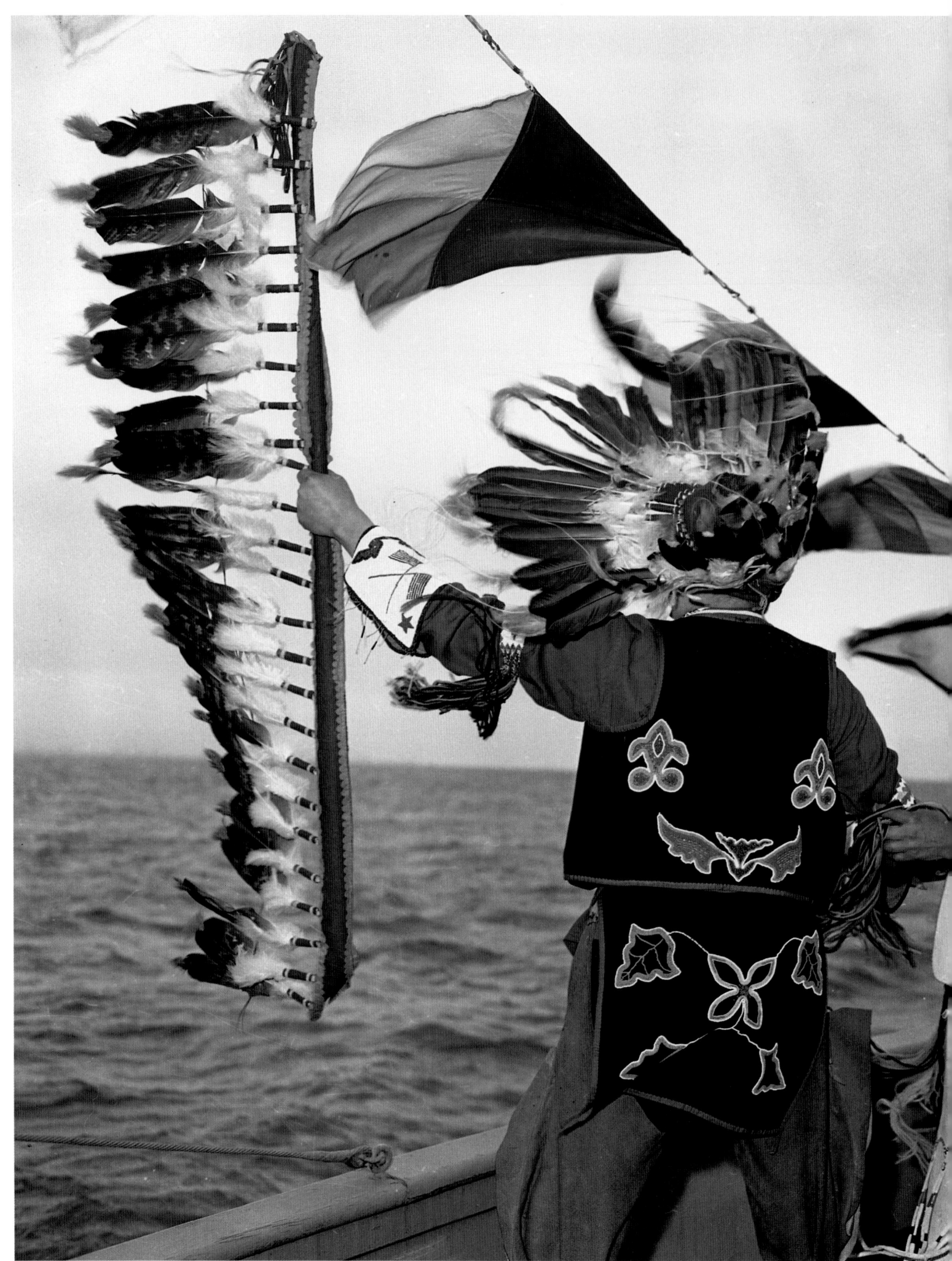
NATIVE AMERICANS WELCOME A DUTCH FREIGHTER AFTER IT SAILED TO CHICAGO VIA SAINT LAWRENCE SEAWAY. APRIL 30, 1959

CROSSROADS OF TRIBAL NATIONS

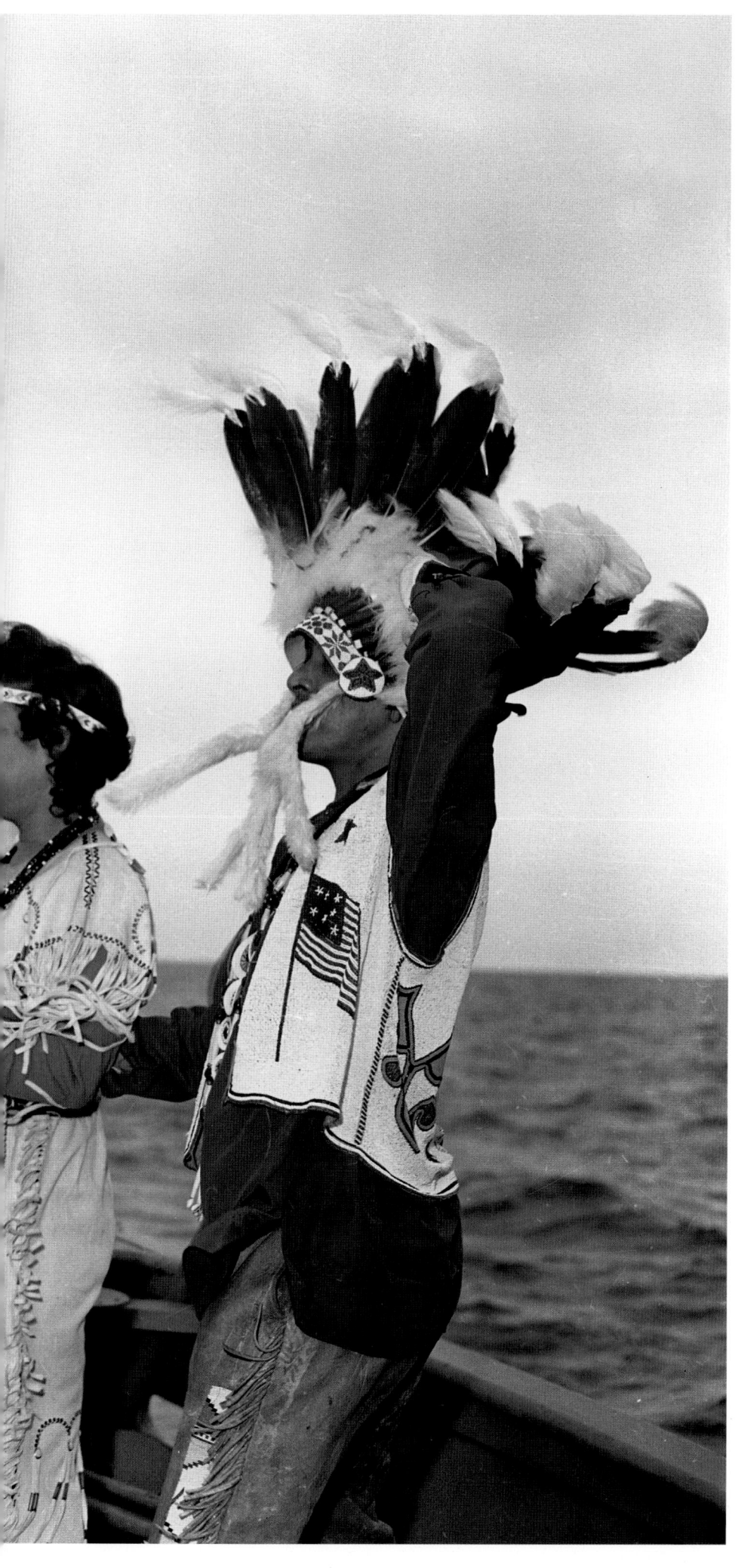

In a windswept scene off Chicago's main port, Native men and a woman greet the arrival of the first ocean freighter to enter Lake Michigan via the Saint Lawrence Seaway. The man on the left—in what appears to be Woodland or prairie-style beadwork of the Potawatomi, Menominee, or Ho-Chunk nations—extends an eagle staff, an important and sacred item in many Native North American cultures. The unnamed individuals wear different forms of regalia, from Plains eagle feather headdresses to Woodland aprons.

The approaching *Prins Johan Willem Friso* ocean freighter, just off camera, was not the first vessel of consequence to traverse the Saint Lawrence seaway. Several hundred years before, French Jesuits arrived in the Great Lakes region. Indigenous peoples travelled the Saint Lawrence in canoes from the northeast coast of North America to "the place where food grows on water." That picturesque reference is to wild rice that used to grow in abundance in the Great Lakes area. Many creation stories of Anishinaabe peoples—one of the Indigenous communities whose homelands are in the Great Lakes region—describe our origins in relation to the Saint Lawrence Seaway and its many tributaries.

The Chicago region has always been a crossroads of many tribal nations. In April 1959, when this photo was taken, Chicago was becoming one of the largest urban centers for Native peoples in the United States. That was due in part to the Indian Relocation Act of 1956, which encouraged thousands of American Indians to leave their reservations and traditional lands to assimilate into the general population in urban areas. The descendants of those families make up a vibrant and diverse urban Indigenous community in Chicago to this day.
—*Blaire Topash-Caldwell, a citizen of the Pokagon Band of Potawatomi, is the public humanities fellow at the Newberry Library.*

ANGER MADE ME SURVIVE

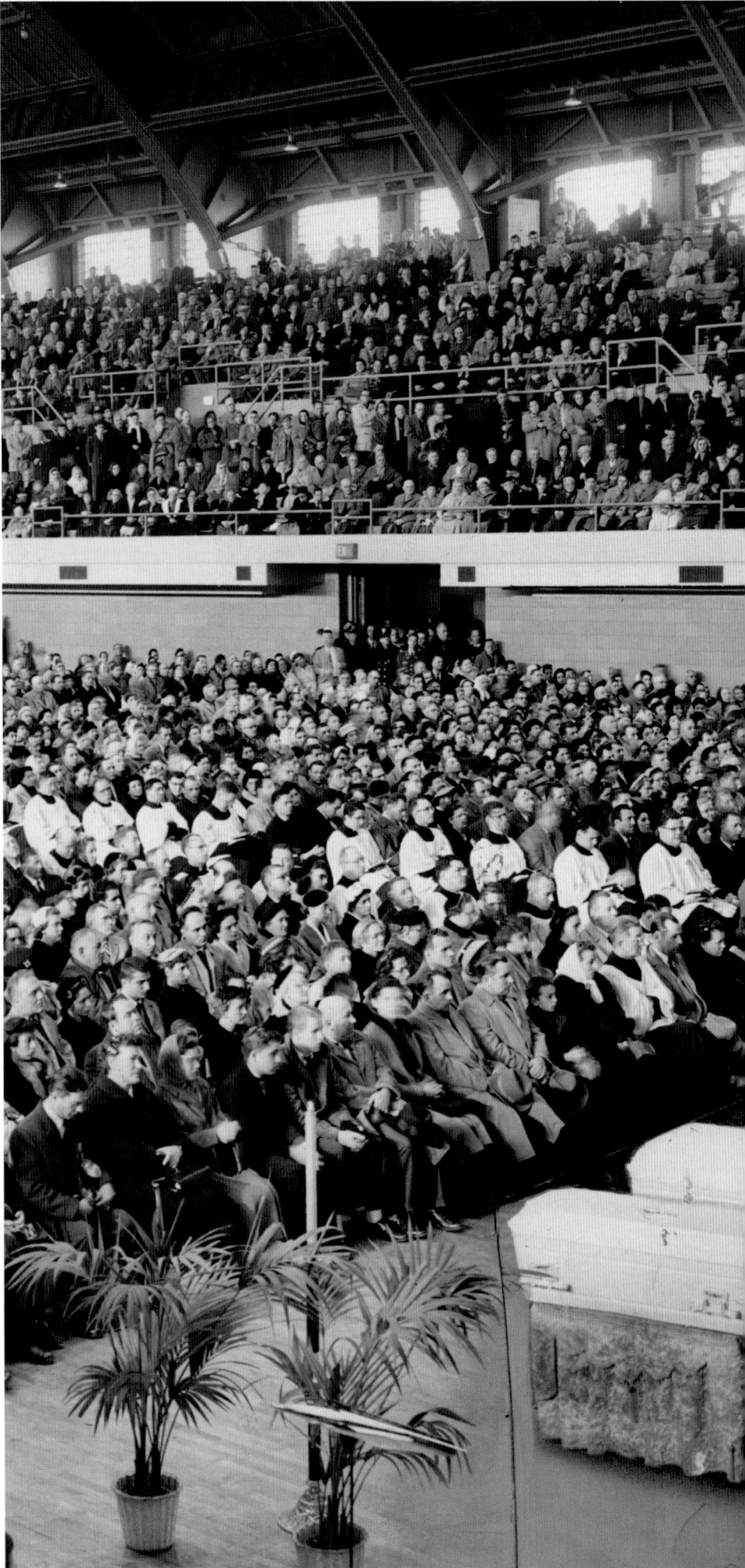

I wish I could say that it was bravery, superhuman courage, some inner, heaven-sent strength that sustained me through the agony, but I cannot.

It was anger, raging anger that made me survive. I was angry at the lack of authority in my classroom when the fire broke out. I was angry because the firemen's ladders fell short of the classroom windows, because I lost the skin of my birthright, because I had to endure ravages of pain that I had thought were reserved for those condemned to the torments of Hell. I was angry for having lived, and I was angry at those who did die and left me behind. I was angry at being treated like a child after I witnessed millions of years of burning all condensed into a single moment. Hellfire, the witches of Salem, the melting skin of Hiroshima—I saw them all, and yet I never left my classroom. All the horrors of the world were presented to me in one brief second and made me realize I am mortal, I shall die.

I have come to terms with many unspoken fears and ideas. It has been difficult, because I was taught very early to think that the fire was a mystical act of a lonely God, and that it should not be talked about or questioned. In my community it was always felt that bringing up memories of the fire would just add new grief to the old. I disagree. I could not recover from the fire until I learned how to mourn, not only for my dead friends but for my skin as well. I think that discussing a disaster and remembering the dead can help to heal wounds and resolve anguish in any stricken community.

Through the fire and its aftermath, I learned that disaster does not breed those strong, jolly, humble heroes that we read about in newspapers and books. Real survivors experience anger, panic, jealousy, guilt, self-doubt—all those feelings people never like to talk about, but which are as important and as powerful as bravery, kindness, and love.
—*Excerpt from Michele McBride's 1979 memoir* The Fire That Will Not Die. *An Our Lady of the Angels survivor, she died at age 56 in 2001.*

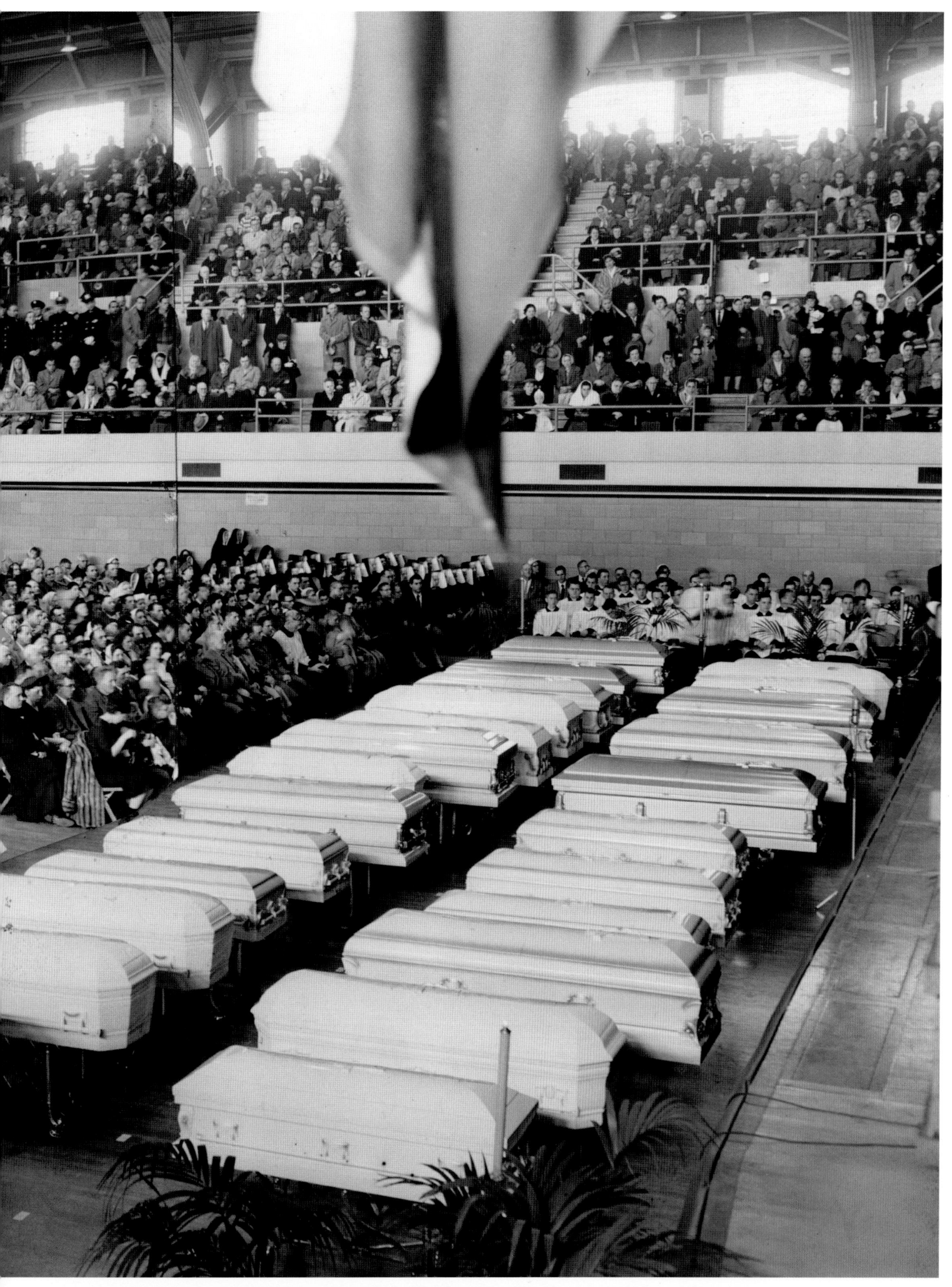

OUR LADY OF THE ANGELS FIRE VICTIMS AT NORTHWEST ARMORY. NINETY-FIVE DIED AND 100 WERE INJURED. DECEMBER 5, 1958/DAVE MANN

PART 2

We just loved taking pictures. We loved pushing the button on our Nikons. That superseded any money that we made.

— Dom Najolia
Sun-Times photographer, 1980–2013

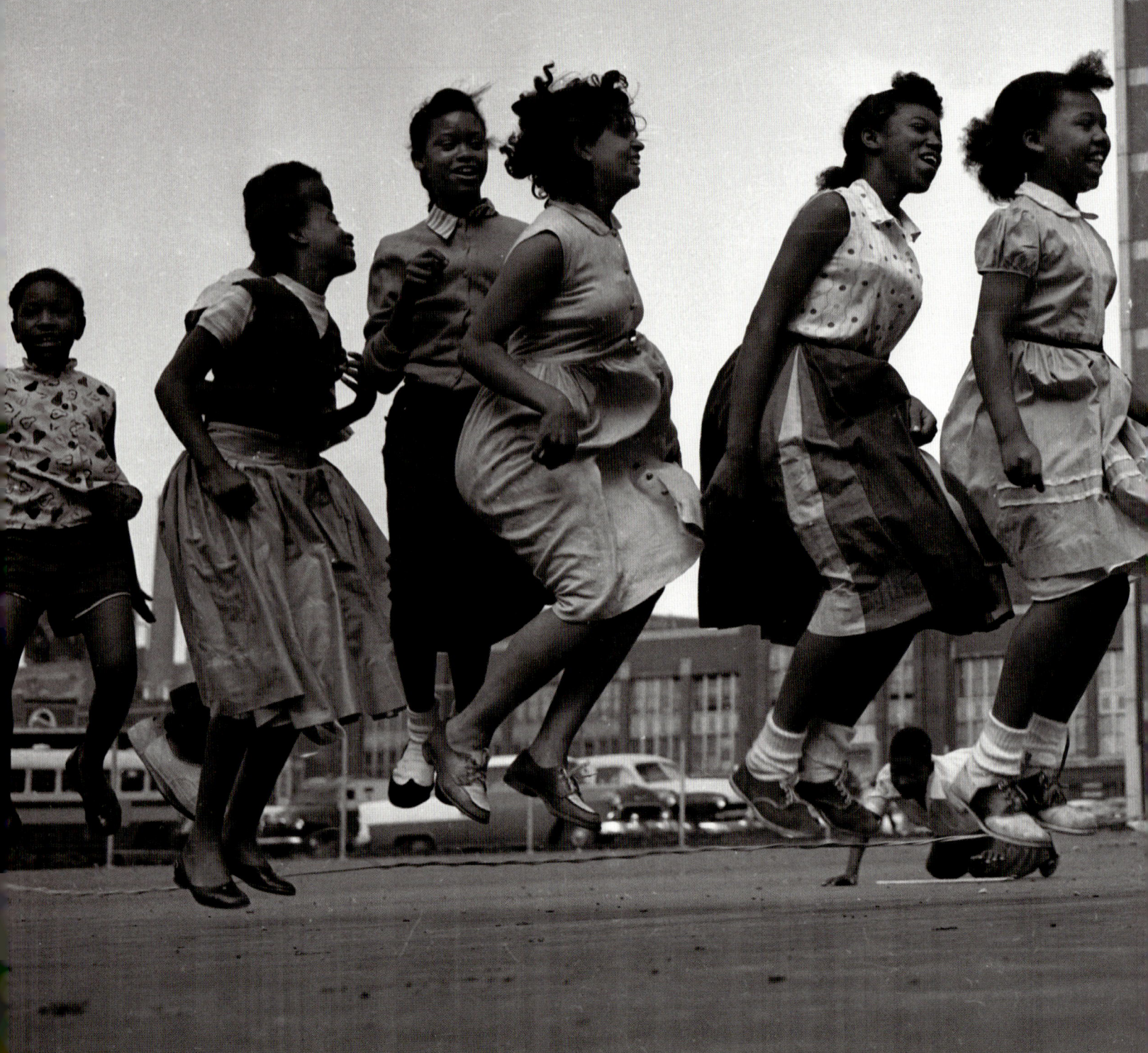

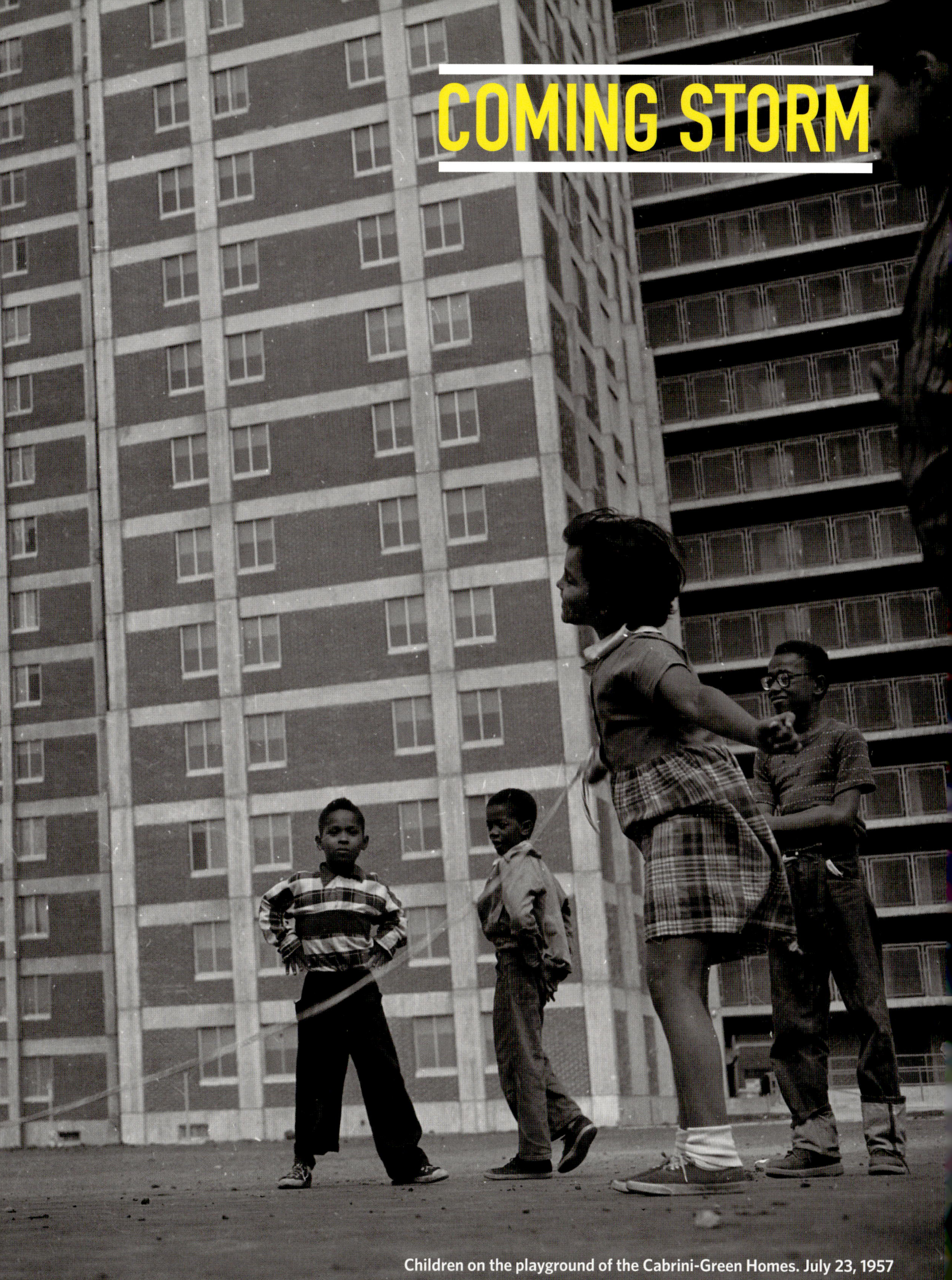

COMING STORM

Children on the playground of the Cabrini-Green Homes. July 23, 1957

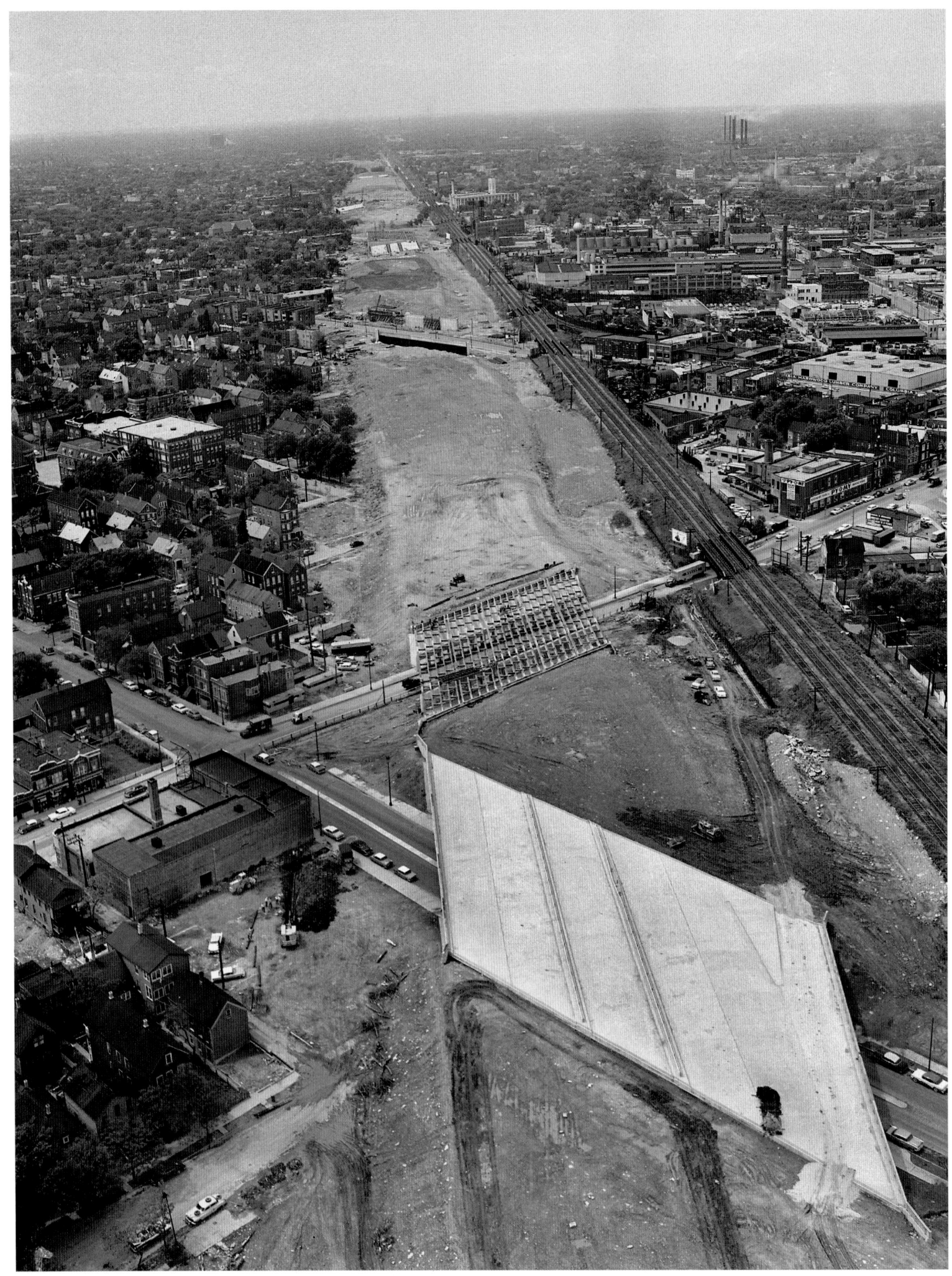

NORTHWEST PASSAGE, NOW KNOWN AS THE KENNEDY. LOOKING NORTHWEST FROM WEBSTER AND DAMEN. JUNE 15, 1959/RALPH WALTERS

THE ROADS MORE TAKEN

My own road begins with these two expressways. On the day I was born—October 21, 1960—a Chicago Tribune reporter raved about another new arrival: the nearly completed Northwest Expressway (later renamed the Kennedy): "We've seen Hitler's autobahns, the elevated highways of San Francisco, New York's tunnels and viaducts, and Los Angeles' miles of speedways, but we'll rate Chicago's Northwest Expressway. . . as the best to date."

The Kennedy offered a fast, eight-lane shortcut between downtown and O'Hare, which soon became the world's busiest airport. The Kennedy's impact has been profound. But it's on the Eisenhower Expressway that my memories travel.

Nine days before my birth, Mayor Richard J. Daley took part in the ribbon cutting for the section of the Congress Expressway that linked my hometown of Downers Grove to the Loop. Growing up in the heyday of White flight, I knew people for whom the Congress, now

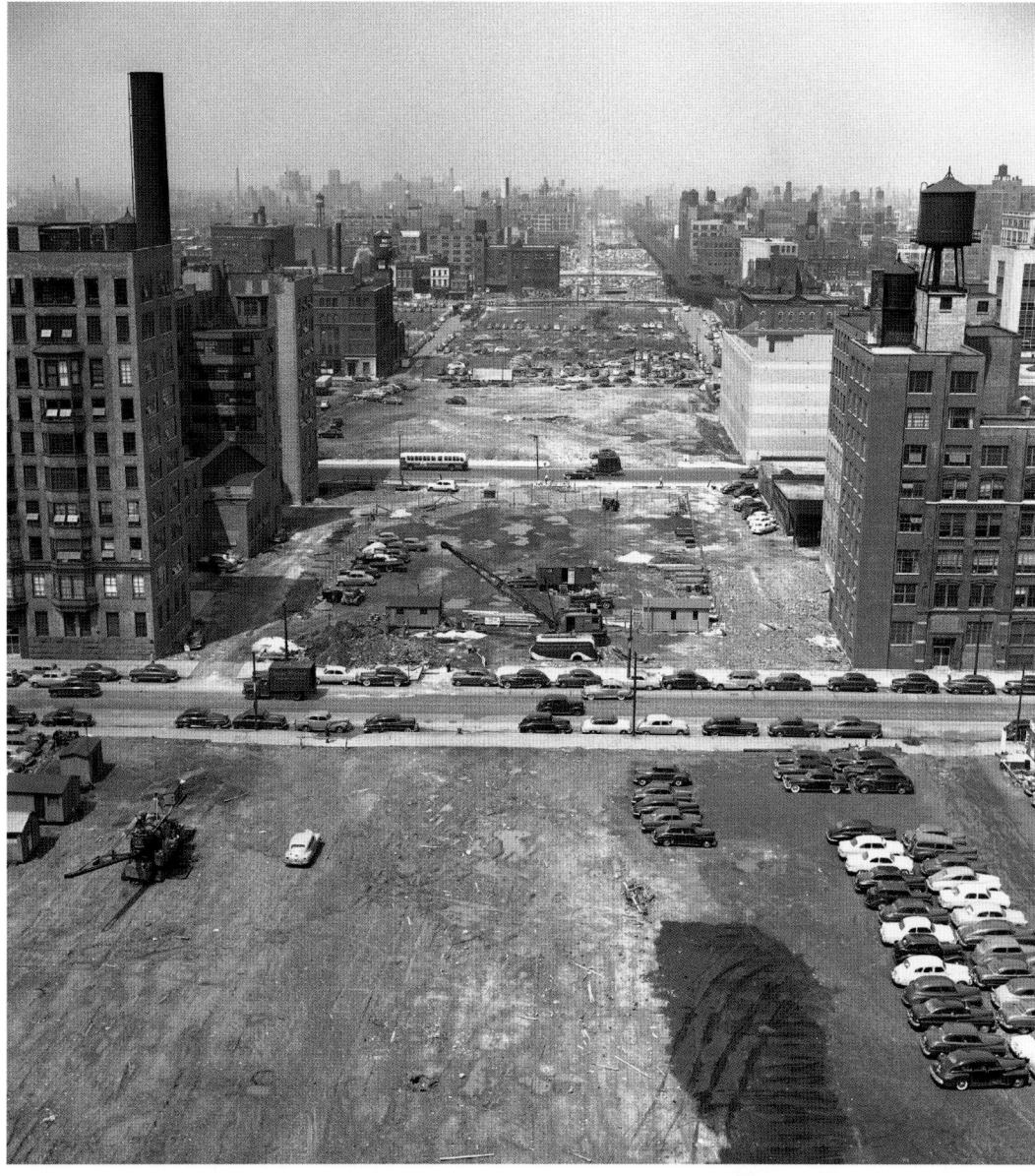

ROUTE OF THE CONGRESS EXPRESSWAY. WEST FROM THE MAIN POST OFFICE. JUNE 29, 1951/WILLIAM DELUGA

the Eisenhower, symbolized escape—the route their families took from increasingly integrated Chicago neighborhoods to a new life in the western suburbs. But for me, the highway always flowed eastward—a pot-holed Yellow Brick Road that led from the homogeneity and small-mindedness of my native environs to the culturally diverse, endlessly enigmatic metropolis at the other end.

Sometimes it feels as if I've been traveling that route all my life—past the "Hillside Strangler," where Interstate 290 merged with the Ike in an unending traffic jam, past the S&H Green Stamps warehouse, a structure so big it contained four soccer fields on its roof, past the Ferrara Pan Candy Company at Harlem Avenue with its intense cinnamon smell of fresh-made Atomic Fireballs hanging over the highway, then past the sultry red lips of the giant Magikist sign just inside the city limits. But the best part of the journey came at the end, where a tunnel took the Eisenhower through the lower part of the old Main Post Office as if carved out of a mountain. For a moment, everything went dark. Suddenly the highway was gone and the city, which a few seconds earlier had seemed distant, engulfed me, beckoned me, frightened me. Here was a magic portal into another world.

I've lived in that world for most of the past four decades. My parents are gone, and the house they owned for fifty years in Downers Grove has been torn down. I live near the Kennedy and have little reason to use the Eisenhower these days. But now and then, returning from a visit to my hometown, I'll take the long way back to the Northwest Side just so I can drive under the old post office once more. It still feels like the future awaits me on the other side.
—*Miles Harvey teaches creative writing at DePaul University and writes books. His latest is* The King of Confidence.

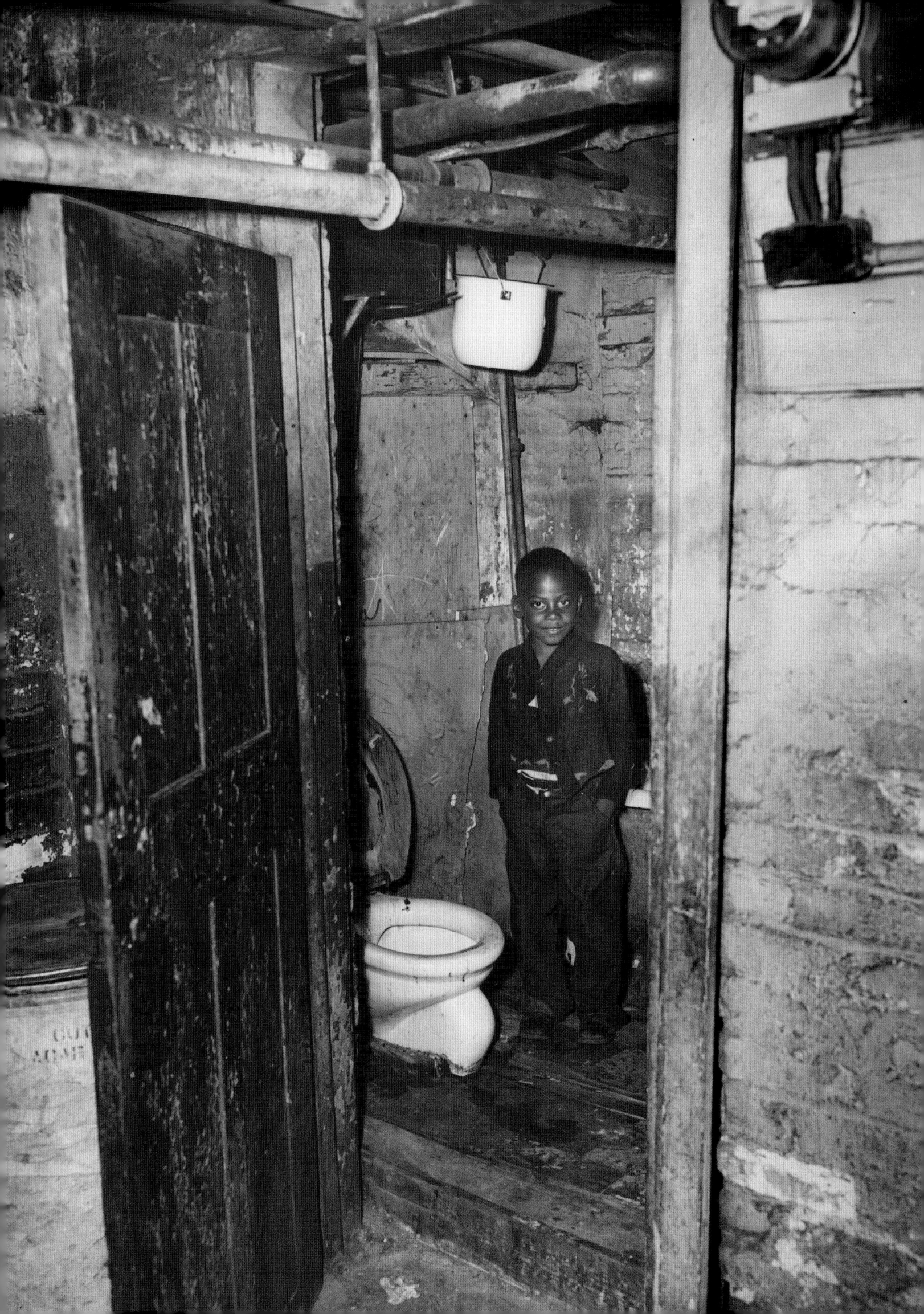

LIFE IN THE BLACK BELT

The Great Migration created a community of people who came to Chicago looking for better lives, jobs, and education—the promise of the North.

The city's largest African-American community was on the South Side. Known as the Black Belt, it doubled in population during the 1920s and people kept pouring in until the 1950s, including thousands returning from World War II. There were severe housing shortages because of limitations on where Blacks could live. Once elegant greystone buildings and stately mansions were broken up and converted into kitchenettes and flats accommodating several families instead of one.

Not surprisingly, the area deteriorated, and many buildings were demolished. How to improve conditions? Local efforts began with legislation that expanded the city's power of eminent domain and assigned certain properties to private developers.

Urban renweal, which was meant to rehabilitate the South Side, meant countless residents had to relocate. Many locals called it "Negro Removal."

My parents moved from the South to Chicago's South Side in the late 1940s. The Bronzeville I remember was a place where you could hear the sound of jazz and the rhythm of the blues day and night. It never occurred to me that it was bleak.

Bronzeville changed in the late 1940s, when the US Supreme Court put an end to restrictive covenants and sales contracts that prohibited White homeowners from renting or selling property to minorities. Now, for the first time, African Americans had a chance to live in other neighborhoods. My family was able to move to nearby Chatham.

Public housing was built in Bronzeville and other areas, but low-cost housing supported and strengthened segregation. African Americans could, for the most part, only take advantage of public housing in Black neighborhoods. When they tried to move elsewhere, they were met with hostility and violence.

Bronzeville did see an example of true urban renewal with the building of Lake Meadows and later Prairie Shores for middle-class tenants. Those apartment complexes brought a modern look to the neighborhood. But to me, the buildings lacked the character of classic Bronzeville.
—*Bernard C. Turner is the author, among several books, of* A New View of Bronzeville.

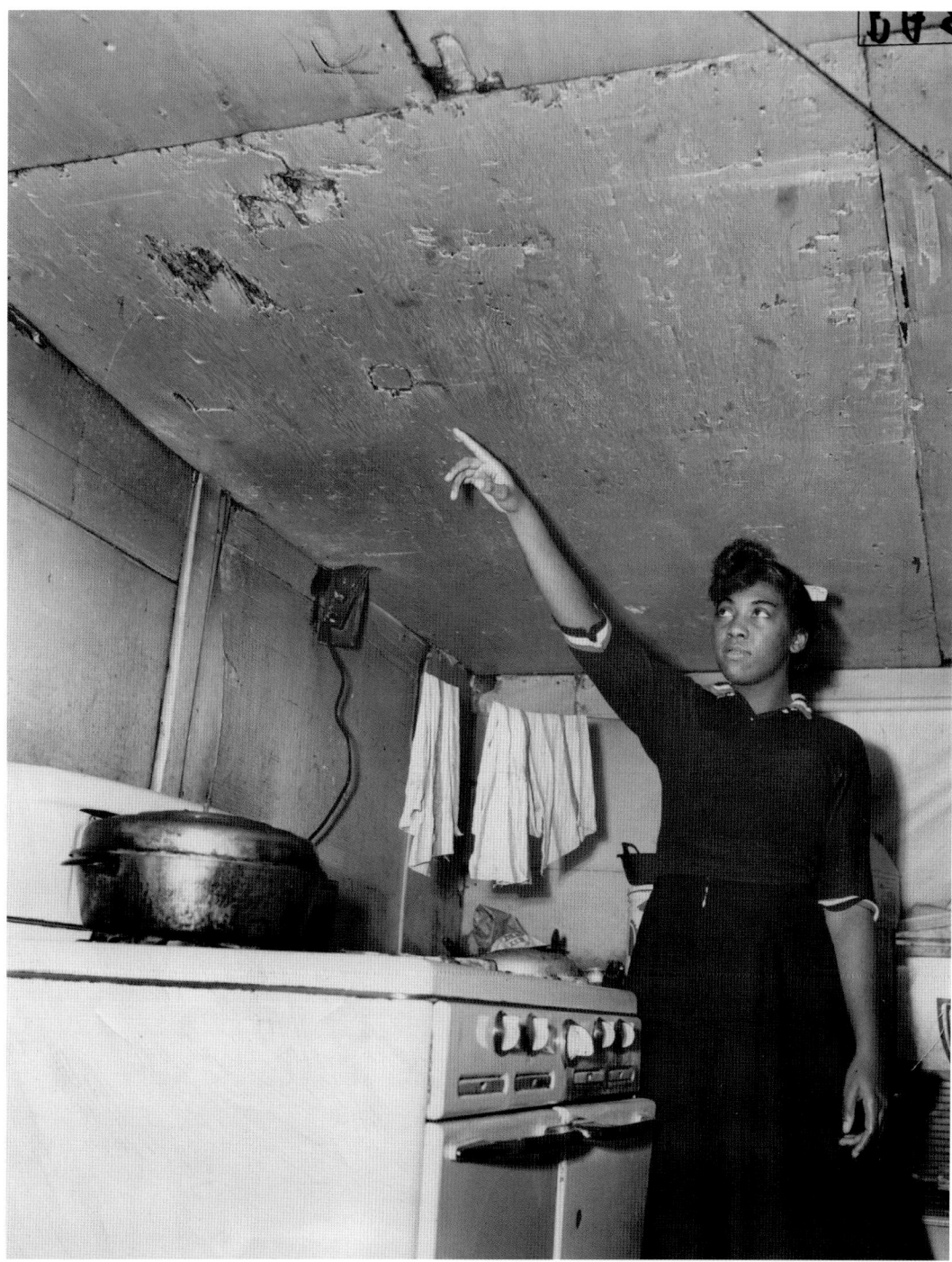

DAMAGED CEILING IN ATTIC FLAT. 1958/RALPH ARVIDSON. OPPOSITE: BASEMENT BATHROOM. 1953

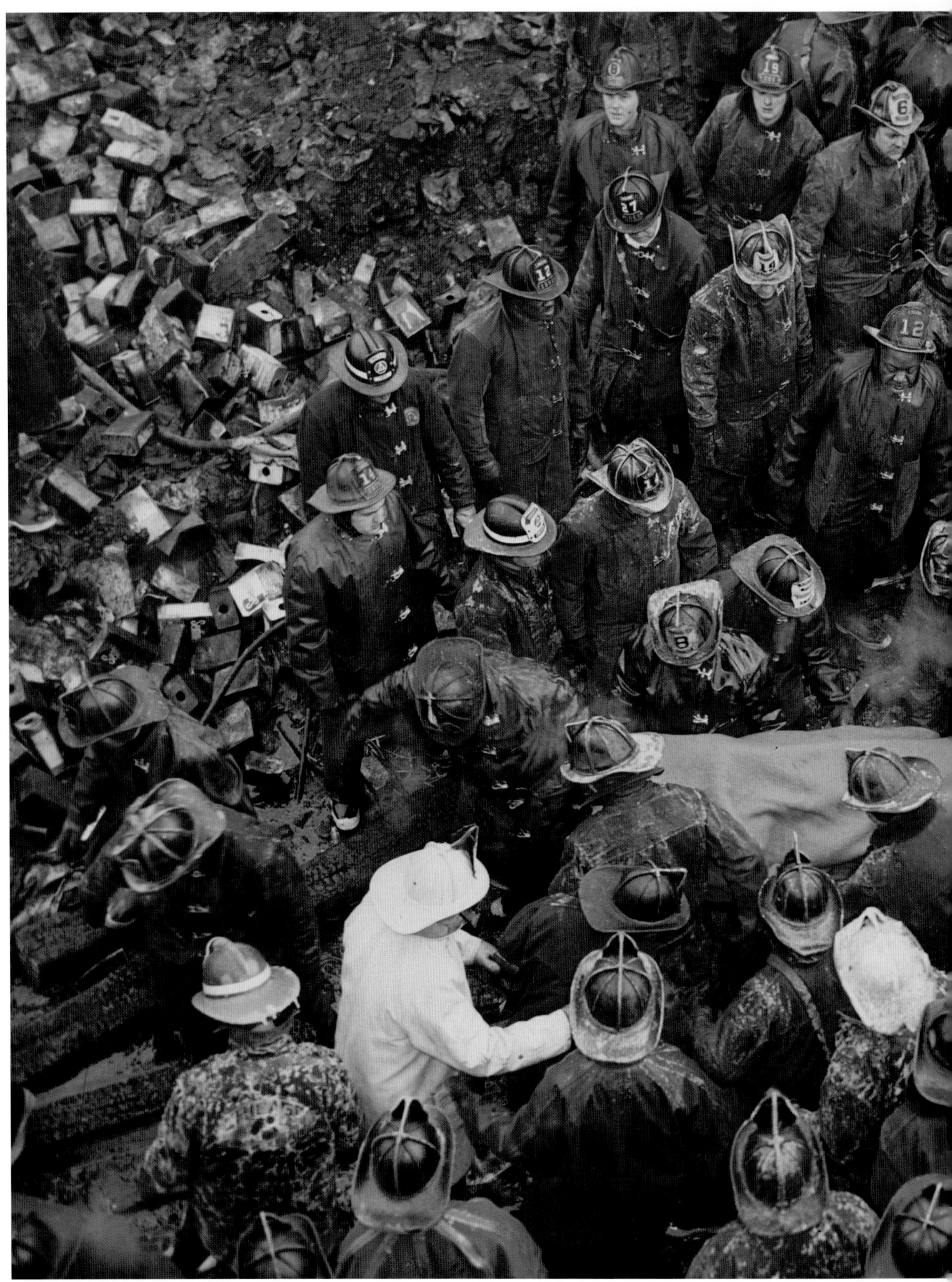

NINE FIREFIGHTERS WERE KILLED AFTER A WALL COLLAPSED AT A WAREHOUSE FIRE AT 614 WEST HUBBARD. JANUARY 28, 1961/BUD DALEY

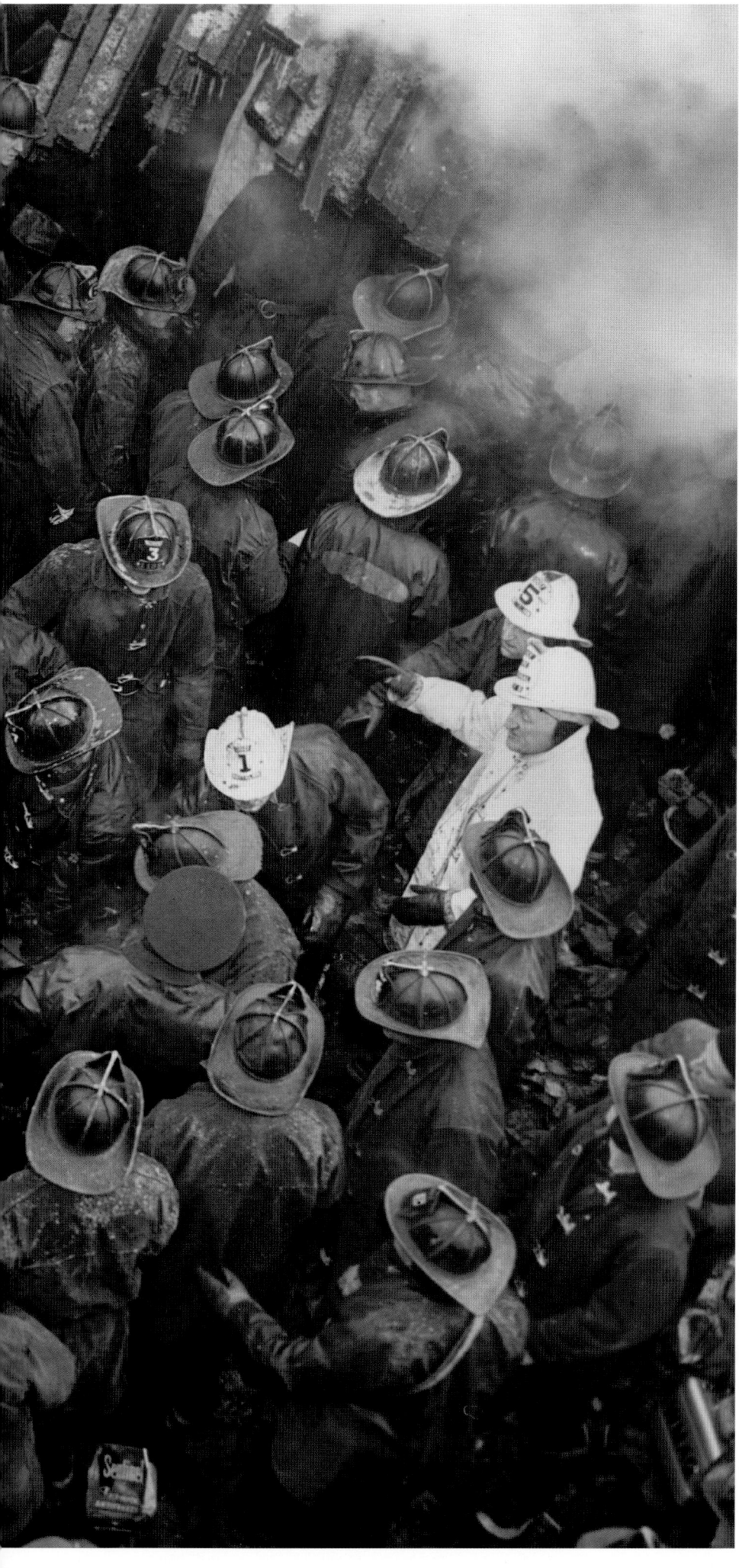

A CITY FORGED BY FIRE

Fire is central to Chicago's identity. The legendary conflagration of October 8–10, 1871, destroyed the entire downtown and most of the North Side, leaving 90,000 homeless. After mourning the disaster, Chicagoans pivoted to celebrating it, boasting of how quickly the city rebounded. Chicago's destruction paradoxically demonstrated it was indestructible.

That self-congratulation and the rush to rebuild ignored an essential lesson: fire would strike again. Improved building codes were delayed, ignored, and unenforced. Less than three years after the Great Fire, another blaze leveled more than 40 acres and destroyed more than 800 buildings in today's South Loop. Improved fire prevention and safety measures followed only when insurers threatened to withhold coverage. These new standards were enacted slowly and unevenly, with deadly consequences.

Though widespread fires became less common, even supposedly sound structures could be firetraps. In 1903, faulty wiring ignited the new Iroquois Theater. More than 600 people perished, most of them mothers and children at a holiday matinee, making it the deadliest single building fire in US history. Seven years later, 21 firemen, including Fire Chief James J. Horan, died fighting a blaze at the Union Stock Yards.

In the decades that followed the Iroquois and Stock Yards fires, the city enacted more serious reforms. Deadly fires nonetheless occur, usually because of a failure to implement safeguards. After six people died in the 2003 fire in the Loop's 35-story Cook County Administration Building, investigators put the blame on the absence of sprinklers and proper rescue methods.

Chicago is justifiably proud of how it rose from the ashes of 1871, but its vitality depends on an awareness that fire may flare up at any time.
—*Carl Smith, professor emeritus at Northwestern University, is author of* Chicago's Great Fire: The Destruction and Resurrection of an Iconic American City.

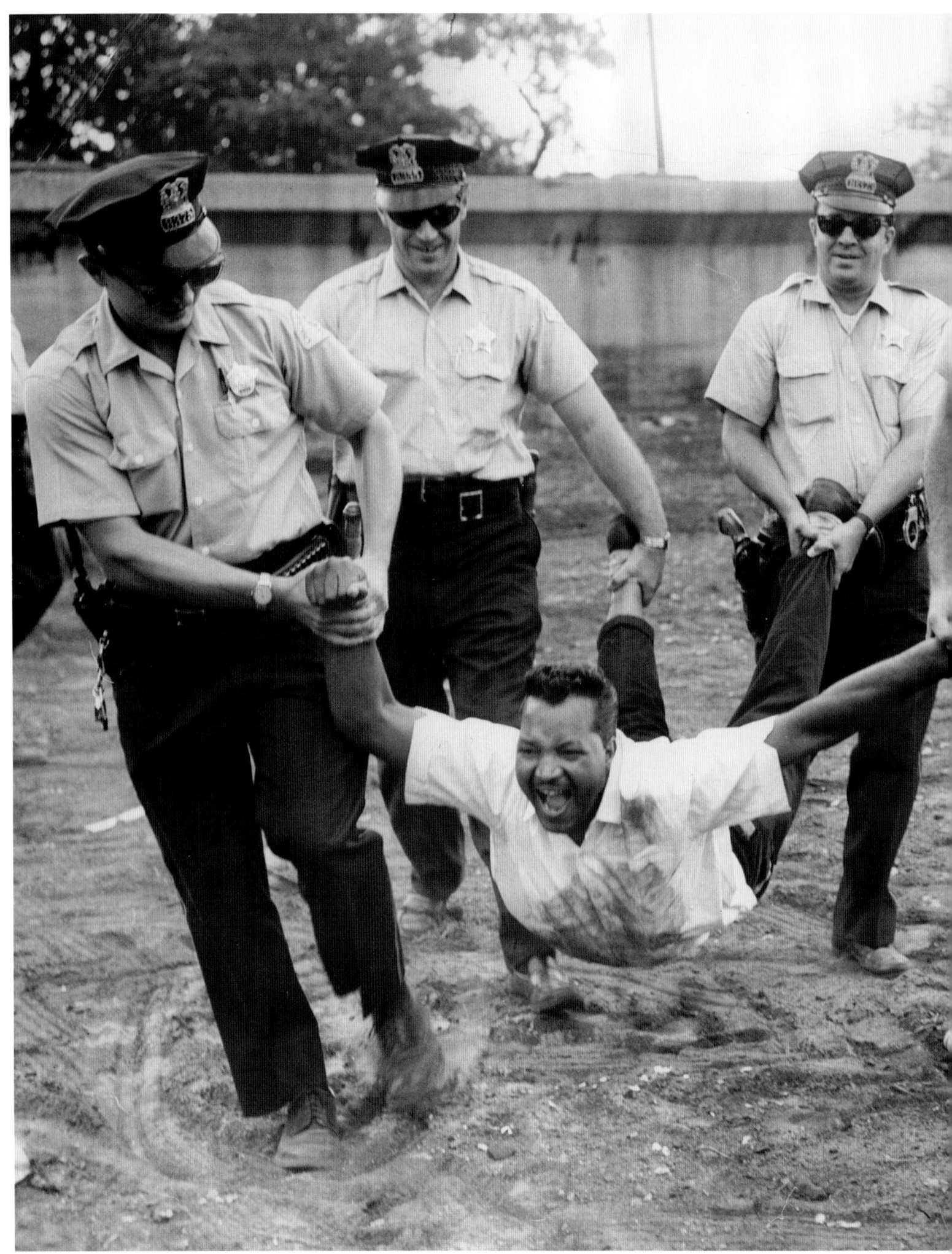
POLICE MAKE AN ARREST AT A PROTEST AGAINST MOBILE CLASSROOMS AT 73RD AND LOWE. AUGUST 12, 1963/DAVE MANN

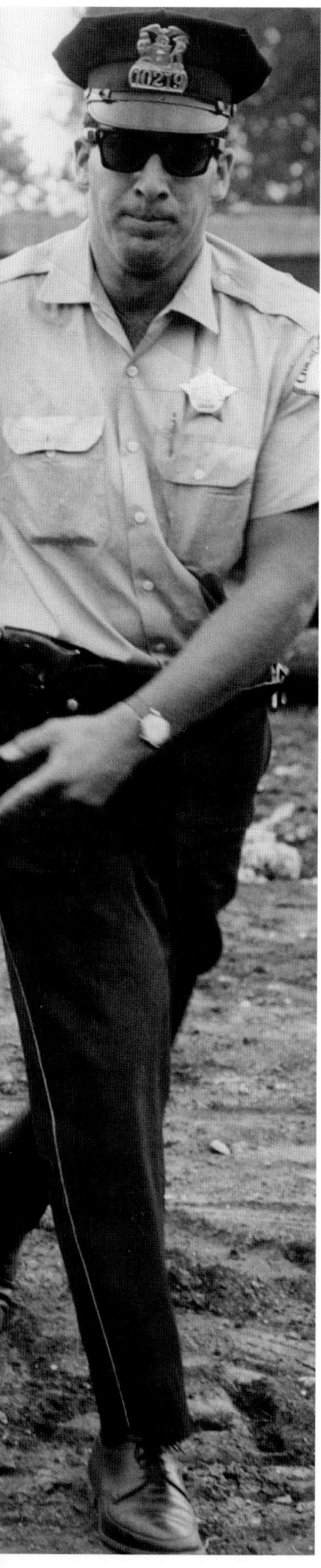

THEY BEAT PEOPLE BLOODY

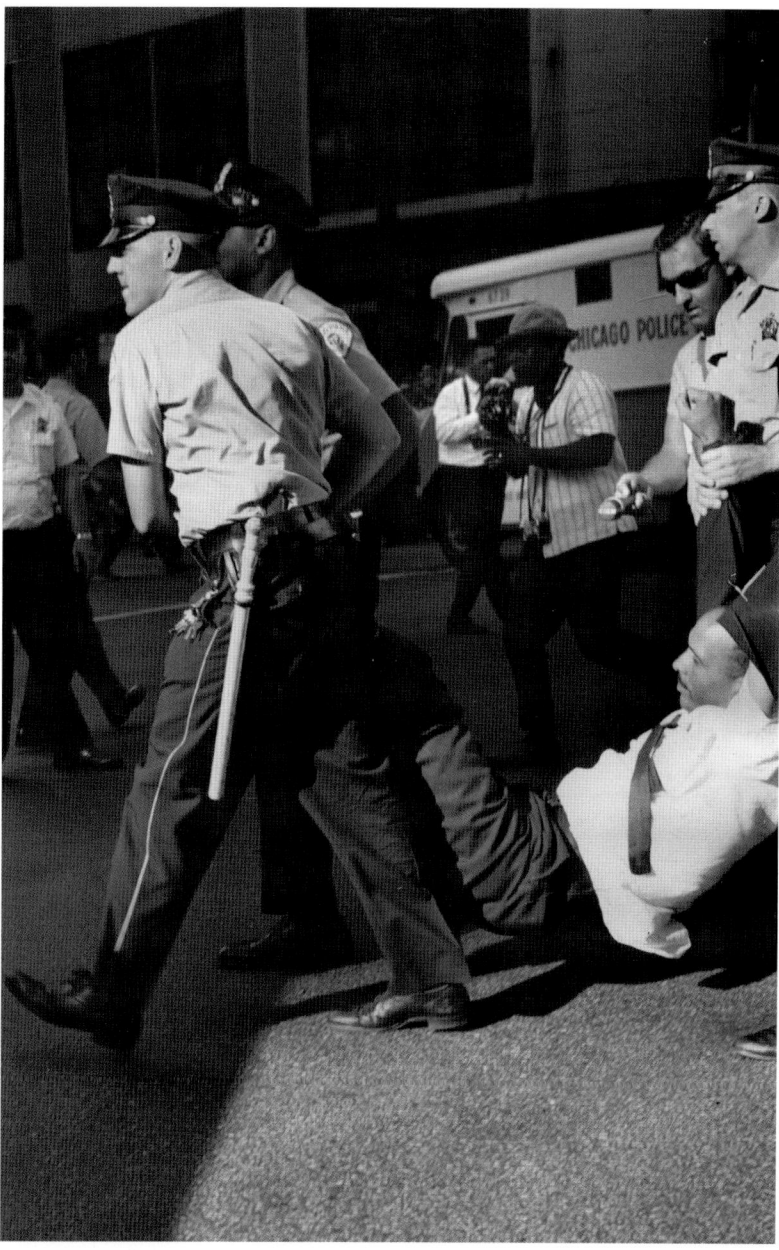

AL RABY IS ARRESTED AT A LOOP ANTI-WILLIS PROTEST. JUNE 28, 1965/MICKEY RITO

The education of my children was very important. In 1963, they were attending an overcrowded school in Englewood on half-day shifts. One day, my children came home and said they were going to start at a new school on Monday. It was in a former Goodwill Industries warehouse at 71st and Stewart.

Parents got together. We organized a freedom school so our kids would not attend a dangerous warehouse near a railroad track. We soon found out that the Chicago Board of Education planned to open an all mobile-unit school nearby, at 73rd and Lowe between a railroad embankment and an alley. Superintendent Benjamin Willis and the board were putting in portable mobile classrooms across the city to provide more space in jam-packed schools. They used those Willis wagons to keep Black students out of White neighborhoods.

We were irate and felt this was a slap in the face when they had empty classrooms west of Halsted Street. It was pouring rain when the first construction trucks arrived. We decided we would lay down so they couldn't get into the alley. We bought chains and locks to lock ourselves to the vehicles. We didn't know what was going to happen. On the first day, 65 of us got arrested for disorderly conduct or resisting arrest. We were muddy. They took us to the police station, asked us to give up our protest. We refused. They put us in jail.

What was most surprising to us was how horrible the police treated us as we continued our protest. One day—the day of this picture—they beat our people bloody. They tossed us headfirst into the police wagons. They would put about eighteen people in a wagon. Instead of taking us to jail, they would park the wagon in the sun. It was a hot August. There was no air. No windows. They treated us like we were criminals. They strip searched us. I will never forget that.

Eventually, the board ended its plan and moved all the trailers. But it was just the start of our fight.

—Rosie Simpson, who was president of the 71st and Stewart Parent Council, helped organize the Freedom Day boycott of Chicago public schools on October 22, 1963. More than 200,000 students stayed out of school and joined in a massive march downtown.

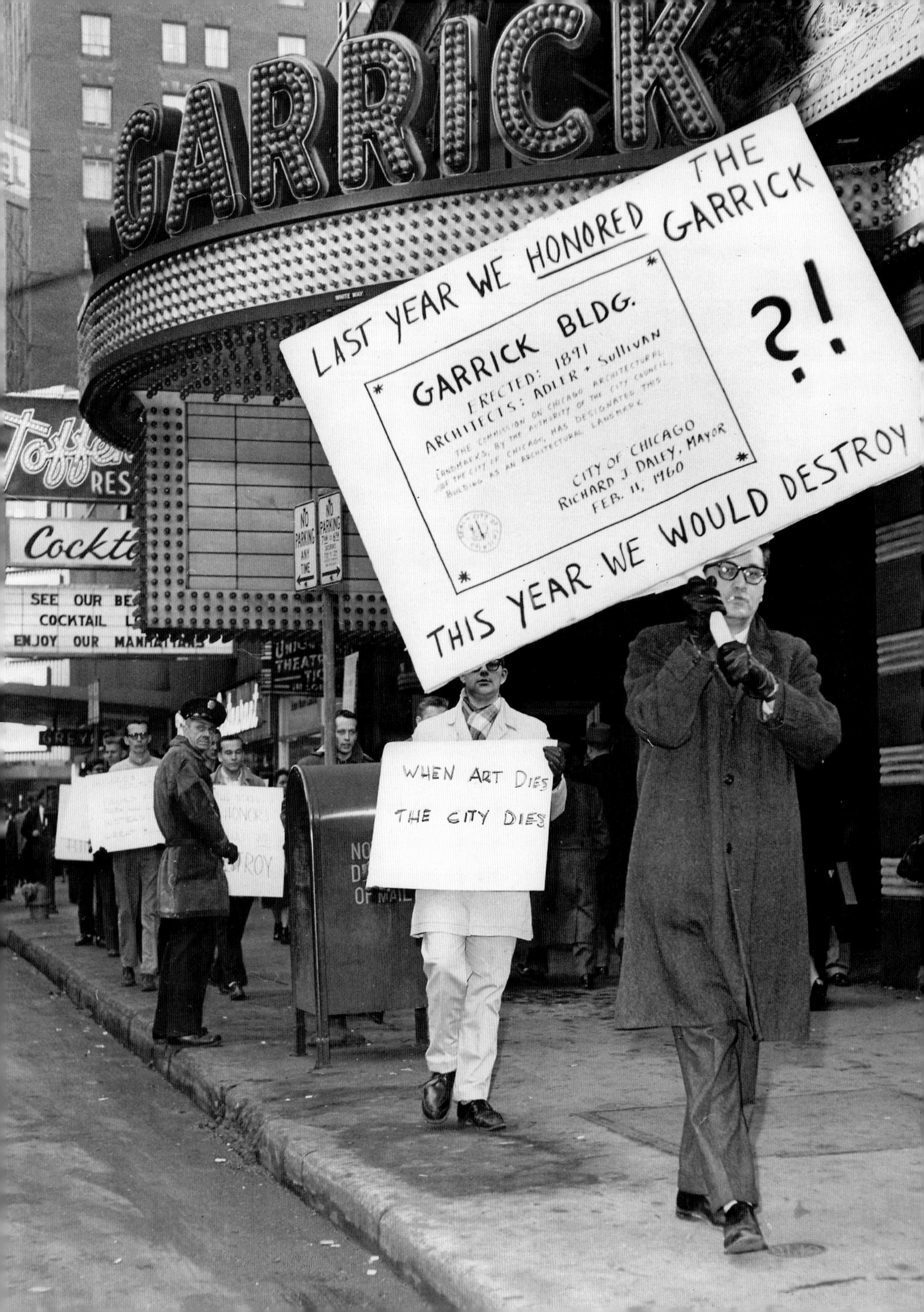

A SCAR ON THE CITY

The fight to save the 17-story Garrick Theater Building was the beginning of a mass movement to protect Chicago's architecturally significant buildings.

The prosperity of the 1950s created a building boom that caused the demolition of downtown buildings designed by architects such as Adler & Sullivan, Burnham & Root, and William LeBaron Jenney.

Photographer and historian Richard Nickel organized a picket line of scholars and friends to protest the proposed demolition of the Garrick. This unprecedented act served as the basis of a legal case to save the building.

At the time, I was working as an architectural intern for Skidmore, Owings & Merrill. I left the office at lunchtime to join the picket line. The Garrick was Adler & Sullivan's tallest building. It was innovative and complex but had been mutilated over the decades with new signage and insensitive remodeling. By 1960, it was hard to make the case for its preservation. Yet, this overt act enlightened the public to the plight of buildings that were significant representations of Chicago's architectural heritage.

I held out little hope because a friend, who worked for the building owner, told me he overheard Mayor Richard J. Daley assure his boss that the Garrick would come down.

The demolition began in 1961. In February, Richard Nickel was assigned to salvage the building's ornament and document its destruction. David Norris and I joined him. The loss of the Garrick left a scar on Nickel's psyche that remained until the end of his life.

The fight motivated preservationists to organize legal methods to save important buildings. Over the next twelve years, Chicago built some of its most iconic buildings: John Hancock, Civic Center, Federal Center, and McCormick Place. But another building, the Stock Exchange by Adler & Sullivan, fell to the wrecking ball in 1972. Richard Nickel, who was inside the building when a collapse occurred, lost his life.

—*Architect John Vinci has played a leading role in Chicago's preservation movement. He is a curator of the exhibition* Reconstructing the Garrick: Adler & Sullivan's Lost Masterpiece.

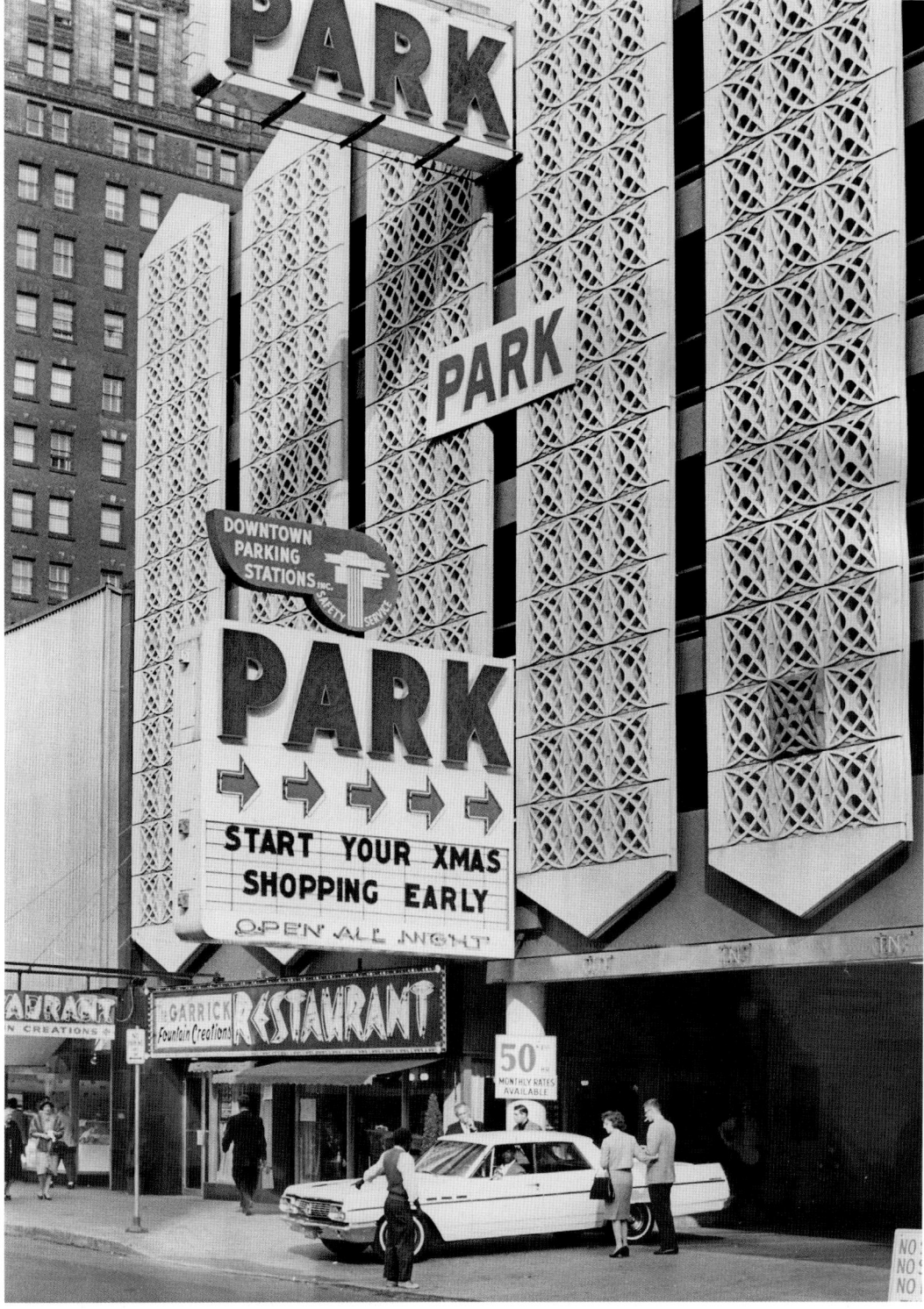

PARKING LOT REPLACEMENT. 1963/HOWARD LYON. OPPOSITE: GARRICK THEATER PROTEST. 1961/HOWARD LYON

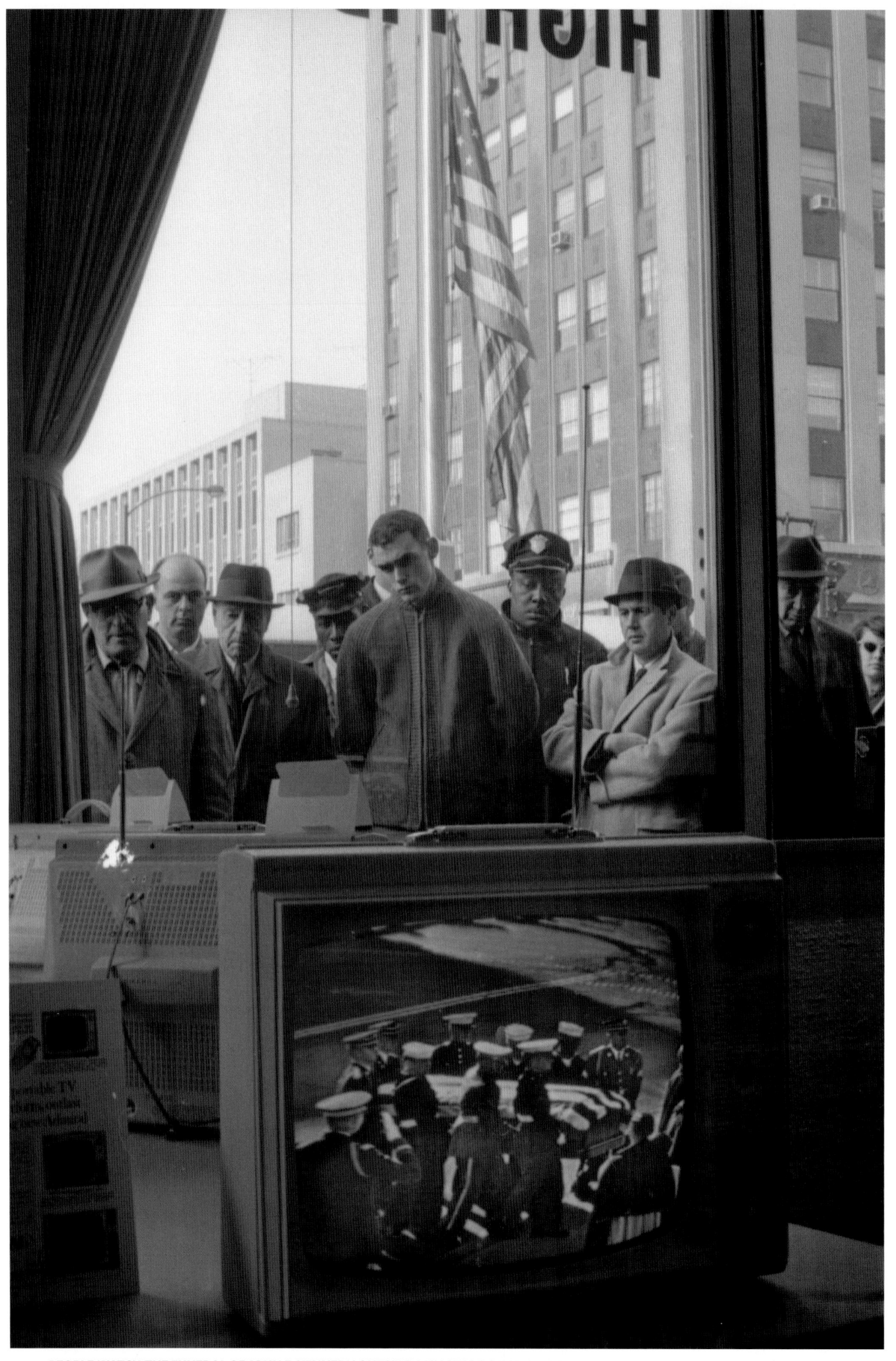

PEOPLE WATCH THE FUNERAL OF JOHN F. KENNEDY OUTSIDE A TV STORE ON MICHIGAN AVENUE. NOVEMBER 25, 1963/BOB KOTALIK

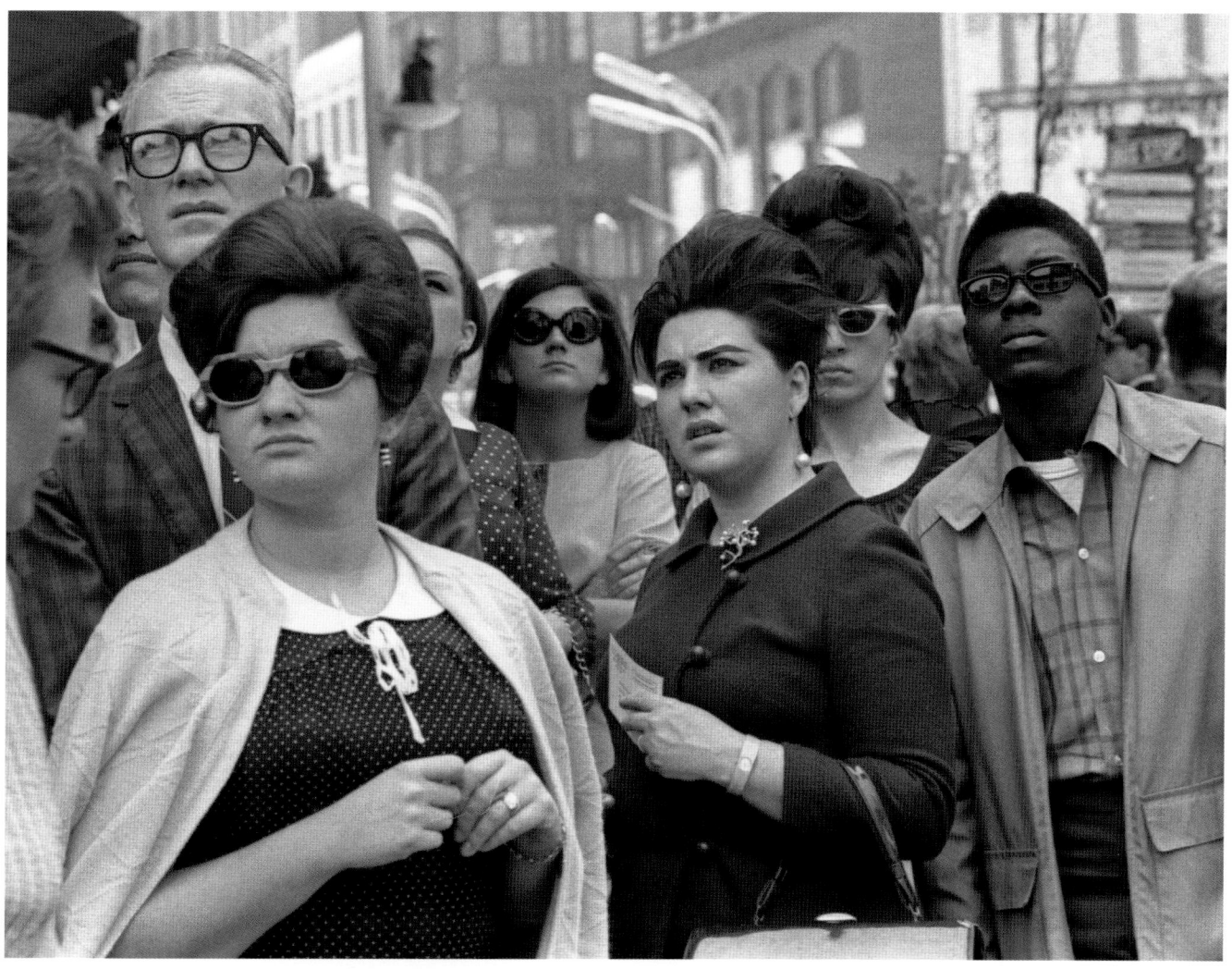

CHICAGOANS AT STATE AND RANDOLPH LEARN ABOUT THE ASSASSINATION OF ROBERT F. KENNEDY. JUNE 6, 1968/CLARENCE PETERS

TEARS FOR OUR NATION

Without preamble or explanation, the loudspeaker in our classroom at Fremd High School in Palatine broke in as we sat in Mr. Botts's sophomore English class. The voice belonged to CBS anchor Walter Cronkite. It was confusing at first—what were we hearing?—then horribly clear.

"From Dallas, Texas, the flash apparently official. President Kennedy died at 1 p.m. Central Standard Time. Two o'clock Eastern Standard Time. Some 38 minutes ago."

President Kennedy had been shot while riding in a motorcade beside his wife.

We froze in our seats.

Mr. Botts, one of my favorite teachers, for once had no words.

Not so some of my classmates.

Strangely, there was some smiling, some soft clapping.

As the bell rang and we moved into the hall, I heard one boy laughing with friends that "the Catholic got what he deserved."

We forget that our nation was divided long before Donald Trump came along.

I am a blue-collar daughter of a devoutly Catholic and Democrat mother. We lived on the wrong side of the tracks in an affluent Republican school district.

That weekend in 1963 we sat on the couch in front of the television, my mother and sister and I, choked and teary.

And then came 1968.

I was a junior that year, this time at the University of Illinois. In early spring, Dr. Martin Luther King Jr. was shot to death in Memphis.

Two months later, as I walked to breakfast, news came that Bobby Kennedy, who was running for the Democratic presidential nomination, had been shot overnight on the campaign trail in California. He would die in less than 24 hours.

What kind of country slaughters its leaders? And why? Is it because they represent a religion or a race or a concept of freedom that drives some to violence?

In the '60s I was young.

Idealistic.

Hopeful.

Six decades later, I hang on for dear life.

Dear Life.

Which insists that I... we... remain... in spite of everything...

Idealistic.

And hopeful.

—*Carol Marin, director of the Center for Journalism Integrity and Excellence at DePaul University, worked as a television anchor, network correspondent, and reporter, and wrote a column for the Sun-Times.*

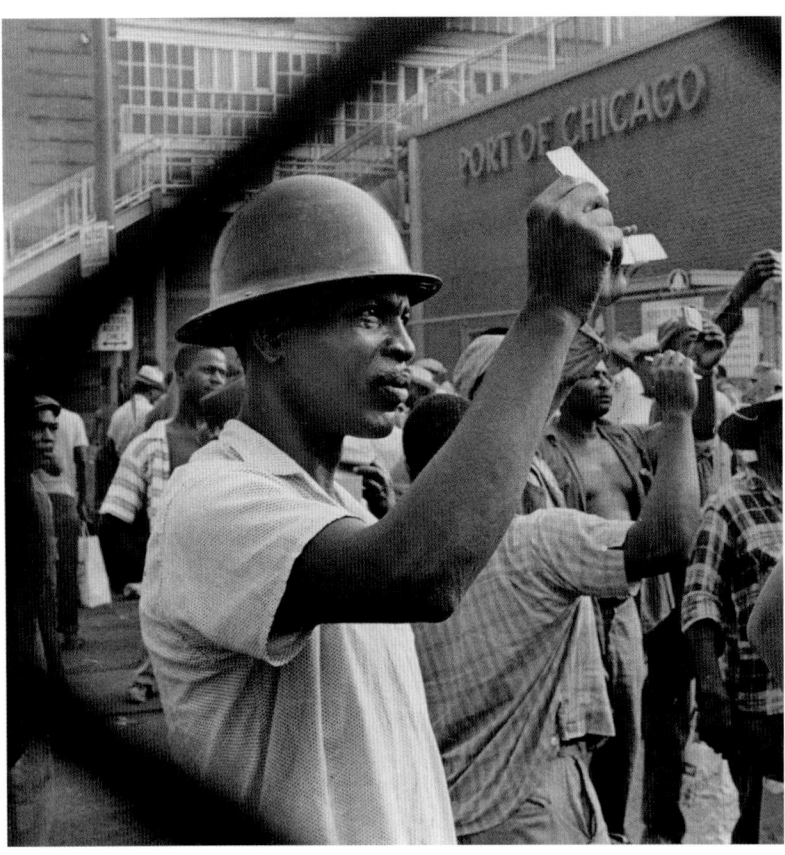

UP AT DAWN

Chicago used to be a thriving inland seaport. After the Saint Lawrence Seaway opened and hundreds of ships from all over the world docked here, Chicago billed itself as the world's largest inland port. Ships were loaded and unloaded at Navy Pier, Calumet Harbor, and along the wharves near the Outer Drive Bridge and the Calumet River.

Dock workers would gather at dawn to get work. The longshoremen vied for jobs every day during the shipping season at what were called shake-ups. They held up their union cards to attract the attention of the union leaders who formed crews. At the time, they earned $23 a day—with $2 going for union dues.

These were changing times for Chicago and for newspaper photography. I took these photos with a 35mm camera. I was the first new photographer hired at the Chicago Daily News in seventeen years. Many of the old-timers dated their careers back to the 1929 Saint Valentine's Day Massacre. They all used large- or medium-format cameras.

They thought this itty-bitty camera was worthless. But when I showed them the results, they couldn't believe it. They could see that this camera made it possible to move around easily and get really close. I always felt comfortable getting close. My camera could see so much more.

It didn't take long for a couple of the photographers to buy the same camera. But they were never comfortable. They would take the small cameras along with their larger ones. Within a few years, when many of those earlier photographers had retired, just about everybody was using the 35mm.
—Henry Herr Gill photographed for the Daily News and Sun-Times from 1963 to 1983. He served as director of photography at both papers.

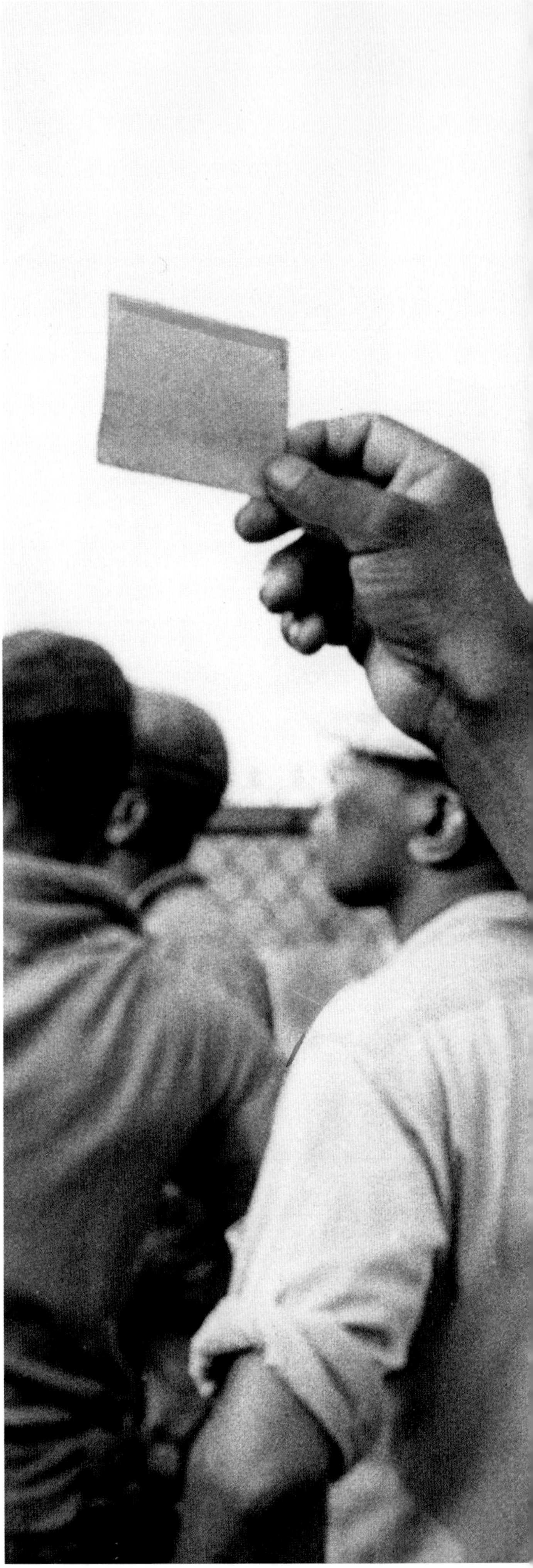

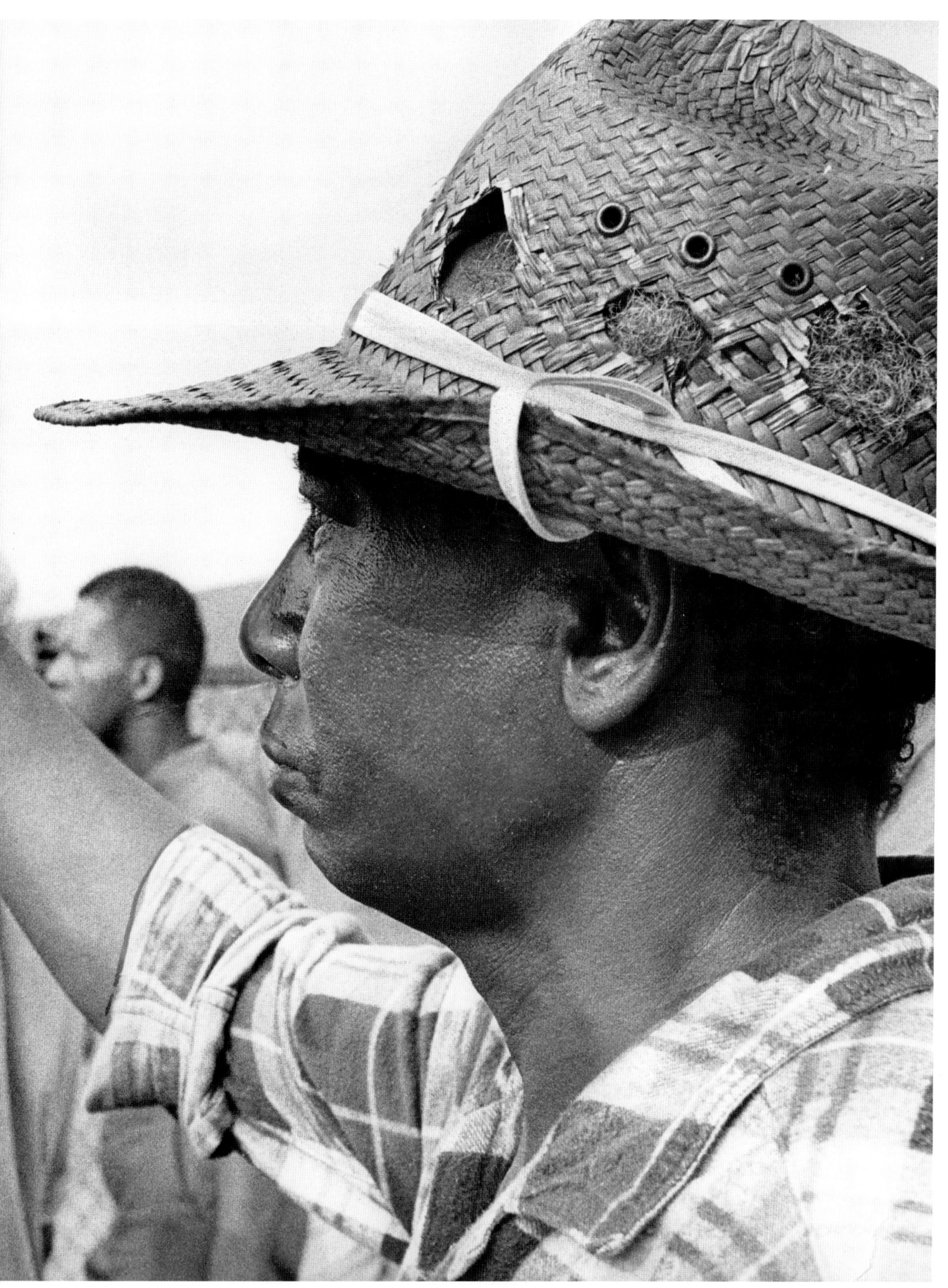
LONGSHOREMEN LOOK FOR WORK AT NAVY PIER. JULY 24, 1964/ HENRY HERR GILL

UNAFRAID OF THE DARK

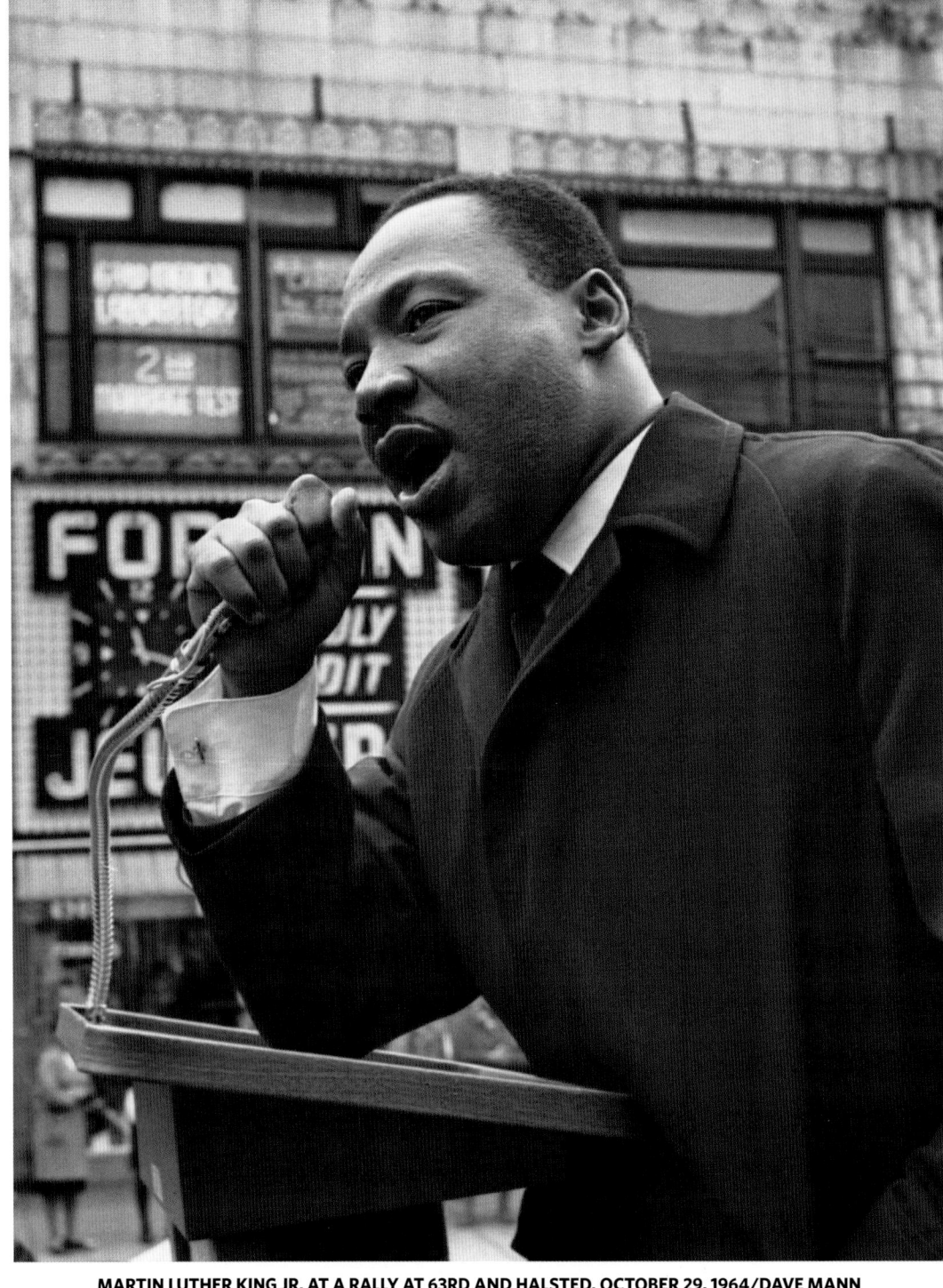

MARTIN LUTHER KING JR. AT A RALLY AT 63RD AND HALSTED. OCTOBER 29, 1964/DAVE MANN

The overarching excitement came from knowing that Dr. Martin Luther King Jr. was actually coming to Chicago.

He spoke all over Chicago that week. I got to see him in a parking lot across from Saint James Church on Forty-sixth Street and Ellis. As kids we were always in that lot, riding our bikes at breakneck speed until dusk. They built a platform for Dr. King to stand on while he addressed a crowd of hundreds of folks who lived nearby. My brother was a Cub Scout and part of the honor guard that welcomed him. I don't remember being jealous, just proud. We had come early because of my brother's duties, and so we were right up front; I was pressed against the platform.

I wish I could remember more of what Dr. King said, but I know he talked about freedom and that was what we wanted most to hear. And I know I touched his shoes, shiny black and plain, because I was at nose level with them, and I wanted to say I touched him.

When the speech was over, he climbed into a black car. I was right next to the window as the door closed. I waved at him. And he smiled—a real smile that a little girl could feel—and waved back at me as the car drove away.

We marched with him that Sunday, my whole family and I. As hot as it was, we dressed as if for church. Daddy wore a suit, his good Florsheim shoes for all that walking, and a hat. We marched all day, through downtown Chicago, to protest against the policies of the Board of Education. Daddy had already lodged at least one protest with the public schools: he refused to let us go to them. But that didn't change his intent to protest on behalf of those children who did attend. "Willis must go," we shouted over and over. On that hot summer day, no one could have told the thousands of us in the streets that the world would not soon be made new. But summer turned to fall, and Chicago's radically segregated world would remain intact for some time longer. It was my first lesson in how hard change really was to achieve.

—From Unafraid of the Dark, *a memoir by Rosemary L. Bray. The Reverend Rosemary Bray McNatt is president of Starr King School for the Ministry in Oakland, California.*

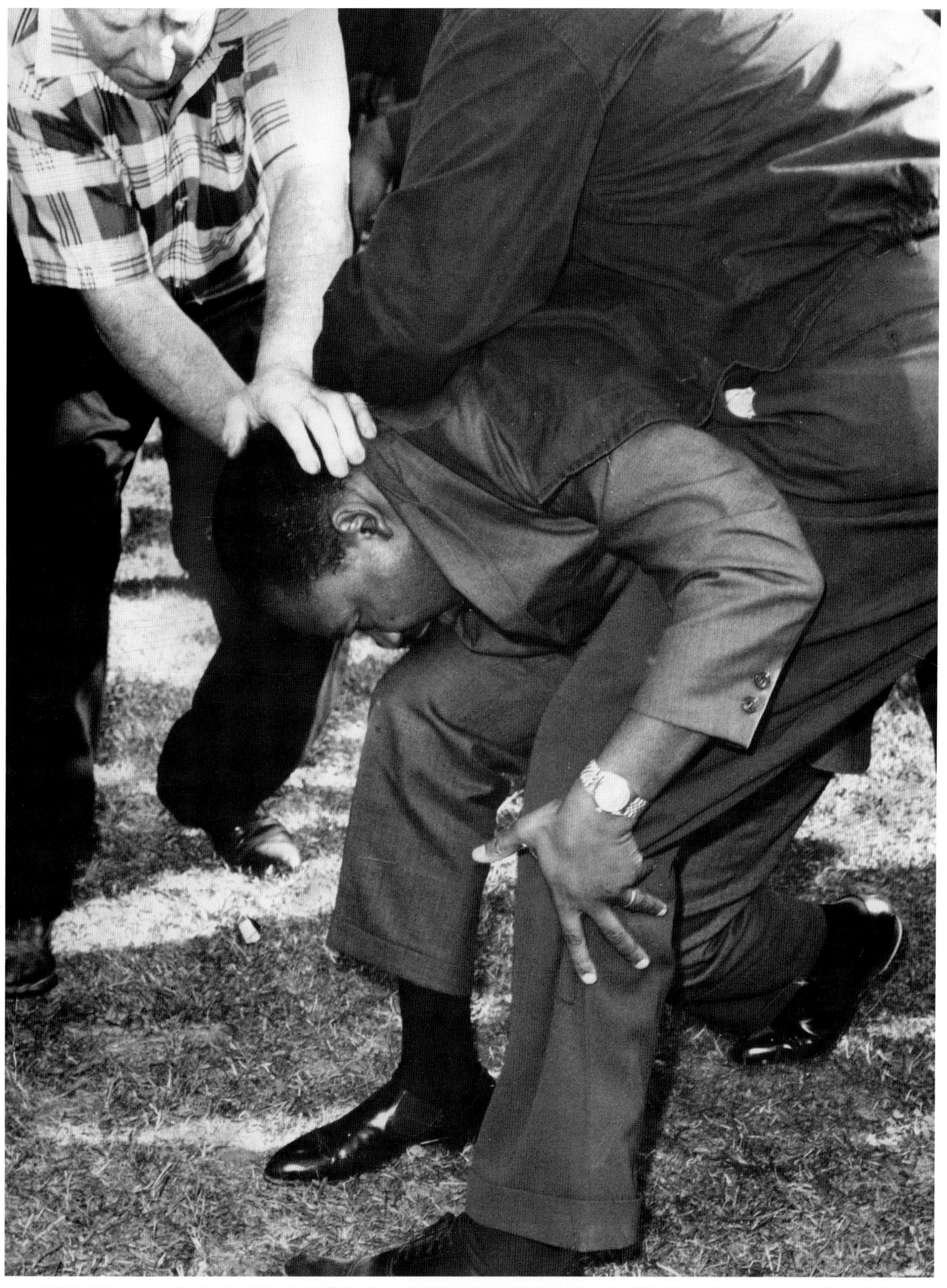

KING IS PROTECTED AFTER BEING STRUCK BY A ROCK FROM A MOB AT A MARQUETTE PARK OPEN HOUSING MARCH. AUGUST 5, 1966/LARRY NOCERINO

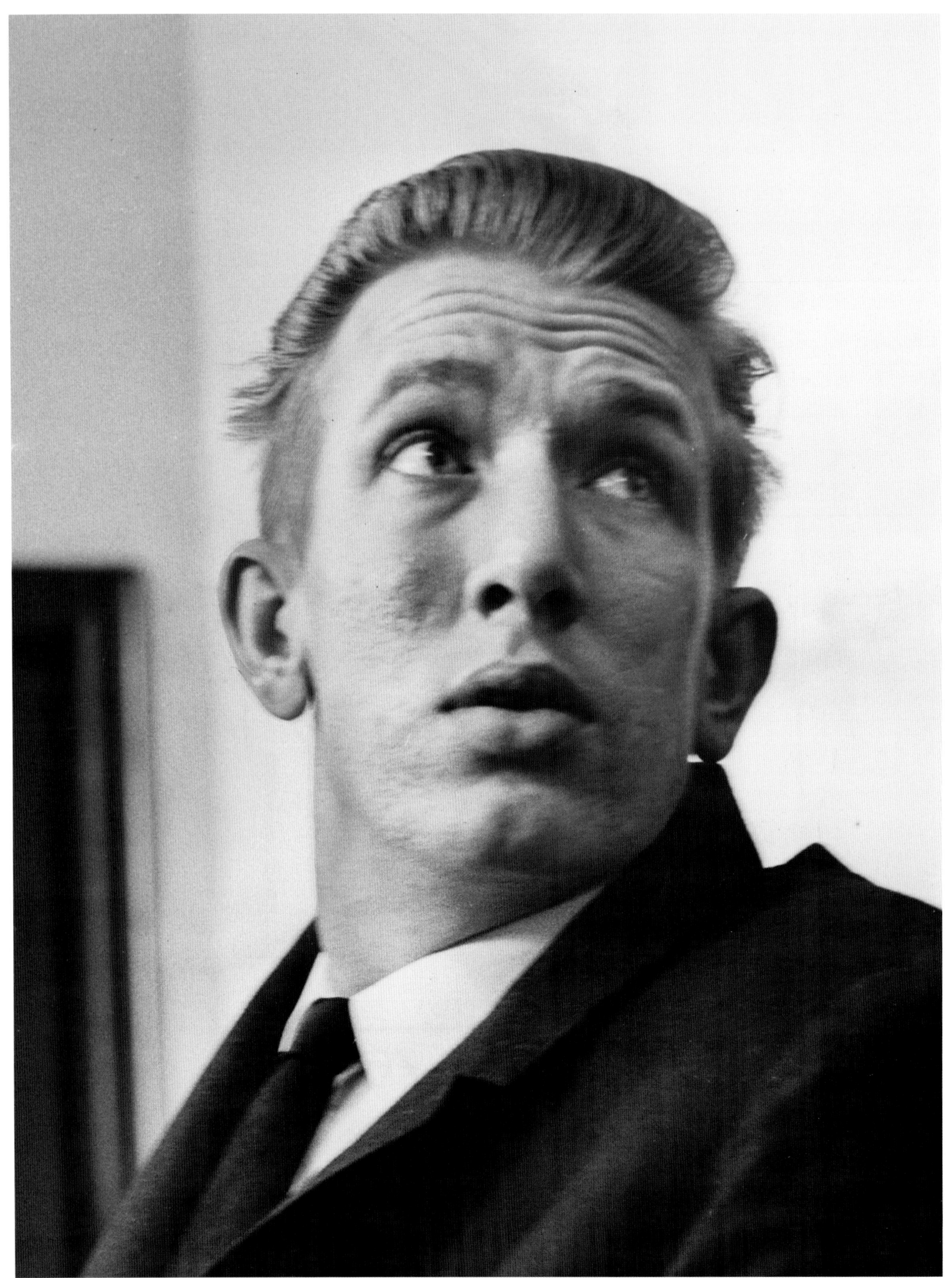

RICHARD SPECK WAITS TO APPEAR IN COURT AT HIS FIRST APPEARANCE SINCE HIS ARRAIGNMENT. AUGUST 18, 1966/RAY BURLEY

'THEY ARE ALL DEAD'

The first alarm clock went off at 5 a.m. Corazon Amurao had been huddled under a bunk bed for two hours. Now she began to untie herself, working her hands back and forth to loosen the double knots of the bedsheet that bound her. Then she untied her ankles. Another alarm sounded. It was 5:30.

Crawling slowly on her stomach, she emerged from her hiding place and with great effort moved under another bunk bed, from where she could peek out the open door. Nothing moved in the hallway. She stood up and began to walk to her own bedroom. She saw the body of one of her roommates lying on the bathroom floor. As she walked across her own bedroom, she stepped over the bodies of three more, covered with blood. She closed her door, fearing the killer might still be in the house.

She climbed into her top bunk, opened the window, and screamed almost continuously for five minutes. There was no reply. Dressed in pajama shorts and top, she crawled out the window and jumped down to a ledge of the townhouse facing 100th Street on the far Southeast Side of Chicago. She stood there screaming for twenty more minutes before anyone came, a scream that shook terror into the very heart of Chicago:

"They are all dead! They are all dead! My friends are all dead. Oh, God, I'm the only one alive!"

It was June 14, 1966, and Chicago awoke on that hot and sticky morning to reports that eight young nurses had been brutally stabbed, strangled, and sexually assaulted. The killings took place as the victims were settling in for the evening in the safety of their own beds. This murder of innocents shocked the conscience of the nation. Doors were locked, strangers were scrutinized, parents checked on their children.

The suspect was little more than a mile east, in the rough Calumet Harbor area of the Southeast Side. Richard Franklin Speck, 24, a heavily pockmarked, tattooed drifter from Dallas, was sound asleep in a small upstairs room at the Shipyard Inn, a tavern-rooming house catering to seamen and steelworkers. A small black pistol was tucked under his pillow. A stale can of beer sat on his nightstand, next to a crumpled pile of dollar bills. What had started out as a $25 robbery had turned into a crime that will never be forgotten.

Speck had swept through the nurses' townhouse like a summer tornado, and his savage murders changed the landscape of crime. Within a few weeks, Charles Whitman would take a rifle to the top of a tower at the University of Texas and kill sixteen; within a few years, Charles Manson would mastermind the "helter-skelter" killings in southern California. Speck's legacy to us is the banality of today's mass murders and serial killings.

This is how it all began.
—*Dennis L. Breo and William J. Martin were the co-authors of* The Crime of the Century: Richard Speck and the Murders That Shocked a Nation. *Martin, an assistant state's attorney, led the prosecution of Speck.*

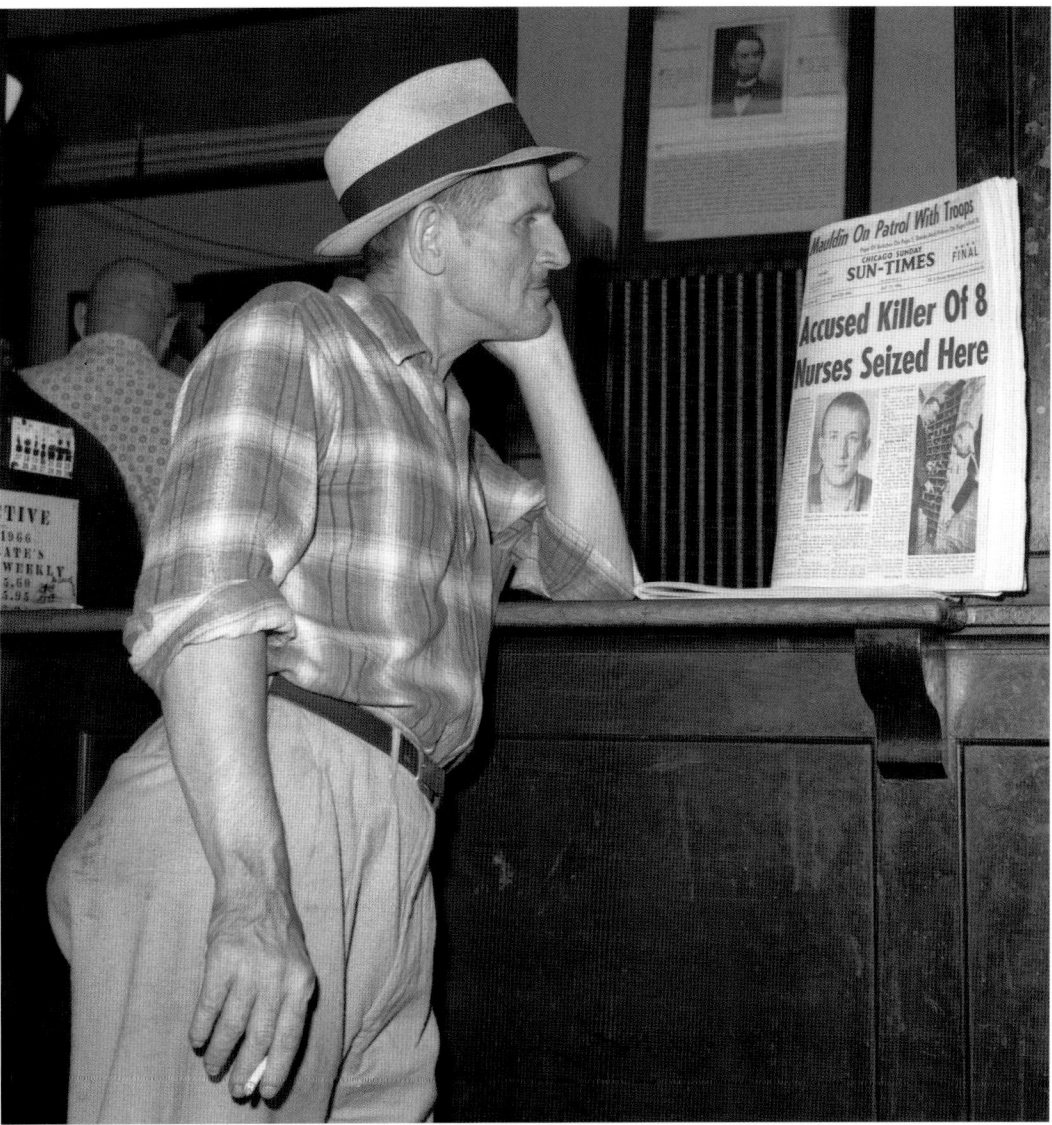

IN THE STARR HOTEL, 617 WEST MADISON, WHERE SPECK WAS ARRESTED. JULY 18, 1966

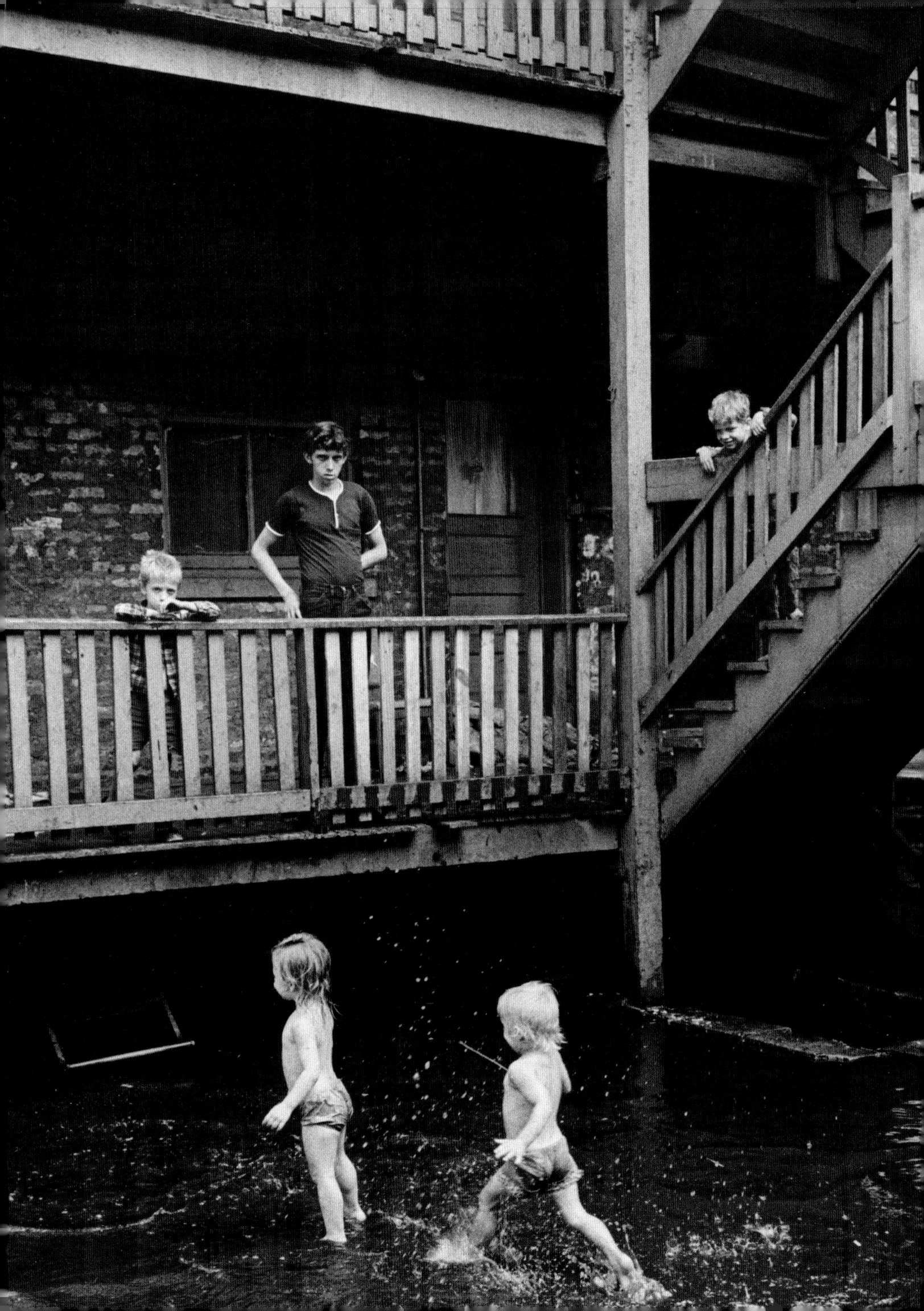

'NO ONE SHOULD LIVE LIKE THAT'

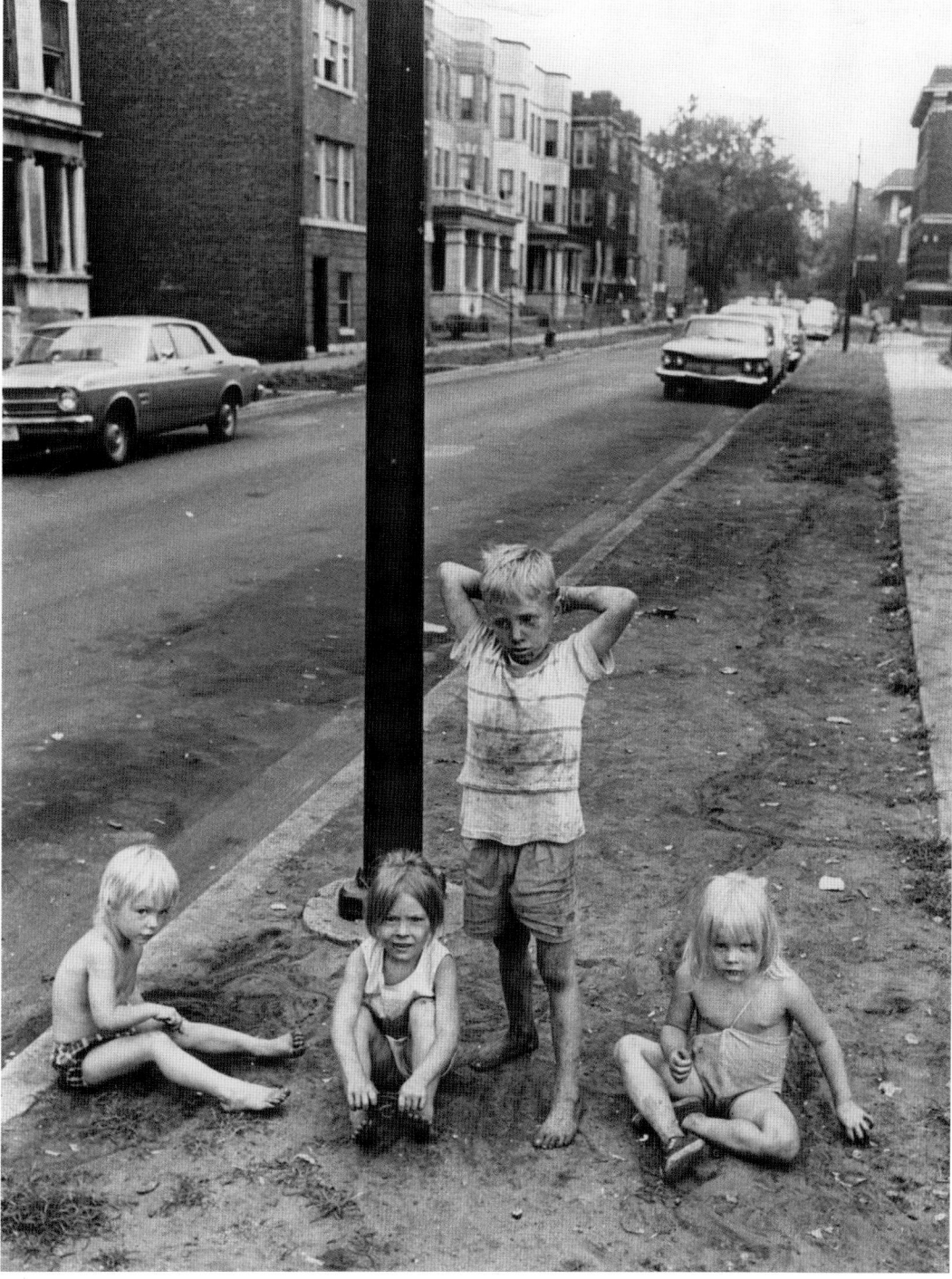

SUMMER DAYS IN UPTOWN. CLIFTON AND MONTROSE. OPPOSITE: NEAR RACINE AVENUE. 1967/JACK DYKINGA

Uptown Chicago was teeming with people when I arrived there in 1972.

Probably the largest concentration of poor White people in an urban area lived in this geographically compact community. Many were from the South. There also were as many Native Americans here as on any reservation. And a significant number of Puerto Ricans—whose fate seemed always to be in the way of some urban renewal plan—had made their way to Uptown from Lincoln Park and from the Near North Side community that became Sandburg Village.

The oldest African-American community outside of Chicago's "Black Belt" was also in Uptown. But that doesn't mean they were welcomed. The first Black resident on the 4600 block of Winthrop Avenue was a chauffeur whose employer had left him his home in his will. That act of generosity would be the catalyst for a 1940s city restriction that, "No Negro person can buy, own, or rent property in this district except on that block which is inhabited entirely by Negros."

Soon Uptown also would become the port of entry for refugees from several war-torn African and Southeast Asian countries.

Much of the housing in Uptown was poorly maintained. Large apartments had been converted into multiple sleeping rooms with shared baths. Many buildings had plumbing and electricity that had been neglected for generations. Lead from flaking paint flowed through the veins of children. Electrical fires were common, as was salmonella poisoning from compromised water and sewer pipes. The people living here were poor. They had few other housing choices.

City planners wanted to tear down what they could. "What's the harm?" they asked. "The conditions are horrible. No one should have to live like that." But while no one wanted to live in those conditions, there was no better housing being offered.

And when buildings were demolished, mounds of unstable bricks and rusty steel debris were often left in the wake. They were dangerous playgrounds that called to children who had no safe places to play.

—*Helen Shiller served as alderman of the 46th Ward, which encompasses the Uptown neighborhood, from 1987 to 2011.*

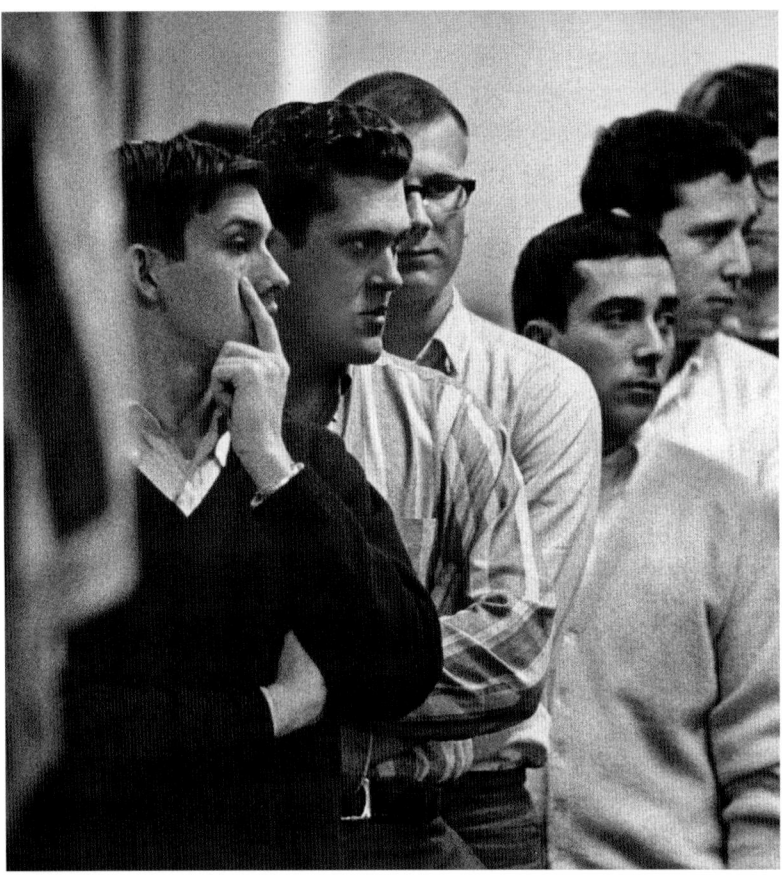

PENSIVE ARMY INDUCTEES ON THEIR FIRST DAY. JANUARY 28, 1968/PERRY C. RIDDLE

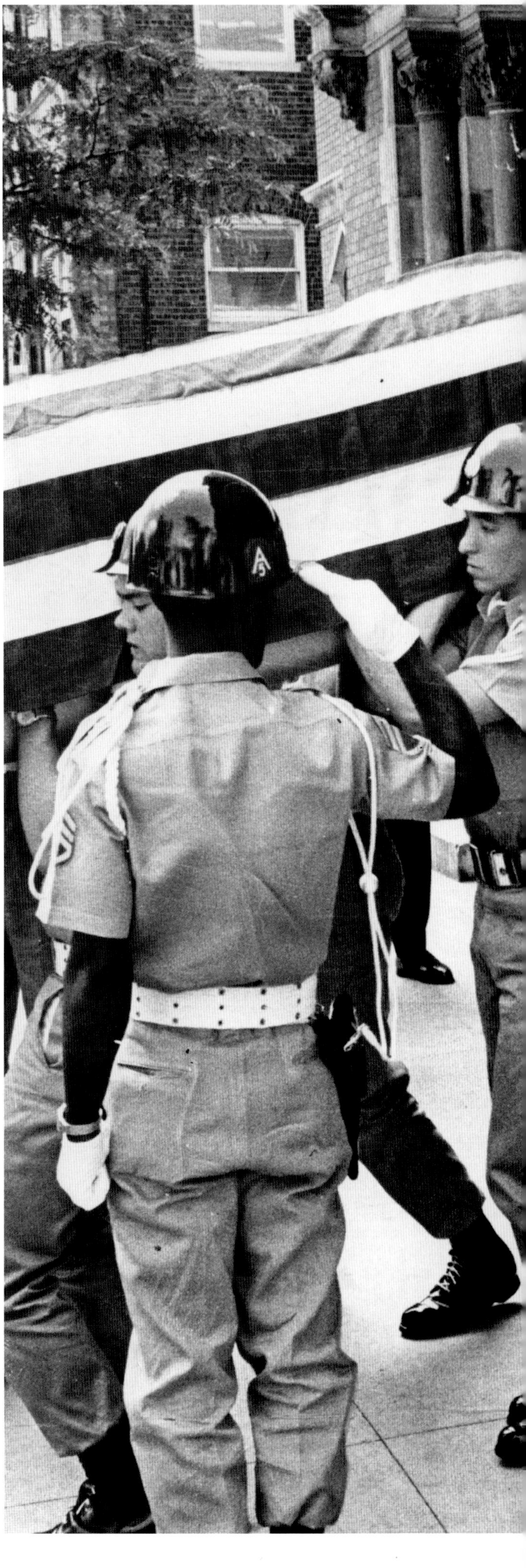

I NEVER FORGOT YOU

Elizabeth C. Scoggin Roberts posted this memory of Robert Aguado on the Vietnam Veterans Memorial Fund's Wall of Faces website in 2005.

I am the Catholic school girl that you wrote letters to from Vietnam. I was eleven years old then. I am 48 now. I never forgot you. I still have the two letters I got from you.

In your first letter dated 3-24-67 you told me that you were going to send the first card I sent you home. These were your words: "There are things, little mementos everyone loves to keep and the card you sent is one of those mementos." Your second and last letter was dated 5-19-67. It was exactly one month before you were killed. You thanked me for my thoughtfulness because I sent you comic books. You described the people and the country of Vietnam to me. You included drawings of the traditional women's clothes because you thought I'd be most interested in them.

I tried to write regularly. The nuns at my school, St. Mary's Parochial School in the Canal Zone, Panama, encouraged us to write so that we could be helpful in some way to the soldiers who were fighting in Vietnam. I wrote you a letter on 8-30-67 and I got it back stamped "Verified Deceased Return to Sender." I have kept your letters with me all these years. They are my mementos of you, a man I never met but who I am so grateful to.

As a child I did not understand why you were at war or really what happened to you. I think I understand now. I hope I do.

I want to thank you for taking the time to write to a child you did not know. You did so with such sweetness and caring in the midst of such a terrible war.

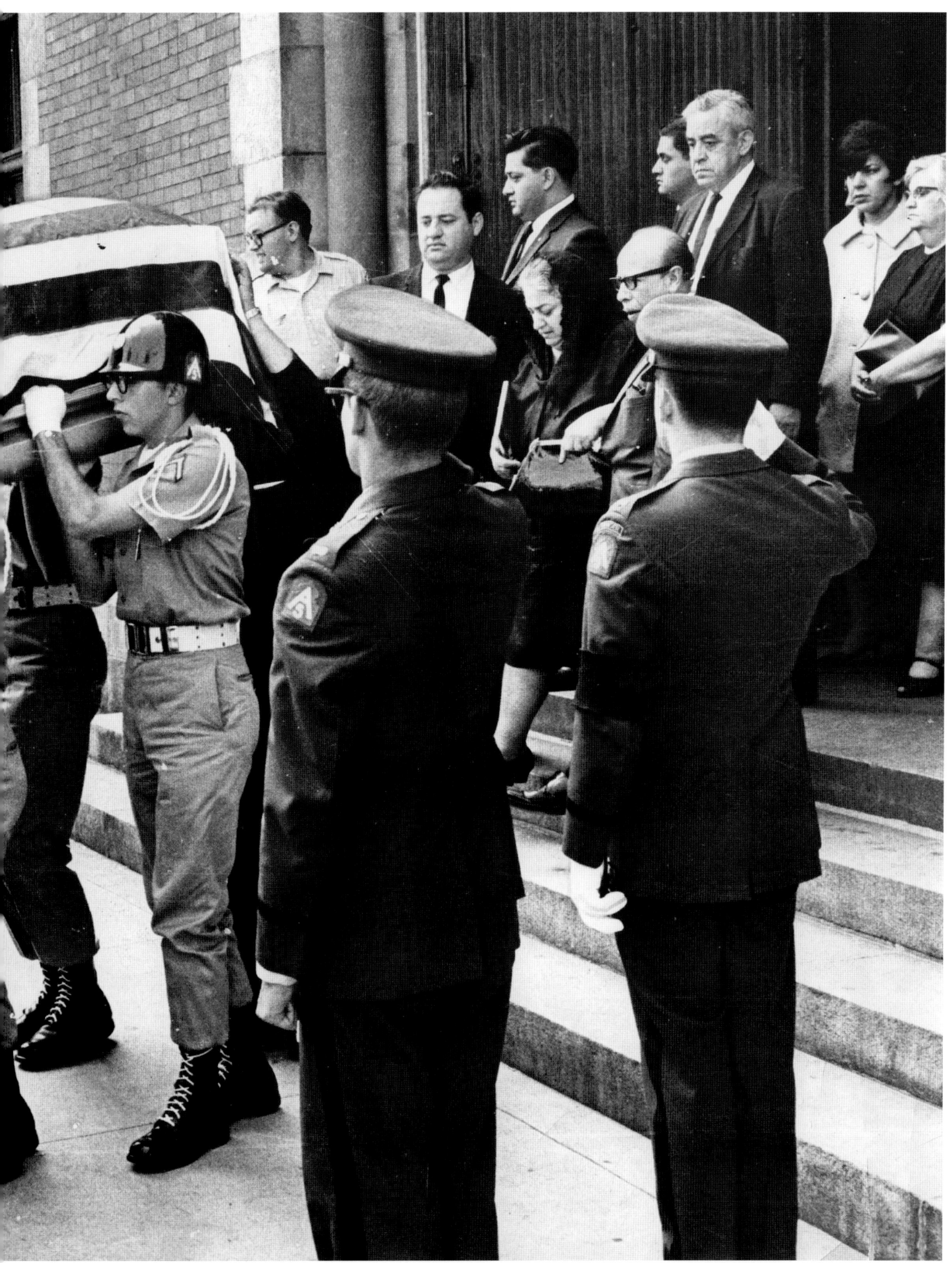
ROBERT AGUADO'S COFFIN IS CARRIED FROM CHICAGO'S SAINT MICHAEL CATHOLIC CHURCH. HE WAS KILLED IN VIETNAM. JULY 3, 1967/JACK DYKINGA

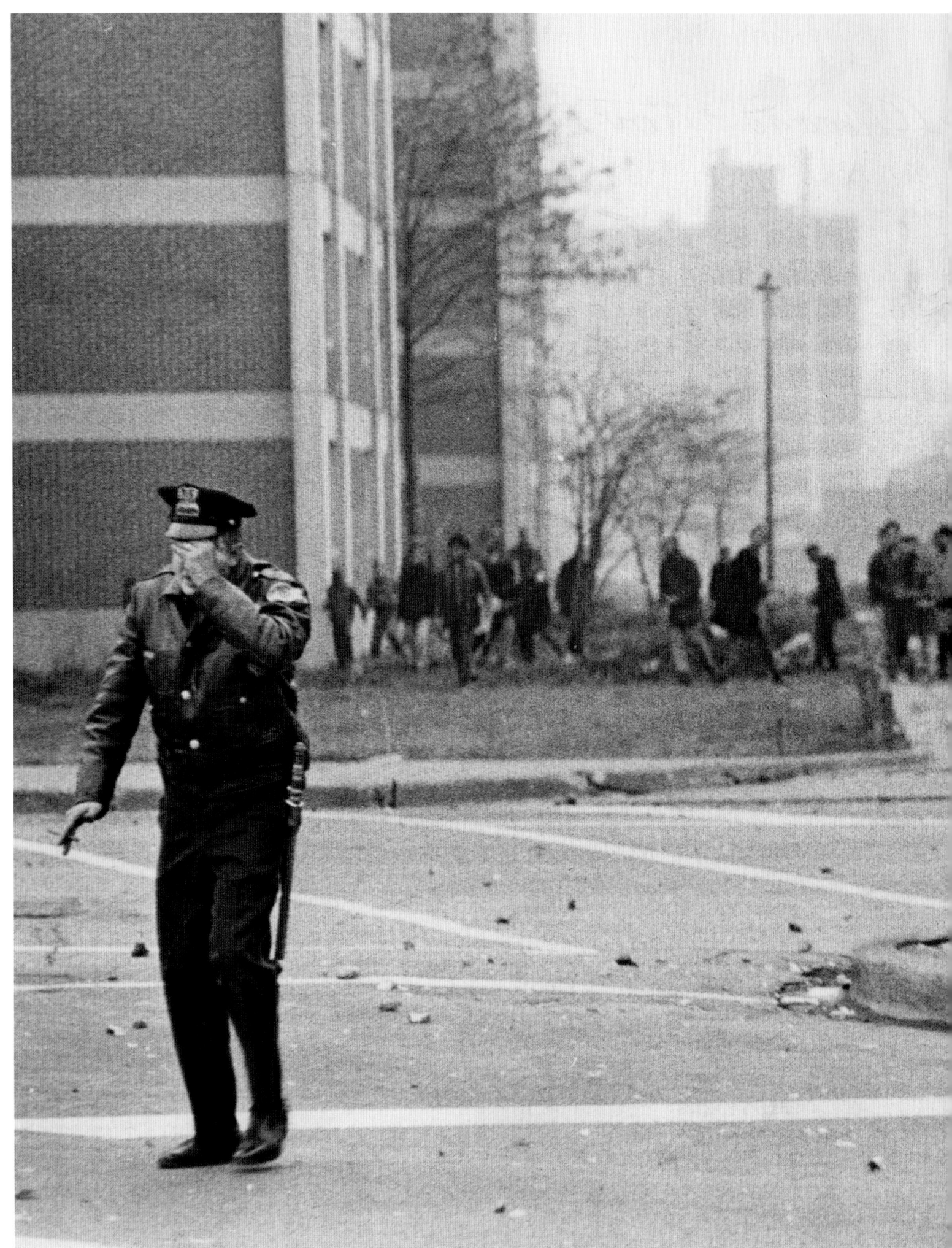

OFFICER ROBERT ASTRAUS RETREATS FROM ROCK-THROWING MOB AFTER BEING HIT IN THE EYE NEAR CABRINI-GREEN. NOVEMBER 21, 1967/JOHN JAQUA

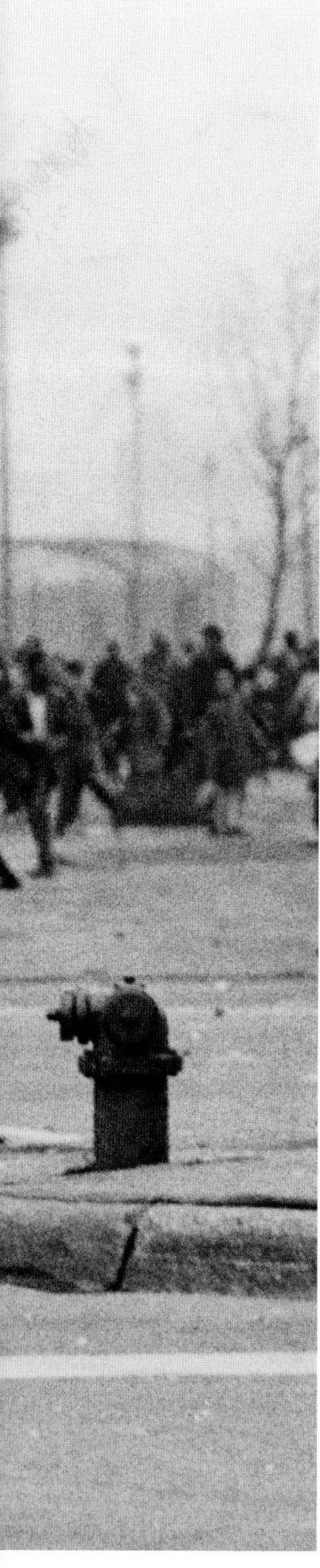

BATTLE FOR THE STREETS

By late in 1967, the relationship between the Chicago Police Department and much of Black Chicago was deeply fractured. For years, policing in Black neighborhoods had been getting more intensive, invasive, and violent. This was especially the case for young people, who were routinely subjected to stop-and-frisk while going about their daily lives and who disproportionately bore the brunt of police violence. When the police department launched its Gang Intelligence Unit in the spring of 1967, it exacerbated this reality.

These photos capture an incident that can only be understood within this context of open hostility between the police and parts of the African-American community.

Throughout the late 1960s and early 1970s, Black and Brown youth in cities across the country violently rebelled against structural inequality, police violence, and harassment. Chicago itself experienced several of these events, on an especially large scale in 1968 following the assassination of Martin Luther King Jr. and sporadically throughout other years.

Images such as this—a badly injured White police officer in focus and a grainy gathering of protesters in the background—scandalized much of White America and prompted a surge in "law-and-order" rhetoric from figures like Chicago Mayor Richard J. Daley and US president Richard Nixon. What critics missed, though, were the political and social underpinnings of these protests. Consider the anger of people who lived in the Cabrini-Green housing development on the city's Near North Side. Opened in the late 1950s and early 1960s with fanfare and great optimism, Cabrini-Green's promise quickly wore off. Neglected maintenance was par for the course. Residents became subject to evermore invasive surveillance practices by housing authorities. The projects were sites of violence and drug use. Opportunities for better futures were hard to come by.

City politicians rarely listened to residents. There was the everyday threat and reality of abusive and harassing policing. When project residents rebelled—destroying property, confronting police—they rebelled against a fundamentally unjust and inequitable social and economic order.
—*Simon Balto teaches history at the University of Wisconsin-Madison. He is the author of* Occupied Territory: Policing Black Chicago from Red Summer to Black Power.

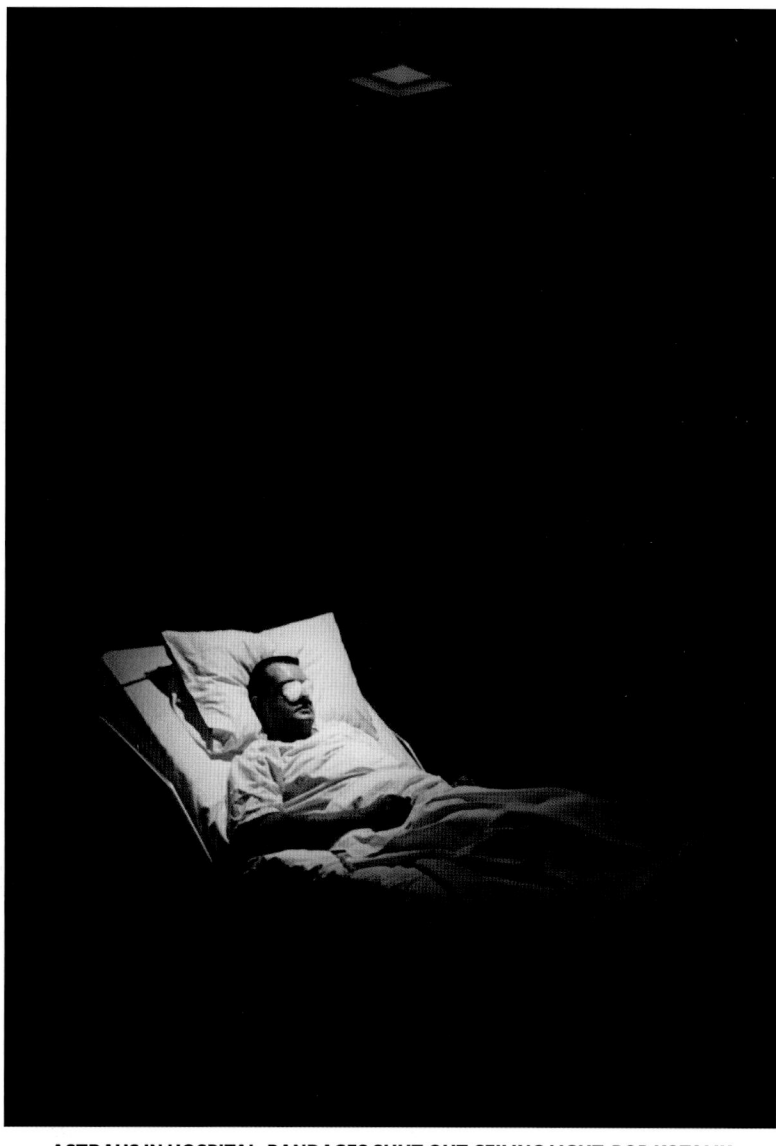

ASTRAUS IN HOSPITAL. BANDAGES SHUT OUT CEILING LIGHT. BOB KOTALIK

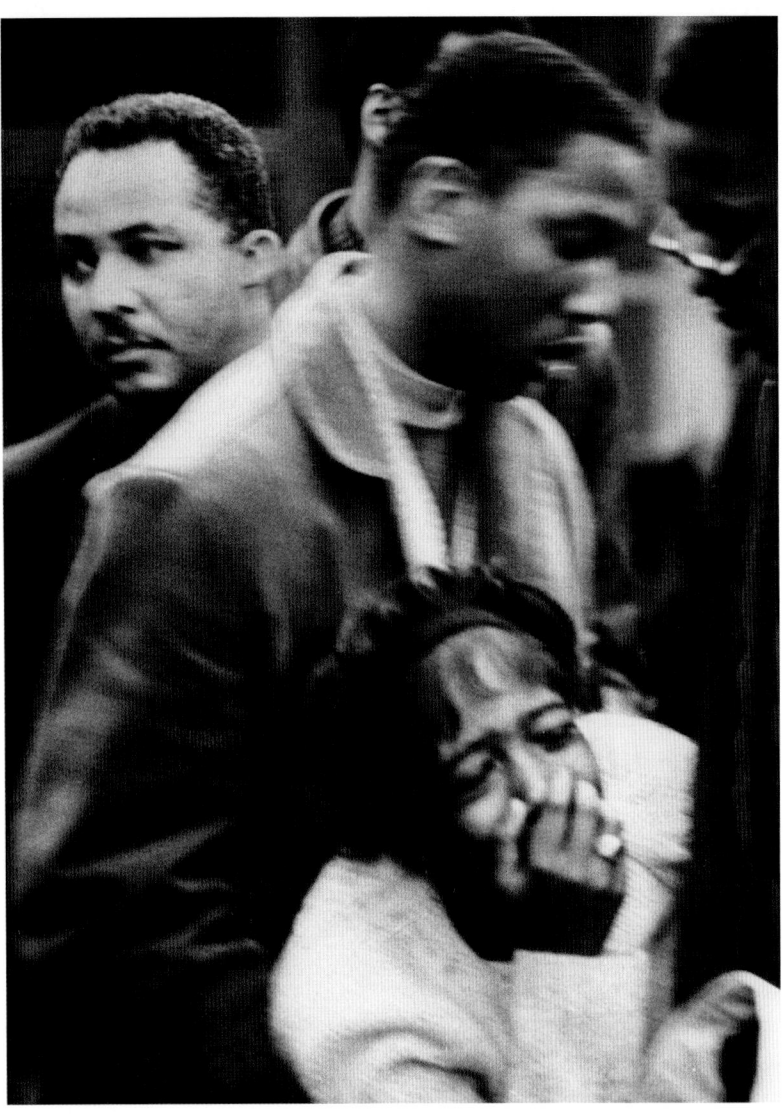

GRIEVING WOMAN AT LIBERTY BAPTIST CHURCH. APRIL 4, 1968/BOB BLACK

WHAT I WAS FEELING

I was driving home when I heard the news flash that Dr. Martin Luther King Jr. had been shot and killed in Memphis.

Overcome, I pulled the car over. The Black radio station I was listening to soon announced that Liberty Baptist Church would open its doors to those who wanted to sit and reflect.

I stopped home, made sure that my wife and baby daughter were okay, and told my wife I was going to Liberty. I wanted to document what I and others were feeling, and I thought I would find it at the church.

I knew that I had to be as low-key as I could. I took one camera and sat by myself at first. I realized that everybody was caught in their own grief, so I decided to move around and take pictures. No flash, just available light.

That's when I saw this young woman whose leg buckled under her as she wept. I took the picture and left. I don't think anyone even knew I was there.

The photo helped me cope. I grew up in this community and was connected to the church. During the next days, I was sent to the West Side and the South Side to photograph looting. I kept asking: Why?
—*Photographer Bob Black worked at the Sun-Times from 1968 until 2006. He was inducted into the National Association of Black Journalists Hall of Fame in 2019.*

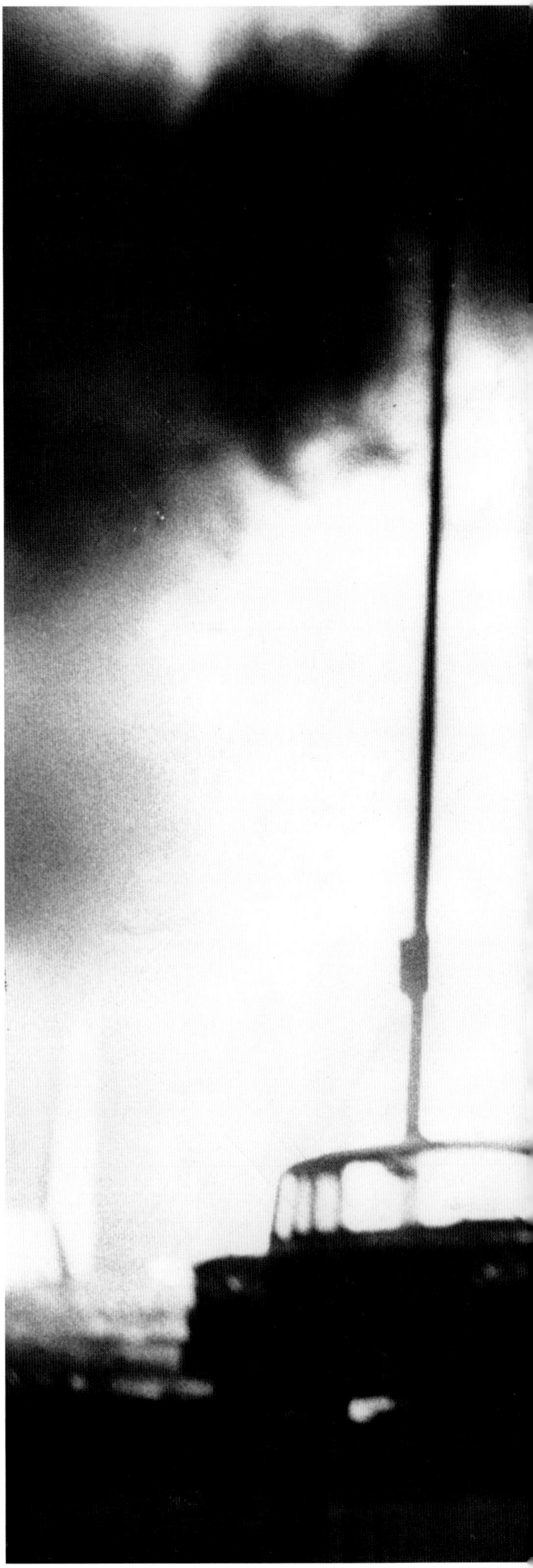

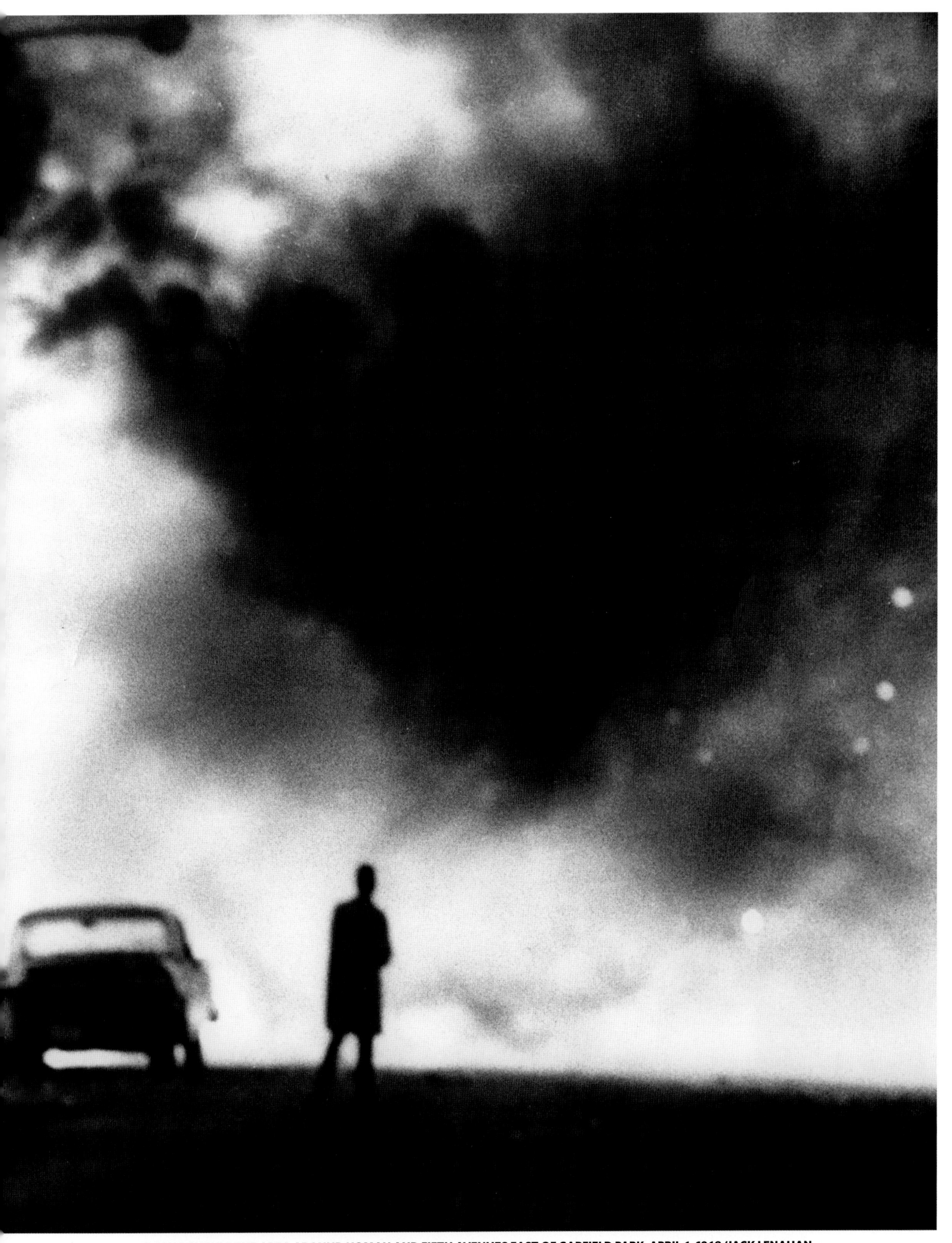
FLAMES ENGULF THE AREA AROUND HOMAN AND FIFTH AVENUES EAST OF GARFIELD PARK. APRIL 6, 1968/JACK LENAHAN

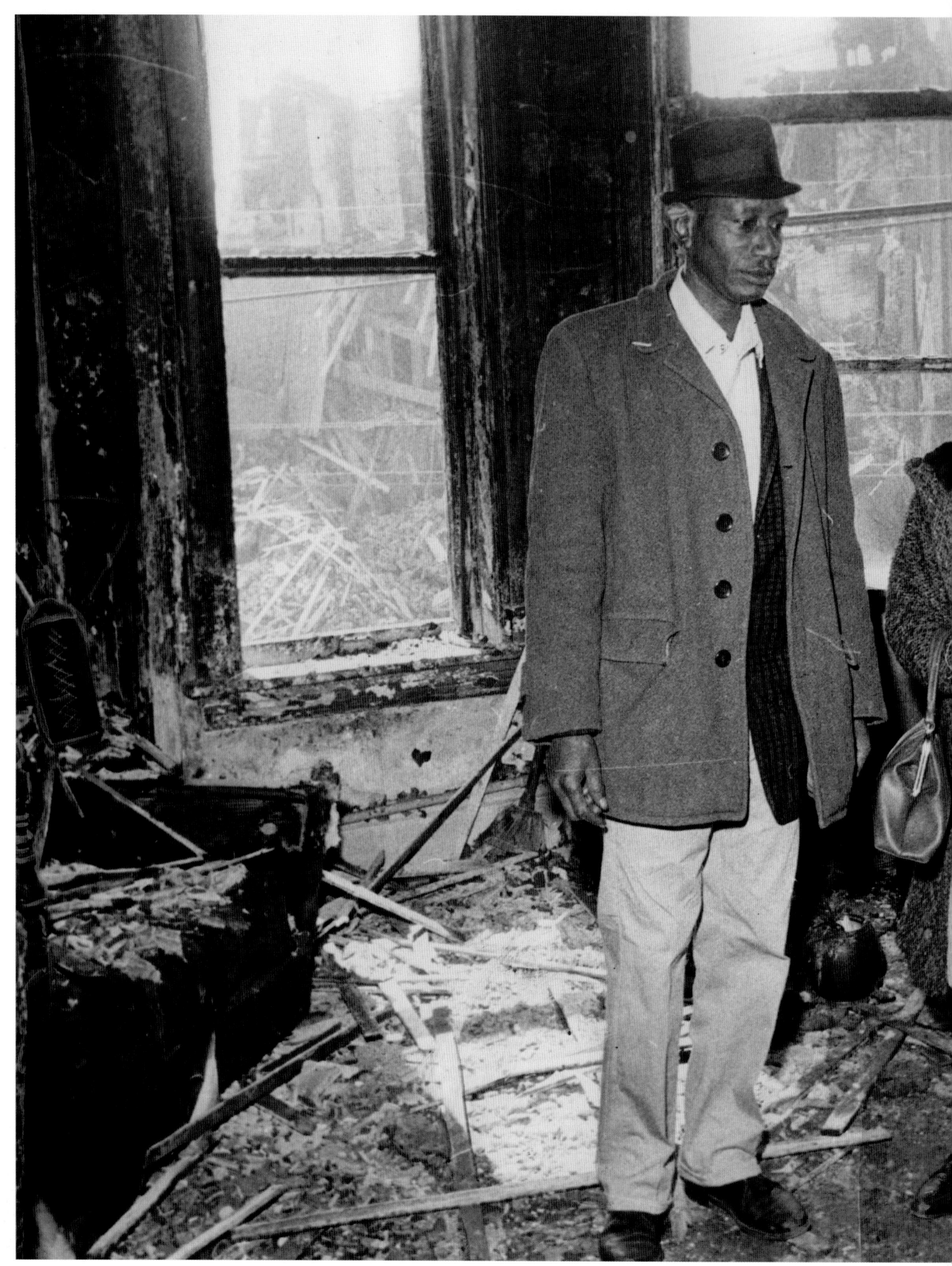

BERTHA AND ARTHUR GARRETT IN THE RUINS OF THEIR FIRE-WRECKED APARTMENT AT 3312 WEST ROOSEVELT. APRIL 9, 1968/DUANE HALL

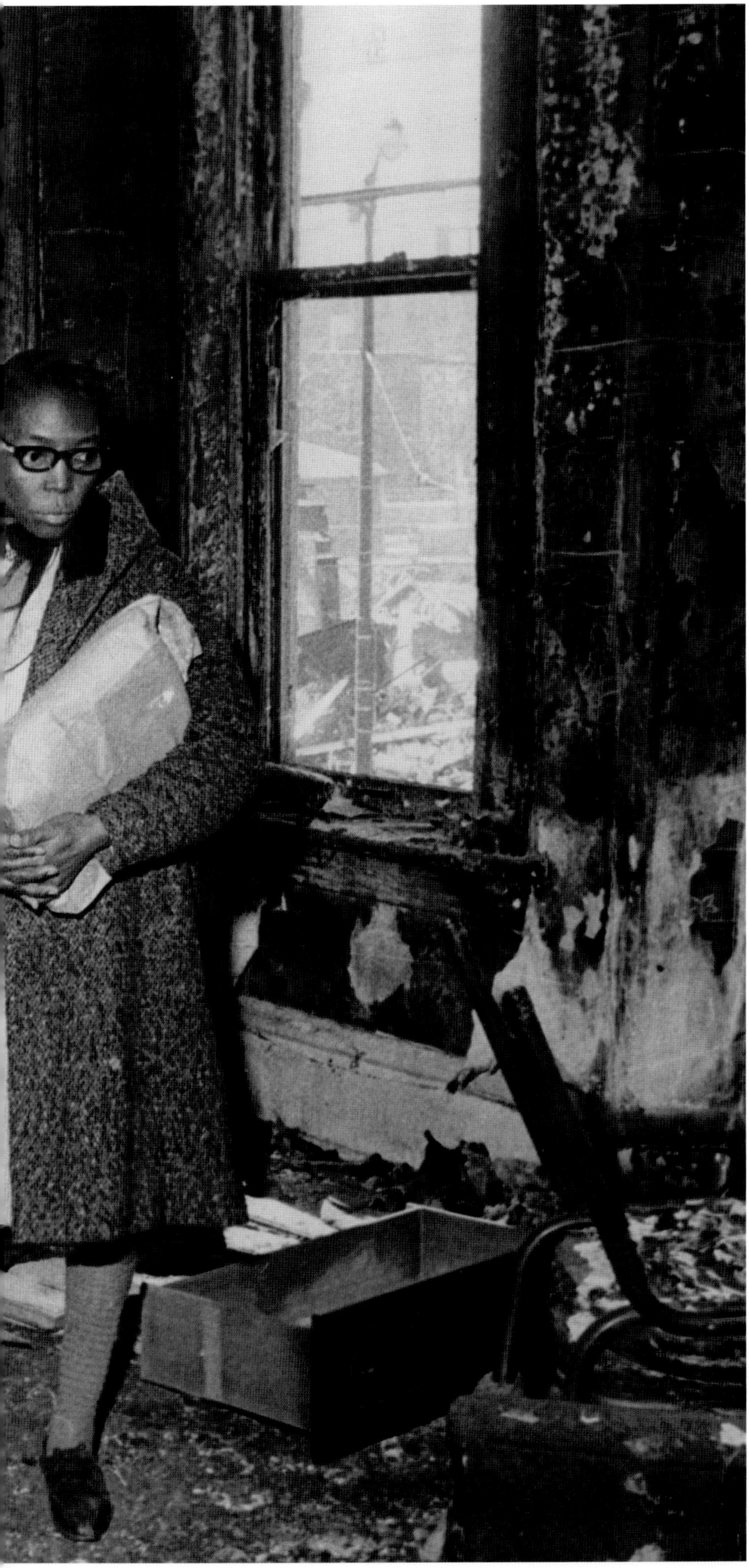

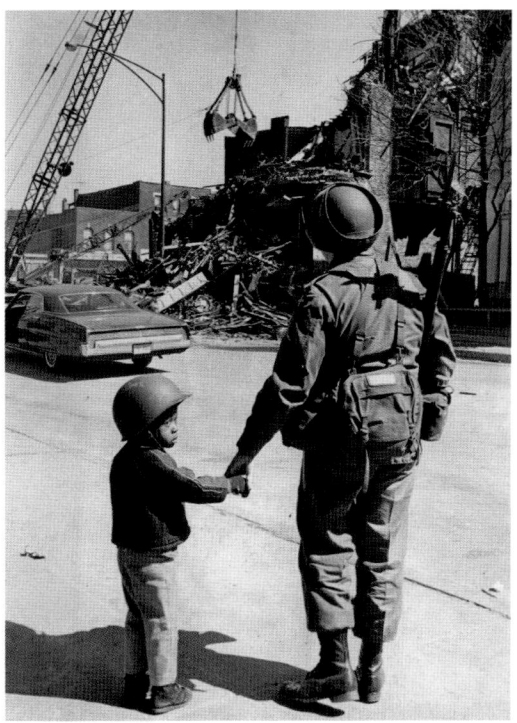

AT MADISON AND OAKLEY. APRIL 9, 1968/BOB KOTALIK

ANGRY FLAMES

These photographs rekindle memories of the fires that flared into the night after Dr. Martin Luther King Jr.'s murder.

I stood barefoot at age seven, watching the fires from our third-floor apartment. Angry flames licked the pale sky above the West Side.

There was an unusual rumbling out on the street, mixed with the voices of unrest and the slapping, sometimes heavy thud of hurried feet in the neighborhood known as K-Town. We were all in the dark.

From the night came the crashing of glass, the blare of sirens. The screams of human anguish. A symphony of chaos.

Smoke seeped into our living room. It settled over the hardwood floor like fine dust and carried the scent of charred mortar and brick. Ablaze were the Jewish-owned clothing stores and businesses along Pulaski Road.

The fire ran up and down Pulaski, from 16th Street to as far north as Madison Street. The fire I witnessed was from hell.

Buildings that burned that night became eternal vacant lots.
The fires are seared into my psyche and soul.
—*A Chicago native son, John W. Fountain is a professor at Roosevelt University and former New York Times national correspondent. He is a columnist for the Sun-Times.*

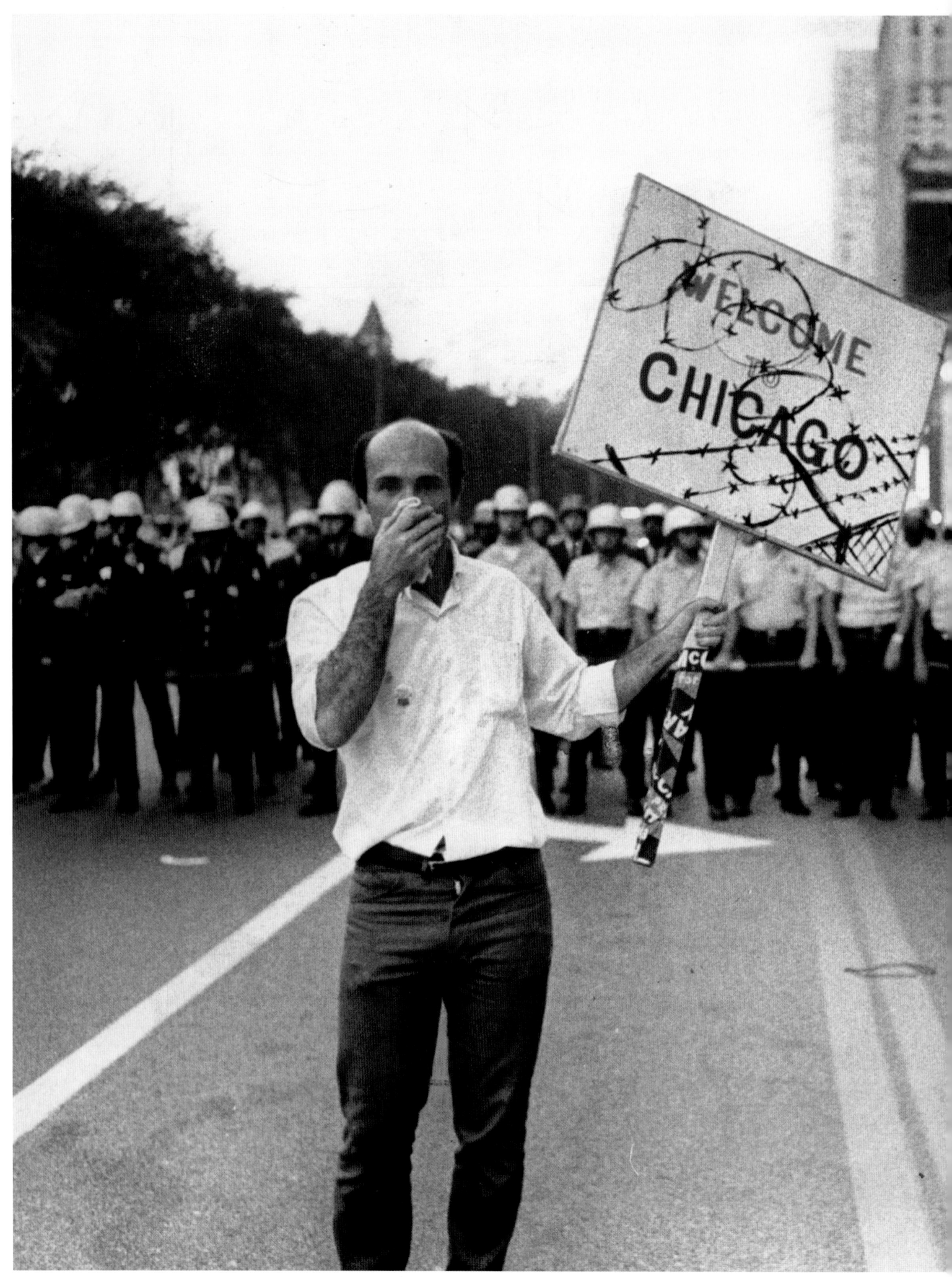
DEMONSTRATOR AT THE DEMOCRATIC NATIONAL CONVENTION FIGHTS OFF TEAR GAS NEAR CONRAD HILTON HOTEL. AUGUST 1968/DUANE HALL

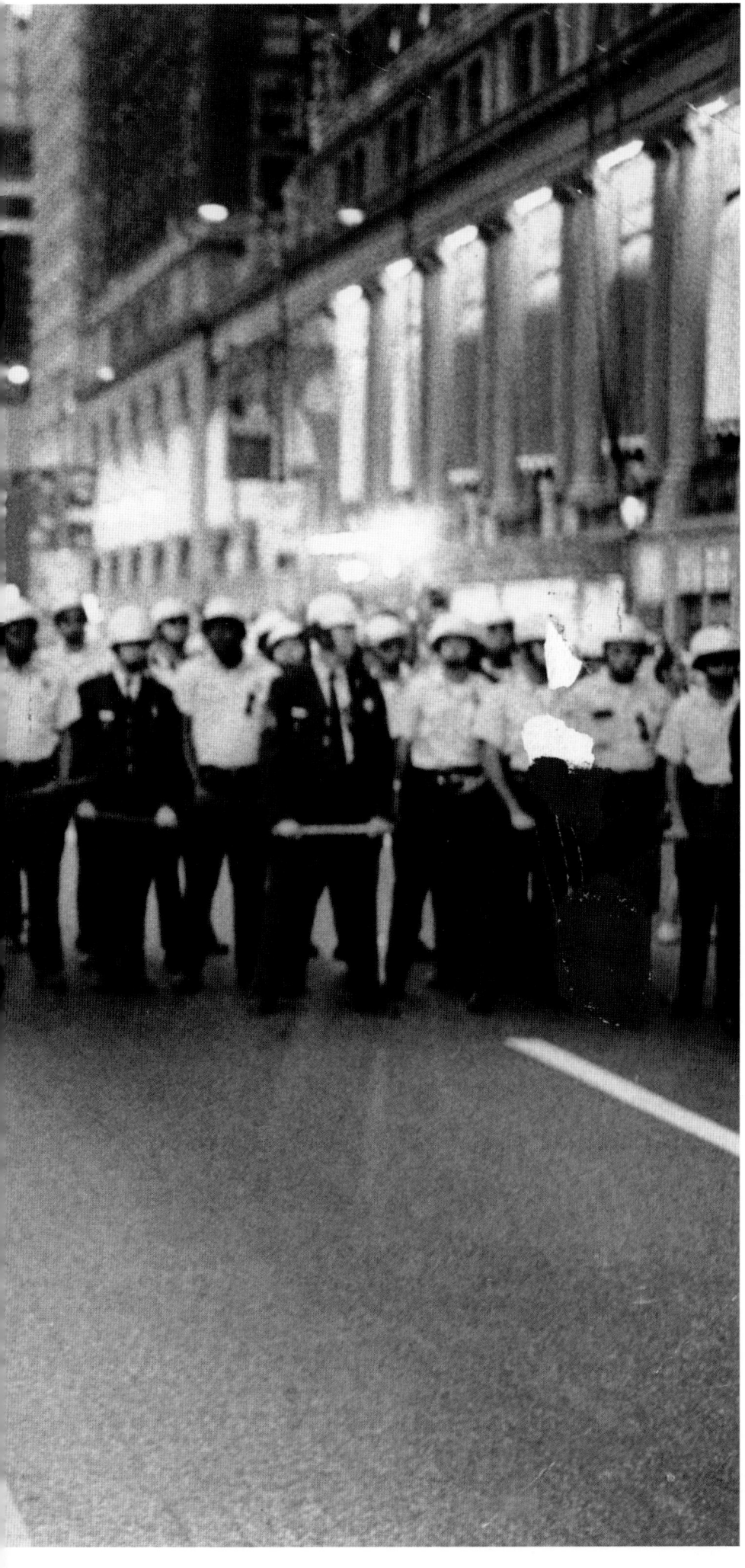

UNWELCOME TO CHICAGO

The year 1968 was a whirlwind time for me. It started with the turmoil after Martin Luther King's murder and continued through the Democratic National Convention. I was in the middle of it all.

This photo was taken on one of the last nights of the Democratic Convention, in front of the Conrad Hilton Hotel. For me, the convention week started on Sunday, August 25, when police pushed Yippie protestors out of Lincoln Park.

I was at the front of the group as they headed toward the Loop. We reporters and photographers were assured that we would be safe if we made clear we were with the press. Not so. As we approached the Michigan Avenue Bridge, a policeman clubbed me with his nightstick.

Three days later, the infamous night when protestors swarmed Michigan Avenue, I climbed to the top of a stoplight at Balbo Drive right across from the Conrad Hilton. Cops told me to come down, but I had a great perch and they couldn't reach me.

I was agile back then, a country boy who knew how to climb trees.

I spent more than an hour photographing police beating protesters.

Months later, eight policemen—including the one who beat me—were indicted on the same day that the Chicago Eight were charged with conspiracy. We provided photographs at the police trials, but all eight of the officers were acquitted.

Chicago in 1968 wanted to be all about love and peace—Wells Street and all that. And at the time, the Sun-Times was the most progressive, liberal newspaper in town. We just rolled up our sleeves, went out on the street, and photographed what we saw. Then I would go home, collapse, and head out the next day.

These were the glory days of photojournalism. I thought it would never end.
—*Photographer Duane Hall worked for the Sun-Times from 1967 through 1977. He purchased a farm in North Carolina and worked as a photographer for news magazines.*

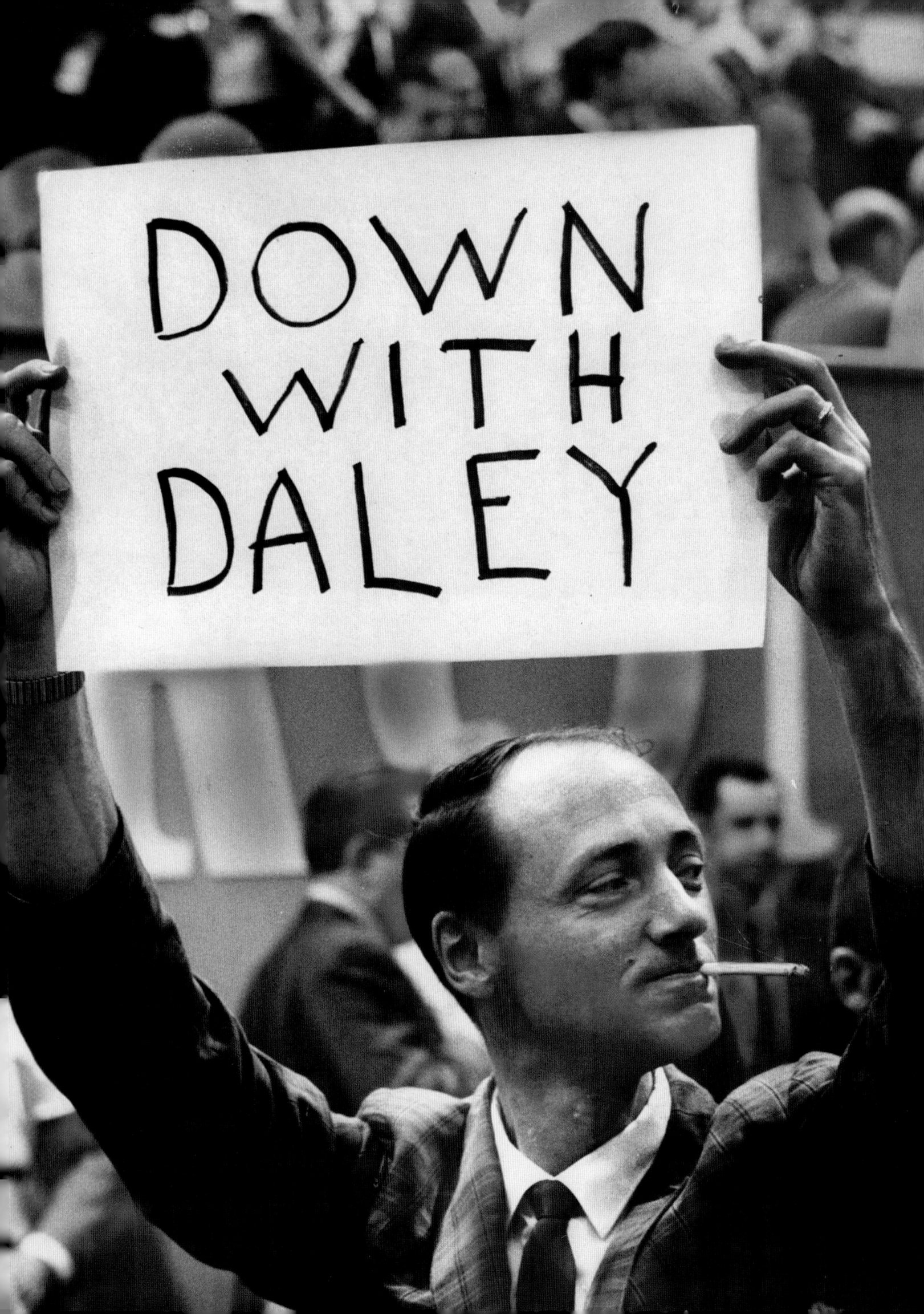

A MATTER OF OPINION

The 1968 Democratic Convention made national and international headlines. Inside the convention hall and in the parks and streets outside, turmoil reigned, spawned largely by opposition to the Vietnam War. A peace plank to end the war was defeated, largely by old-line political bosses led by Mayor Richard J. Daley. In the end, the events of August 1968 doomed the presidential candidacy of Hubert Humphrey and led to the election of Richard Nixon.

But there was a major Chicago political impact as well. Prior to 1968, the Chicago Democratic patronage machine controlled virtually all political activity in the city, except for the Fifth Ward, which included Hyde Park and the University of Chicago.

North Side residents, particularly those living along the lakefront, had long accepted and supported machine politics as the price of stability and growth in the city. Fissures in that relationship had been starting to grow. But they were not deep enough to cause a fracture.

The convention changed all that. People across the city, including North Siders, were shocked by police beatings and the indifference of politicians.

The first election following the convention was for alderman of the 44th Ward in Lincoln Park. The independent candidate—that was me—beat the Daley-backed candidate. The upset attracted nationwide attention.

The independent movement was born. In short order, another ward elected an independent alderman, and independents won seats in the Illinois General Assembly and Senate and as delegates to the 1970 Illinois Constitutional Convention.

Today, much of the machine has been dismantled. The beginning of the end was that North Side independent movement that sprung up in reaction to the 1968 convention.
—*Attorney William Singer, former alderman of the 43rd and 44th wards, was defeated by Richard J. Daley in the 1975 Democratic mayoral primary.*

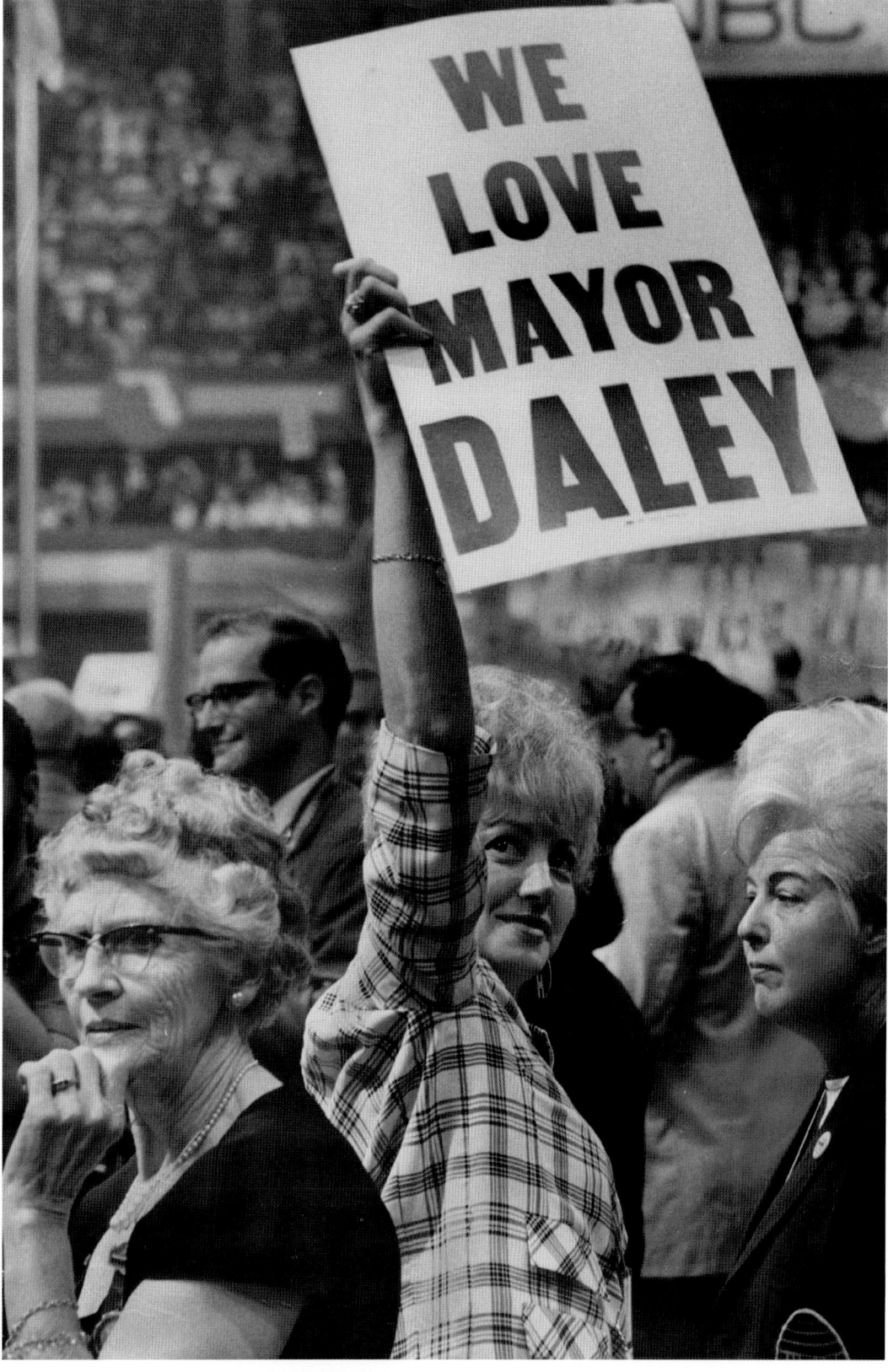

DEMOCRATIC DELEGATES ON THE FLOOR. AUGUST 29, 1968/HENRY HERR GILL

THAT WAS THE SPARK

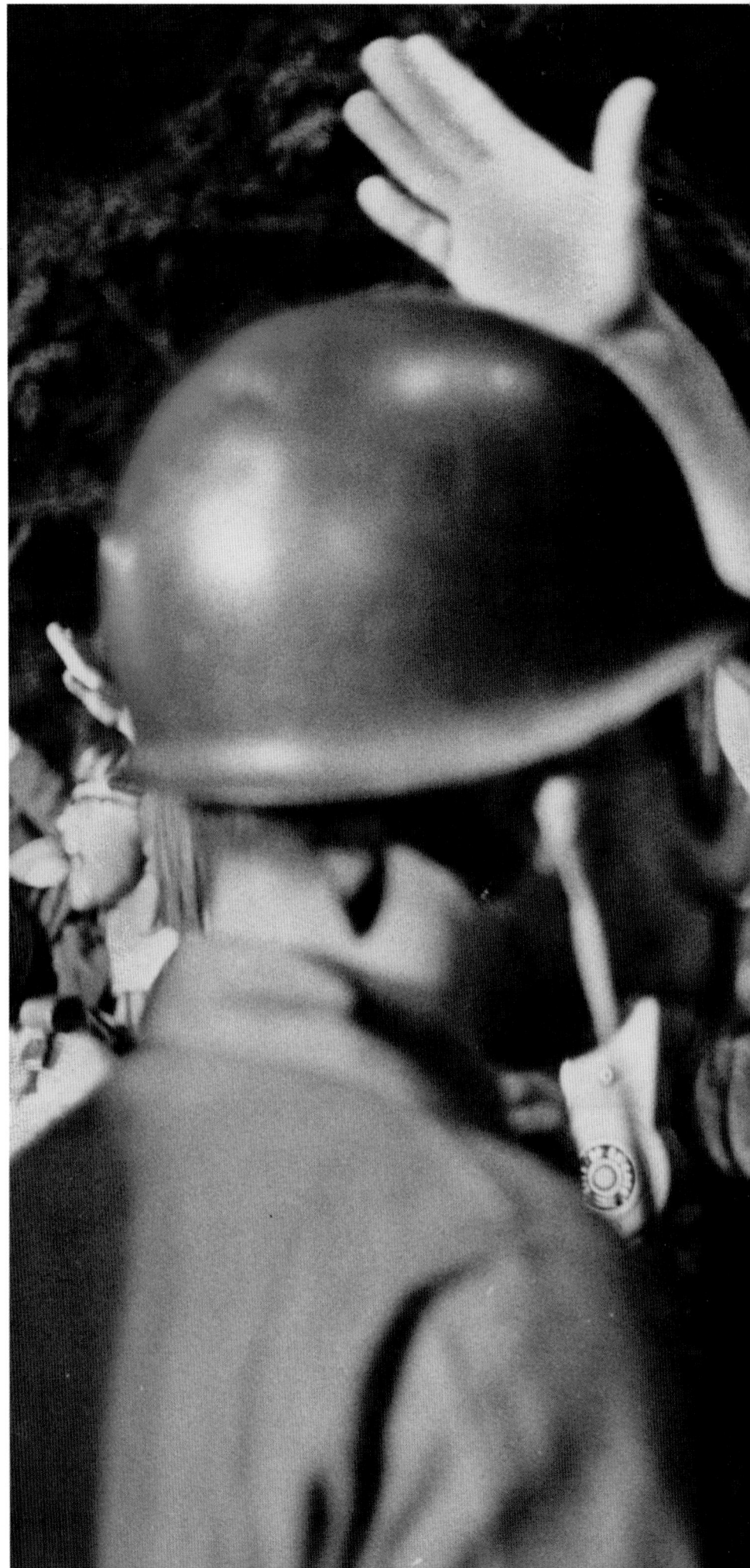

Outrage had been brewing a long time. The assassinations of Martin Luther King Jr. and Robert F. Kennedy. An unending war against an unknown people. A young generation watching the American myths of freedom and democracy unravel before our eyes. Yet in the days before the Democratic Convention, it seemed that our protests would attract only the usual few thousand demonstrators.

Despite official accounts, those gathered in Lincoln Park were mellow. We listened to music, the occasional speech, and learned the "snake dance" to protect us from the police. Some munched on Yippie-supplied brownies or chanted with Allen Ginsberg.

At 11 on Saturday night, August 24, when a phalanx of police tried to clear us from Lincoln Park, most ran (well, except for Ginsberg, who remained seated and chanting), fleeing our first encounter with tear gas and batons. But the police attack backfired. Enraged by TV images of unarmed youth being brutally beaten, hundreds more joined us the next day.

When the police attacked again on Sunday night, the crowd ran at first. But then we turned and fought back with whatever objects we could find.

That was the spark. What strikes me is how quickly the protests grew. The next days as we moved from Lincoln to Grant Park across from the Hilton Hotel we were joined by thousands.

It seemed that every youth who opposed the war or the draft, championed civil rights, or was just tired of all the rules had traveled from neighborhood or neighboring states to join the fray and take a stand. As Tom Hayden, Rennie Davis, and Abbie Hoffman predicted, Richard J. Daley and his overzealous police created the events that the whole world watched.
—*Public policy consultant Marilyn Katz was a member of the Students for a Democratic Society in 1968.*

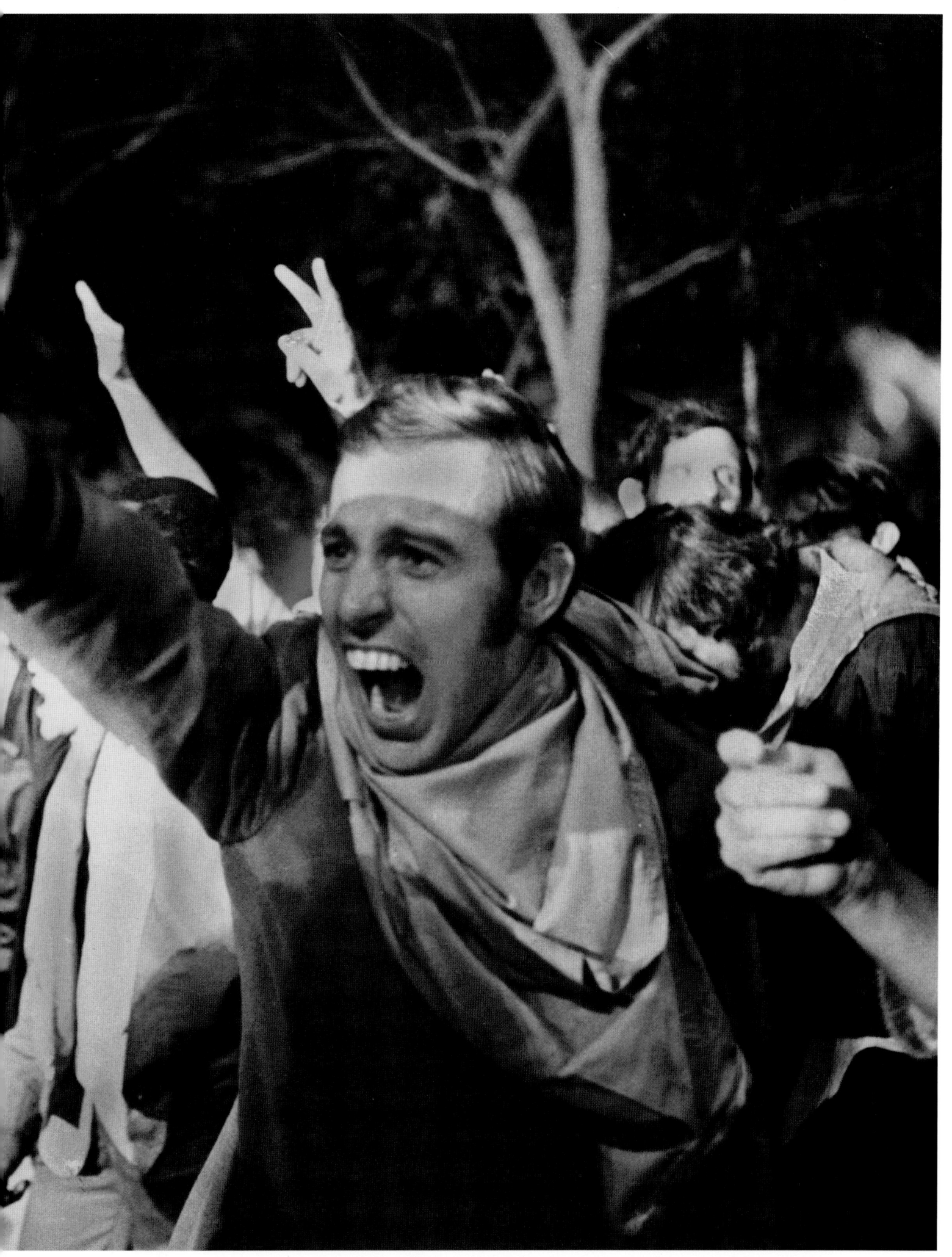
THE BATTLE OF CHICAGO: PROTESTERS BAIT NATIONAL GUARDSMAN WITH "SIEG HEIL." AUGUST 28, 1968/PERRY C. RIDDLE

IS THIS YOUR KING?

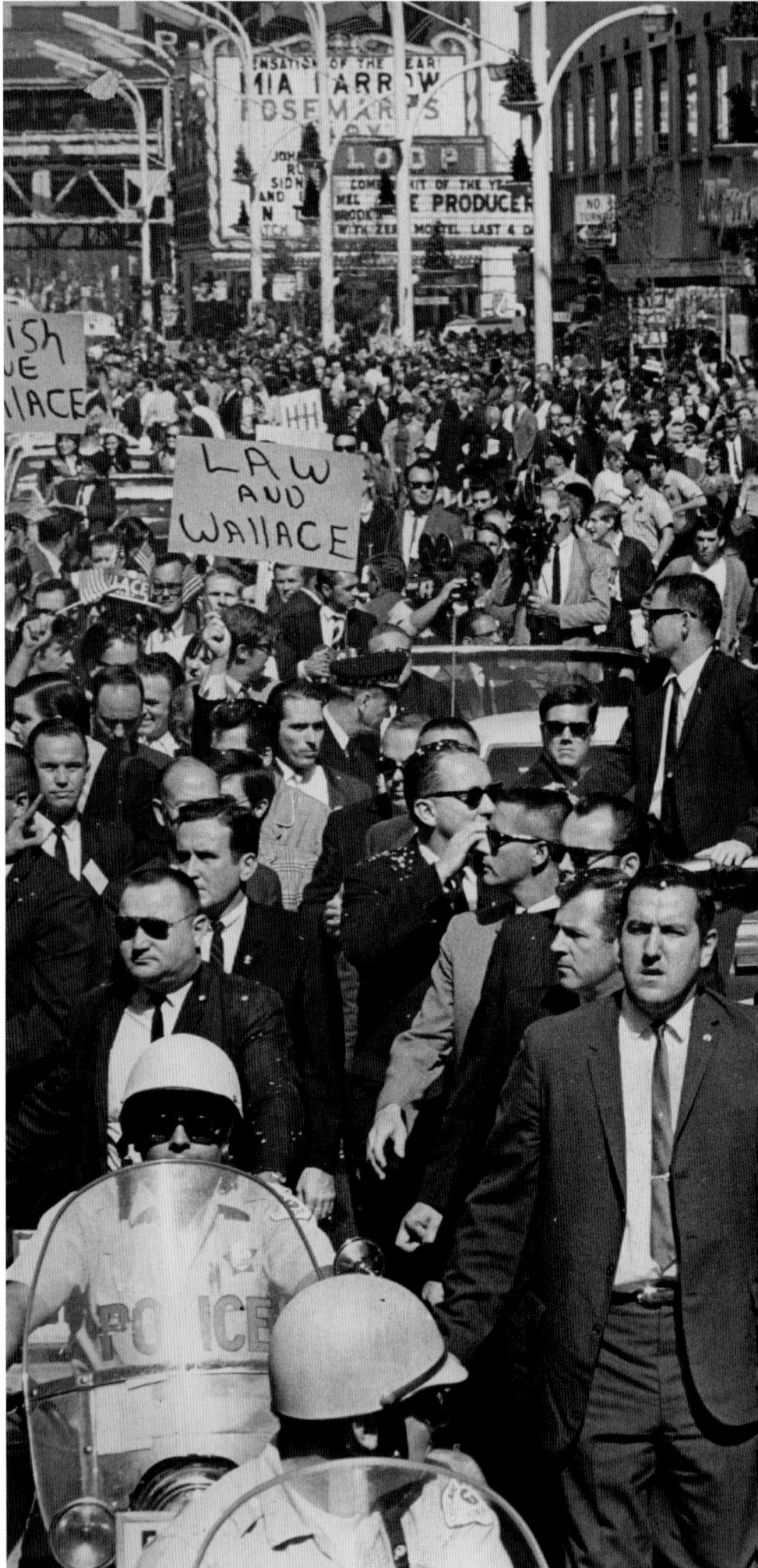

An impenetrable sea of whiteness surrounds segregationist George Wallace during this downtown State Street parade in support of his third-party candidacy for president in 1968.

To me, a Black woman born the year before, this image feels like so many archival photos (think: lynching parties) of White people supporting the wrong things at the wrong time for the wrong reasons.

The respectability politics suggested by stone-faced men in sharp suits can't disguise what Wallace represented. He made it his mission as Alabama governor to thwart integration and equality for African Americans. Wallace furthered a grotesque racial climate that persists today when he declared, "Segregation now, segregation tomorrow, segregation forever" at his 1963 inaugural address.

Later, on September 15, 1963, six African-American children were killed in his home state—four girls at Birmingham's 16th Street Baptist Church bombing by the Ku Klux Klan and two boys shot in separate incidents—because of the hateful climate Wallace stoked and normalized.

Despite the Wallaces of the world, the civil rights movement clinched several victories, including the Civil Rights Act, Voting Rights Act, and Fair Housing Act.

Still, in this year of 1968, Black America hurt. Uprisings in the wake of Dr. Martin Luther King Jr.'s assassination ripped through cities. We were consumed by Vietnam War violence. We also lost Robert F. Kennedy.

In a decade where Wallace doubled down on White supremacy, a Loop street overflowing with White followers belies the mythology that racism was a preserve of the South.

This ethos still lives in the so-called progressive North, where Great Migration African Americans sought to be rid of all that.

For White society, this photo evokes the question: Is this your king?
—*Journalist Deborah D. Douglas is author of* U.S. Civil Rights Trail: A Traveler's Guide to the People, Places, and Events That Made the Movement.

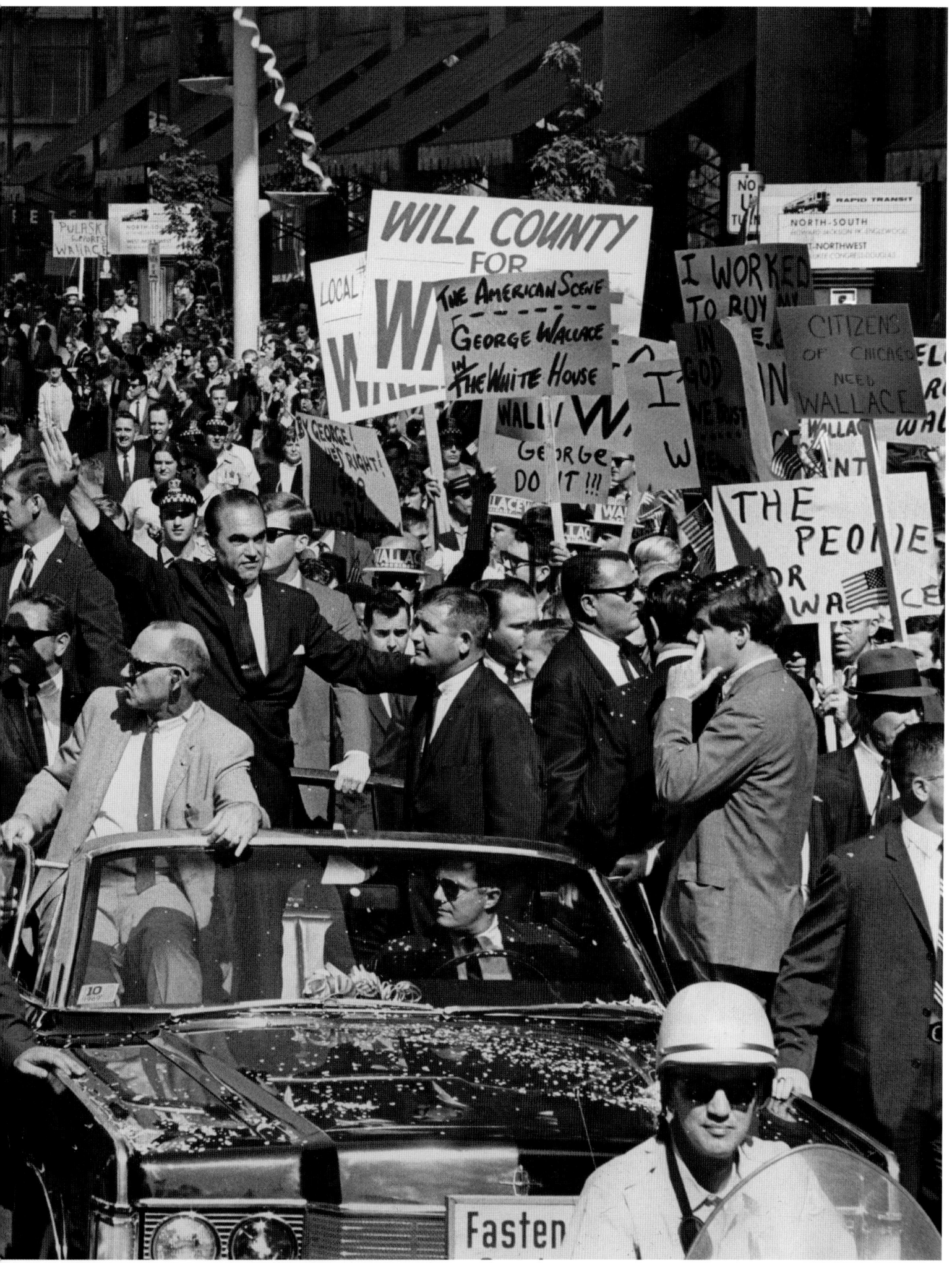

GEORGE WALLACE WAVES TO LOOP SUPPORTERS. HE RECEIVED ALMOST 10 MILLION VOTES FOR PRESIDENT AND 46 ELECTORAL VOTES. SEPT. 30, 1968

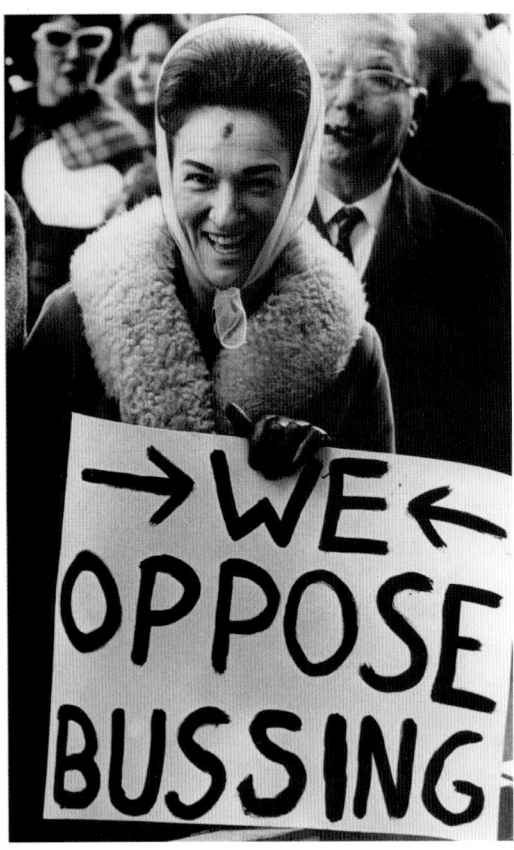

ASH WEDNESDAY. FEBRUARY 27, 1968/JACK DYKINGA

BUSING BONFIRE

I remember that rally as if it were yesterday.

Those were very difficult times for everyone. We had just moved into our first home in South Holland. I was working for Illinois Bell, but on strike since May. My wife was about eight months pregnant. We had moved to the suburbs for a better life with better education and overall better living conditions than Chicago provided. The city was divided by nationalities because of languages and religious beliefs.

We went to that rally because we wanted our children to attend our local schools and not be bused to some other area. We moved to South Holland because our friends lived on the same street. We visited them, liked the area and schools, and decided to move there.

Busing brought out the worst in people because they were afraid of change and the unknown. Instead of bringing people closer together it drove people apart.
—*Larry Moisan Sr. was the father of the two children pictured at this rally.*

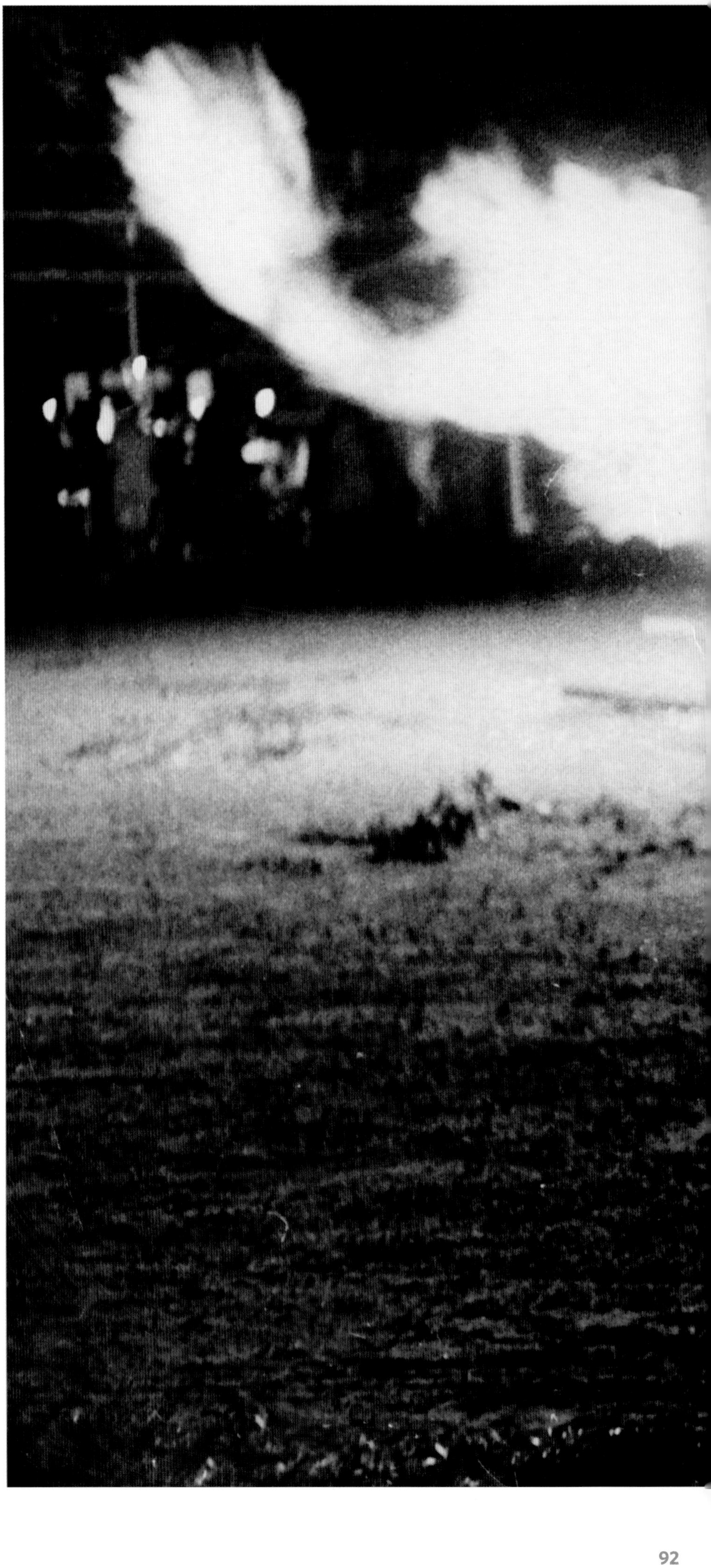

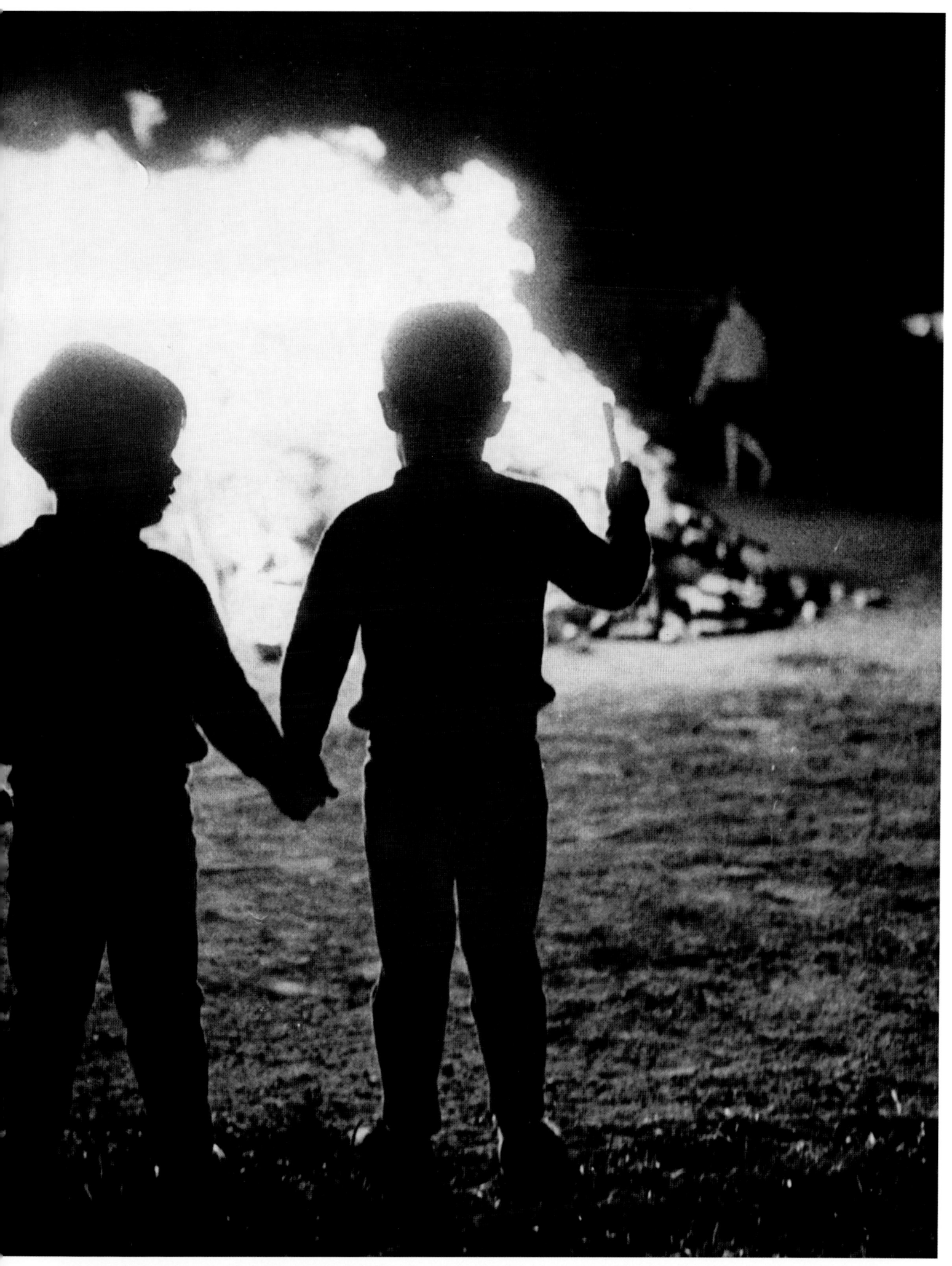
LORI AND LARRY MOISAN JR. AT BONFIRE PRAYER IN SOUTH HOLLAND TO PROTEST SCHOOL DESEGREGATION. SEPTEMBER 16, 1968/LARRY NOCERINO

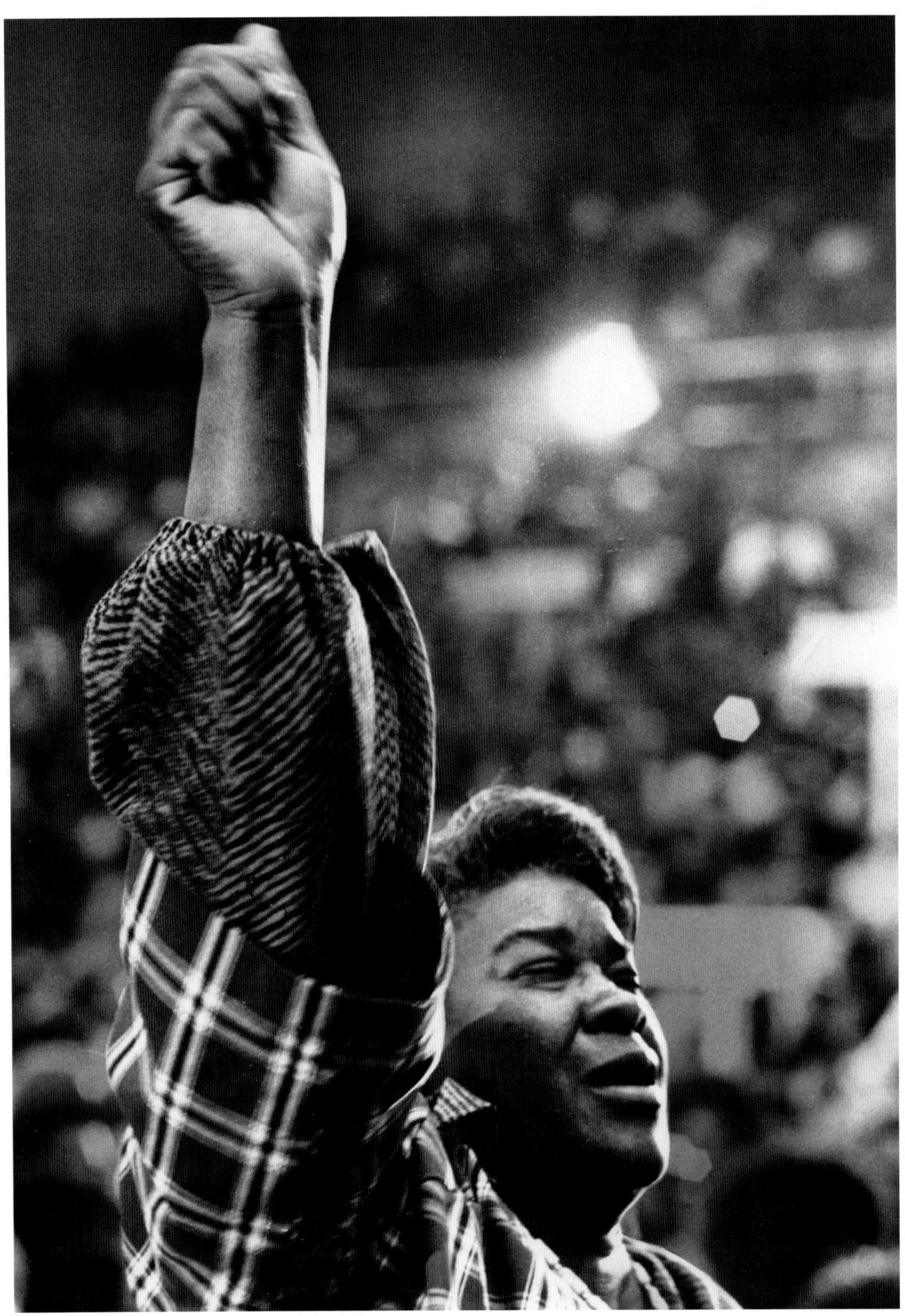
DELEGATE REACTS TO SPEECH AT THE FIRST NATIONAL BLACK CONVENTION IN GARY, INDIANA. MARCH 11, 1972/HOWARD D. SIMMONS

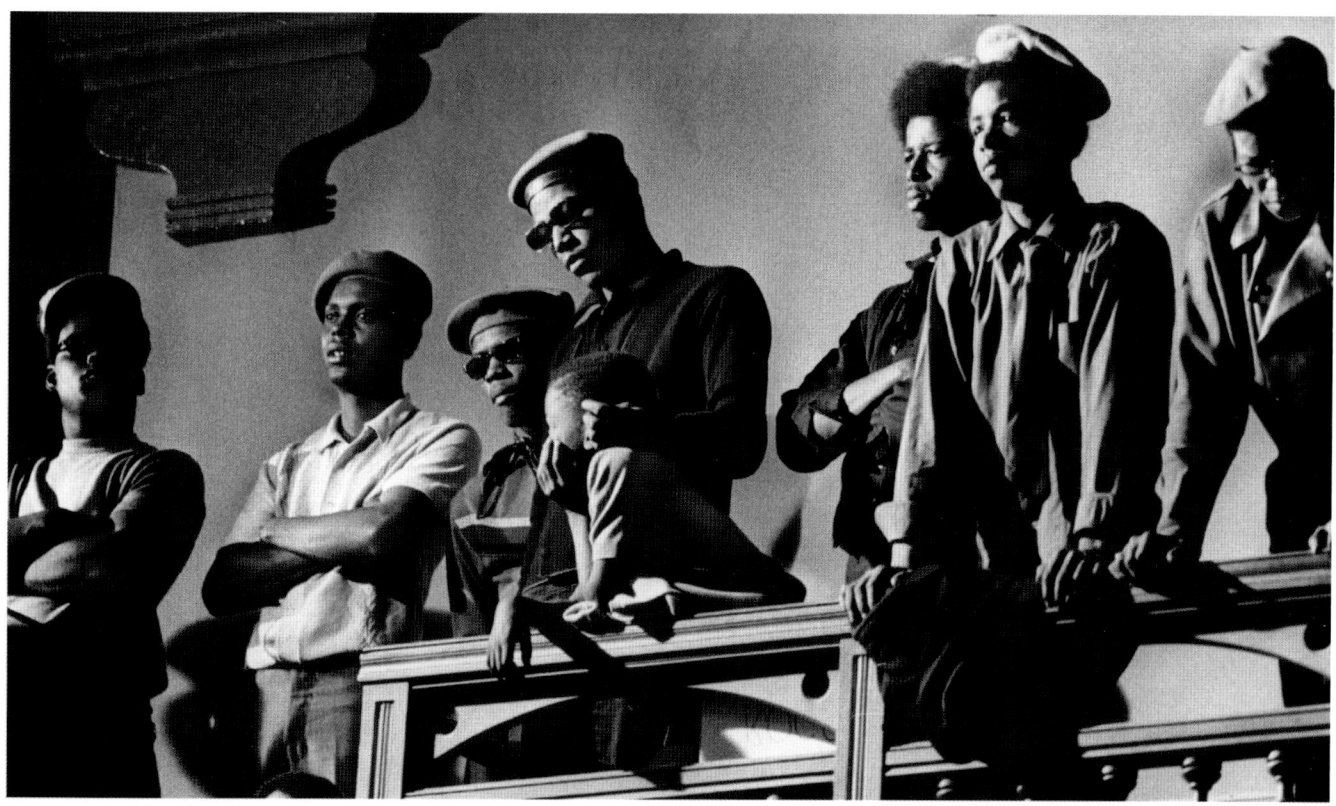

BLACKSTONE RANGERS, AT THE CAPITOL IN SPRINGFIELD, WATCH DEBATE OVER THE FUTURE OF WELFARE. MAY 6, 1969

BORN UNIQUE AND BEAUTIFUL

I did not expect a single university class to so influence my identity and shape the trajectory of my 1970s journalism career. But one did. It was a Black history course taught by Lerone Bennett Jr., the social historian and senior editor of *Ebony* magazine.

Bennett, well known for his seminal *Before the Mayflower*, was a visiting professor at Northwestern University when I was an undergraduate.

His teachings affirmed that as a Black woman I was born unique and beautiful. No need to mimic the style or identity of others. He taught me about the substantial role African Americans played in the nation's development. He showed me that I descended from a brilliant and innovative ancestry, African Americans who succeeded in a malicious nation.

His teachings were transformative. My inner confidence grew. My Afro hairstyle became my signature. No need to straighten my hair with chemicals or a hot comb to mimic sleek, long hairstyles of White women on magazine covers.

And my mission was clarified. I could use my background to find and report stories that might otherwise be overlooked and pave the way for other African Americans.

I heard Bennett's message when I was eighteen years old. I was from East St. Louis, Illinois, a city reeling from the aftereffect of racial violence in 1917, as industries steadily left and the tax base dwindled. In 1971, my father was elected the first Black mayor of the city in a grassroots campaign.

Like Bennett, who was raised in Mississippi, my ancestral roots were imprinted by the South. I grew up next door to my maternal grandparents, children of ex-slaves who saved money to send my mother to Wilberforce University in Ohio, the nation's oldest private Black college. My mother, who became an award-winning teacher, said she was expected to step off the sidewalk and bow her head when a White person approached in the Jim Crow South. My father grew up poor in Kentucky-Ohio border towns, met my mother at Wilberforce, and attended law school at night.

Bennett's course taught me that if I persisted, I—like my parents—could compete successfully.

I redoubled my efforts in Northwestern's tough journalism program, participated in internships, and earned undergraduate and graduate journalism degrees.

When I stepped into the Sun-Times newsroom that first day in 1973, I was the only Black woman reporter and only the second ever hired. Though I felt confident, inexplicably that day I lost my voice—literally. I could not speak. It was something that never happened before and never happened again. I went on to win recognition for reporting, including extensive coverage of Harold Washington, the city's first Black mayor.

I found my voice.
—*Lillian Williams worked at Sun-Times until 1991. She later worked as a TV reporter in Cleveland, as a tenured professor at Columbia College Chicago, and earned a PhD.*

WHO WAS MANUEL RAMOS?

Manuel Ramos, you were gunned down by an off-duty police officer in Bridgeport in 1969. At age twenty. You also were my grandfather.

I don't know much about you, other than that we share a name. But I always admired you.

You and other founding members of the Young Lords Organization fought to uplift the Puerto Rican diaspora in Lincoln Park. You wanted your heritage celebrated instead of forgotten for the sake of assimilation.

You helped fight for better housing, improved access to fresh food, and you stood up against urban renewal, which was pushing Puerto Ricans out of Lincoln Park.

This is the story I was told about the events that led to your death:

Your two kids—my father and aunt—were asleep when someone knocked on your Lincoln Park apartment door. It was a friend asking you to go to a party, but you were hesitant. You looked at my grandma, who gave you a look that said: Stay home. You told your friend no.

But he was relentless, and you gave in.

At the party, you heard a commotion outside and went to see what was going on. You saw a man yelling at your friends. You didn't know he was an off-duty police officer.

You tried to break up the argument but failed. The man pulled his police-issued gun and shot you and your friend, José Rivera. He lived. You died.

After the shots rang out, several Young Lords jumped on top of the man to hold him down until police arrived. He was not arrested. They were.

You were unarmed, but the off-duty cop said you pointed a gun at him. Numerous eyewitnesses told police that was a lie. The officer was questioned and quickly released.

Three weeks later, a coroner's inquest found the killing justifiable.

The Chicago Sun-Times and Daily News both covered the civil unrest it inspired.

But the handful of stories published in both papers failed to answer a simple question: Who was Manuel Ramos?

Your death sparked thousands to protest police violence against young Black, Brown, and poor White people. More than 3,000 people overflowed the funeral home. Hundreds gathered in front of police stations, demanding charges.

At no point did the papers feel the need to humanize your life, despite all the unrest that followed your death.

There was no interest in learning what you stood for or why the Young Lords were so wounded by your death.

The media didn't care that you were a young father. They didn't ponder the impact your death would have for two generations.

Your death is something my father has never fully grasped. He often thinks his life would have been different if you were around. You could have helped him avoid the gangs and the drugs.

In a lot of ways, you're the reason I'm a journalist. My dad always said real power comes from the pen.
—Manny Ramos has covered minority communities as a reporter for the Sun-Times since 2018.

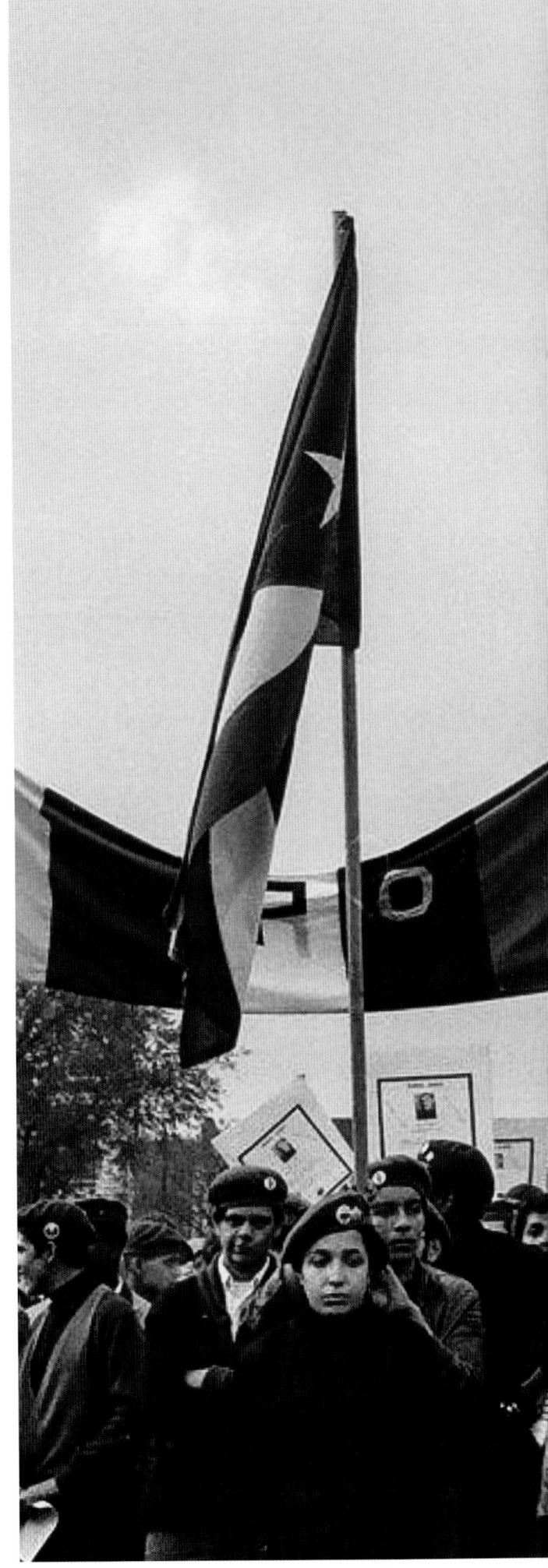

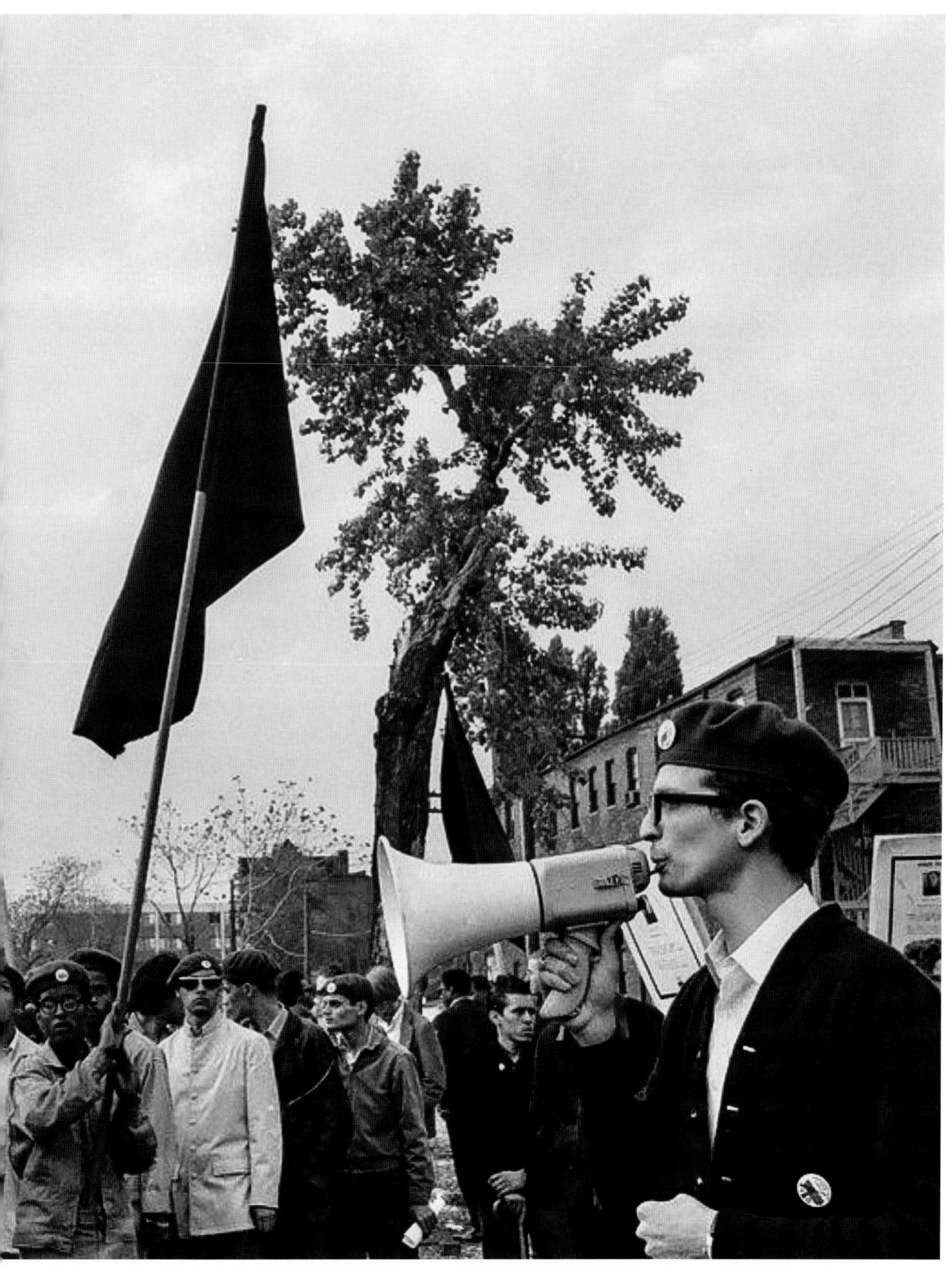

YOUNG LORDS, COBRA STONES, BLACK PANTHERS, YOUNG PATRIOTS, AND THE SDS PROTEST THE FATAL SHOOTING OF MANUEL RAMOS. MAY 5, 1969

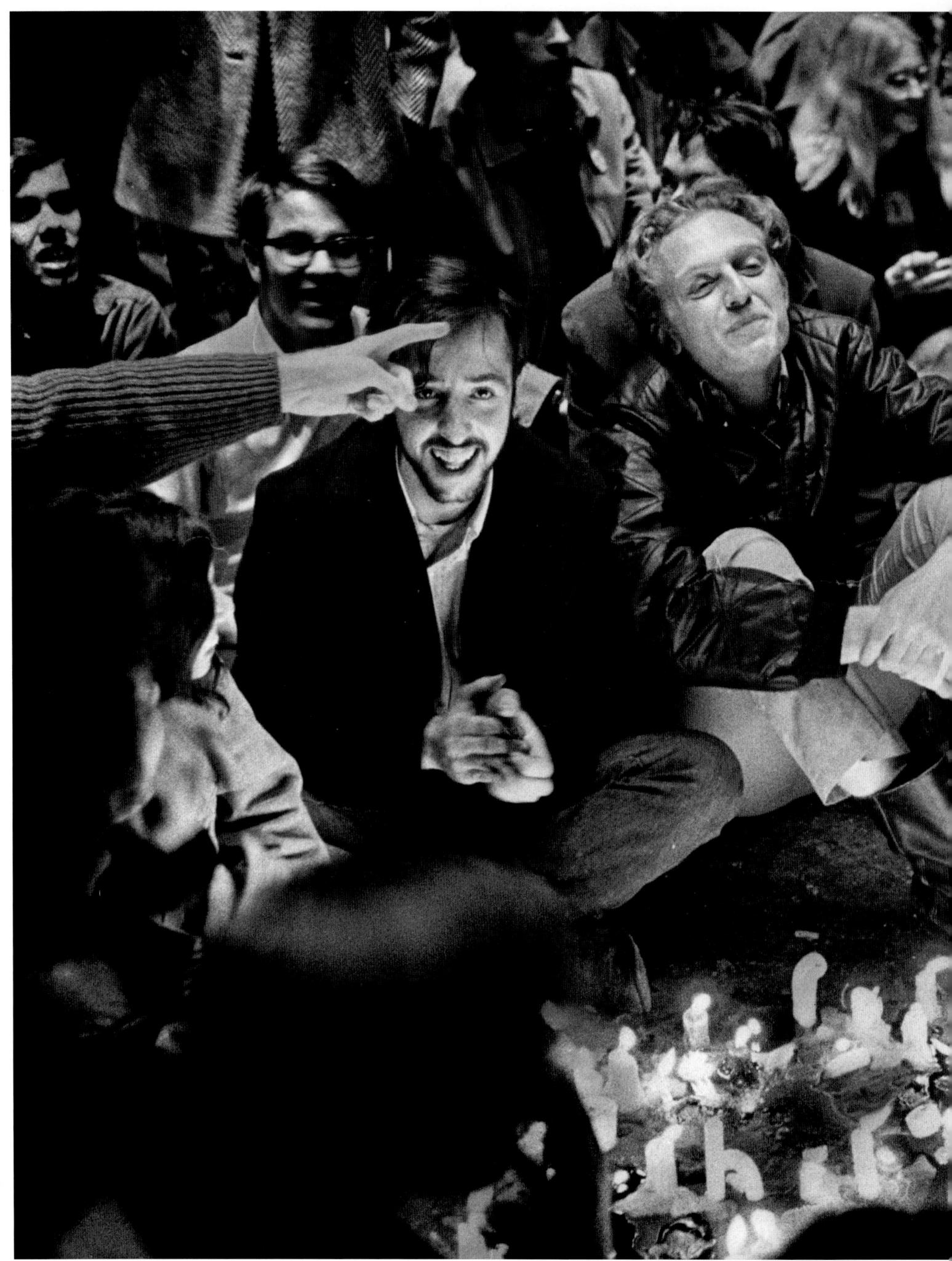

DEMONSTRATORS GATHER IN LINCOLN PARK TO PROTEST THE CHICAGO EIGHT TRIAL. SEPTEMBER 23, 1969/DON BIERMAN

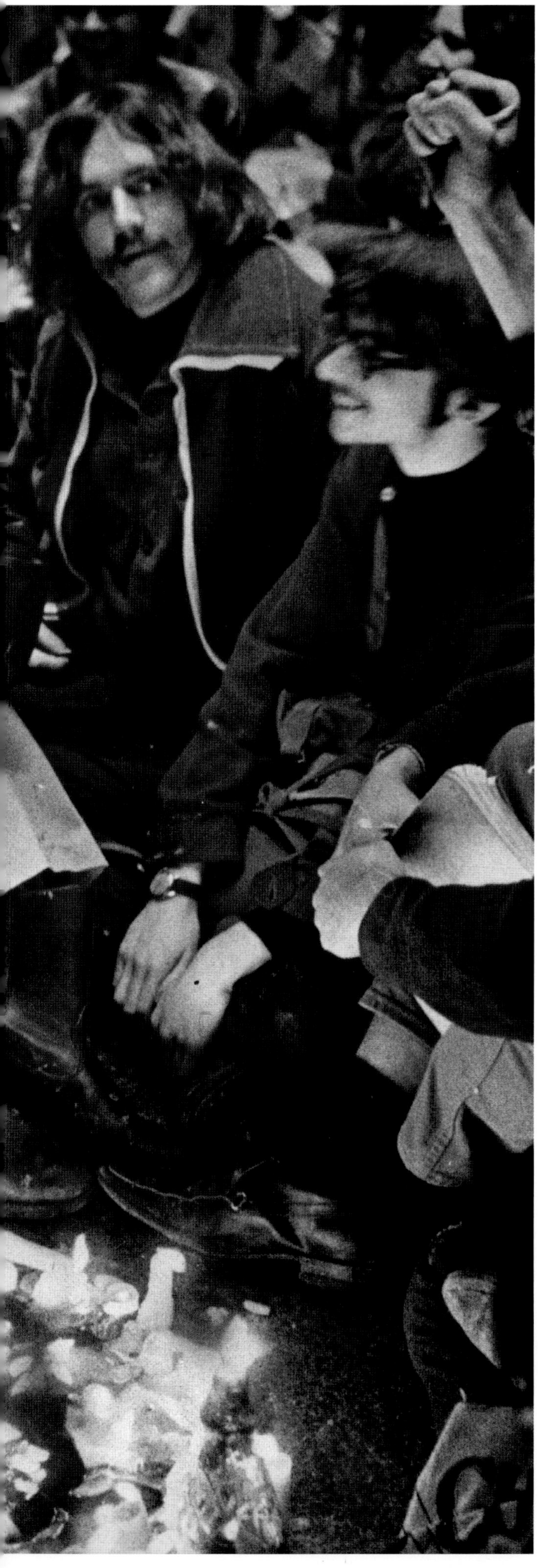

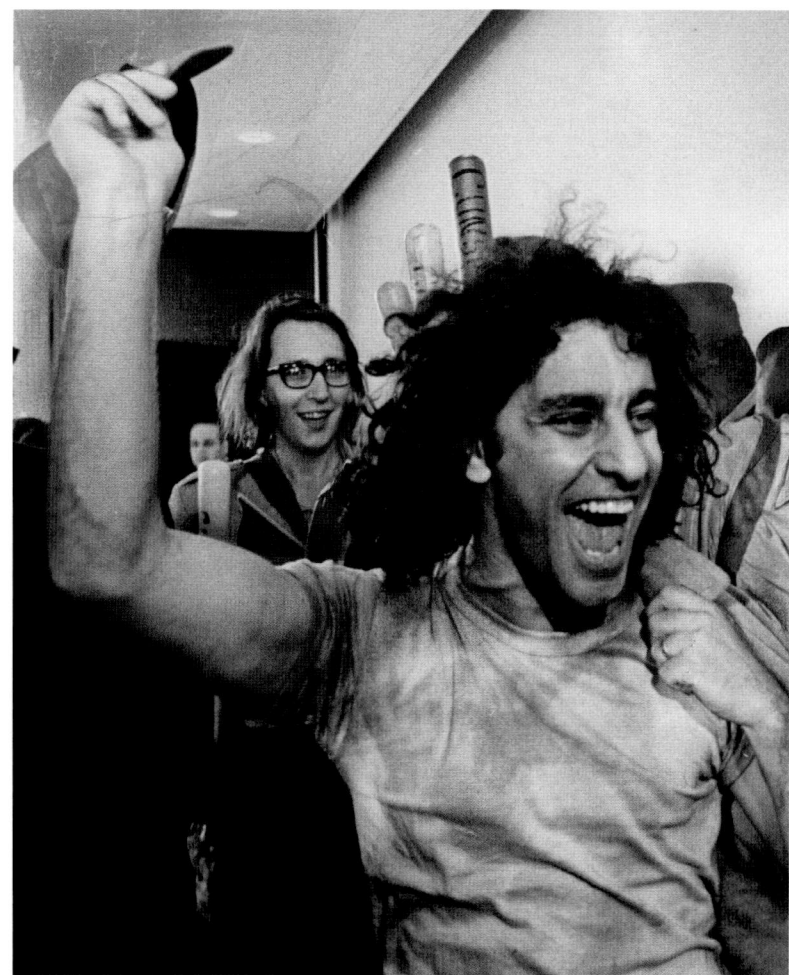

YIPPIE ABBIE HOFFMAN ARRIVES FOR TRIAL. SEPTEMBER 21, 1969/BILL MARES

THE RETURN OF CHICAGO 8

I don't recall this night, but I certainly recall the times. We photographed so many demonstrations during the late '60s they all seem to blur together.

Chicago was the city to be in if you were a photographer or reporter.

Nobody at first took seriously the gatherings in the parks in 1968 as the Democratic National Convention was ramping up. The people who congregated there were a bunch of kids. Their words hardly mattered; it was almost like Bughouse Square.

I was amazed that the police gave them the platform they needed to become a national story.

Everything changed during the convention. The intensity of the Chicago Police Department's violent reaction to the demonstrators and retribution toward the press was shocking. It was prevalent among the supervisory personnel all the way up to the mayor's office.

The police had always given photographers preferential treatment, such as the ability to park wherever necessary when covering news. They turned on us almost overnight. Several photographers were beaten.

So by 1969, I was empathetic to people who were demonstrating against the abuse of power during the conspiracy trial.

I think our photographs had a strong effect. People did not want to believe what was happening, but here it was in front of their eyes.

—*Photographer Don Bierman worked for the Chicago Daily News from 1965 until 1968 and later for the Sun-Times and Tribune.*

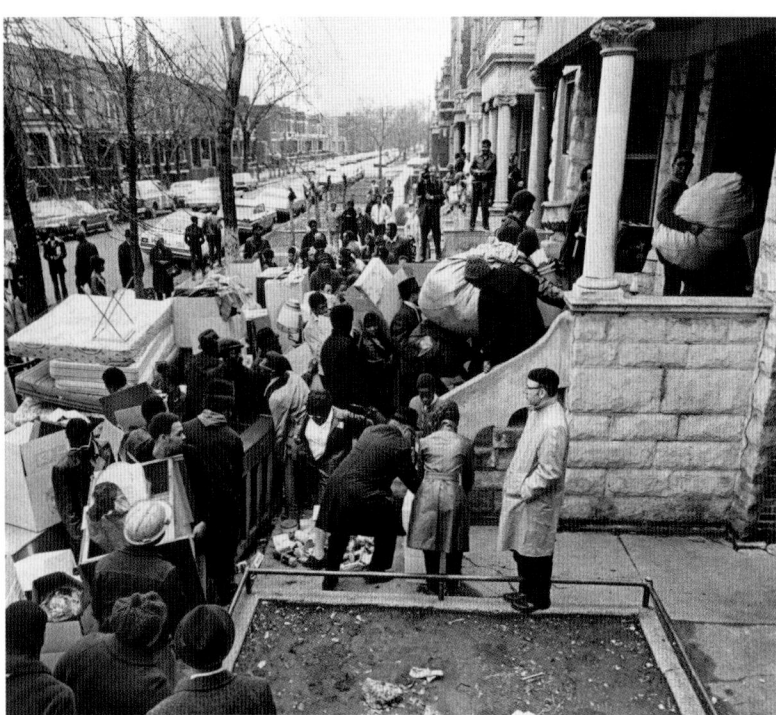

POSSESSIONS ARE MOVED BACK INTO A HOME. APRIL 21, 1970/JACK DYKINGA

'THEY AIN'T GOING TO COME IN MY DOOR'

On January 29, 1970, Cook County Sheriff Joseph Woods supervised the eviction of Mr. and Mrs. Johnnie Moss and their four children. Almost 200 helmeted deputies, most carrying "truncheons and gas masks," massed in a morning snowstorm to evict them.

It was a disaster. The deputies dragged furniture out of the Moss family home. They dumped the family's plastic Nativity scene in the bushes and chased their dog into the yard, where it pranced around the deputy sent to control it.

Like most Black Chicagoans of their era, the Mosses had bought their home "on contract," or on an installment plan. Contract buyers could be evicted for missing one payment. Most were grossly overcharged for their homes.

In 1968, they formed a Contract Buyers League. In 1970, the league went on a strike, refusing to make their payments until their housing contracts were renegotiated. Now the Mosses were being evicted for participating in the payment strike.

A crowd of 200 league members and supporters confronted the deputies. Some in the crowd admitted that they would not hesitate to use violence to defend their homes. As one told the Chicago Defender, "They ain't going to come in my door. I've got a couple of guns and I'll blast them." Suddenly two shots were fired—both by security guards who were posted inside the Moss house. The guards abandoned the property, and the crowd moved the Mosses' furniture back inside.

The result was that Johnnie Moss, a man whom reporters described as "so busy trying to pull himself up by his bootstraps" that he'd never had time for a civil rights march, now faced jail for living illegally in his own home.
—*Beryl Satter describes a Contract Buyers League skirmish in* Family Properties: Race, Real Estate, and the Exploitation of Black Urban America.

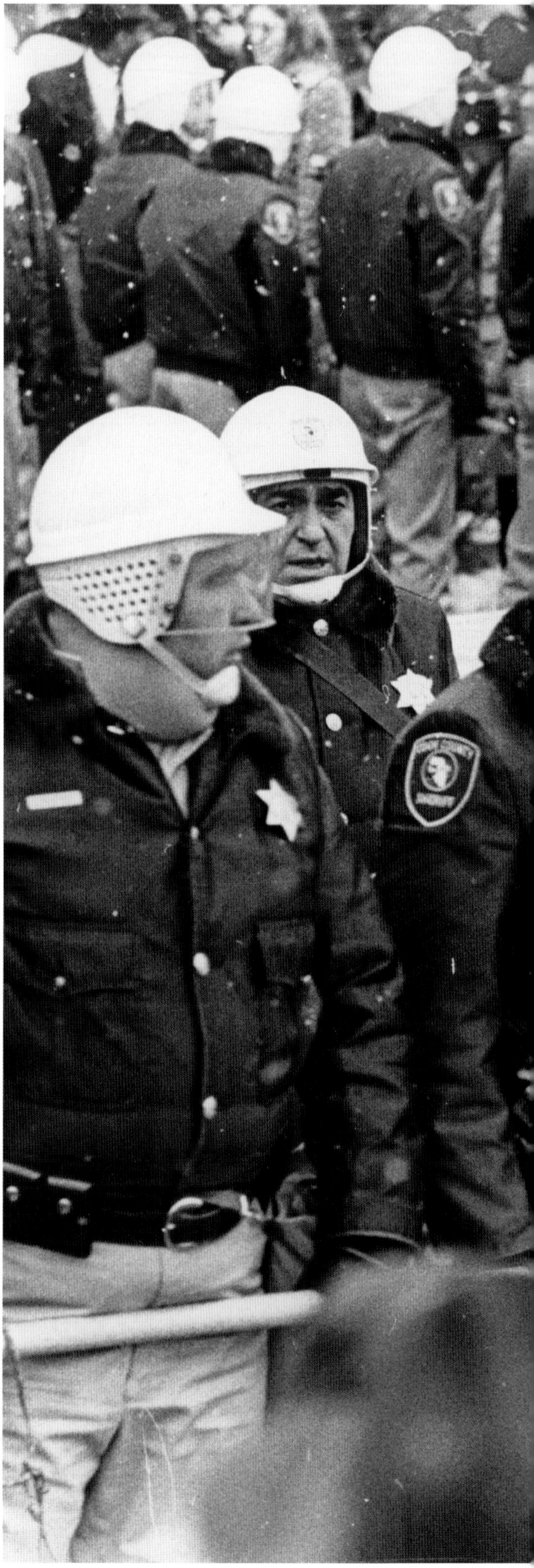

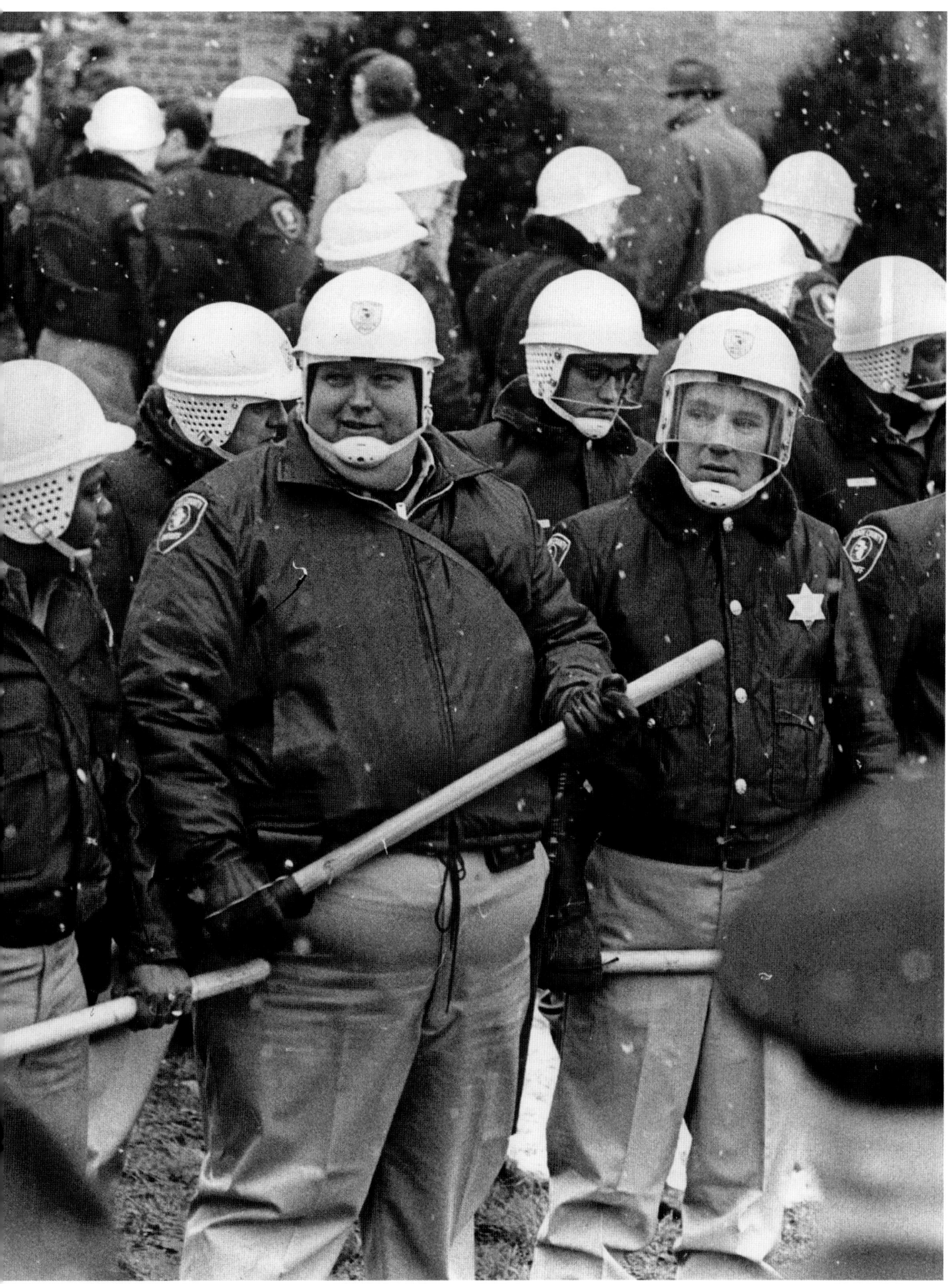

SHERIFF'S DEPUTIES HOLD RIOT CLUBS—LONGER THAN BILLY CLUBS—TO EVICTION OF MR. AND MRS. JOHNNIE MOSS. JANUARY 29, 1970/PAUL SEQUEIRA

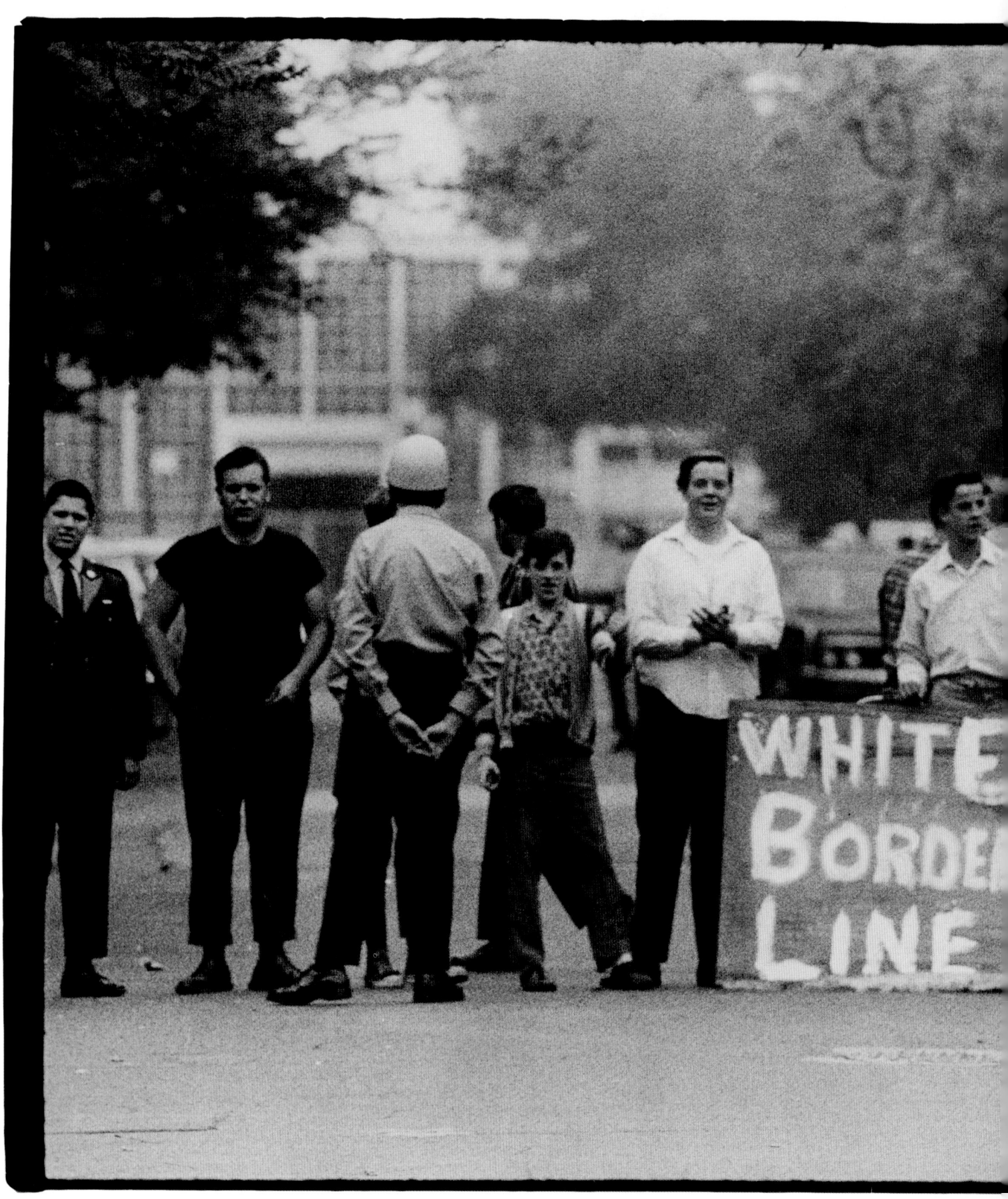

POLICE KEEP WHITE AND BLACK STUDENTS APART AT TILDEN HIGH SCHOOL, 4747 SOUTH UNION. OCTOBER 6, 1969/JOHN H. WHITE

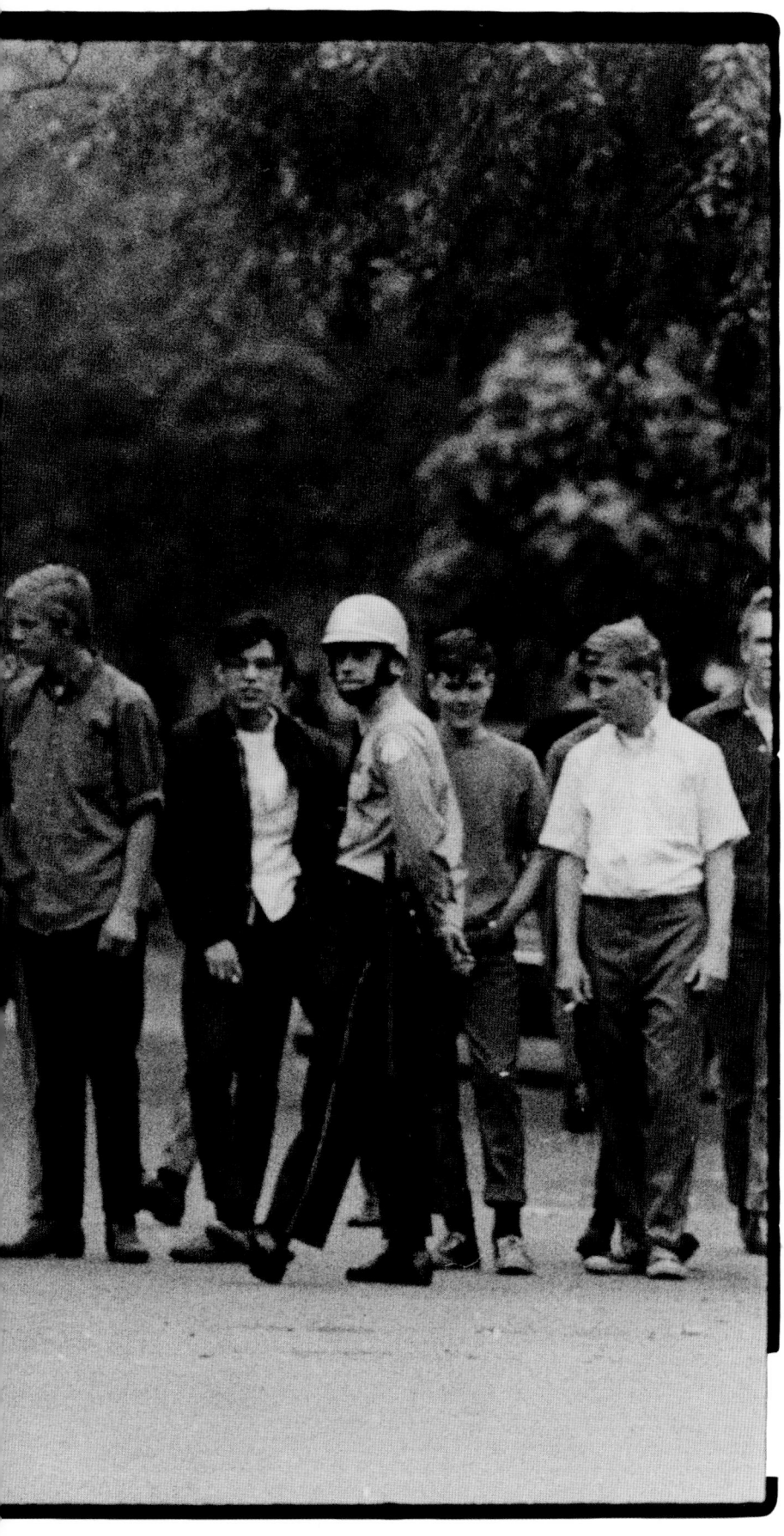

WHERE RACISTS DREW THE LINE

Racism was as integral a part of our lives in the 1960s as baseball, Mickey Mouse, and vacations at the lake.

I grew up in a southwest suburb just like the town where Dick and Jane lived in our elementary school readers: No African Americans lived in Evergreen Park. The only Blacks I knew about were professional baseball players whom my uncles mocked at family parties and picnics. I grew up believing Larry Doby was an awful player. When one of my brothers dropped a ball, we called him Larry Doby. The same Doby who's in baseball's Hall of Fame.

Before I ever met an African American, I repeated racial jokes heard from my friends who heard them from their elders. So when I finally encountered Black people on a CTA bus or at the Evergreen Park Plaza, I viewed them with a mix of wariness, even aversion.

At Saint Bernadette Parish School, no one disabused me of these notions. Not the Dominican nuns. Not the priests. Change occurred after I took a job teaching English alongside African-American teachers at Chicago Vocational High School. You can't help unlearning stereotypes and forming friendships with people you live and work with every day.

Because my school colleagues had endured myriad social and economic obstacles all their lives, they shared lessons about judging character, motivating youth, overcoming tragedy, and withstanding daily slings and arrows while still maintaining optimism with humor, faith, and love.

That's why I subscribe to Dr. King's belief in the imperative for integration. The goals behind it, including enlightenment, transformation, and racial harmony, are as valid as ever today.
—*David McGrath is the author of* South Siders.

A LION'S COURAGE, A LION'S ROAR

Fred Hampton was assassinated because FBI Director J. Edgar Hoover was afraid of him.

Fred was a self-proclaimed revolutionary, a charismatic, talented 21-year-old Black man who helped set up community health clinics, free breakfasts for children, and critical social services in communities that had been overlooked and underserved for far too long. He had the ability to create a political force that would liberate and emancipate people who had long been ignored. He had conviction and he was effective. He had a lion's courage and a lion's roar.

Fred Hampton was assassinated along with fellow Black Panther Party member Mark Clark in the early morning of December 4, 1969, in a raid by agents of the Cook County State's Attorney Office, the Chicago Police Department, and the FBI.

I believe the orders came directly from J. Edgar Hoover and that this was the only political assassination instituted by the federal government on US soil. The Chicago police wanted Fred dead, too. They wanted revenge after two police officers were shot and killed in a South Side gun battle with two Black Panther Party members less than a month earlier. Retribution, revenge, and political ambition were state's attorney Edward Hanrahan's primary motivations.

I recently wrote the US attorney general requesting the release of unclassified and unredacted versions of Department of Justice and FBI files related to the assassination. And I introduced legislation that would make all COINTELPRO files public. I want to fully understand what happened. I want to know the totality of the federal government's involvement and who made the decision. This state-sanctioned murder was not done to take Fred off the streets.

He was supposed to return to prison only a few days later. They did not want him to live. They wanted him dead. I want to know who paid and who received the bounty money for Fred's murder.

I have often thought about what would have become of Chairman Fred had he not been gunned down. He understood the power of law and understood the power of his voice. He knew he could move people. I believe he would have been a talented lawyer or a gifted preacher. He had all the skill to become a significant national leader. He wanted to live an effective life and make a difference for those who were left out.

His murder changed Chicago and it changed America. The inextricable bond between the Democratic Party and the Black community was finally broken by his assassination. Three years later, the community helped defeat Edward Hanrahan when it voted in a Republican state's attorney. That eventually led to the 1983 election of Harold Washington, whose victory provided the momentum that bolstered Barack Obama's bid to become president.

Fred Hampton inspires me each and every day. His prophetic words still apply: "You can murder a revolutionary, but you can't murder a revolution."
—*Congressman Bobby L. Rush cofounded the Illinois chapter of the Black Panther Party.*

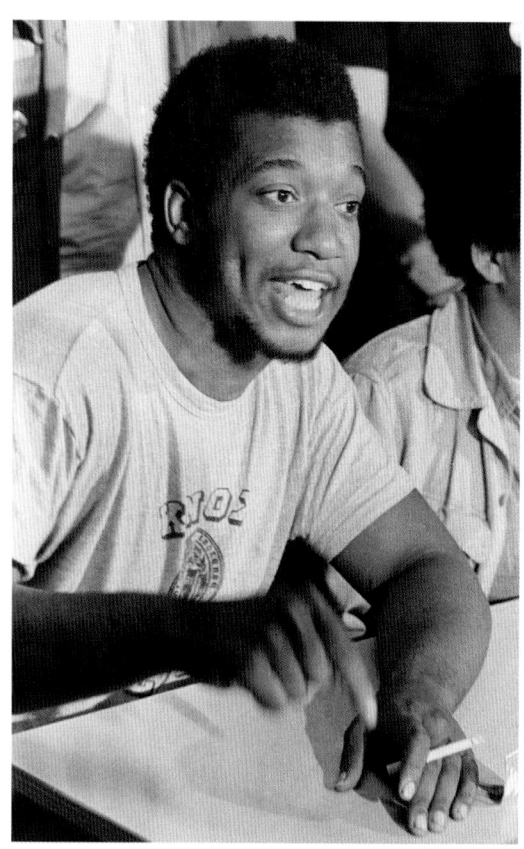

FRED HAMPTON. 1969/HOWARD D. SIMMONS

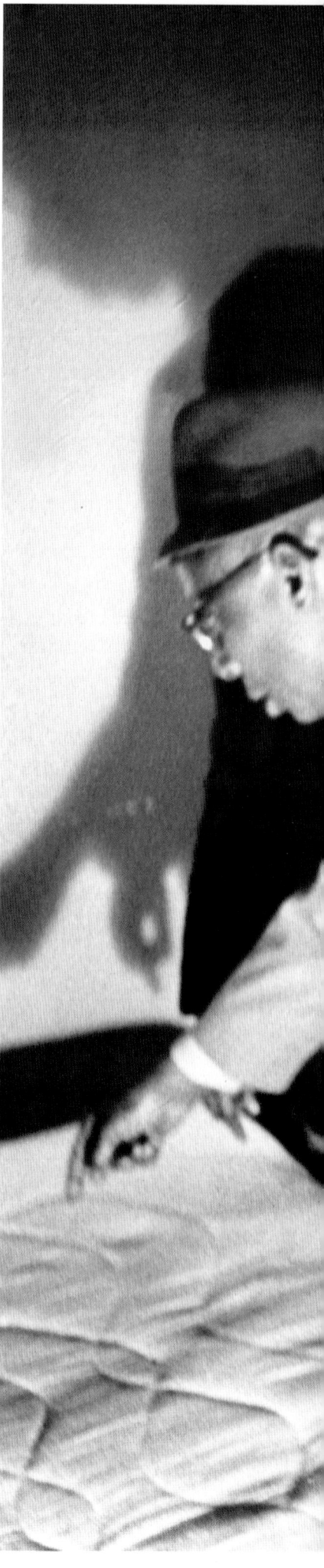

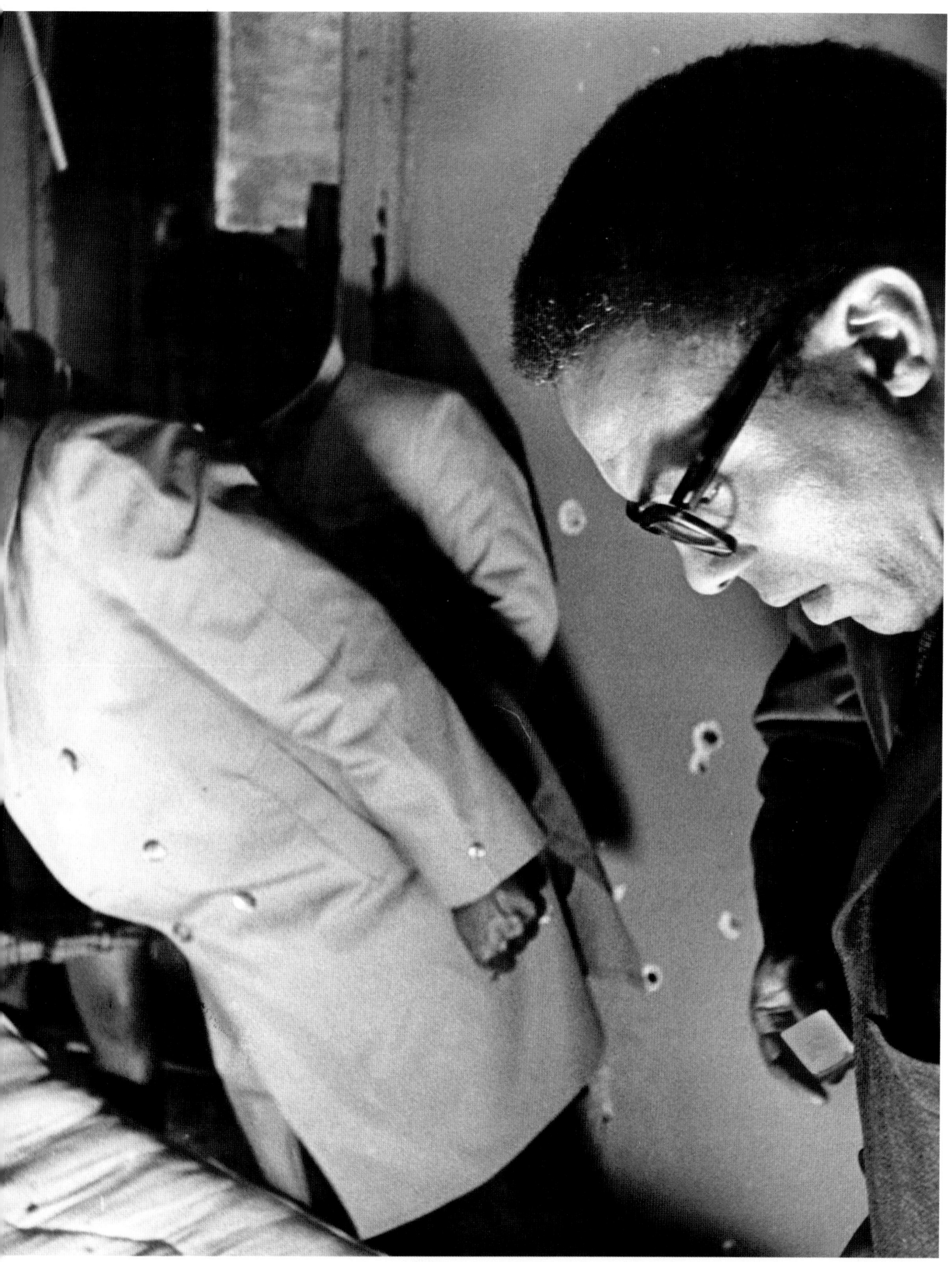
STATE SENATORS CHARLES CHEW (LEFT) AND RICHARD NEWHOUSE INSPECT THE BED WHERE FRED HAMPTON WAS KILLED. DECEMBER 5, 1969/JOHN H. WHITE

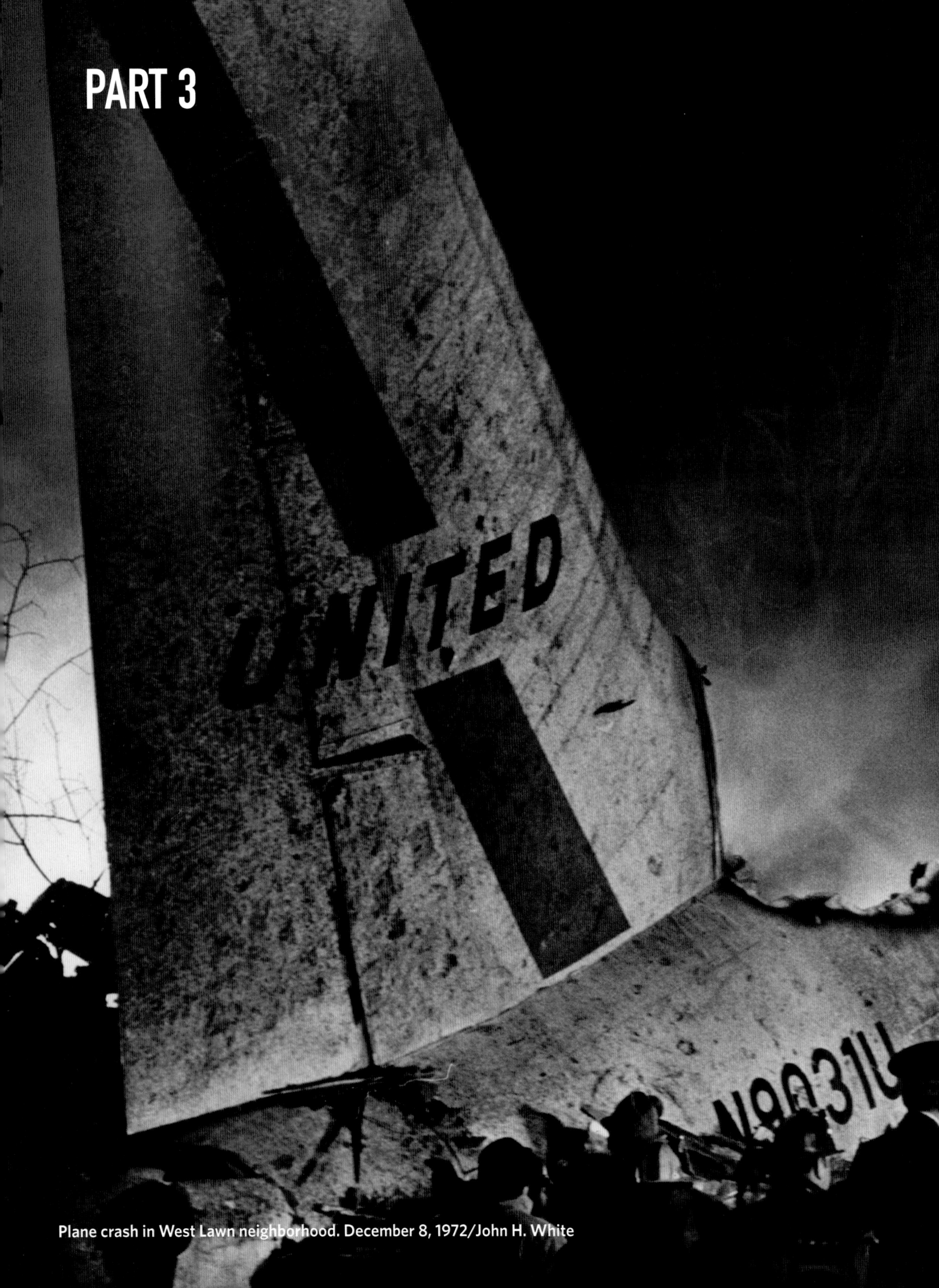

PART 3

Plane crash in West Lawn neighborhood. December 8, 1972/John H. White

SHOCKING NEWS

We photojournalists are human beings. We see difficult things. I sometimes used the camera as a shield.
— **Scott Stewart**
Sun-Times photographer, 1985–2013

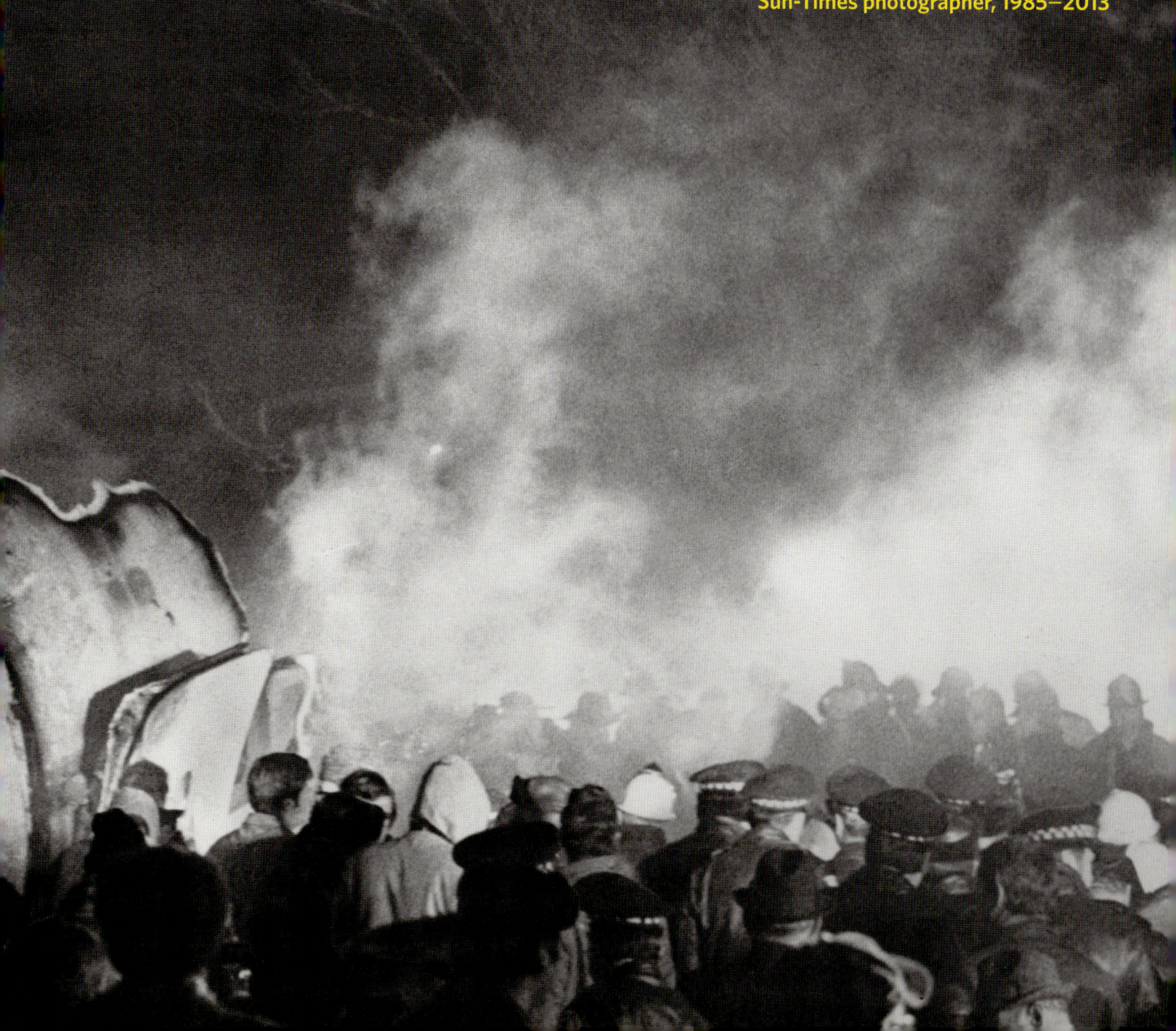

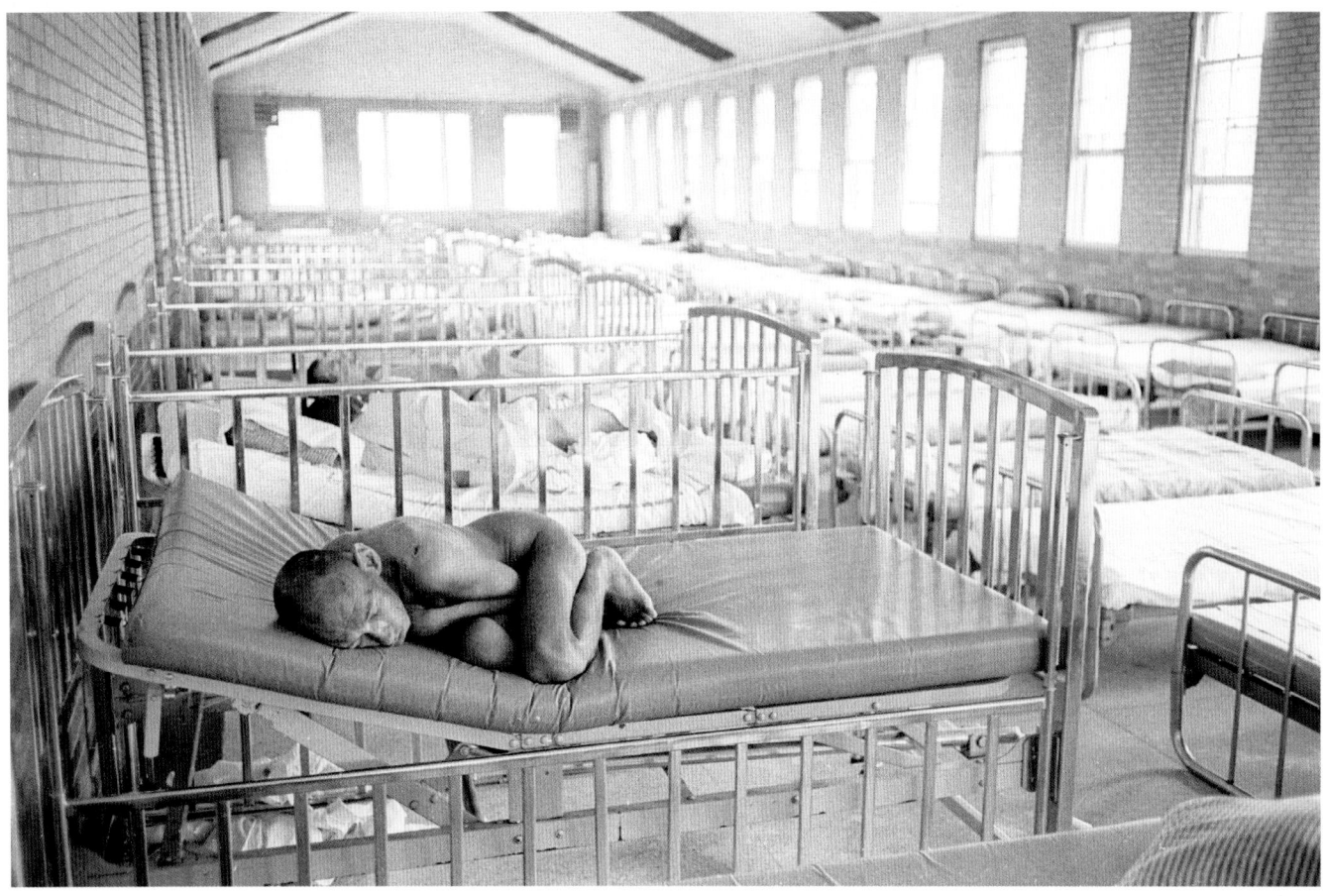

STATE SCHOOLS FOR PEOPLE WITH INTELLECTUAL DISABILITIES IN DOWNSTATE DIXON AND LINCOLN. APRIL AND JULY 1970/JACK DYKINGA

NOTHING COULD HAVE PREPARED ME

I was a 27-year-old kid. Cocky, ambitious, and a product of a fiercely competitive four-newspaper town. Yet I was naïve when it came to journalism and the power of images.

When chief photographer Ralph Frost assigned me to join writers Sam Washington and Jerome Watson to document the purported "warehousing" of developmentally challenged patients at Illinois state institutions, I had no idea what was ahead.

Parent groups informed the Sun-Times about abysmal conditions at Lincoln and Dixon State Schools at a time when Republican Governor Richard B. Ogilvie was proposing massive cuts to an already financially starved system.

It was this situation that led Watson and me to head to downstate Dixon. Surprisingly, we were greeted by staff eager for us to bear witness to their daily working conditions.

Nothing could have prepared me for the shock to all my senses as I entered the first ward. Fecal and urine smells and near-constant screaming caused me to reel back. I felt I needed context in an upside-down world. My cameras dangled uselessly at my shoulders as I just stared. The concrete floor was slick with urine. Half-dressed inmates wandered aimlessly.

Many with excrement-smeared hands reaching to touch me or my cameras. A young patient with Down Syndrome became my self-appointed guardian. He would shout at inmates to stay clear.

Gradually, I began photographing. My mind began to sort out scenes and moments within the horror. At some point, muscle memory kicked in and I became a fly on the wall surveying the desolation and despair around me.

This routine was repeated at Lincoln State School along with days spent documenting successes in rehabilitation centers where challenged men and women received treatment.

When I got home from that first visit, I was drained. My face was vacant, and my clothes reeked. My ears were still ringing. I wept. My wife, Margaret, a psych nurse during her training, had some idea of what I'd been through. Being there was a different matter.

Those memories endure to this day.

There was, of course, jubilation when the governor reinstated funding. I entered the Sun-Times newsroom a year later to standing applause upon winning a Pulitzer.

The work forever changed my life. I was fortunate to learn early the power of photojournalism to tell stories that can effect change.
—*Jack Dykinga won a 1971 Pulitzer Prize in feature photography for documenting the Dixon and Lincoln State Schools. He worked at the Sun-Times from the mid-1960s to the mid-1970s.*

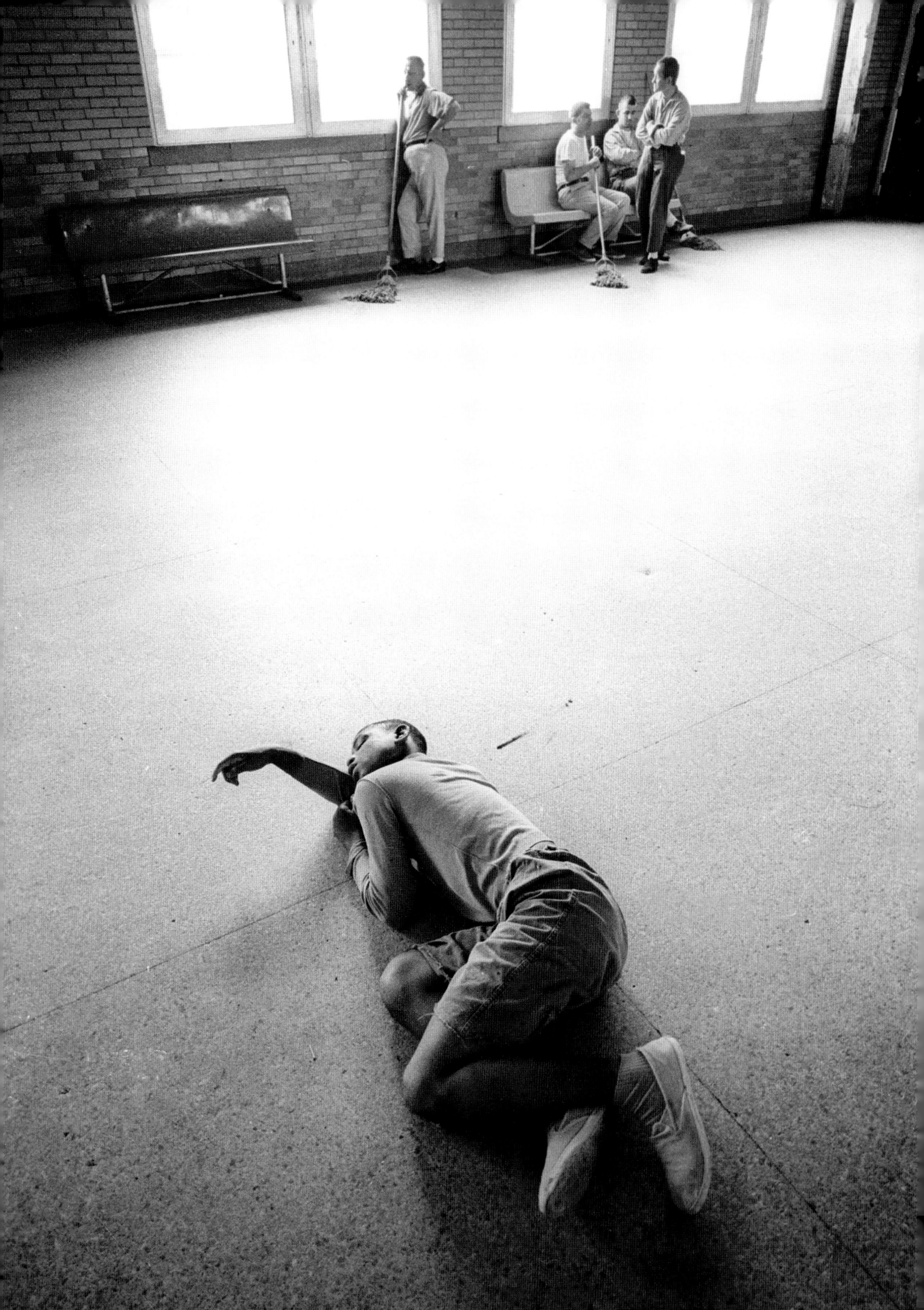

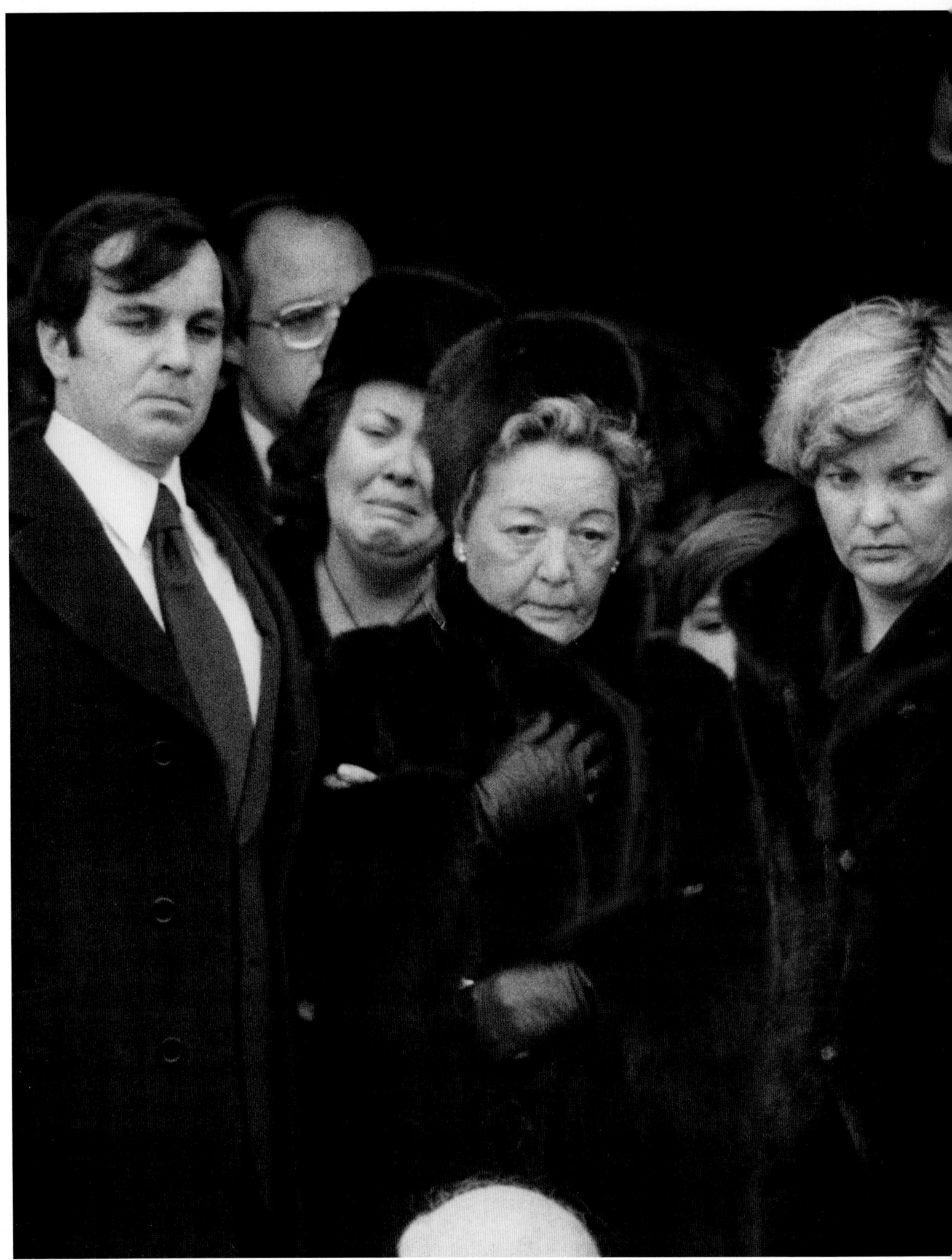

DALEYS BIDS FAREWELL. FROM LEFT: SON RICHARD M., DAUGHTER PATRICIA, WIFE ELEANOR, AND DAUGHTER ELEANOR. DECEMBER 22, 1976/PERRY C. RIDDLE

A CITY MOURNS

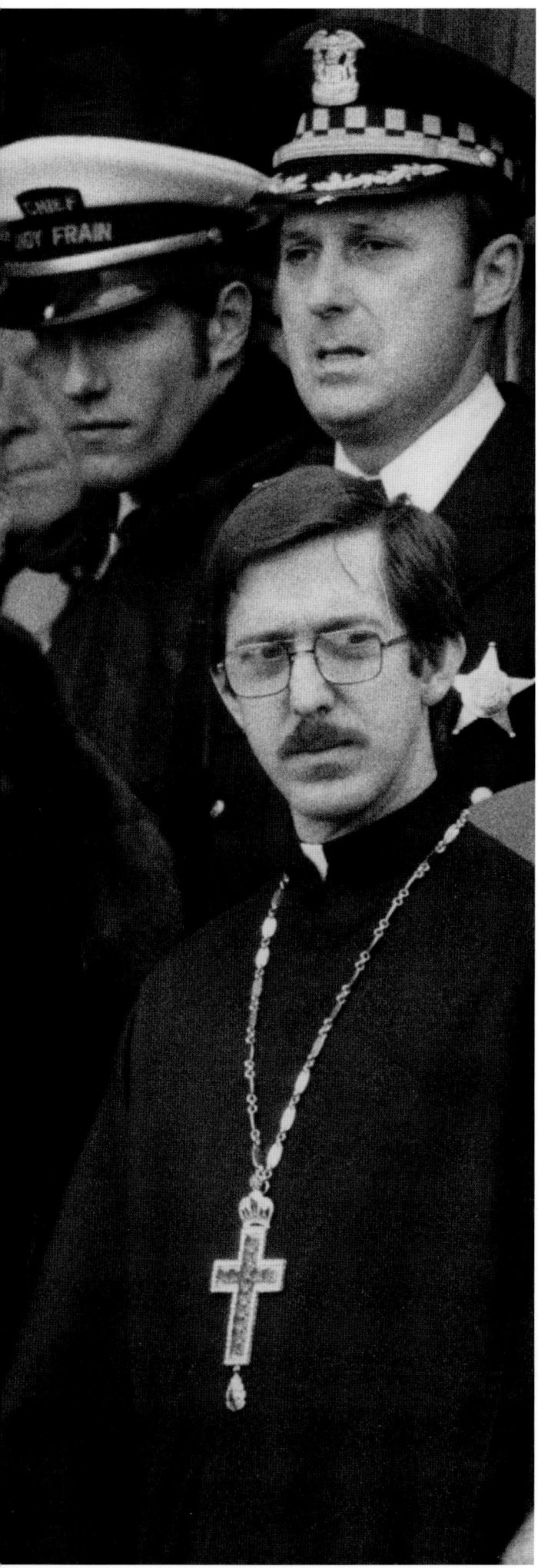

If a man ever reflected a city, it was Richard J. Daley and Chicago.

In some ways, he was this town at its best—strong, hard-driving, working feverishly, pushing, building, driven by ambitions so big they seemed Texas-boastful.

In other ways, he was this city at its worst—arrogant, crude, conniving, ruthless, suspicious, intolerant.

He wasn't graceful, suave, witty, or smooth. But then, this is not Paris or San Francisco.

He was raucous, sentimental, hot-tempered, practical, simple, devious, big, and powerful. This is, after all, Chicago.

Sometimes the very same Daley performance would be seen as both outrageous and heroic. It depended on whom you asked for an opinion.

For example, when he stood on the Democratic National Convention floor in 1968 and mouthed furious crudities at smooth Abe Ribicoff, tens of millions of TV viewers were shocked.

But it didn't offend most Chicagoans. That's part of the Chicago-style—belly to belly, scowl to scowl, and may the toughest or loudest man win.

Daley was not an articulate man, most English teachers would agree. People from other parts of the country sometimes marveled that a politician who fractured the language so thoroughly could be taken so seriously.

Well, Chicago is not an articulate town, Saul Bellow notwithstanding. Maybe it's because so many of us aren't that far removed from parents and grandparents who knew only bits and pieces of the language.

So when Daley slid sideways into a sentence, or didn't exit from the same paragraph he entered, it amused us. But it didn't sound that different from the way most of us talk.

Daley was a product of the neighborhoods and he reflected it in many ways—loyalty to the family, neighbors, old buddies, the corner grocer. You do something for someone, they do something for you. If somebody is sick, you offer the family help. If someone dies, you go to the wake and try to lend comfort. The young don't lip off to the old, everybody cuts his grass, takes care of his property, and doesn't play his TV too loud.

That's the way he liked to live, and that's what he thought most people wanted, and he was right.

But there are other sides to Chicago neighborhoods—suspicion of outsiders, intolerance toward the unconventional, bigotry and bullying.

That was Daley, too. As he proved over and over again, he didn't trust outsiders, whether they were longhairs against war, Black preachers against segregation, reformers against his machine, or community groups against his policies. This was his neighborhood-ward-city-country, and nobody could come in and make noise. He'd call the cops. Which he did.
—Columnist Mike Royko worked for the Chicago Daily News and Sun-Times from 1959 to 1984 before moving to the Tribune. He won the Pulitzer Prize for commentary in 1972. This excerpt is from his column the day after mayor Richard J. Daley died.

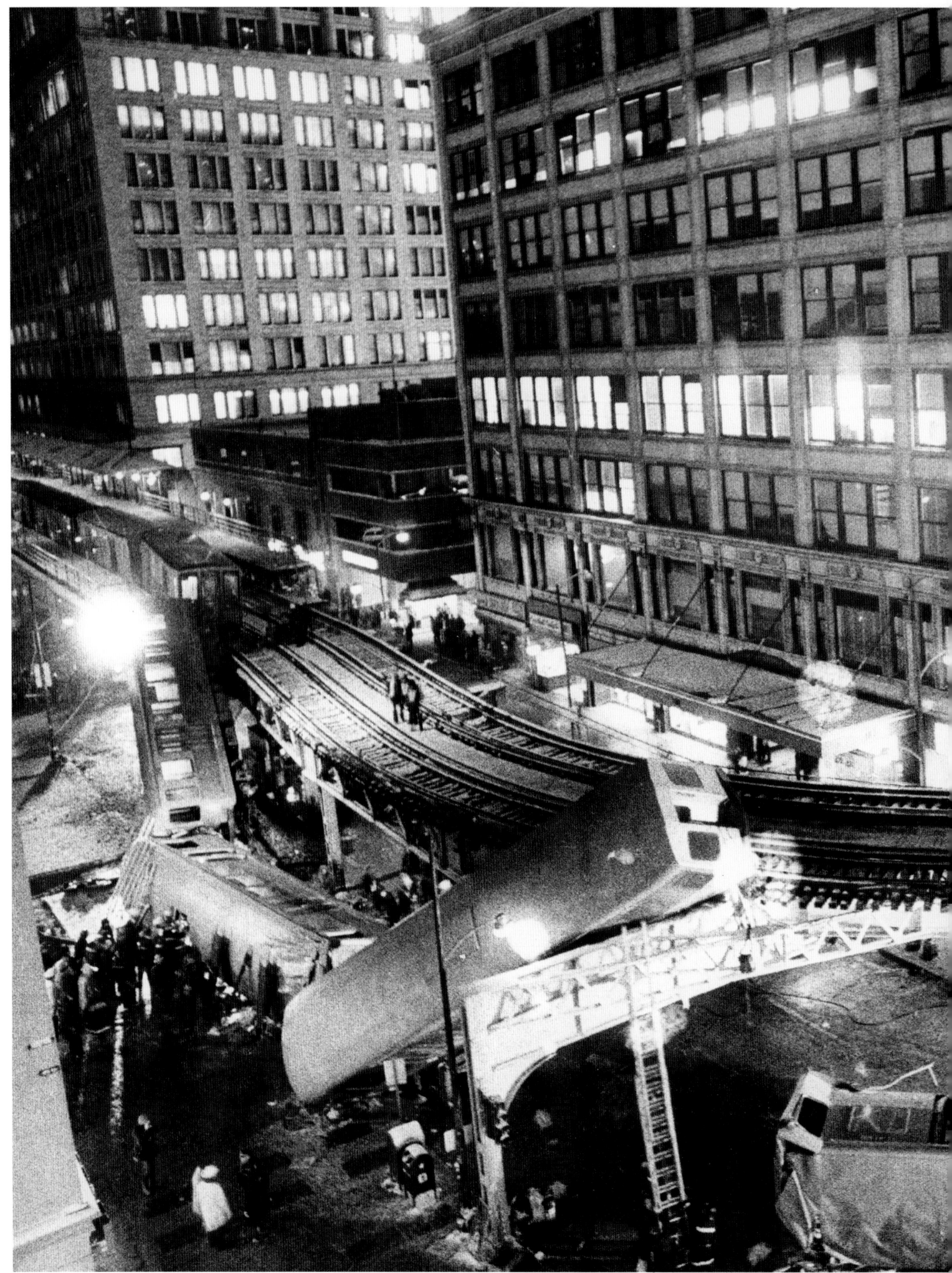

FOUR CARS OF A LAKE-DAN RYAN L TRAIN DERAIL AT LAKE AND WABASH DURING THE EVENING RUSH HOUR. FEBRUARY 4, 1977/JACK LENAHAN

THE MEMORIES STILL SEEM UNREAL

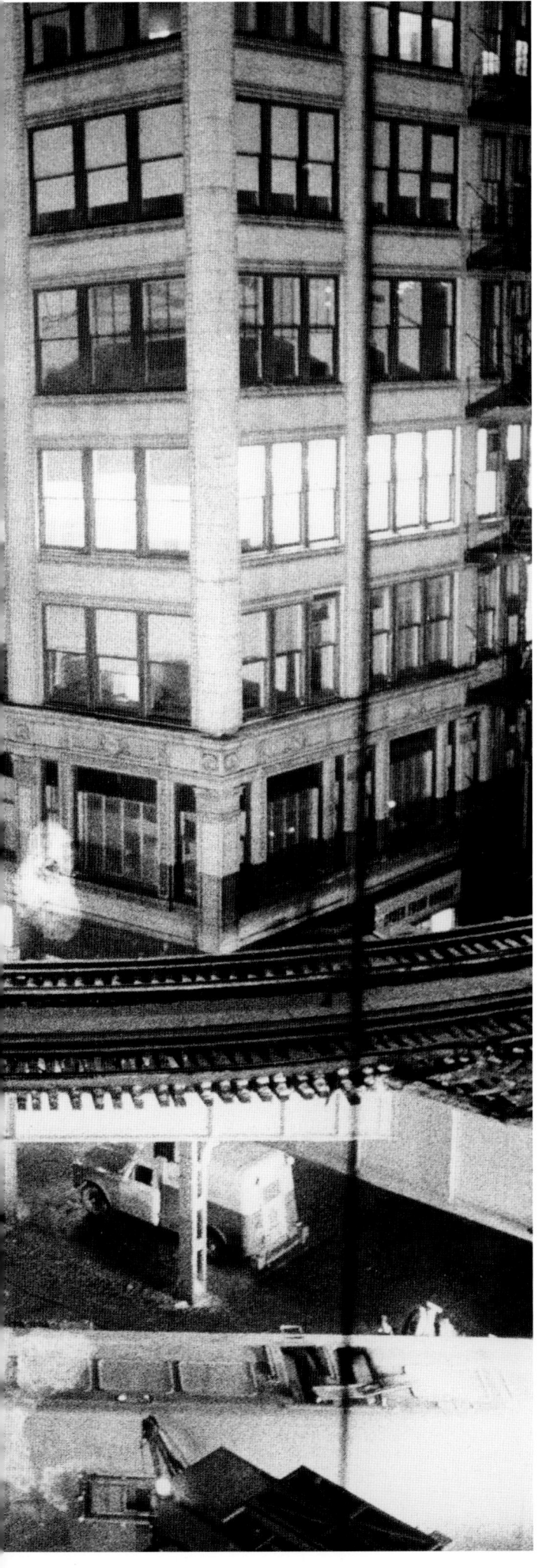

Chicagoan Donald MacCorquodale was one of the first to arrive when L trains collided at Lake Street and Wabash Avenue killing eleven and injuring 180 people. Here are excerpts from his account written four days later.

The two trains came together with a dull thump. From my vantage point, the silhouettes of the passengers in the first and second cars were clearly visible. Despite the sealed windows of the air-conditioned cars, the terrified screams were quite audible.

For a moment, the train was almost motionless. It had lost all forward headway and the cars were gently rocking. The cars remained stationary for a period of at least two or three seconds, possibly longer. Then, in quick succession, an unforgettable sequence of events began to take place.

The first indication of a derailment was four distinct bursts of arcing from the rear of the lead car, #2043. Slowly, ponderously, the 2043 rolled over and left the structure rear-end first. The car fell to the street with a crash that defies description.

For a split second, I thought only the 2043 was going to fall. Perhaps my mind was refusing to accept the enormity of what I was seeing; the memories still seem unreal.

Then the other cars began to go. The sound of falling equipment was deafening. As the last cars came to rest, the awful cacophony subsided and was replaced by an utter silence which seemed unreal.

On the sidewalk ahead of me, a girl turned around, her face distorted with hysteria. She threw her arms around me, sobbing uncontrollably. I guided her back to the lobby of the building at 203 North Wabash where she quickly regained her composure.

I then returned to the street. Some instinct told me to help get those people out. A small cluster of pedestrians had formed around each of the end train doors of 2043. Thinking there was little I could do there, I hurried over to #2044.

With the door open a few inches, I could hear people moving around inside, trying to get themselves untangled. While there were grunts and coughs, I noted with surprise that there was no hysterical screaming. The trapped passengers in 2044 were remarkably calm considering the experience they had been through.

A side window across from the cab of 2044 had broken out, and a man was lying on the pavement. He was doubled up in agony and a pedestrian was telling him not to move. Behind the window opening, I could see an incredible tangle of arms, legs, and seat cushions.

With the mass of 2044 hanging above him, the victim on the pavement was pleading for someone to pull him away; he was afraid the suspended car would shift and crush him. I tried to reassure him that the car was wedged solidly and that it would not move any farther. This was a lie; I had no idea whether or not it would break loose, but I knew any attempt to move him might do grievous harm.

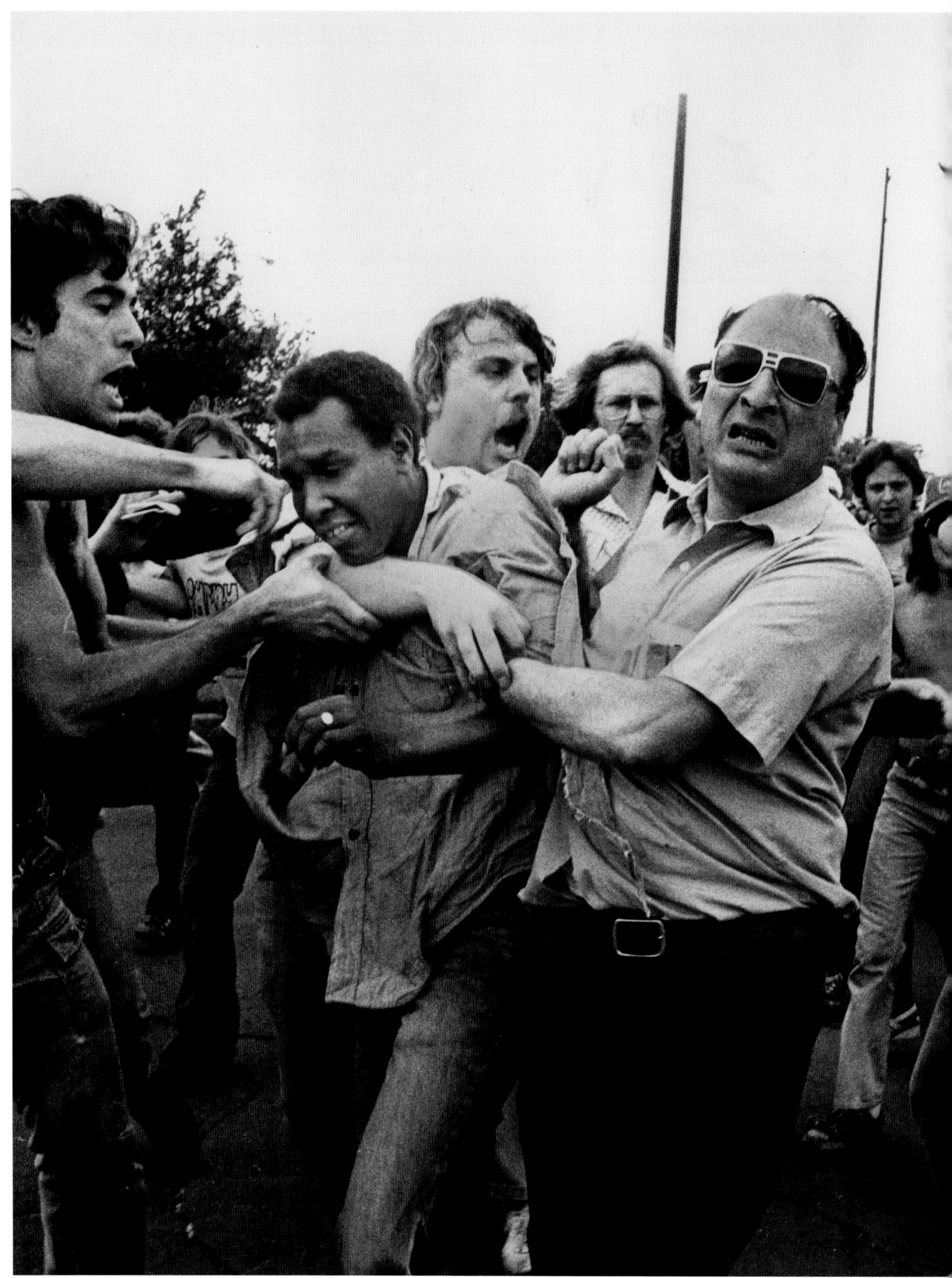

RESCUE FROM A MOB NEAR MARQUETTE PARK. THE TWO RESCUERS WERE INJURED BUT DID NOT REQUIRE HOSPITALIZATION. JULY 9, 1978/JAMES DEPREE

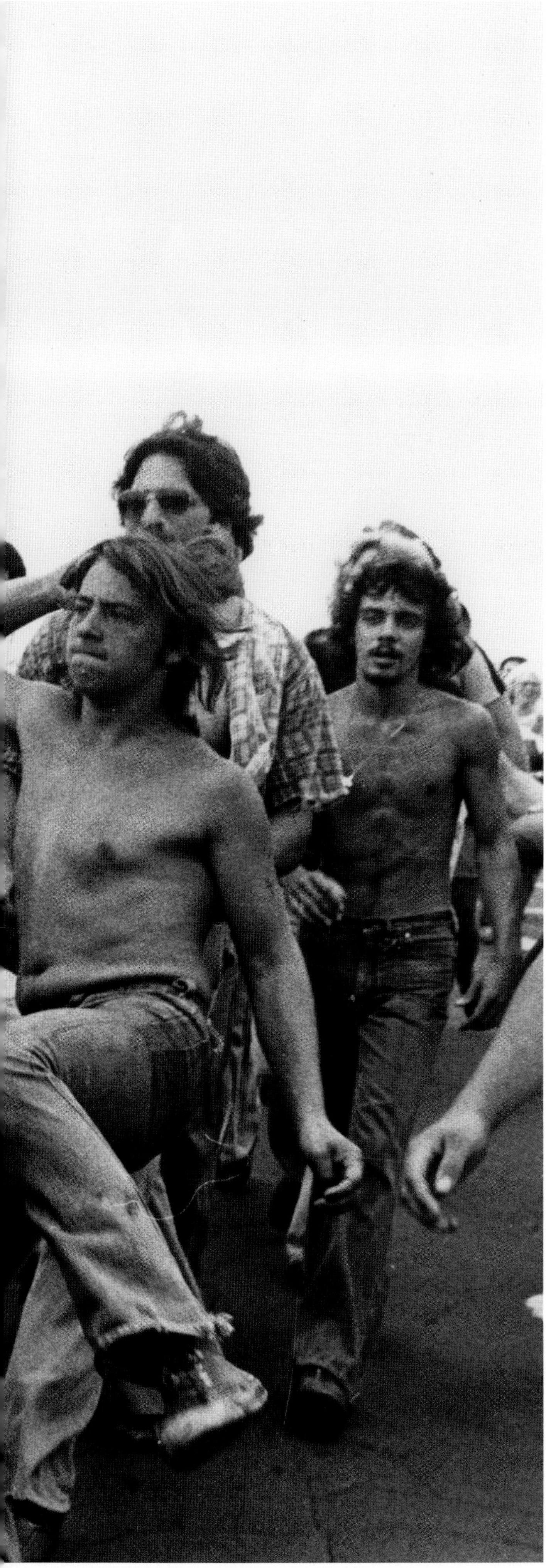

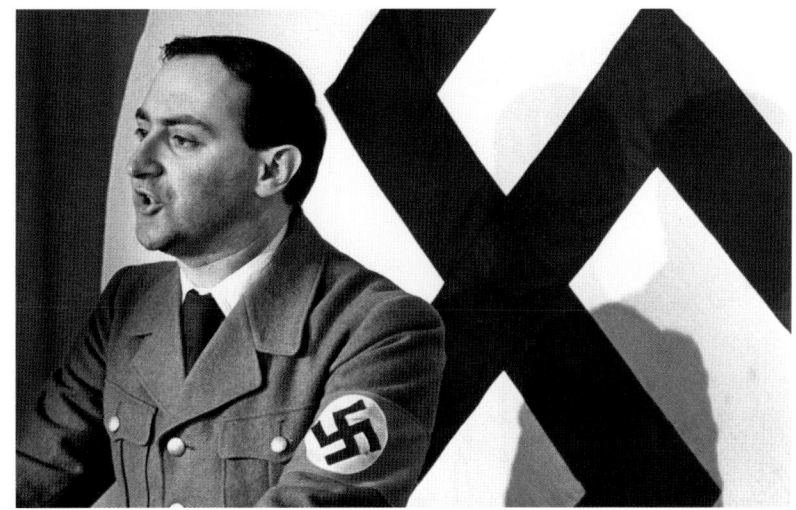

NEO-NAZI FRANK COLLIN. JUNE 22, 1978/JACK LENAHAN

EVERYONE WAS THERE BECAUSE OF THE NAZIS

Less than a year before my father, James DePree, died, I sat with him and a voice recorder. It was early 2020. He had scanned hundreds of photographs from his years as a photographer, and we wanted to talk about them. We spent twelve hours—over six days—looking over his work.

I was born after my father left the Sun-Times. The older he got, the more he reminisced about those years. He talked about many things, including the day in 1978 when he was assigned to photograph a rally led by Chicago Nazi leader Frank Collin in Marquette Park on the Southwest Side. Here is his edited account:

"I was sent there by the newspaper because it was going to be a big story. The crowd was large and growing bigger. Everyone was there because of the Nazis.

I started at Rockwell Hall in their headquarters with Frank Collin before everything began in the park. Eventually the protesters started to march down the street and I photographed them as they came to me. It was quite a violent demonstration. There were fights and people were throwing rocks and bottles. A man with a sign marching near me was hit in the head and was knocked out. There were hundreds of police and thousands of people.

I always worked by myself. I could see them throwing stuff at me, but they never hit me. You just do what you can do to get your picture and try and be safe. It was a trying time in Chicago. I will never forget the excitement of it all."

This photo, according to its printed captions, shows two "neighborhood residents" (the man in sunglasses and the shouting man with a mustache) rescuing a young Black man caught in a crowd of angry young supporters of Collin. Now, decades later, I wonder if those rescuers were plainclothes Chicago police officers.

After the Sun-Times, my father bought and managed apartments in the Lake View neighborhood. He looked back at these newspaper years with great fondness. He lived with a police scanner. If there was action, he was there.
—*Matthew DePree graduated from DePaul University with a degree in history. Like his father, he is a property manager and lover of history.*

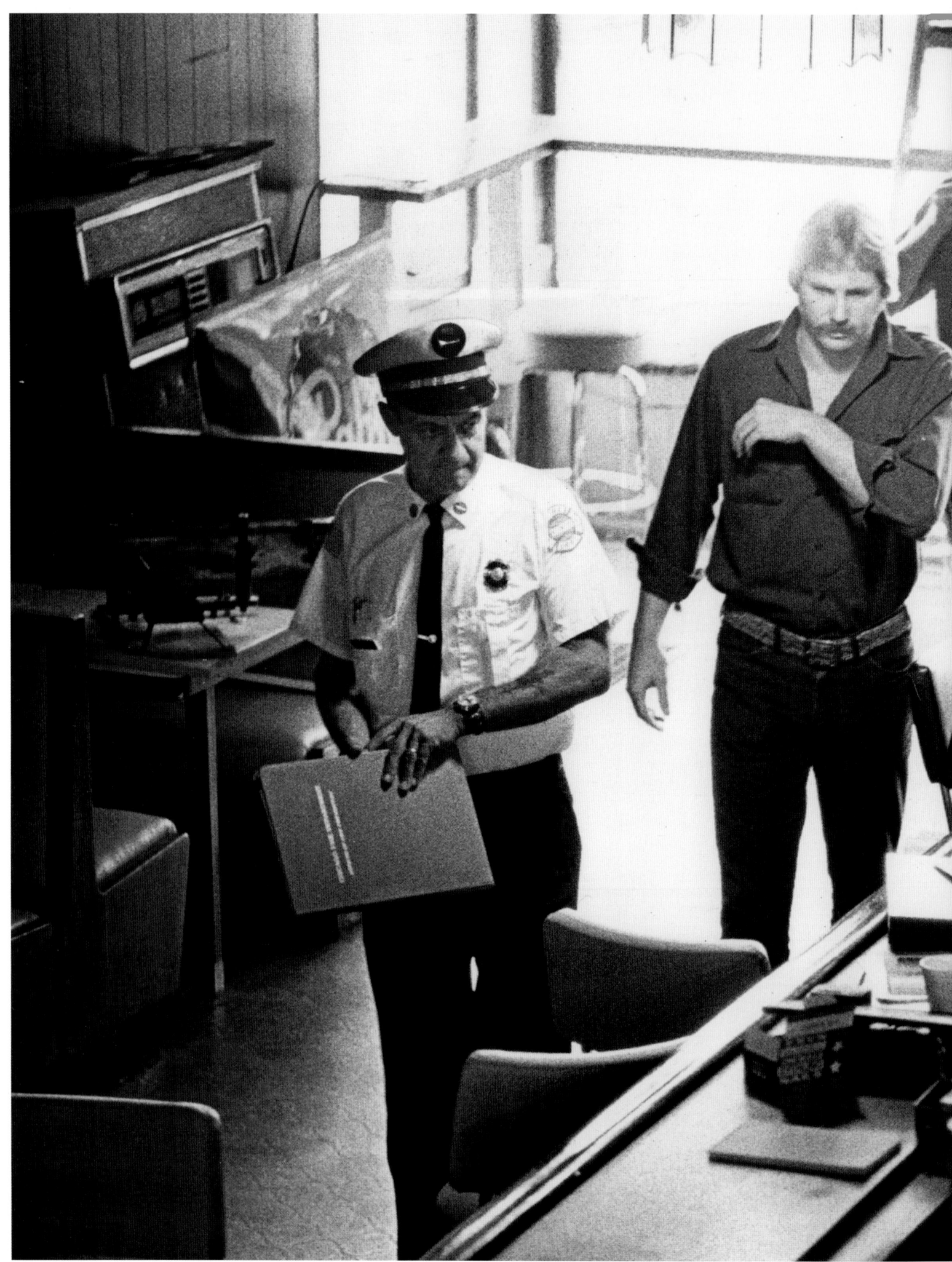

FIRE INSPECTOR BENJAMIN JUNGMAN ARRIVES TO SURVEY THE MIRAGE. HE IGNORED FIRE HAZARDS—FOR A $10 PAYOFF. JULY 27, 1977/JIM FROST

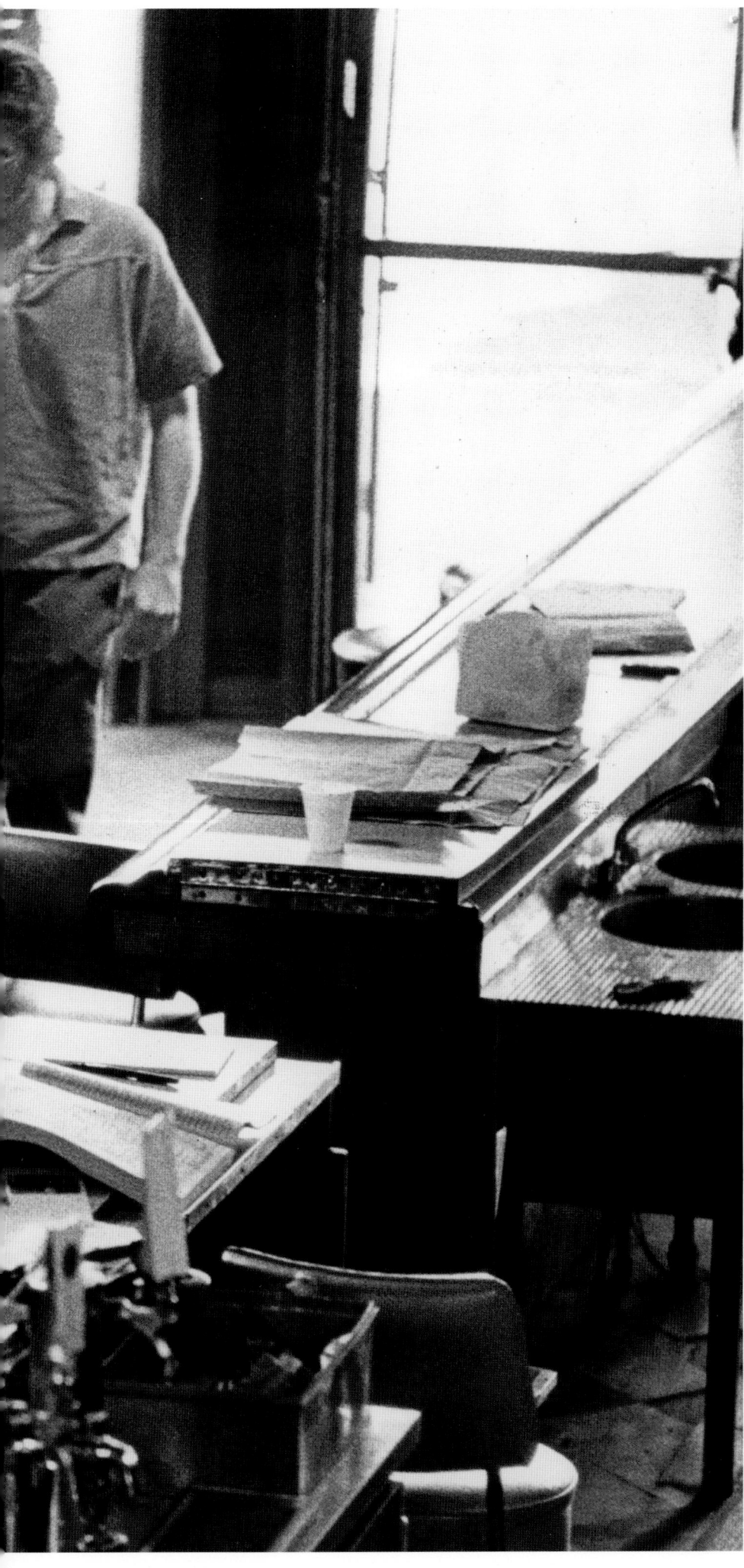

THE PICTURES WERE ESSENTIAL

I was a rookie at the Sun-Times, still learning everyone's name and how a big city newsroom functions when I was called into the managing editor's office.

Editor Stuart Loory told me I had been chosen for a high-profile undercover investigative project. The Sun-Times had purchased a bar—full of code violations—at 731 North Wells. The paper bought it, I was told, to document an open secret: that city inspectors routinely shook down business owners. The bar was a journalistic sting. It was appropriately named the Mirage.

I was instructed not to discuss "The Special," as we called it, with anyone, including my immediate boss or my family. And that I was to respond day or night to any assignment at the bar. I was chosen because I was the new kid in town and none of the City Hall types would recognize me.

Working at the Mirage were Sun-Times reporters Pam Zekman and Zay N. Smith and Better Government Association investigators Bill Recktenwald and Jeff Allen. Gene Pesek and I photographed a parade of payoffs made to health, plumbing, building, electrical, and fire inspectors to keep the bar open and in business. We photographed the cash exchanges through a peephole from an upstairs loft in back. The pictures were essential. Images were evidence and brought the story to life.

To keep our cover, Gene and I posed as repairmen. We would walk into the bar, say something like, "That fuse box again?" and disappear into the back room. We wore workmen's coveralls, a suitable cap, gloves and carried a large toolbox to conceal our cameras.

Four months after we opened, the Mirage was "closed for remodeling." On January 8, 1978, the story broke: "Our 'bar' uncovers payoffs, tax gyps" the headline read. The 25-part series ran for weeks. It finally documented Chicago's culture of corruption.

After months of wondering where I kept running off to, my wife—along with the rest of the country—had the full story.

—*Jim Frost was a staff photographer at the Sun-Times from 1977 to 2006.*

JUST A FEW FEET AWAY

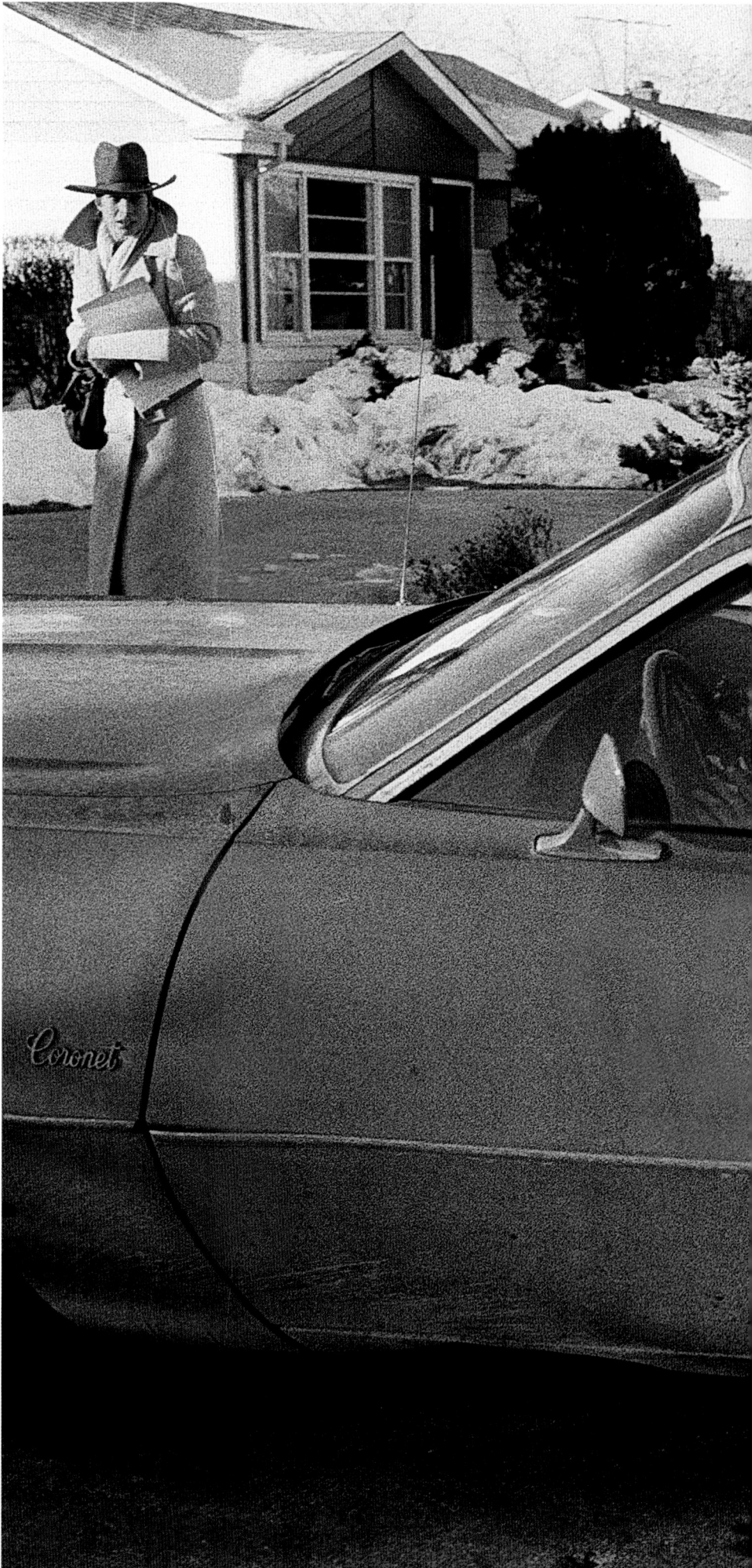

The desk called about 5 a.m. with an address: 8213 West Summerdale on the far Northwest Side. Lots of police activity.

I was the early morning shooter. It was still dark and very cold. I was one of the first photographers there. Plainclothes police were closed-mouthed. At some point, news leaked out that this was a mass murder investigation.

I photographed the scene before other reporters and photographers arrived. There was little to see. After a while, officers emerged from the house holding large trash bags. I shot several pictures as they carefully transferred the bags to an ambulance. I knew something was up.

I was standing by the driveway when an unmarked car pulled up. I photographed the beat-up, two-door Dodge Coronet as it pulled in front. One officer told me that the guy in the car was the suspect. I didn't know it, but I had the first images of John Wayne Gacy—glaring out the rear window—after his arrest.

I called the office and told them I was coming in with the film. By the time I got there, the photo department Christmas party had just begun. I processed my film; the lab made prints. A reporter confirmed it was Gacy in the car.

That Christmas gathering was quite strange. I spent most of my time explaining that the trash bags contained the body parts of Gacy's victims. I had just stood a few feet from the most notorious mass murderer in the nation's history.

Gacy was convicted of 33 murders. He buried almost all his victims in that ranch house on Summerdale Avenue. That first cold morning remains a strong memory.
—*Photographer Richard Derk worked at the Daily News and Sun-Times from 1977 to 1984. He later worked as a photographer and picture editor at the Los Angeles Times.*

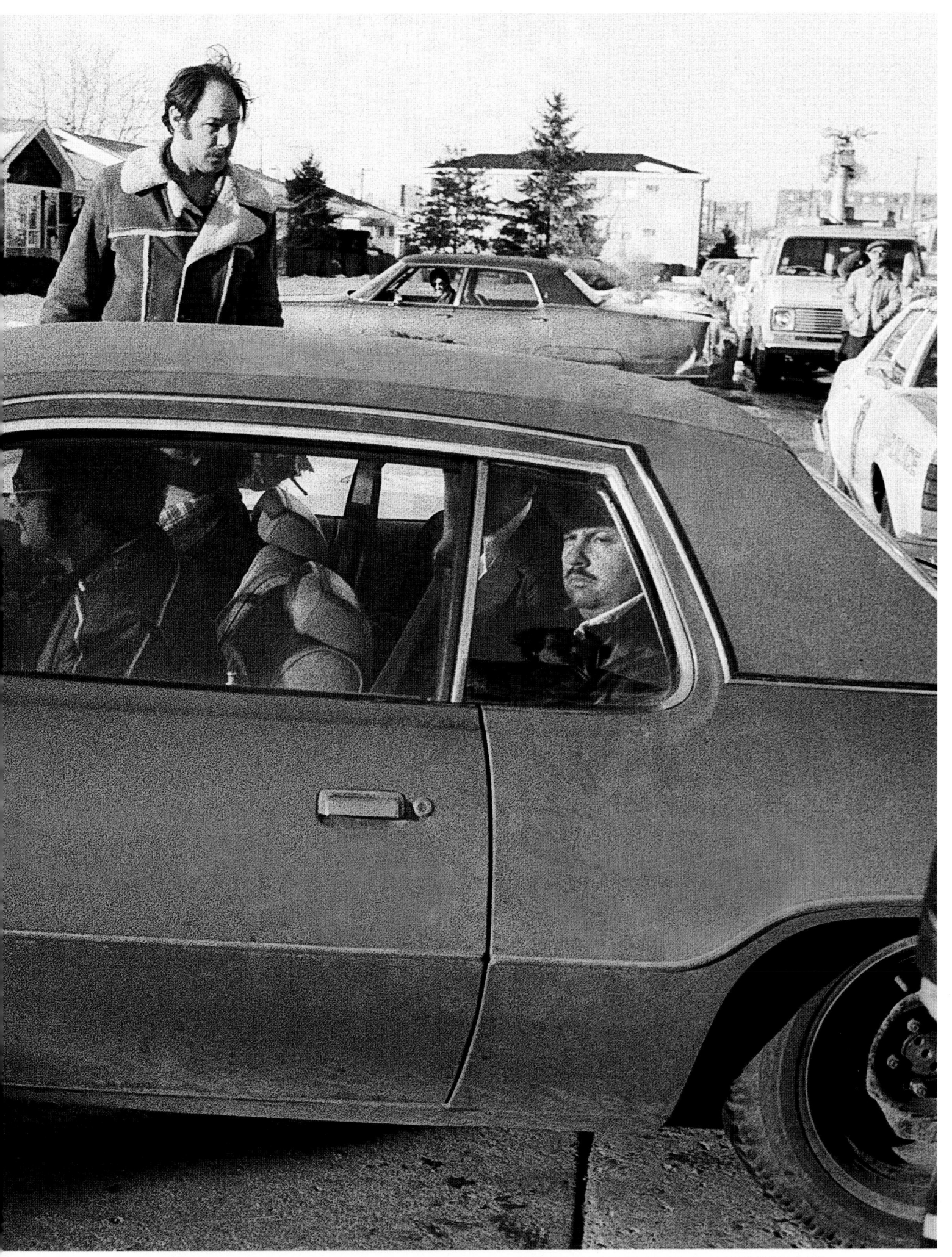

FIRST PHOTOGRAPH OF JOHN WAYNE GACY, IN THE BACK SEAT OF UNDERCOVER CAR. DECEMBER 22, 1978/RICHARD DERK

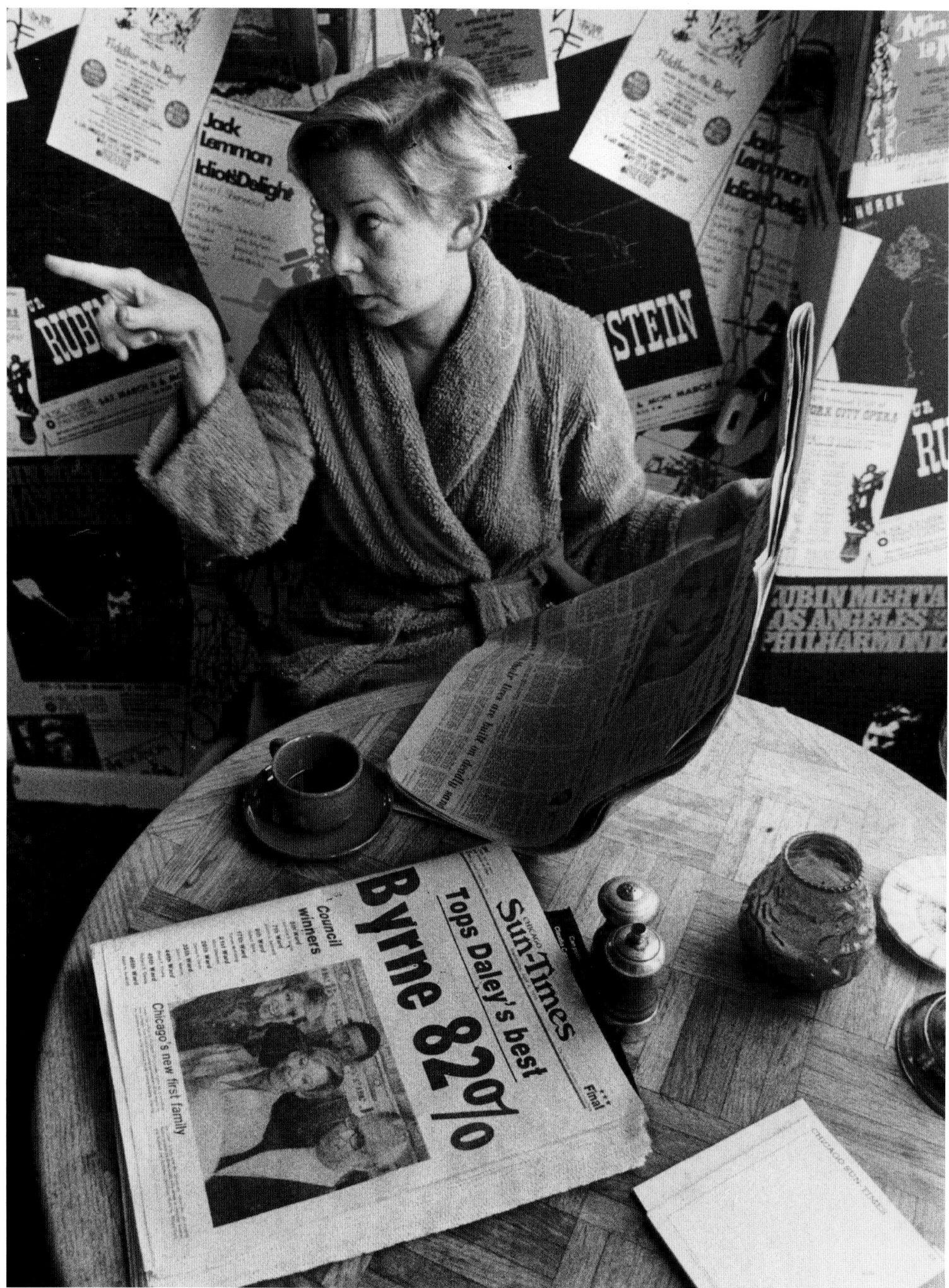

THE MORNING AFTER JANE BYRNE WON ELECTION AS CHICAGO'S FIRST WOMAN MAYOR. APRIL 4, 1979/RANDY LEFFINGWELL

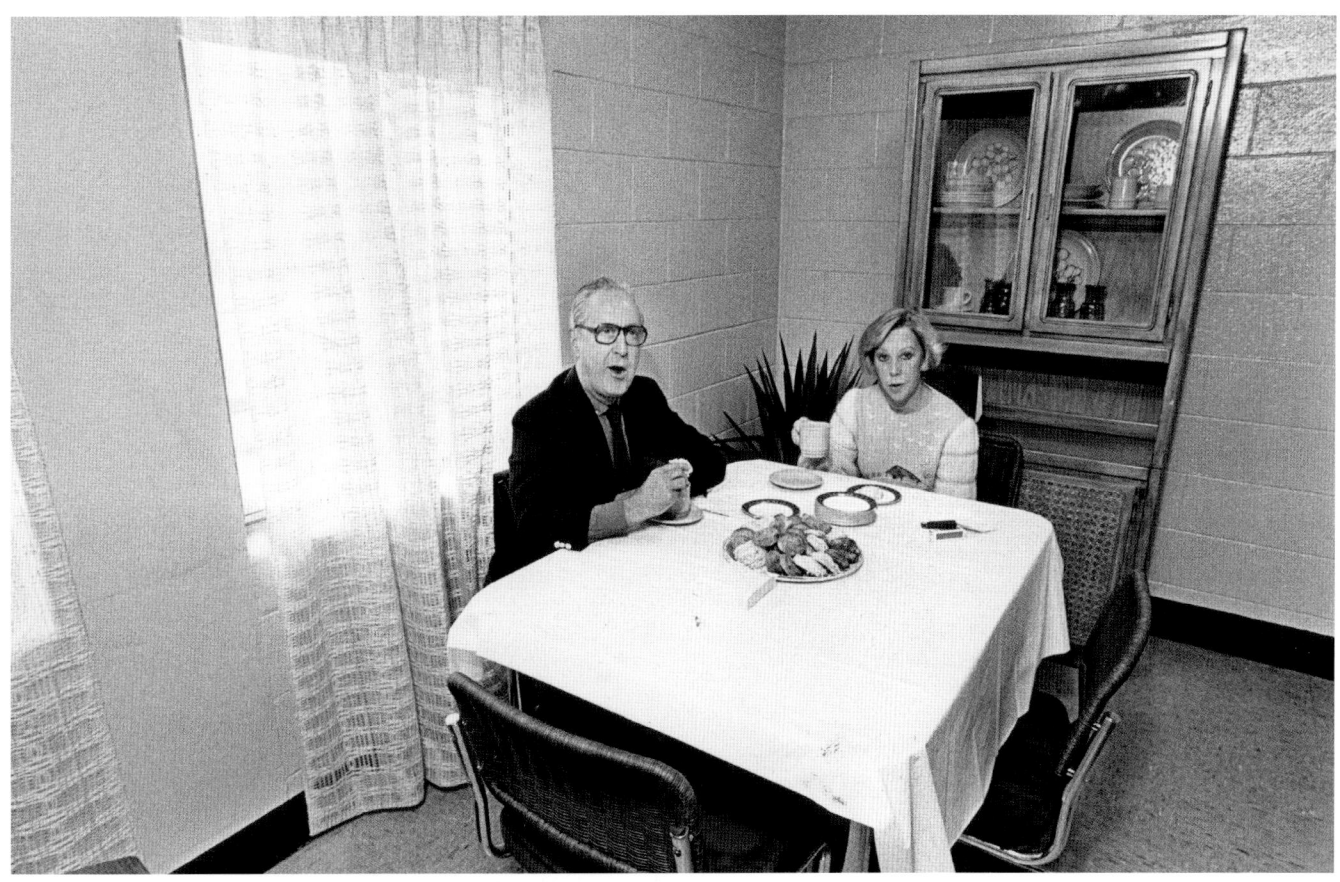

MAYOR BYRNE AND HUSBAND JAY MCMULLEN IN THEIR CABRINI-GREEN APARTMENT. APRIL 3, 1981/KEVIN HORAN

MAYOR BYRNE MOVES INTO & OUT OF CABRINI GREEN EASTER SUNDAY, APRIL 19, 1981

the first night
the mayor & her husband
watched the academy awards,
april fools in a two-bedroom
apartment furnished
by montgomery ward
in the most infamous
project on the planet
protected by 2 bodyguards
6 squad cars, her publicist
said she'd return to her gold
coast apartment a few blocks
east for a change
of clothes or perhaps a week
end, thou residents saw her sneak
in every morning & out each night
    for three weeks   she lasted.

& such is whiteness

the ability to de-robe
a life/style & return to privilege
awash in skin, adorned in birth
rite. a retreat, a return
back across heavily patrolled
borders of wealth
& white / working & not   white

on easter the mayor's blonde
ambition presides over an egg
hunt, the residents picket,
chant: *we need jobs, not eggs
jane byrne is the ku klux klan*

The mayor as invader
conquistador, missionary:
idyllic words backed by force.

on the last day Jesus returns
the mayor flees.

—*Poem by Kevin Coval
from his 2017 collection
A People's History of
Chicago.*

IT WAS ODDLY PLACID

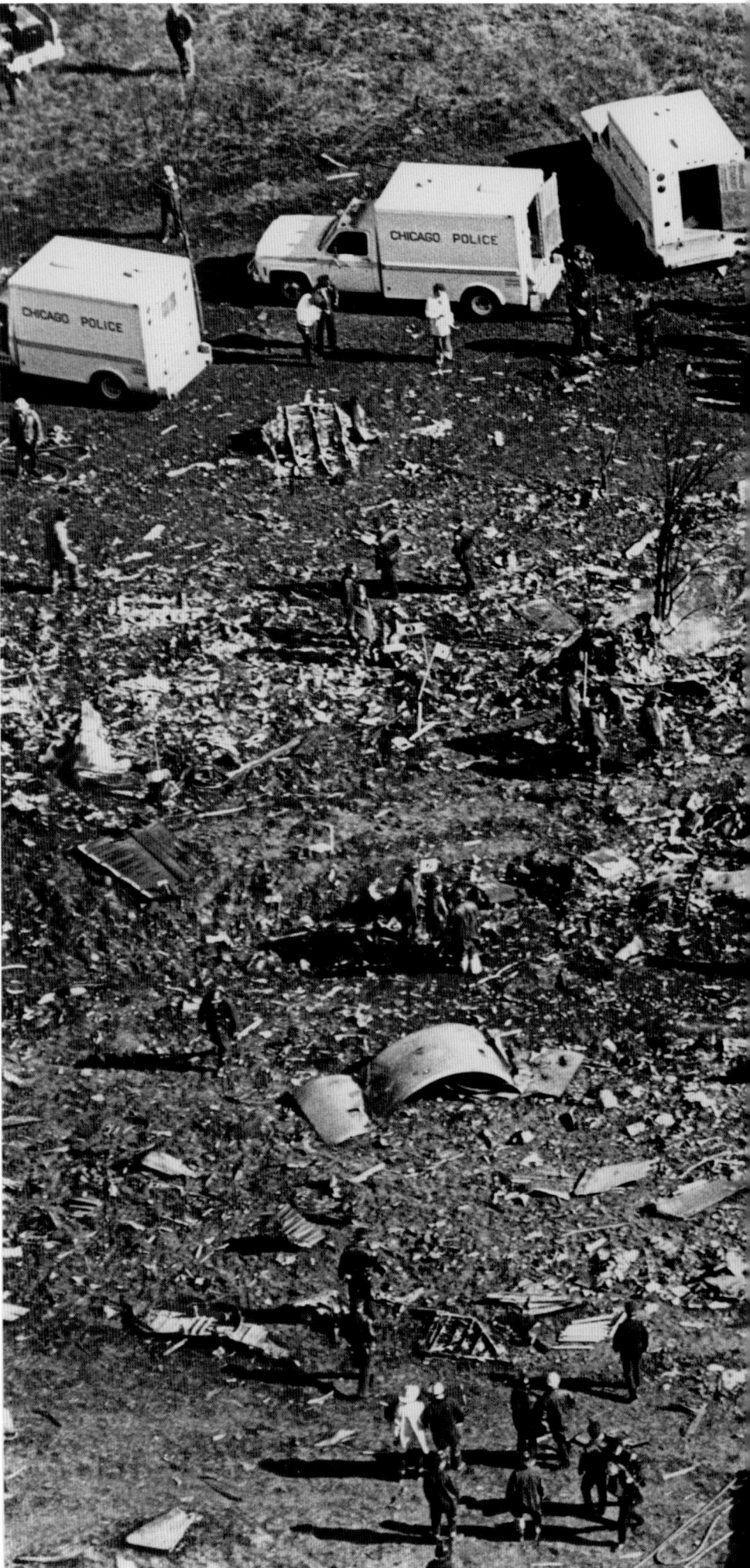

An airline crash in your own city scrambles the entire news staff. With most photographers sent speeding to O'Hare, I was sent in the opposite direction—to Meigs Field, to hop on a chartered helicopter so we could photograph from the air the plane crash of American Airlines Flight 191.

The pilot and I thought we would see the wreck from a distance, but we found there was no plane to see. The fireball was long gone by the time we flew over the scene. The plume of black smoke created by the crash had already disappeared. We wondered why we couldn't find the DC-10—and finally realized the plane had been almost entirely vaporized. Nothing but the tail engine resembled an aircraft.

We circled the site a few times during the next fifteen minutes—constantly in communication with the control tower. We were on the same flight path as Flight 191. I was surprised we could buzz around so close to the airport but that was because O'Hare had been shut down.

Looking at the prints decades later, I can see from the relaxed body language of the first responders that there was little sense of urgency. By the time we arrived, there was nobody to save.

When you are photographing an epic event, you often wish you could be in the air to see what's really going on. But from the helicopter, I wished I could be on the ground, closer to the action. Up here, I was safely removed from the carnage. It was oddly placid. I remember thinking as we headed back to Meigs that I didn't have the photo that would stop the presses. The scene looked more like a landfill than a plane crash. It was a document. A simple document.

After the Sun-Times, I spent a lot of time on commercial aircraft. Almost every time I got on a plane, I had the same attitude as the 271 people who boarded Flight 191. No problem. Just another flight.

But after seeing that crash site, I always also thought, "This might be the day."

—*Kevin Horan worked as a staff photographer for the Daily News and Sun-Times and later as a photographer for U.S. News and World Report and other magazines.*

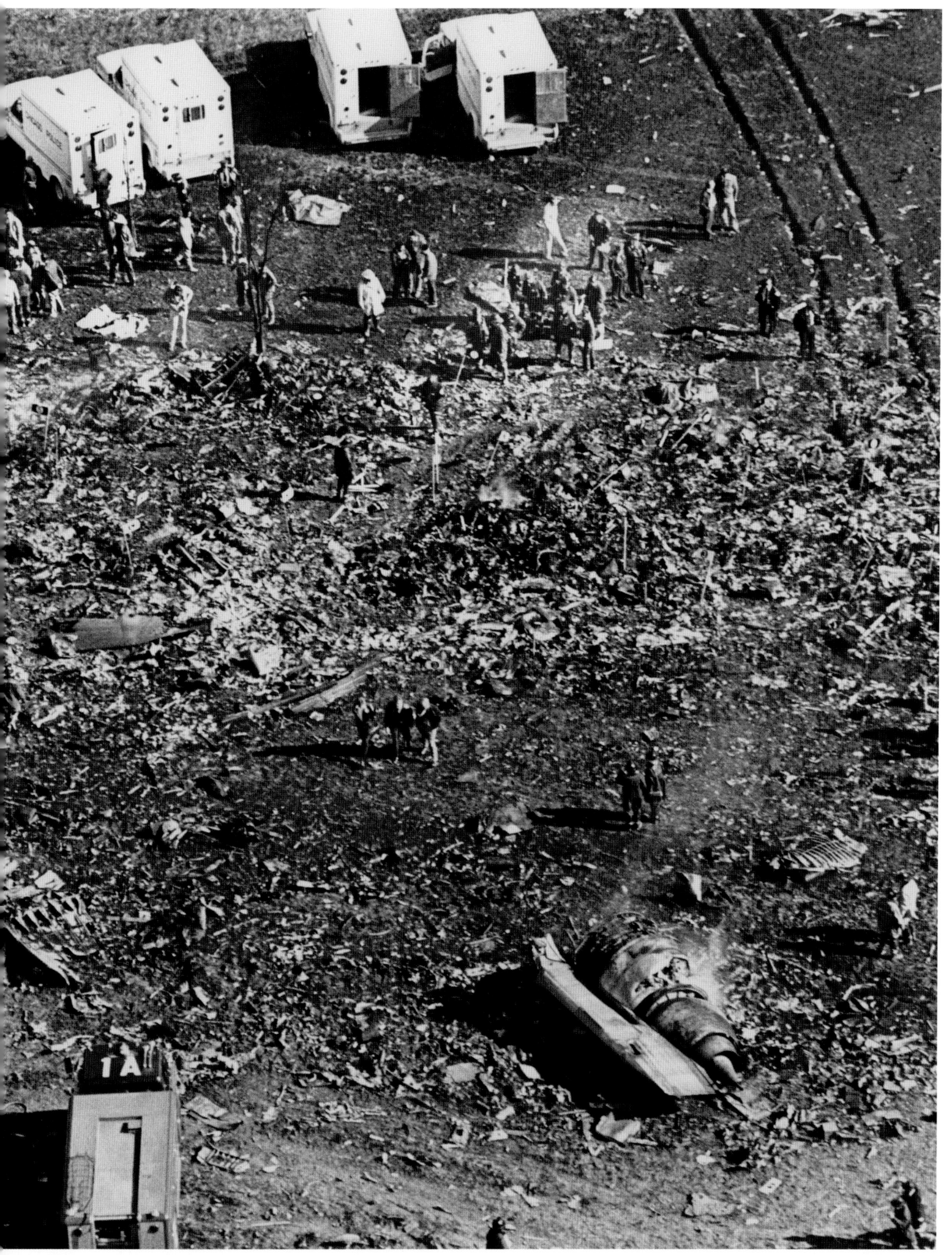
CRASH SITE OF AMERICAN AIRLINES FLIGHT 191. AT THE TIME, IT WAS THE DEADLIEST AVIATION ACCIDENT IN US HISTORY. MAY 25, 1979/KEVIN HORAN

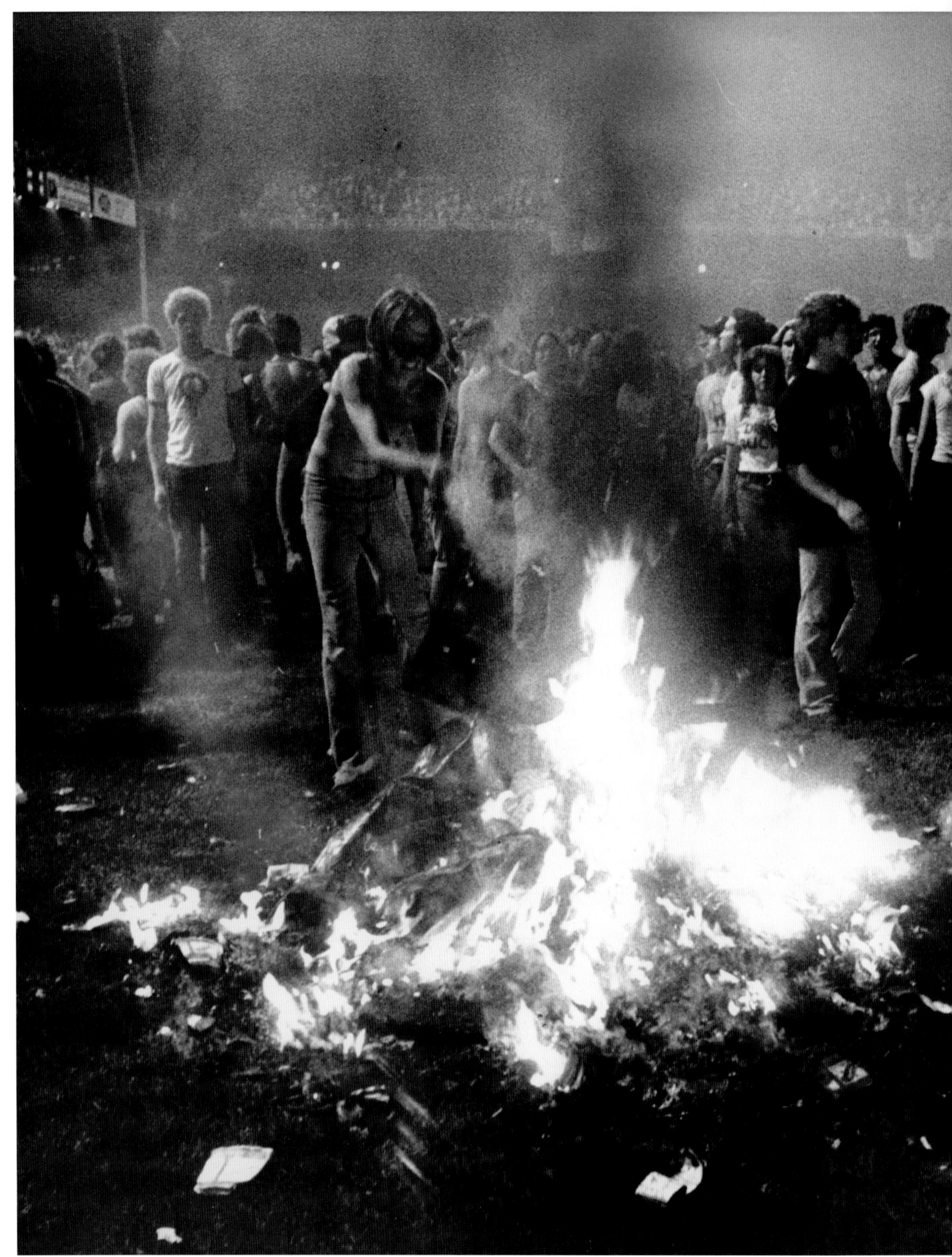
CROWDS SET REJECTED RECORDS ON FIRE AT COMISKEY PARK ON DISCO DEMOLITION NIGHT. JULY 12, 1979/JACK LENAHAN

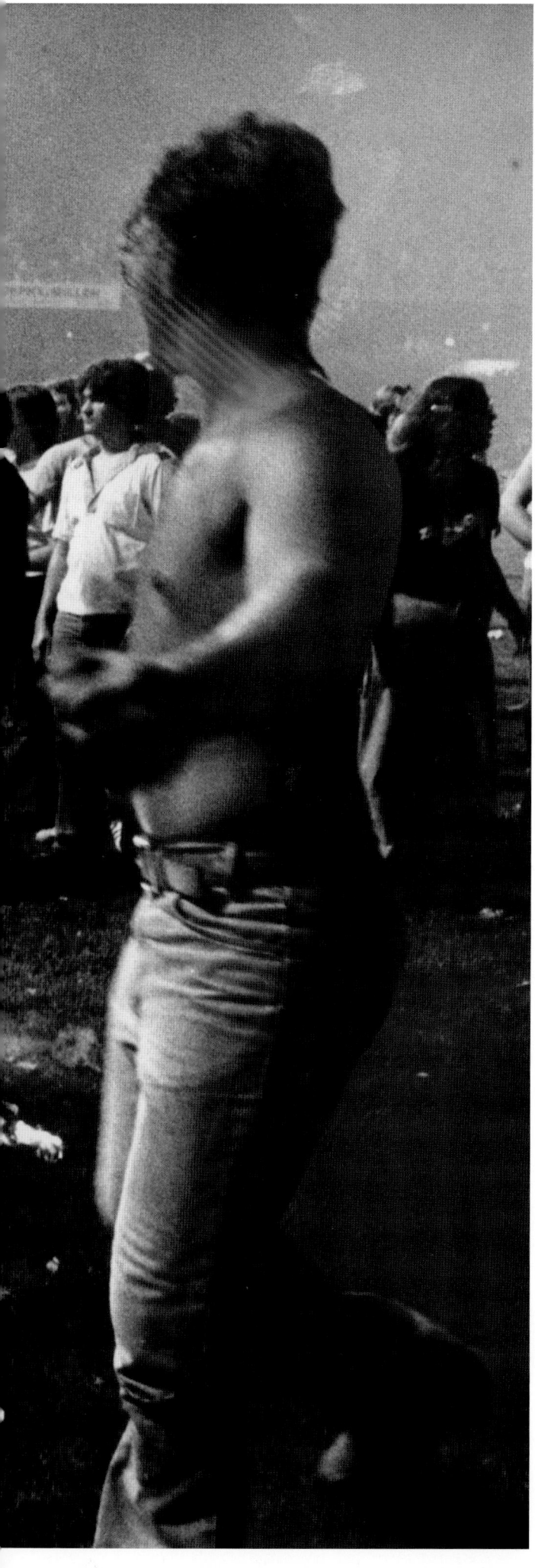

DO YA' THINK I'M SEXY?

The ill-fated Disco Demolition promotion never would have caught fire at Wrigley Field. Originally constructed as "Teen Night" at Comiskey Park by WLUP personality Steve Dahl and Mike Veeck, son of White Sox owner Bill Veeck, the event was rooted in the cultural divide between Chicago's South Side and its North Side—a split that exists today.

WLUP-FM was a hard rock station that spoke to South Side muscle. Dahl and sidekick Garry Meier were irreverent guys who lampooned soft pop culture, radio guru Wally Phillips, the sequined outfits of the Bee Gees, and glam nightclubs. Poking at the establishment was catnip for their underdog listeners.

The Cubs? They were WXRT, Jack Brickhouse, and Old Style beer. I know because I was there. I was a Cubs fan who showed up at the Disco Demolition doubleheader because I love baseball. I had no issues with disco.

Bill Veeck spun his magic on the spirit of incongruity, and that was part of my baseball DNA. In his 1962 *Veeck as in Wreck* autobiography, Barnum Bill wrote that "all kids are tickled by the incongruous" as an explanation for sending a person with dwarfism up to bat for his St. Louis Browns.

I was a Cubs fan who incongruously should have been a White Sox fan. My father was a purchasing agent for Swift & Company, beginning his career as a gofer at the Union Stock Yards, a few blocks from Comiskey. He took me to my first major league game when I was ten: 1965. Sox-Yankees. In the right field upper deck, not far from where I took in Disco Demolition.

Yet I became a Cubs fan because of the star-crossed Cubs in the electric summer of 1969. The Cubs were on WGN-TV. The White Sox were on the then-obscure WFLD-TV.

And my family lived on the North Side. That's where the action was. The stock yards had closed in 1971. The White Sox neighborhood was struggling. The International Amphitheatre, at 42nd and Halsted, was on its last legs as a convention hub because conventions had moved north to McCormick Place. But in 1979, rock acts like Kiss, Rush, and Alice Cooper all played the forsaken Amphitheatre.

Even before nearly 50,000 footloose fans attended Disco Demolition, old Comiskey embraced a Wild West environment. I remember fans drinking from open bottles of Jack Daniel's and smoking endless packs of cigarettes. Wrigley was Frosty Malts and Coca-Cola. White Sox fans had tattoos before tattoos were cool. Cubs fans wore sunscreen.

Disco Demolition was an accident waiting to happen, just like the Great Chicago Fire, Jerry Springer, and Rod Stewart's "Do Ya' Think I'm Sexy," the record I happily sacrificed for Disco Demolition.

—*Dave Hoekstra was a Sun-Times staff writer between 1985 and 2014. In 2016, he co-authored* Disco Demolition: The Night Disco Died *with Steve Dahl.*

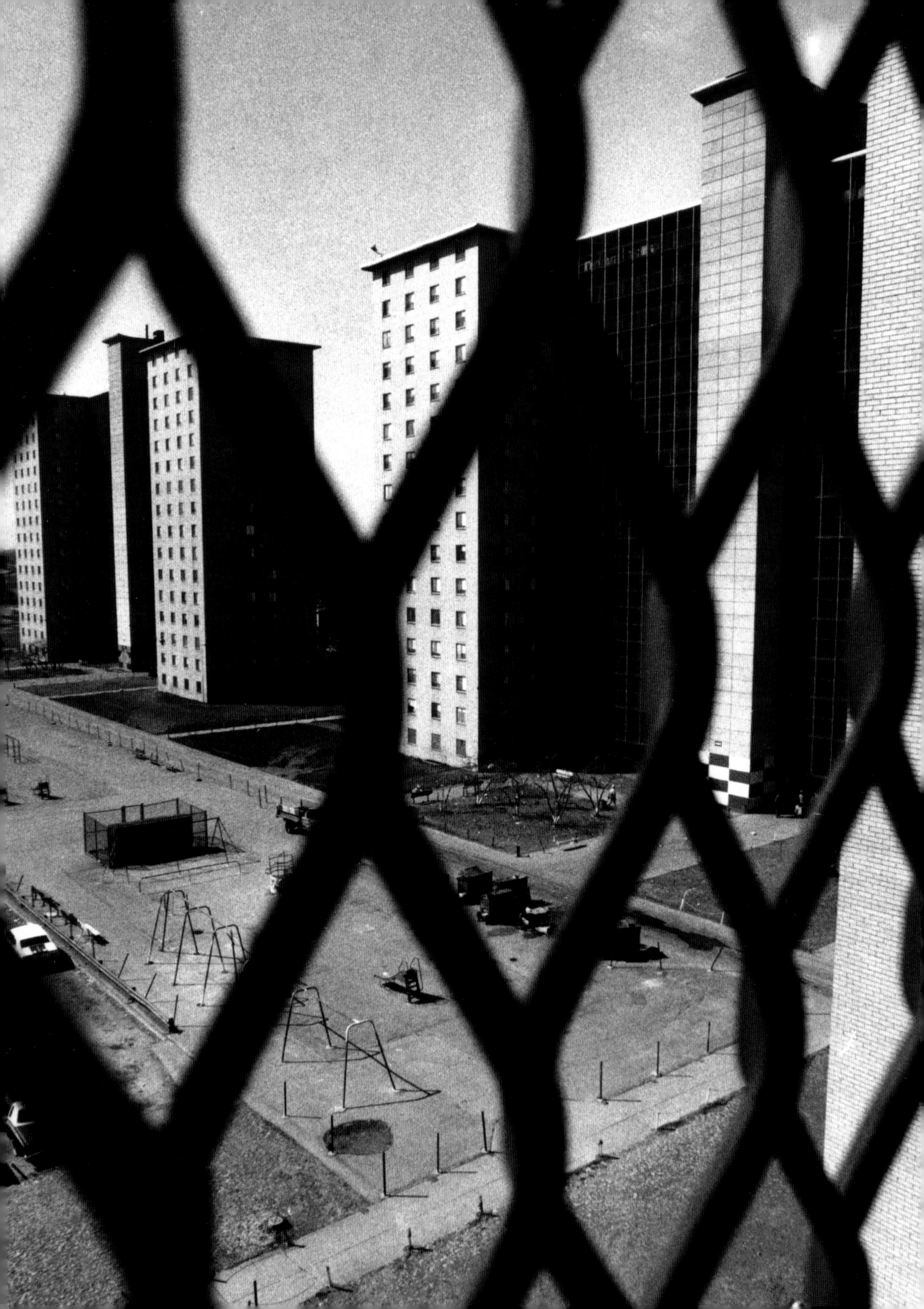

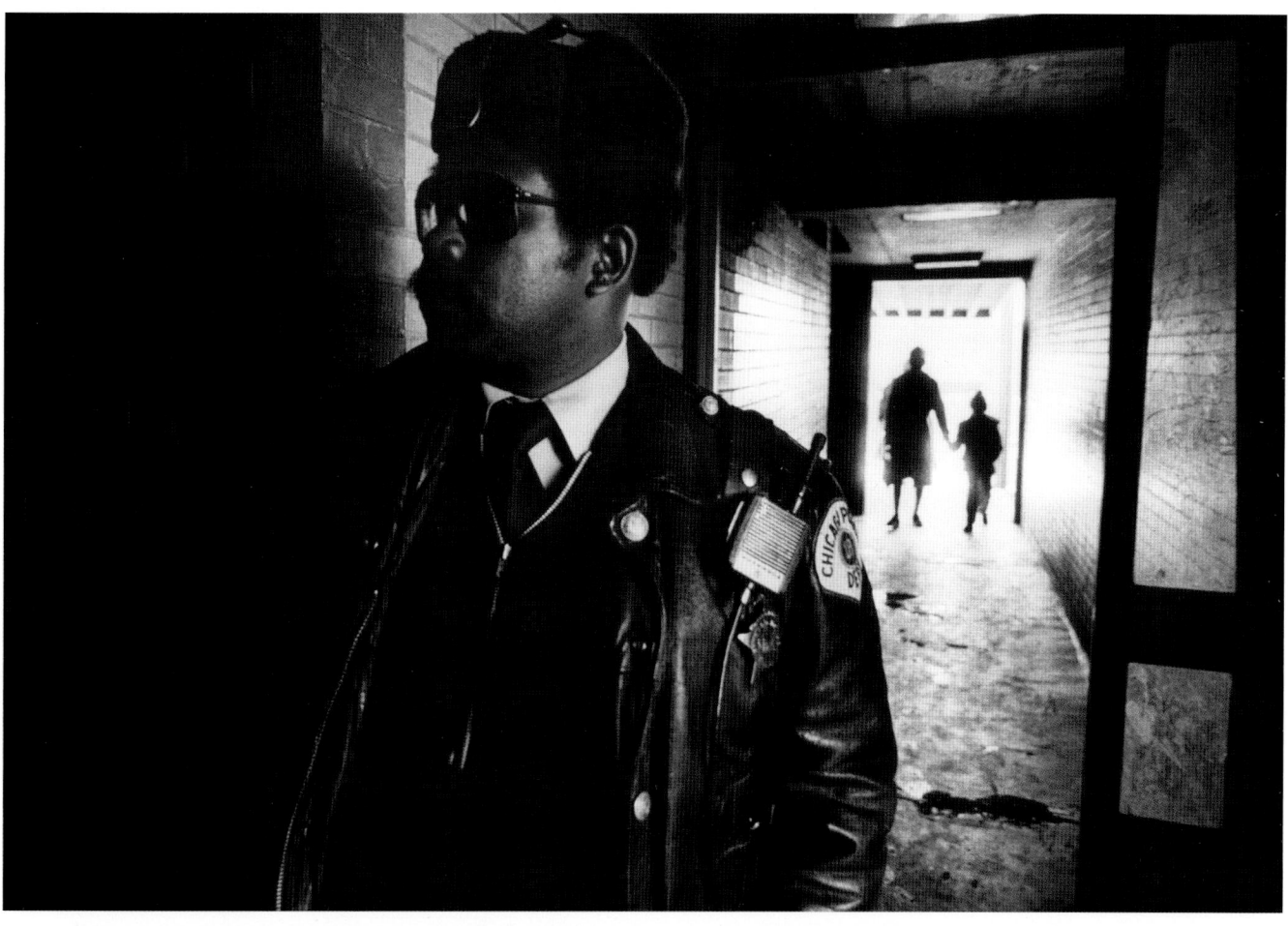

OUTSIDE AND INSIDE THE ROBERT TAYLOR HOMES, PART OF THE 1982 PULITZER PRIZE-WINNING PORTFOLIO. 1981/JOHN H. WHITE

HE SHOWED WHAT RESIDENTS SEE

Everybody who meets photographer John H. White has a story.

Reporters talk about how he guided them or watched out for them. His photojournalism students talk about how he inspired them.

Readers who admire him—and there are many—marvel at his remarkable work. In 1998, when a natural gas main exploded on a North Side street spewing a 15-story fireball, people ran as fast as they could to escape. White ran toward it—to take pictures.

I had never heard of White when I started at the Sun-Times. Already legendary, he was one of the first Black photojournalists on a Chicago metro paper. And he was the most honored photographer—winning hundreds of awards and the Pulitzer Prize for a portfolio that includes these scenes of Cabrini-Green.

I remember driving past the Robert Taylor Homes when I moved to Chicago—looking up at the units from the highway. White gave us a view from inside. He showed what residents see—the presence of police surveillance and debilitated, vacant spaces. His images, although stark, emphasize humanity. Somehow, he can see the soul of a person or the essence of a place. His photos help me see.

White is known for his God-talk, which is not all that common among journalists. Yet, those who view journalism as a calling might understand his insight, regardless of their faith.

I got to know White at the Sun-Times and at church. He had the unusual habit of showing up at the early Sunday service of my First United Methodist Church at the Chicago Temple even though he was not a member. He would appear at the Loop skyscraper before his morning shift, wearing his signature sports jacket and slacks, comfortable shoes, and—of course—a camera or two. He attended so often I did a feature story about him for the church newsletter.

I knew that spirituality is an essential part of his life. White is known for telling just about everybody to "Keep in Flight." He informed me during that interview that he adopted the saying after William J. Walls, a prominent bishop in the African Methodist Episcopal Zion Church, offered him encouragement in 1975 by saying, "And John, may God keep you in flight."

Walls died two weeks later. Said White: "'Keep in Flight' became God's signature for me."

And that is *my* John H. White story.
—*Lisa D. Lenoir worked as a reporter and editor on the Sun-Times from 1997 to 2007.*

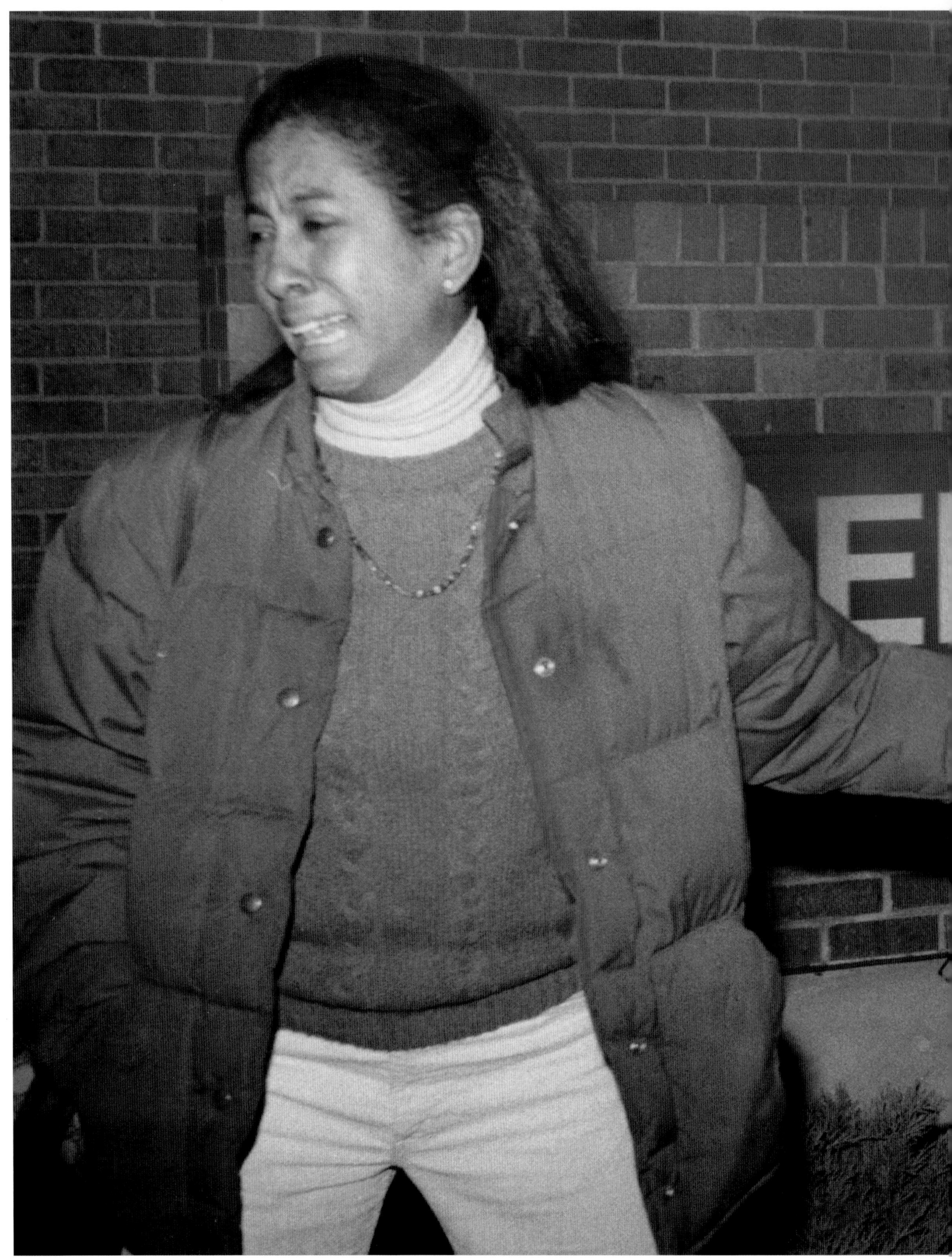

BEN WILSON'S FRIENDS OUTSIDE THE SAINT BERNARD HOSPITAL EMERGENCY ROOM. NOVEMBER 20, 1984/JOHN H. WHITE

FOR ANYBODY WHO KNEW BENJI

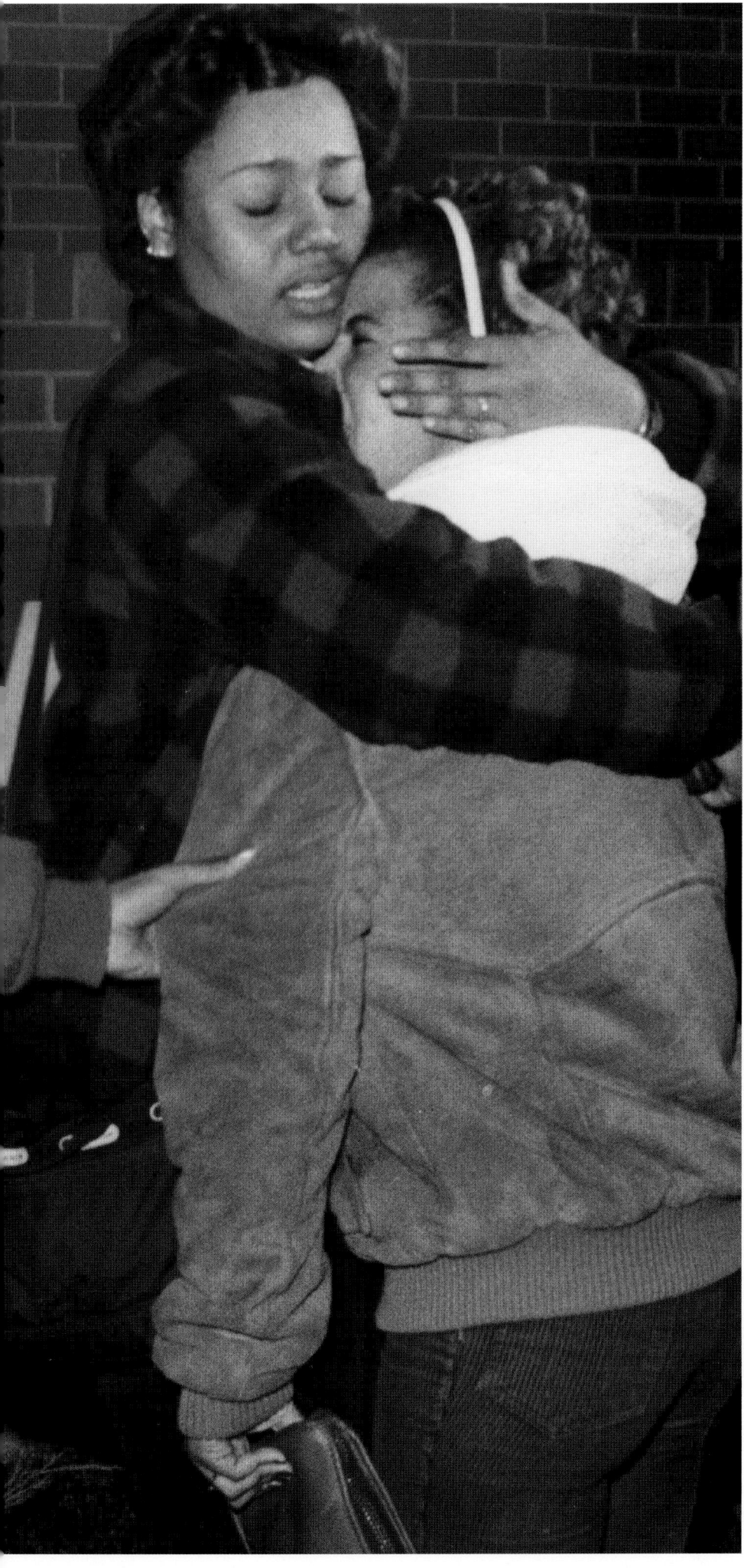

People still walk down the 81st block of South Vincennes Avenue and stare. Cars slow up when they get to 8139 and curious eyes peer out at the School Store. Sometimes the passengers blink, sometimes they dab their eyes with tissue.

It's been nearly two weeks since Ben Wilson was shot and killed in front of the School Store. But Vincennes Avenue still seems to be the most desolate, lonely place in the world, especially for anybody who knew Benji.

Lots of seventeen-year-olds get shot and killed in the streets of Chicago, thirteen this year alone. Chances are nobody even remembers their names. But they remember Ben Wilson, who was 6 feet 8 and called the best high school basketball player in the nation.

This cold, hard city probably hasn't mourned so much since Mayor Richard J. Daley died nine years ago.

The neighborhood where Ben Wilson went to school has always been a pretty quiet place. It's a middle-class area with no history of tragedy. Boys fight, yes. But shoot each other, no. I didn't know Benji—he lived in an adjacent neighborhood. But I do know some of the kids he hung out with, and they say he didn't belong to any of the gangs that have turned the fringe areas of my old neighborhood into an all-out battleground.

The kids at Simeon aren't gangsters. Al Scott, the football coach, said his program sends more players to college (and has more graduates) than any other high school in the city. Simeon has rules that no student can wear any gang insignias in its halls. Students with tattoos have been taken to hospitals to have them removed.

From all indications, the person charged with killing Wilson didn't even know he was a basketball player.

But those who did know Wilson marveled at his potential.

—Excerpt from Michael Wilbon's Washington Post column, December 3, 1984. He is now a host on ESPN.

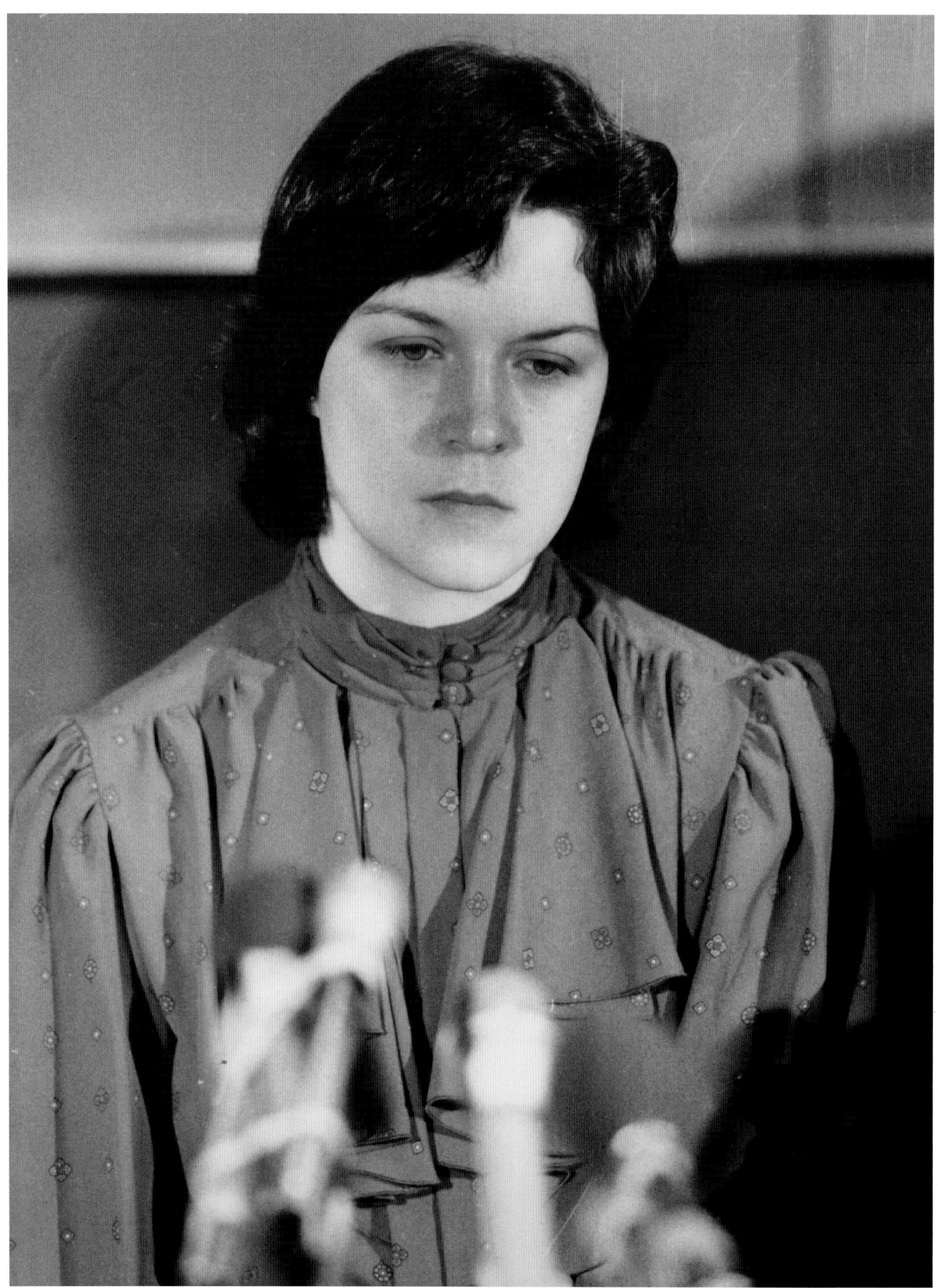

"I'D LIKE THE COURT TO TRY ME NOW [ON PERJURY]," SAID CATHLEEN CROWELL WEBB, WHO HAD ACCUSED GARY DOTSON. APRIL 12, 1985/AL PODGROSKI

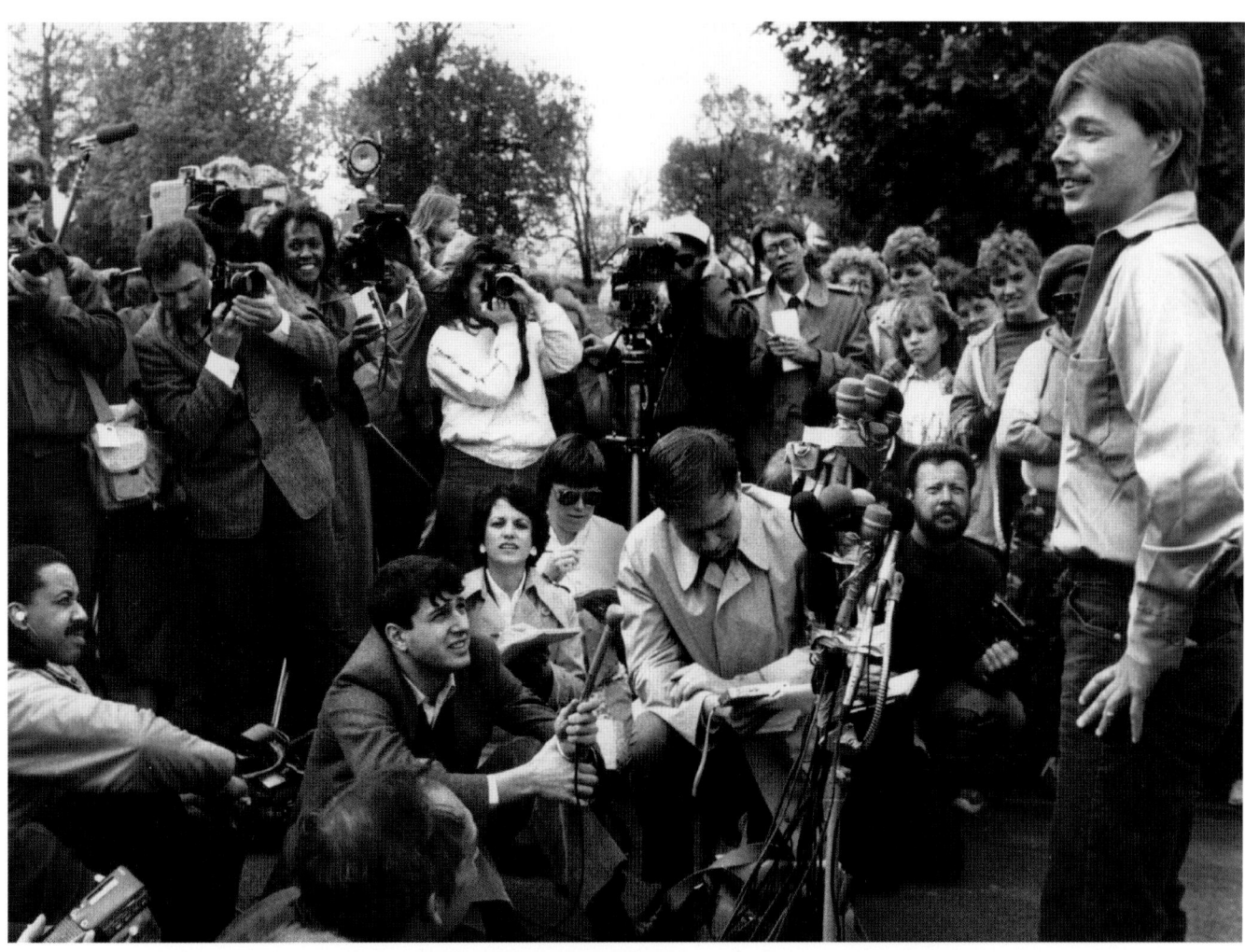

DOTSON MEETS REPORTERS FOLLOWING HIS RELEASE FROM DIXON CORRECTIONAL CENTER. MAY 1, 1985/JIM KLEPITSCH

A QUESTION OF CREDIBILTY

In March 1985, I received a phone call from a woman named Barbara Dotson, who asked me to represent her son. Gary Dotson had been convicted six years earlier of kidnapping and raping a woman who now admitted she had made up the charges. Dotson, who was 27 when we met, had been convicted by a jury and sentenced to serve two consecutive prison terms of 25 to 50 years.

I took the case as a favor to Barbara Dotson's boss, a friend. Within minutes of our talk, reporters started calling me. To understand the case, I reviewed the original transcript and spoke to Dotson's first attorney. I met Gary Dotson, who seemed believable, and met Cathleen Crowell Webb, the accuser who was clearly remorseful. The case, which I took pro bono, filled me with anxiety because there was no roadmap. I had not practiced criminal law in years.

There had been only two prosecution witnesses at the 1979 trial. One was Webb. The other was a state crime lab specialist, who gave false forensic testimony and turned out to be dishonest about his credentials.

Because both witnesses lacked credibility, I thought we had proved our case. But Governor James R. Thompson, acting as chair of the Illinois Prisoner Review Board for the first time, announced that he agreed with the original verdict. Thompson commuted Dotson's sentence—out of mercy, he said—to time served. But this left Dotson with a felony conviction that made him unemployable. As my representation of Dotson came to an end, I felt that I had failed him even though he was released from prison.

We have 2.5 million people in custody. If you think the criminal justice system is right 99 percent of the time, then 25,000 people in jail are innocent.

Dotson's conviction was vacated several years later based on DNA evidence.

He was the first person in America to be exonerated through genetic testing. Worldwide news coverage awakened law schools and legal clinics to investigate cases of possible wrongful convictions. As a result, lives have been saved and years of imprisonment have been avoided.

So maybe Gary Dotson won after all.
—*Warren Lupel served as Gary Dotson's attorney until Dotson was freed from custody.*

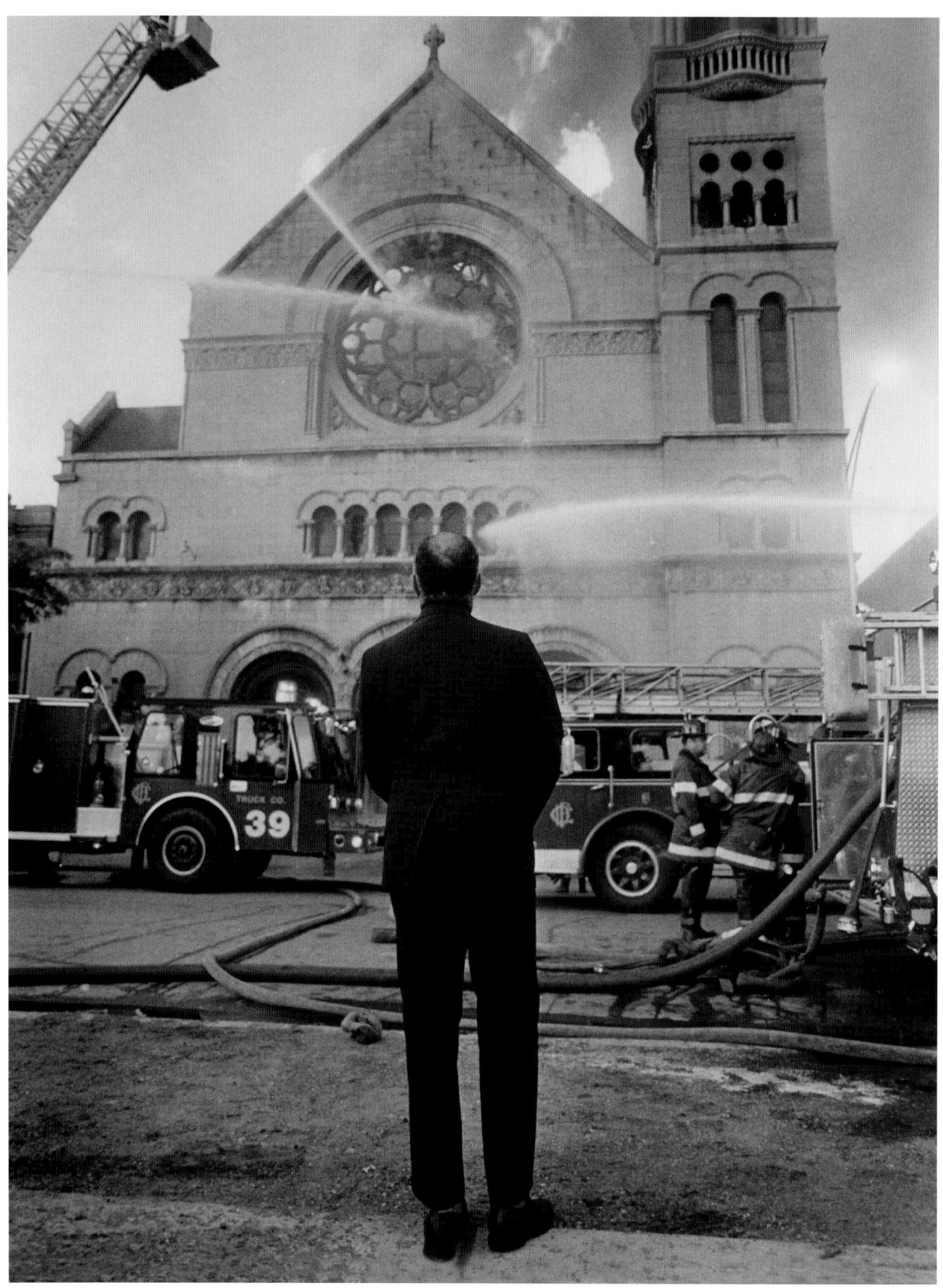
FATHER GEORGE CLEMENTS WATCHES AS HOLY ANGELS CHURCH AT 607 EAST OAKWOOD IS DESTROYED BY FIRE. JUNE 9, 1986/KATHLEEN REEVE

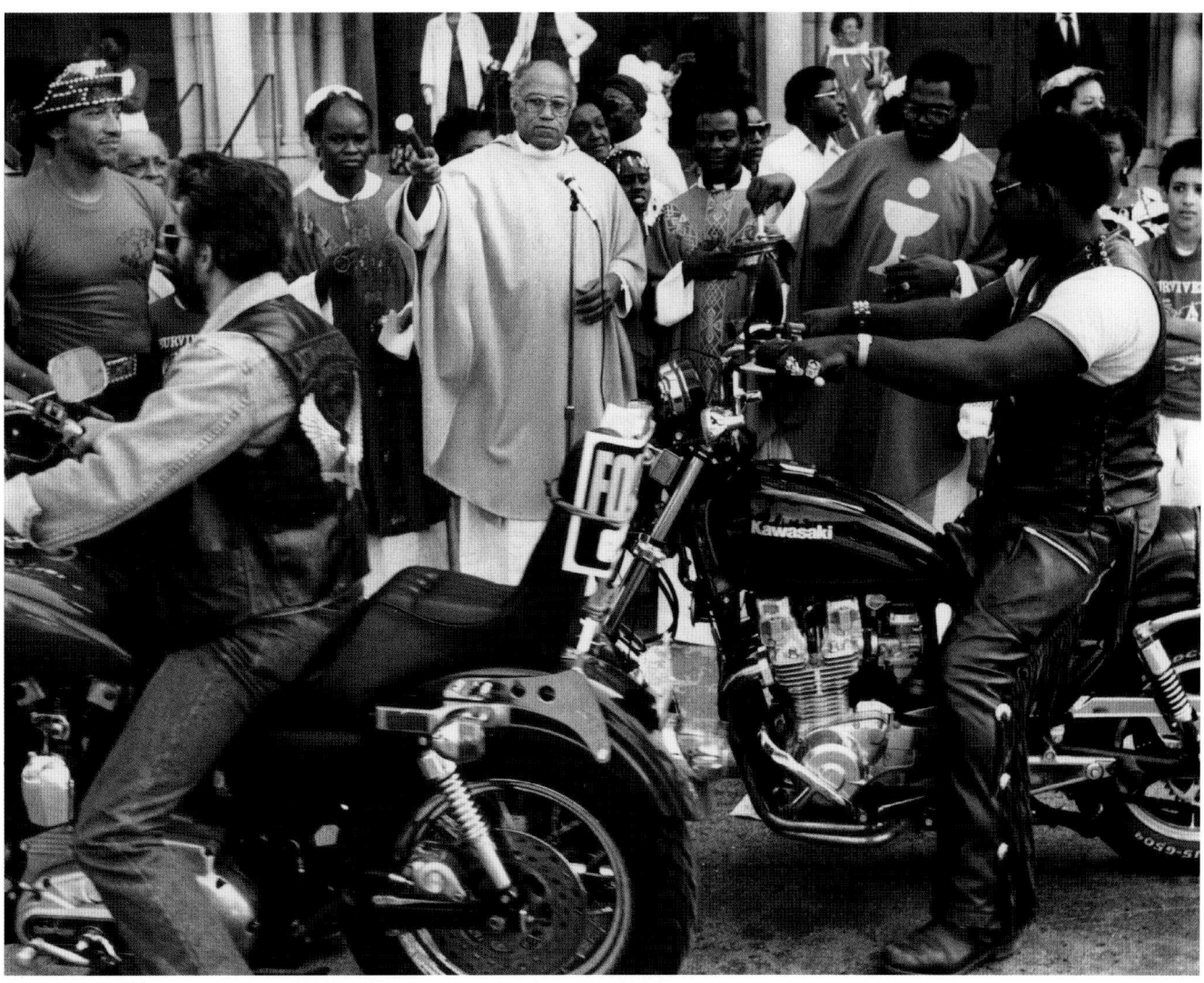
FATHER CLEMENTS BLESSES MOTORCYCLE RIDERS WHO HELPED RAISE MONEY TO BUILD THE NEW CHURCH. AUGUST 24, 1986/AL PODGORSKI

A MAN FOR ALL SEASONS

Father George Clements was a groundbreaker. In 1980, he started a program called One Church One Child, which encouraged Black churches to find and support parishioners to adopt Black children. The next year he became the first Catholic priest to adopt a child and later adopted three other boys.

I photographed Father Clements three or four times. I had a special interest in him because I was considering adopting children, too. I talked to him about the possibility of doing a picture story about the adoptions. He met with me but didn't want to play it up. He was very humble. He didn't consider what he was doing to be out of the ordinary.

These two photographs, one by a colleague and one by myself, were taken during Father Clements' most challenging year—1986, when he watched his church burn. "No one can replace a human being," he said. "Buildings can be replaced."

Contributions to rebuild began that very day. I photographed a motorcycle rally two months later that raised more than $1,000. The new Holy Angels Church opened in 1991. Two weeks later, Father Clements stepped down, his work at the parish complete. Being Catholic was always a part of my life. I grew up in the Bucktown neighborhood, around Ashland and Paulina. In those days, Catholic schools made mass attendance mandatory, and I still have many good memories of those early years. I saw the church—especially institutions like Catholic Charities—as a powerful force in the city.

I remember when Harold Washington passed away in November 1987. City Hall was open around the clock as his body lay in state. I figured if I arrived in the middle of the night, I might get a picture of the cleaning crew near his casket. Instead, I found a long line of people waiting to pay their respects (pages 136–137). At the head of Washington's casket was a curtained area with a ladder. I climbed it and used a very long exposure to show the flow of the somber crowds. It was like a river of people.
—Al Podgorski worked as a photographer for the Sun-Times from 1983 to 2015.

A MOMENT PACKED WITH HISTORY

It was actually a routine assignment: Harold Washington gets sworn into office. But I knew it was also packed with history: Chicago's first Black mayor.

I don't remember if we were put on risers in the Navy Pier auditorium or how far we were from the podium, but I do remember that I positioned myself so that I could see Washington and Judge Charles Freeman, who administered the oath, as well as Jane Byrne, the city's outgoing mayor. We had good access. I was right in front of them and used a short telephoto lens. I was concentrating on Washington; I was looking for expression. Would he be stoic? Or give you a grin?

But it was Jane Byrne's expression that made the photo. I'm not sure if I knew I got it when I shot the picture. But I was pleasantly surprised to see it when I looked through the negatives back at the office. Whenever you get an assignment like this, you are always looking for something a little different. A unique moment. That's what we photojournalists do everyday.

The Washington years were a very proud time for African Americans in this city. He was our guy. He fought for us. He represented us. I covered a lot of City Council meetings and saw Ed Vrdolyak and Edward Burke do everything they could to stop Washington in every way they could. They tried to make him look bad, to make it look like he couldn't do the job. And the "Vrdolyak 29" blocked just about everything that Washington brought forward.

But Harold stood up to them. Harold was Harold. He had charisma and a take-charge attitude. He was known all over the city and all over the country by one word: Harold.

I see many young people taking charge today. Whether they know it or not, they are following in his footsteps. They should be reading history books to see what he did. He was a voice. He fought for the little guy. He was the right person at the right time.
—*Photographer Keith Hale worked on the Daily News and Sun-Times from 1977 to 2011.*

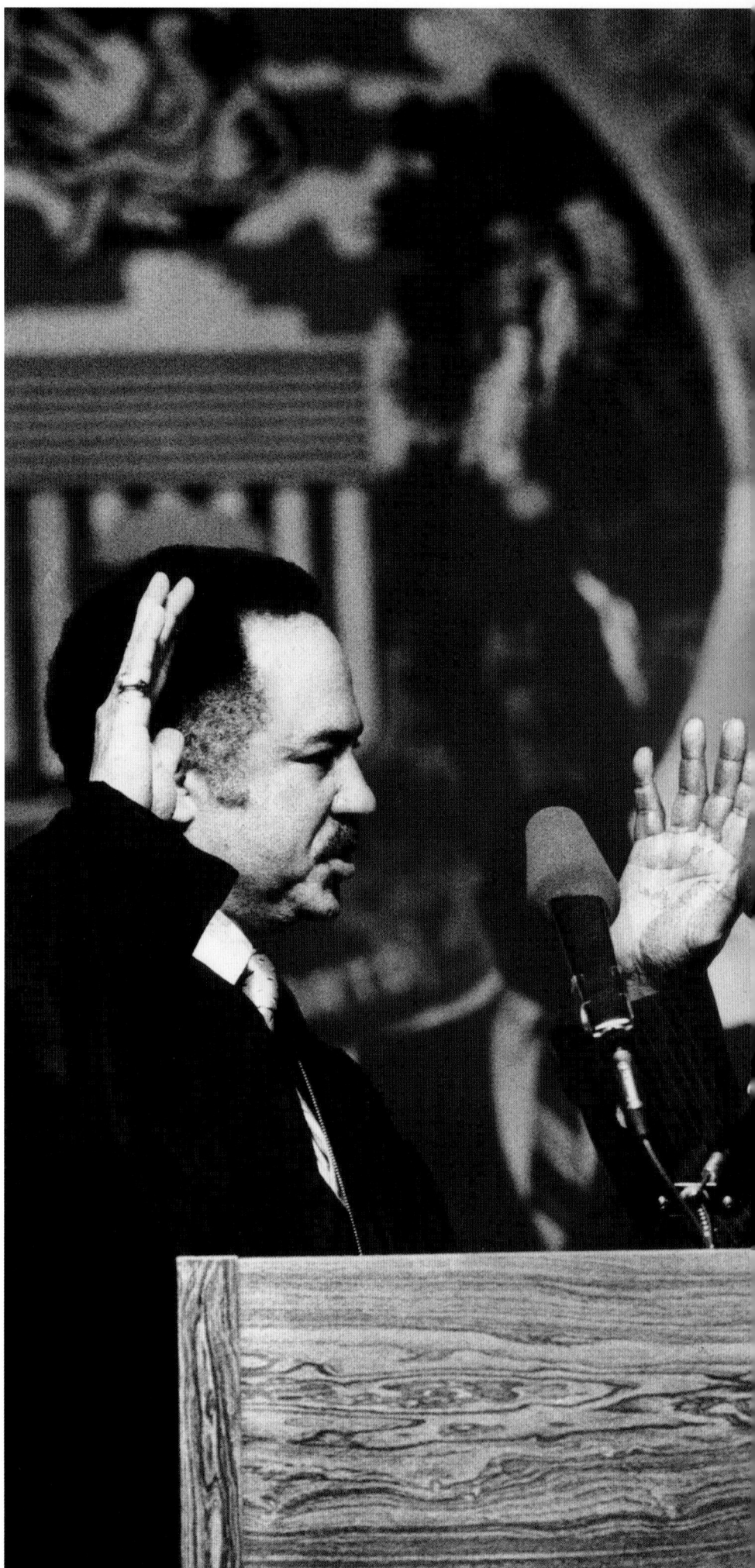

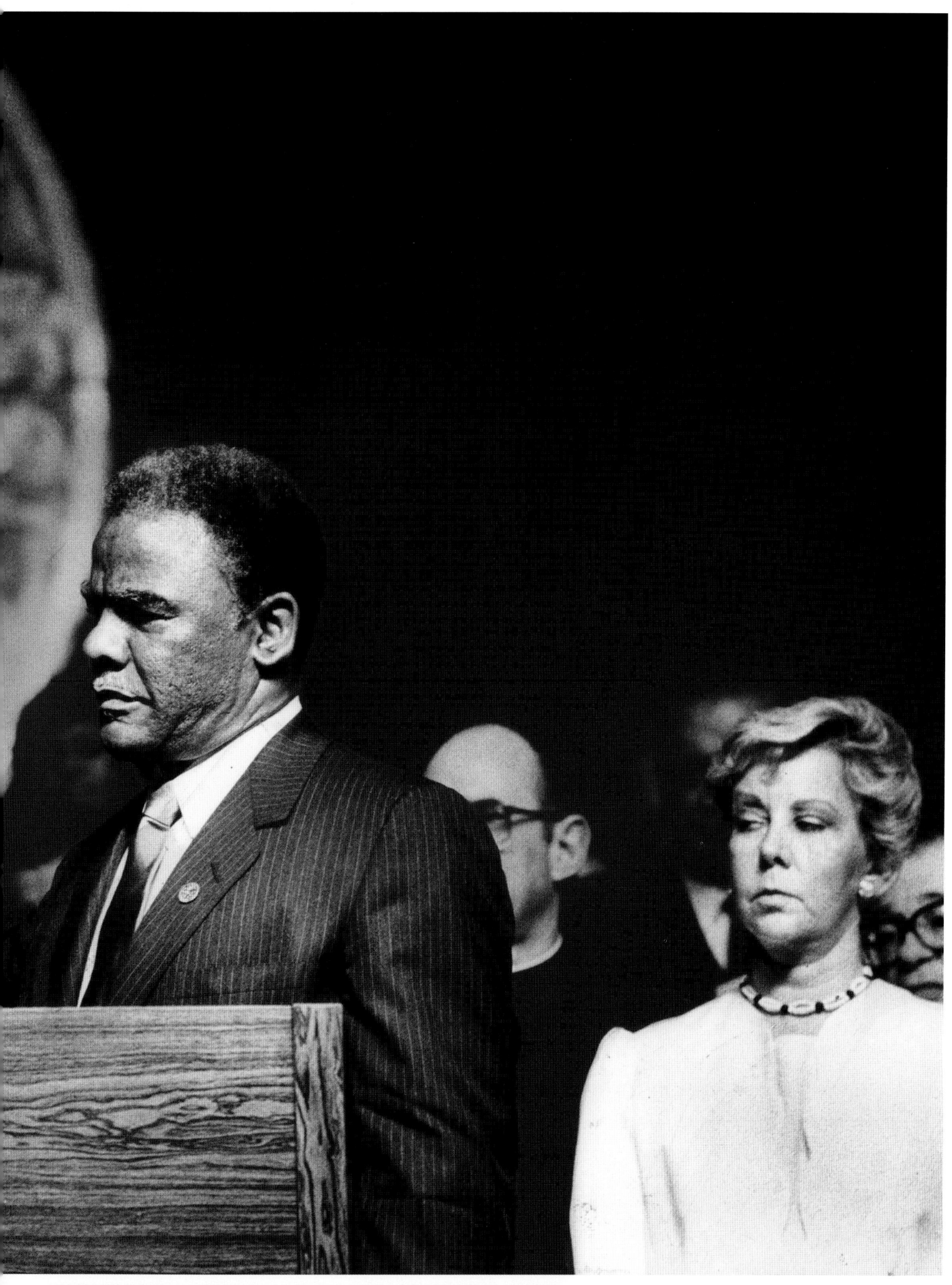

HAROLD WASHINGTON IS SWORN IN AS MAYOR BY JUDGE CHARLES FREEMAN AS MAYOR JANE BYRNE WATCHES AT NAVY PIER. APRIL 29, 1983/KEITH HALE

ALL-NIGHT VIGIL

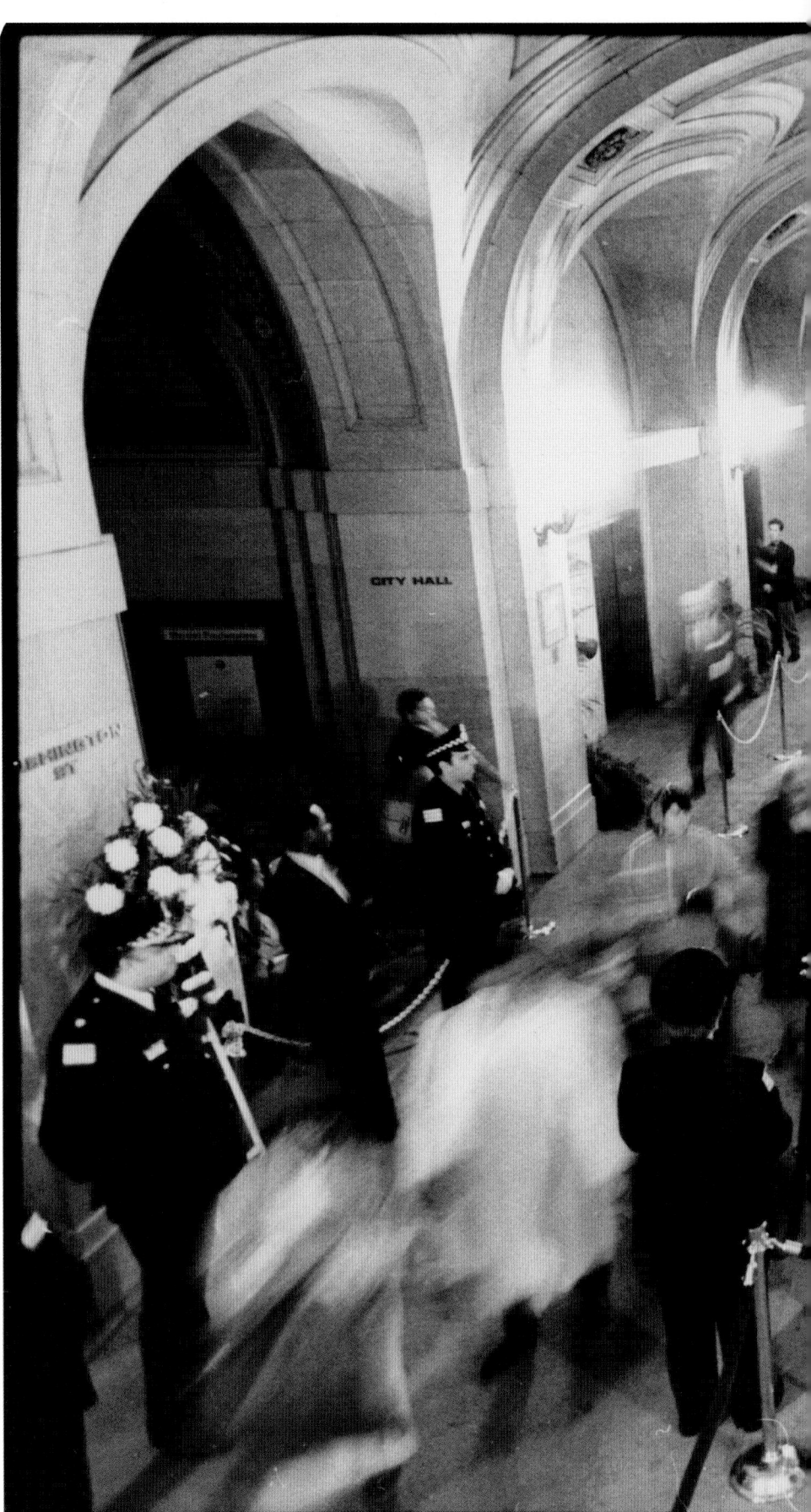

I grew up dreaming of racial justice and equity.

I grew up on Chicago's segregated South Side, where inequity was a fact of life, where the political establishment's racist and exclusionary policies always left behind people of color.

To Harold Washington, we mattered. His 1983 mayoral victory sparked a never-before-seen drive for fairness and truth.

As a young reporter, I covered Washington's historic mayoral campaign. Later, I was honored to serve as his deputy press secretary.

Washington's charisma and uncanny political instincts inspired and charged voiceless men and women. At campaign rallies, he would grin and shout: "You want Harold?" "Yes!" the crowd would roar. "You got him!" He fiercely believed that Chicago was richer and stronger when all could walk through the corridors of power.

At his inauguration and beyond Washington declared: "No one—but no one—in this city, no matter where they live or how they live, is free from the fairness of our administration. We'll find you—and be fair to you wherever you are!"

Imagine a politician saying that *now*, much less meaning it?

More than 150,000 new African Americans registered to vote in the 1983 primary election. Nearly all voted for Washington.

My father, Andrew N. Washington, was a mail carrier for the US Post Office, but believed the government would never work for him. Until that freezing February day in 1983 when—his mail route completed—he headed to the polling place to pull the lever "for Harold."

It was the first time he had voted in twenty years.

Harold Washington inspired a remarkable moment—the confluence of an extraordinary man, a unique time, and a political movement. He proved that politics could be a powerful force for change.

We got Harold. Chicago has never been the same.
—*Laura S. Washington is a columnist for the Sun-Times and political analyst for ABC 7-Chicago.*

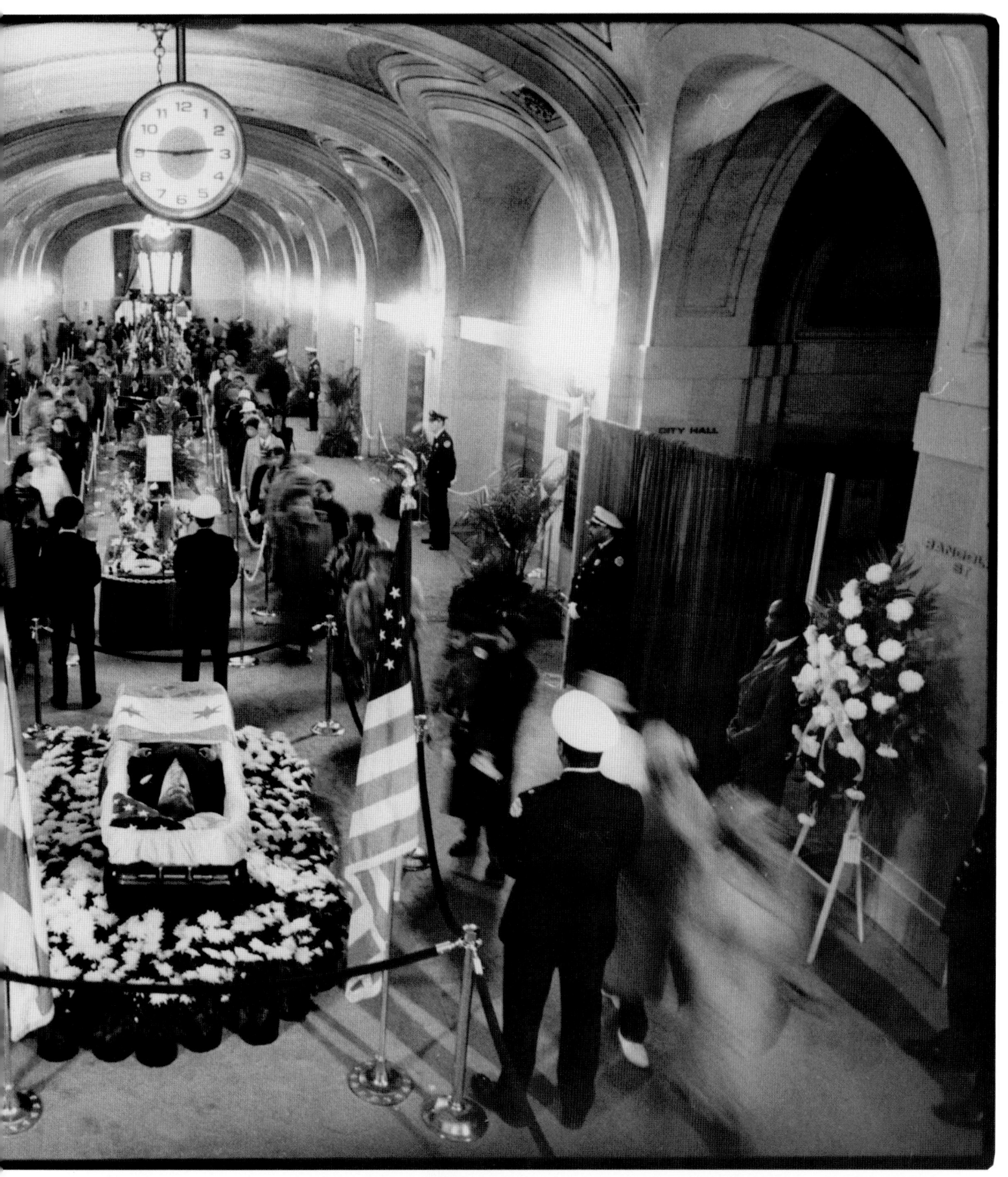

MOURNERS FILE INTO CITY HALL THROUGH THE NIGHT TO PAY RESPECTS TO MAYOR HAROLD WASHINGTON. NOVEMBER 29, 1987/AL PODGORSKI

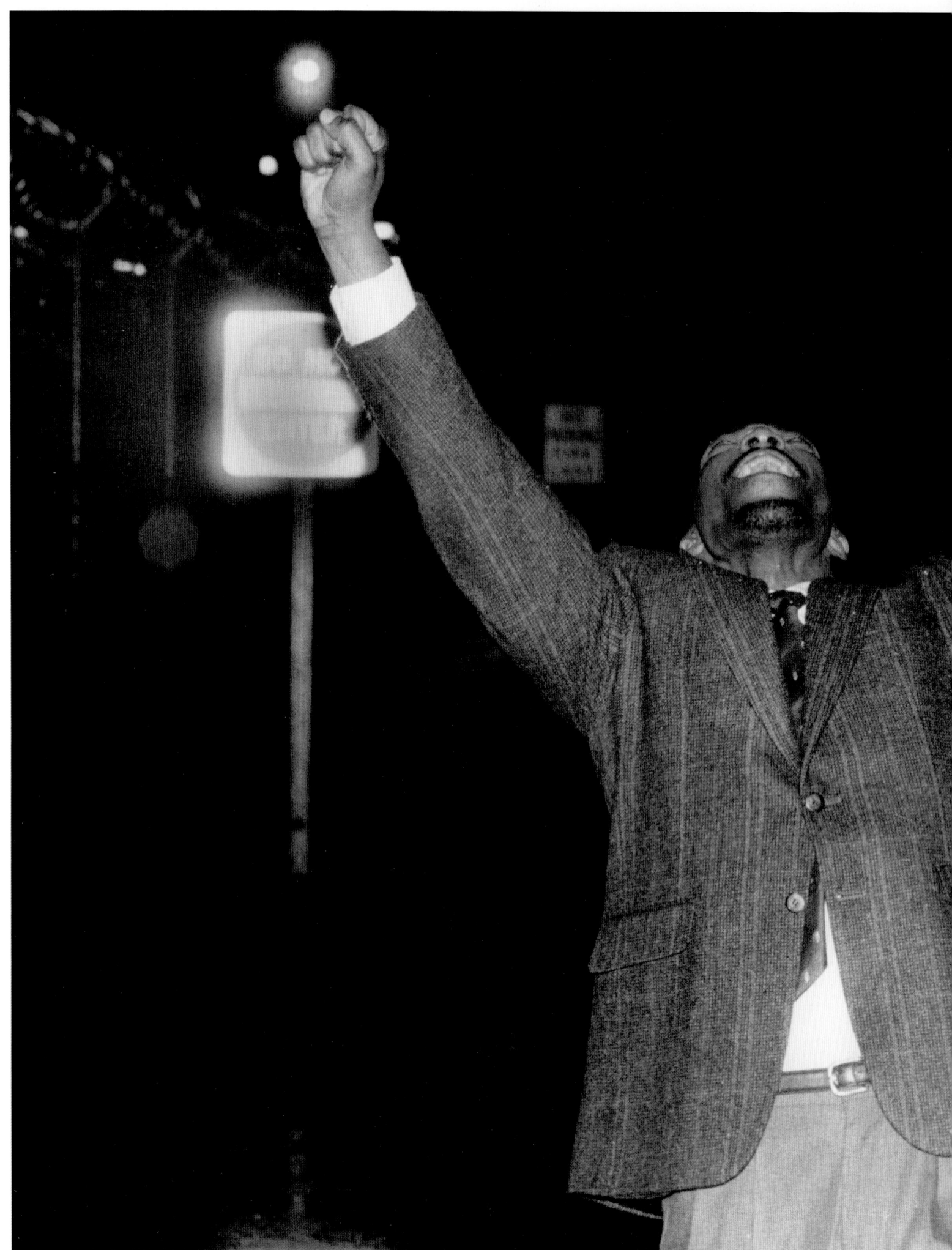

ROBERT BROWN LEAVES COOK COUNTY JAIL—ALONG WITH ELTON HOUSTON—AFTER SERVING FIVE YEARS IN PRISON. OCTOBER 30, 1989/BARRY JARVINEN

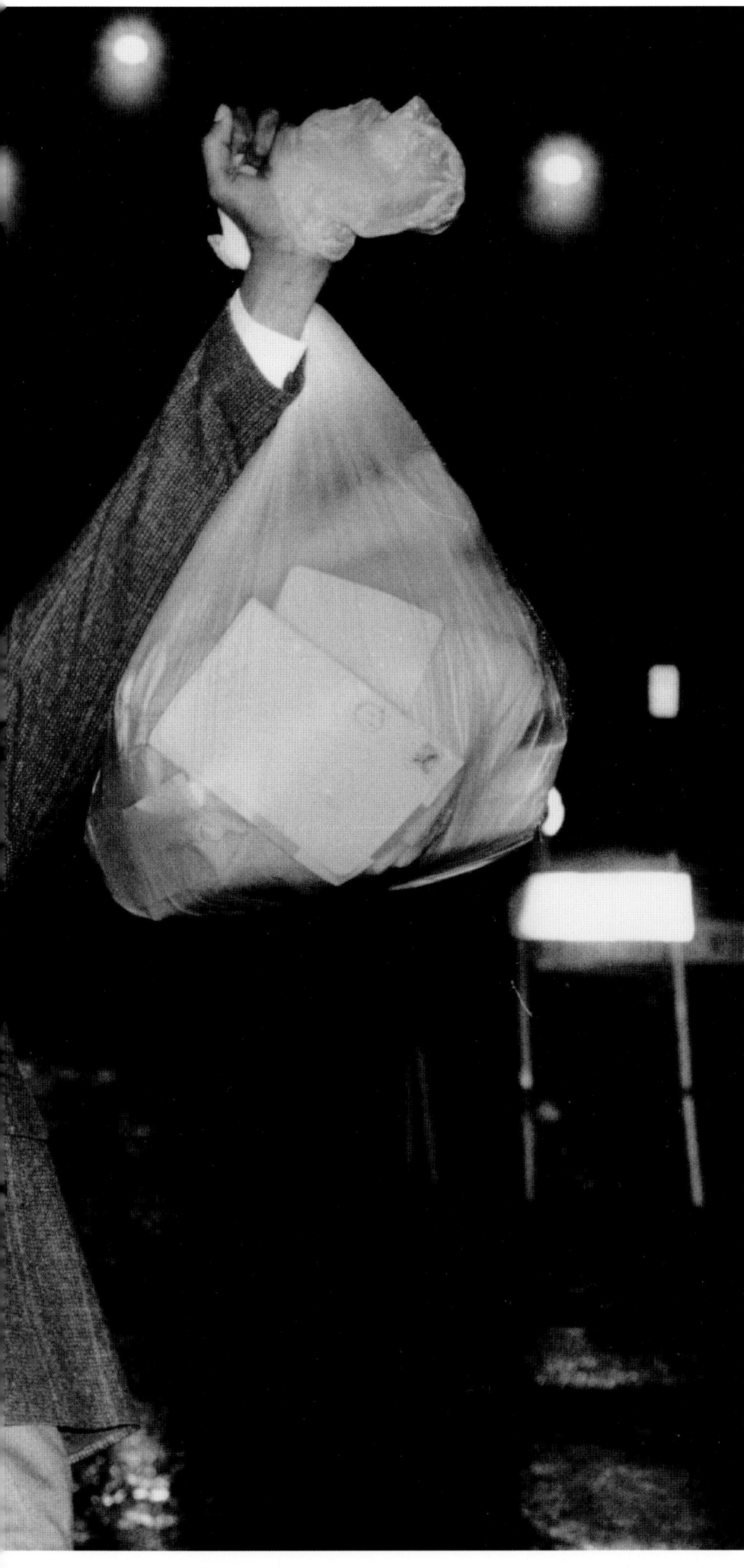

I SHARED THAT JOY

The sheer joy evident in this photo of Robert Brown leaving Cook County Jail on October 30, 1989, was obvious—especially to me. He was leaving after five years behind bars for a murder that prosecutors belatedly acknowledged he had not committed.

I shared Robert's joy because I was his codefendant, freed the same night. We were falsely convicted in 1984 of the gang-related murder of a young man named Ronnie Bell, who died in a hail of gunfire on the South Side the previous year.

Robert and I obviously knew all along that we were innocent. What we didn't know was that prosecutors had evidence of our innocence a year after we were convicted. They kept it secret. As a result, taxpayers paid $1.1 million to settle our civil claims in 1993. Robert wasn't around to enjoy the money. He was murdered in 1991. His share of the settlement went to his family.

We were in the vanguard of what's become known as "the innocence movement," which has spawned 67 university-based projects dedicated to identifying and rectifying false convictions.

Since our release in 1989, there have been 350 documented exonerations in Illinois and 2,780 nationally.

The exonerations have been the impetus for meaningful criminal justice reform. For one thing, police lineup procedures in Chicago have been changed to reduce erroneous eyewitness identifications, as happened in 28 percent of the exoneration cases, including ours.

While no one who's been exonerated would volunteer to become fodder for reform, there's solace in knowing that something positive came from our misfortune.

But, to my disappointment, the prosecutors who kept Robert and me behind bars for four years knowing that we were innocent were not held to account.
—*Elton Houston, who is disabled because of an injury he suffered in prison, lives in west suburban Forest Park.*

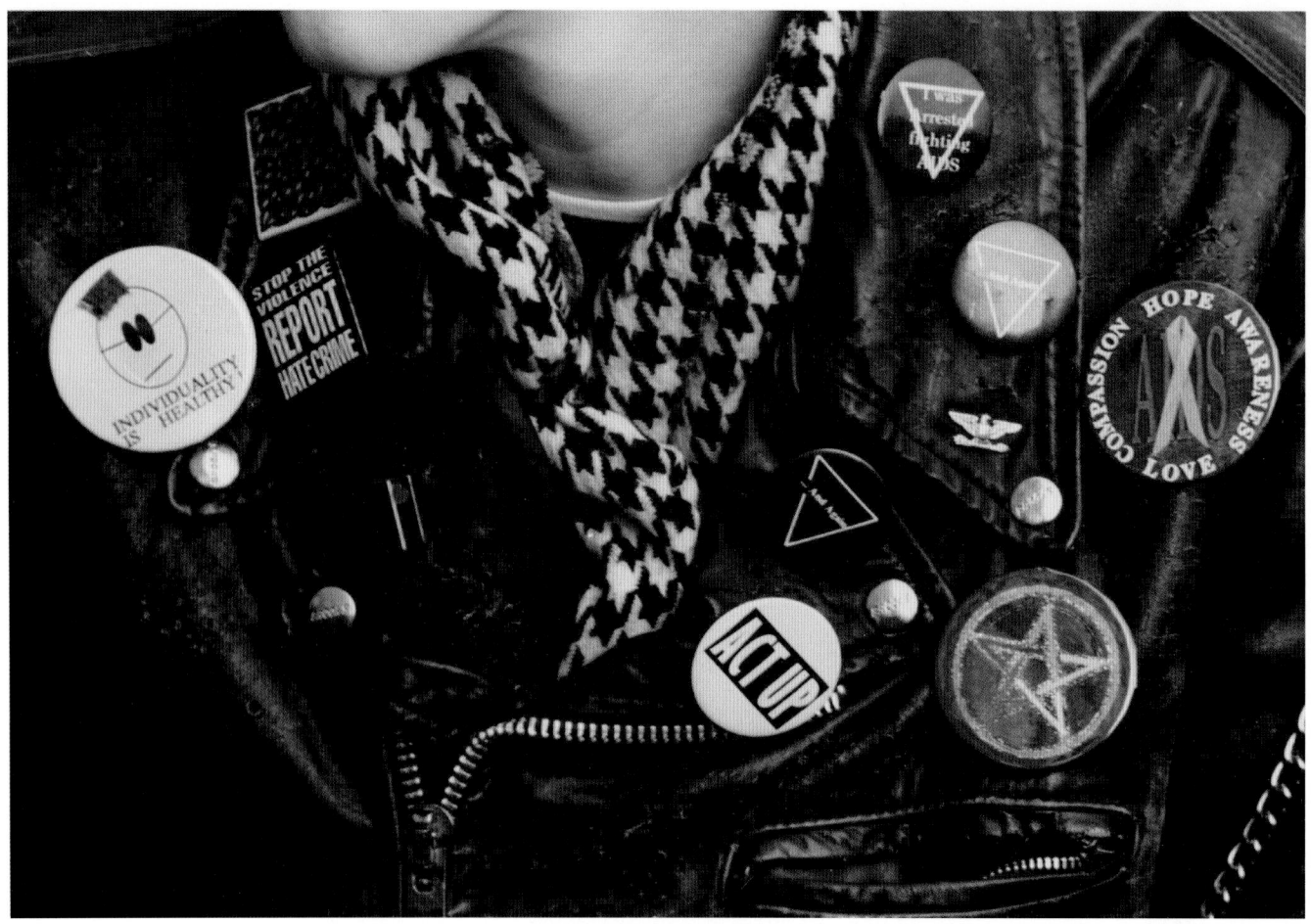

JACKET WORN AT ACT UP DEMONSTRATION. DECEMBER 4, 1993/ROBERT A. DAVIS

STREET ACTIVISM WAS SCREAM THERAPY

I attended my first ACT UP meeting out of sheer frustration.

It was 1989 or 1990. AIDS was decimating the queer community. The disease was holding us in this bubble of pain and fear. And we had already been there for years. No help was coming. The powers that be expected us to accept their lack of action—and ACT UP, the AIDS Coalition to Unleash Power, promised change.

AIDS revealed a diseased society. We had allies—and we had those who wanted us dead. The epidemic was a ripe time for attack, for saying HIV was deserved, for fanning the flames of homophobia, for price gouging, and for calling AIDS the will of God. The behavior of the Reagan administration, the Catholic Church, televangelism, insurance and pharmaceutical companies, and the so-called Moral Majority was abysmal.

Being good little queers had gotten us nowhere. Outrage was a big motivator. Street activism was scream therapy. I was purging as much as protesting. Shouting myself hoarse got rid of the anger, the fear, and the grief. For a while.

ACT UP Chicago was filled with people—like Danny Sotomayor, Ortez Alderson, and Ferd Eggan—who inspired me. Meetings could be volatile, but the group got results. ACT UP achieved things like getting additional hospital beds and lower drug costs. Our superpower was shaming politicians and businesses by spotlighting their greed and inhumanity.

Attending big demonstrations, like ACT UP's National AIDS Actions for Healthcare held in Chicago in April 1990, was the equivalent of being plugged into a socket. We came together with a focused purpose. You could feel the air pulsating. You felt the waves of energy. We were blood pulsing through an artery. We were this incredible force. We gave power to the protest. And the demo returned energy multiplied.

Looking back, what I saw in protests and in the mass volunteering and caregiving was the beauty of a community coming together to protect and care for its own. This was love in action.

So amid all the horror, there were these moments of profound tenderness and personal sacrifice. Seeing that courage and compassion in the face of such pain and loss was what made me fall in love with Chicago's LGBTQIA+ community. And that has only deepened over time.
—*Owen Keehnen is a queer writer and grassroots historian specializing in Chicago LGBTQIA+ history.*

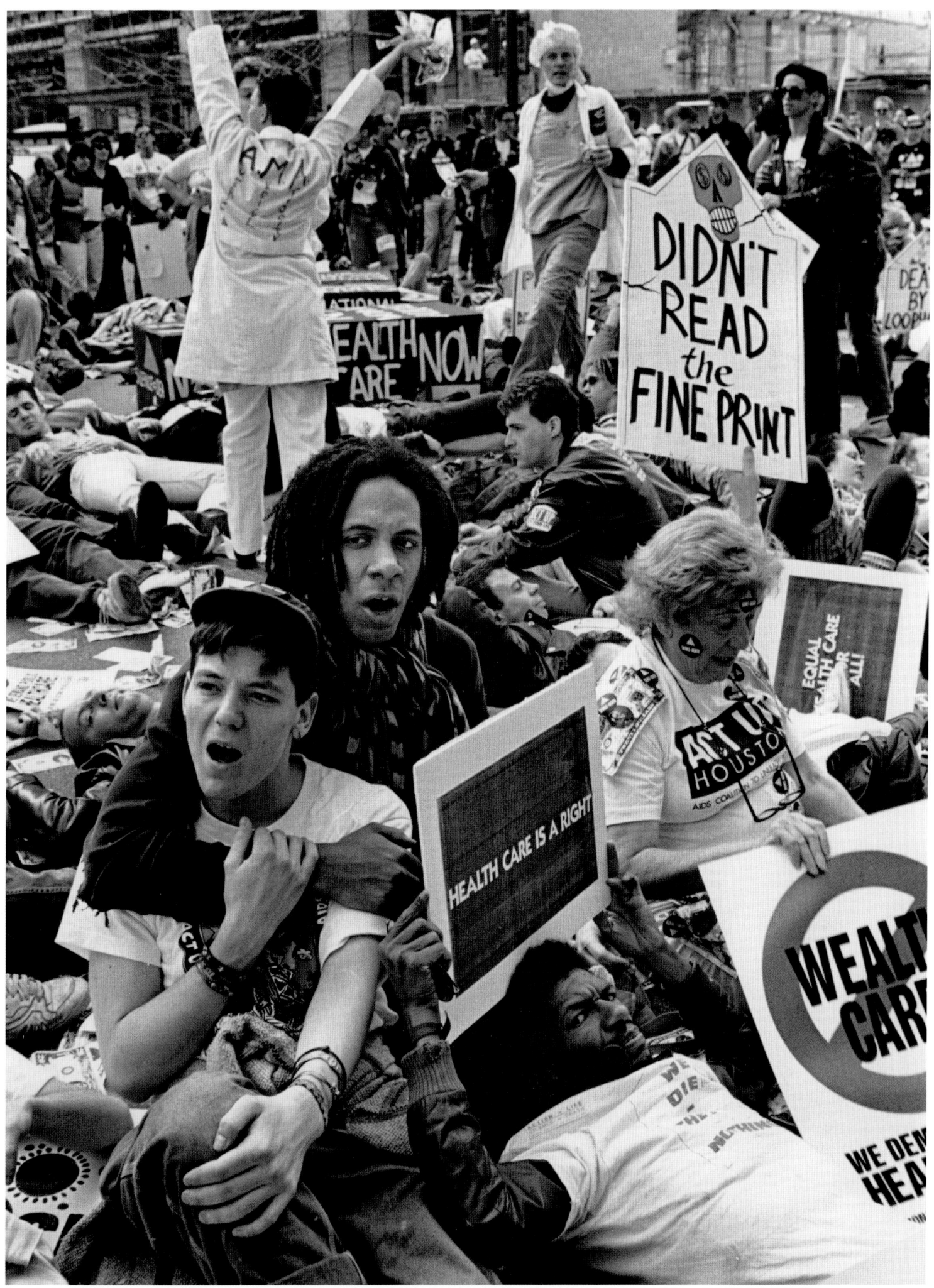

THE CITY'S LARGEST AIDS DEMONSTRATION. ABOUT 150 WERE ARRESTED. APRIL 23, 1990/AL PODGORSKI

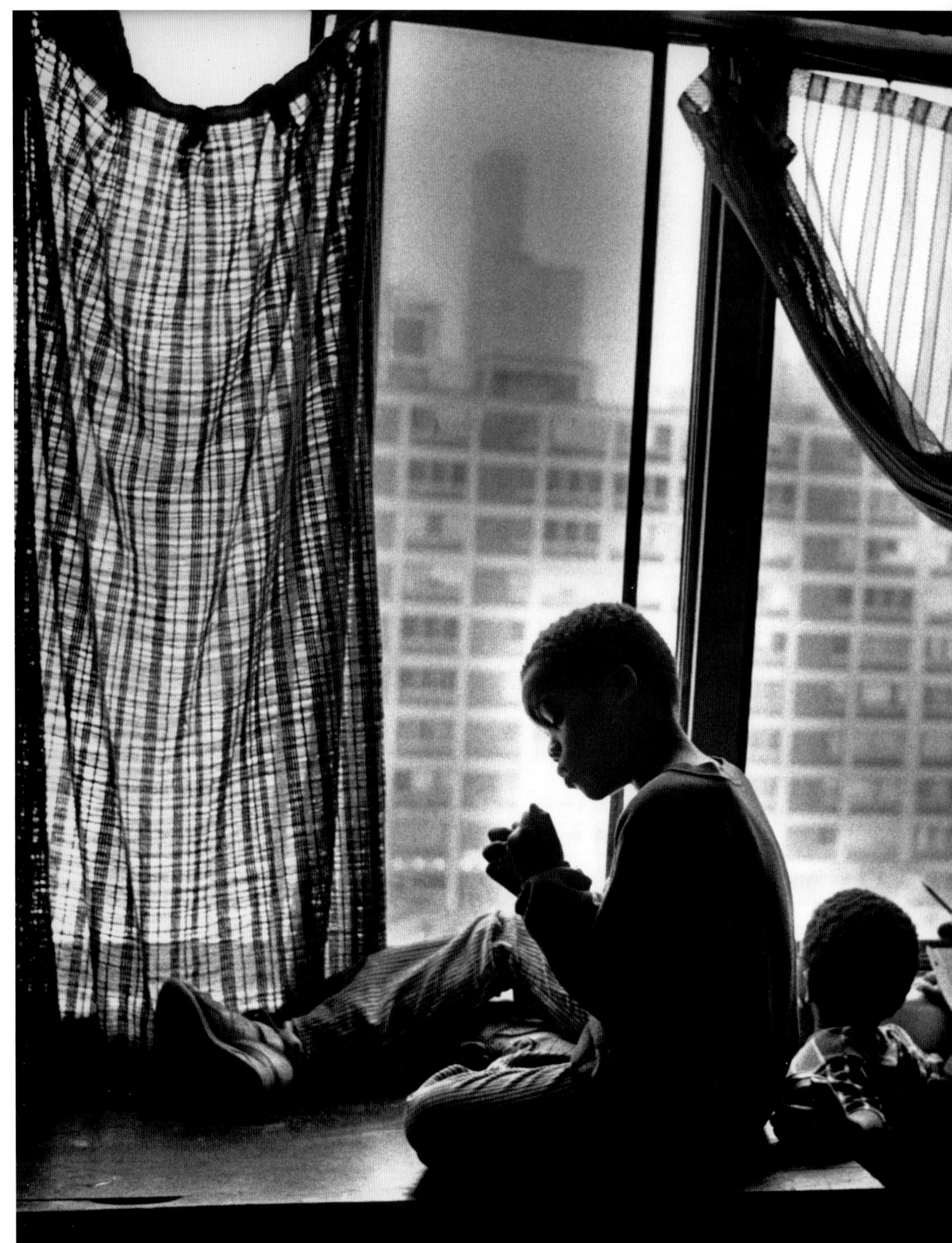
FRIENDS OF DANTRELL DAVIS IN THEIR NINTH-FLOOR CABRINI-GREEN APARTMENT. DECEMBER 1992/JOHN H. WHITE

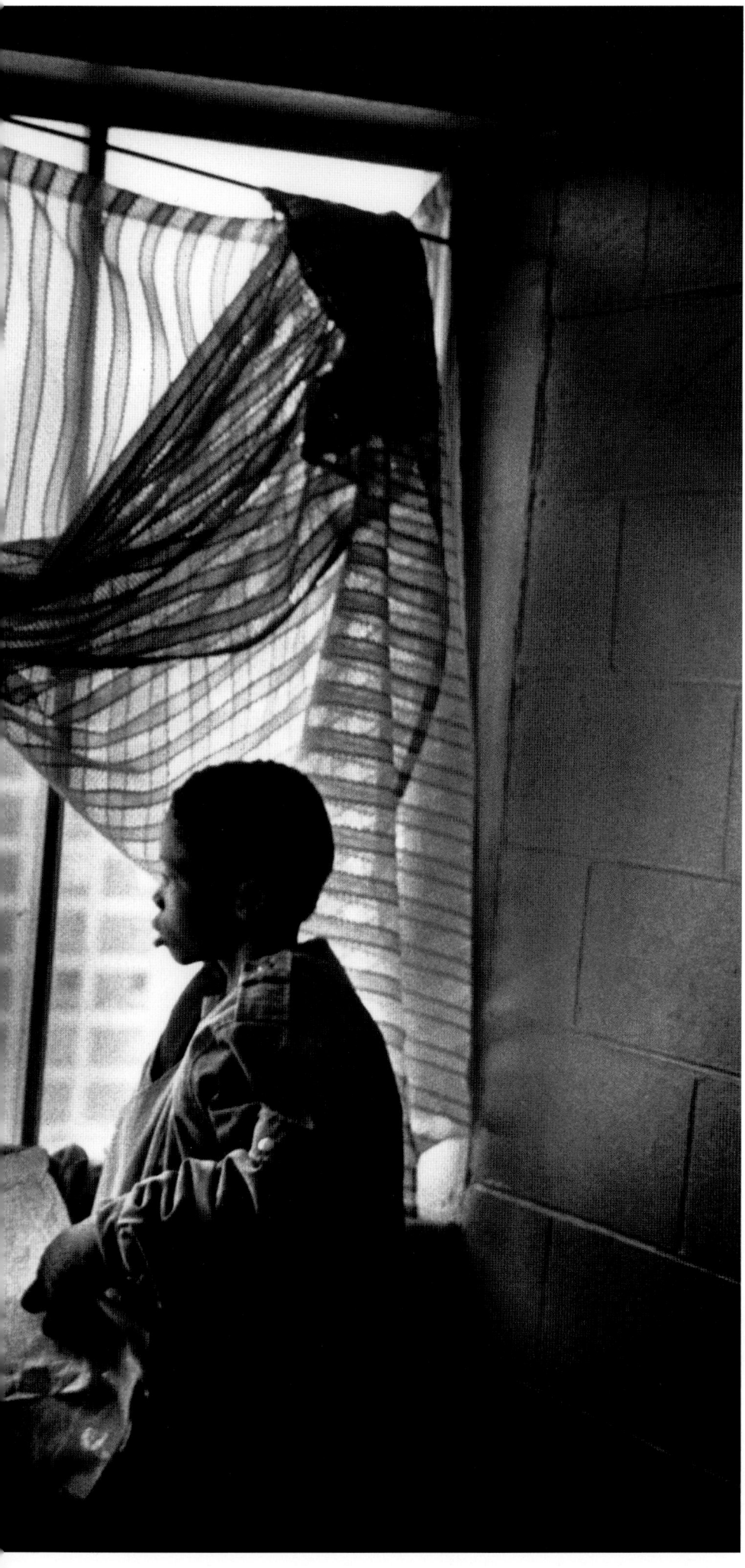

BRINGING DOWN THE PROJECTS

A first grader's 1992 death became known as the shot that brought down the projects.

Dantrell Davis held his mother's hand one fall morning as she walked him to Jenner Elementary, a Cabrini-Green neighborhood school. From a vacant tenth-floor Cabrini apartment, a sniper fired at rival gang members but struck seven-year-old Dantrell. The little boy with apple cheeks was the third Cabrini resident from Jenner Elementary shot to death that year.

Outrage exploded internationally. The city's establishment rallied around Dantrell's murder, and conversations about overhauling public housing hit a fever pitch. A strategy for redevelopment of public housing—known as the Plan for Transformation—was approved around the year 2000.

The crux of the plan involved razing the high-rises for happily-ever-after mixed-income communities where a third of the apartments rented or sold at market rate, a third were affordable for working-class families, and a third were public housing. No social science research informed the Chicago Housing Authority mix of housing.

Officials argued that higher-income families could be good role models for poor families. CHA also wanted to break the cycle of intergenerational poverty; families shouldn't feel that signing a lease to an apartment guaranteed they'd have it for life.

Most public housing residents refused to embrace the Plan for Transformation and argued that CHA spurned their input. They skeptically viewed the demolitions as land grabs and unequivocal gentrification designed to push them off prime land.

Originally, the Plan for Transformation had a 2010 date of completion. That date was extended to 2015. CHA missed that deadline, too. Out of 16,000-plus families who lost their homes when the high-rises were razed, only 1,468 permanently live in mixed-income communities with names like Legends, Oakwood Shores, and Park Boulevard.
—*Natalie Y. Moore, reporter for Chicago Public Media, is the author of* The South Side: A Portrait of Chicago and American Segregation.

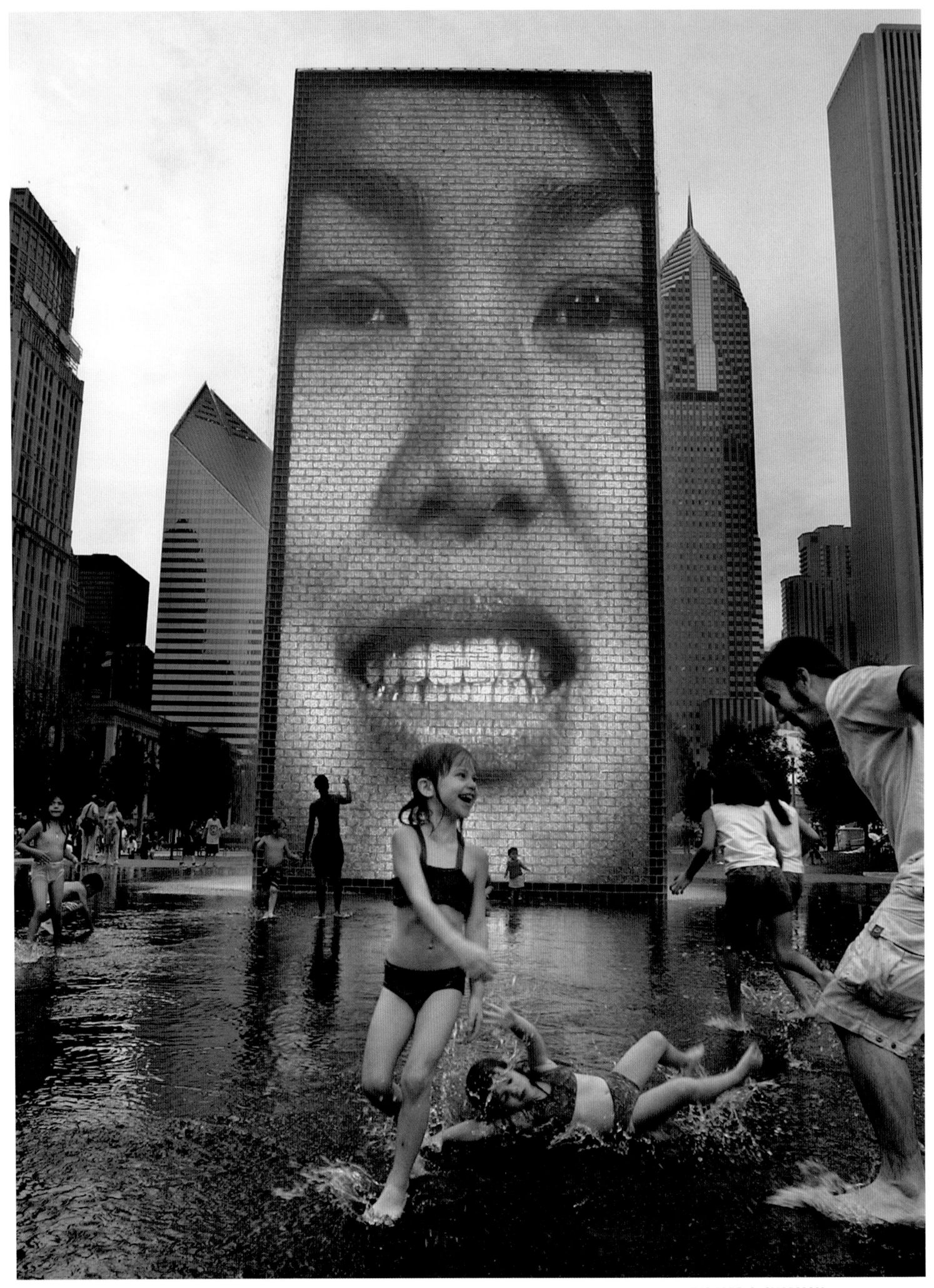

CHILDREN PLAY IN THE WADING SECTION OF MILLENNIUM PARK'S CROWN FOUNTAIN. AUGUST 3, 2004/RICHARD A. CHAPMAN

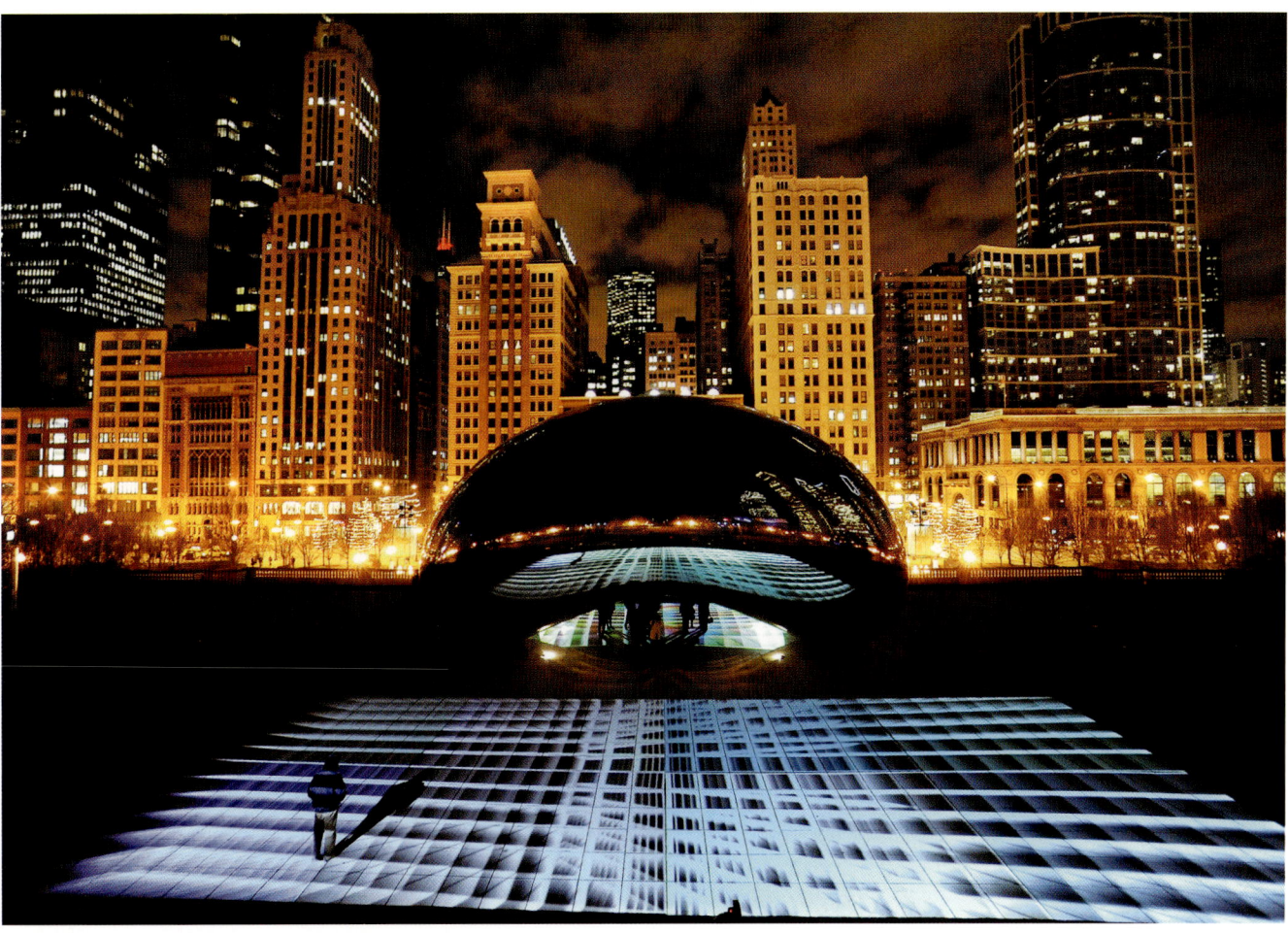

THE LIGHT EXHIBIT "LUMINOUS FIELD" AT CLOUD GATE IN MILLENNIUM PARK. FEBRUARY 7, 2012/TOM CRUZE

A SHOWCASE OR A MIRAGE?

Reflections. That's what Crown Fountain and The Bean (Cloud Gate, if you want to be formal) in Millennium Park are all about. They are in shimmering pools, mirrored surfaces, and sometimes in our minds.

There's much to see in the 24 acres that make up Chicago's premier park downtown, but visitors—who come from across the globe—flock to those two attractions.

And who can blame them? The fountain and The Bean are a special brand of fun. Places that hit tourists with ever-changing images, leaving them to wonder: What all am I seeing here?

Standing before Crown Fountain, many a relieved child has thought: Finally, after being dragged to everything my grown-ups want, we're somewhere I can have fun. Off go the shoes. Let the shenanigans begin!

You can't play in that fountain or settle onto the nearby benches and not feel part of the fun. Kids make fast friends in the reflecting pool. And laughter fills the air, especially when a particularly expressive face—each one belongs to a Chicagoan—pops up on those massive glass towers spouting a stream of water.

If Crown Fountain is the territory of the young, The Bean's the spot for all of us to get a little silly or simply drink in the beauty of Chicago's skyline. Get up close and crack your goofiest face or hug that BFF while checking out your strange likenesses.

It's here you also can practice a slightly different style of people watching. You're not looking *at* them, you're witnessing the action reflected off The Bean's glimmering, sloping shape. Stand before it on a quiet night and The Bean looks downright magical.

And yet. . .

As much as I marvel at both, I can't help but consider how the popularity of Millennium Park and its star attractions has made it easy to pat ourselves on the back for our striking downtown while turning our focus away from the pockets of the city riddled by unending gun violence, generational poverty, worn housing, and long-vacant stores.

That sort of inequity can exist for only so long. Someday—and the ongoing unrest here suggests that the time is upon us now—Chicago must put the same type of energy and dollars that created the wonders of Millennium Park into figuring out how to help those communities that struggle the most.

Now that's something to reflect on.

—*South Side native Sue Ontiveros worked thirty years as an editor and columnist at the Sun-Times.*

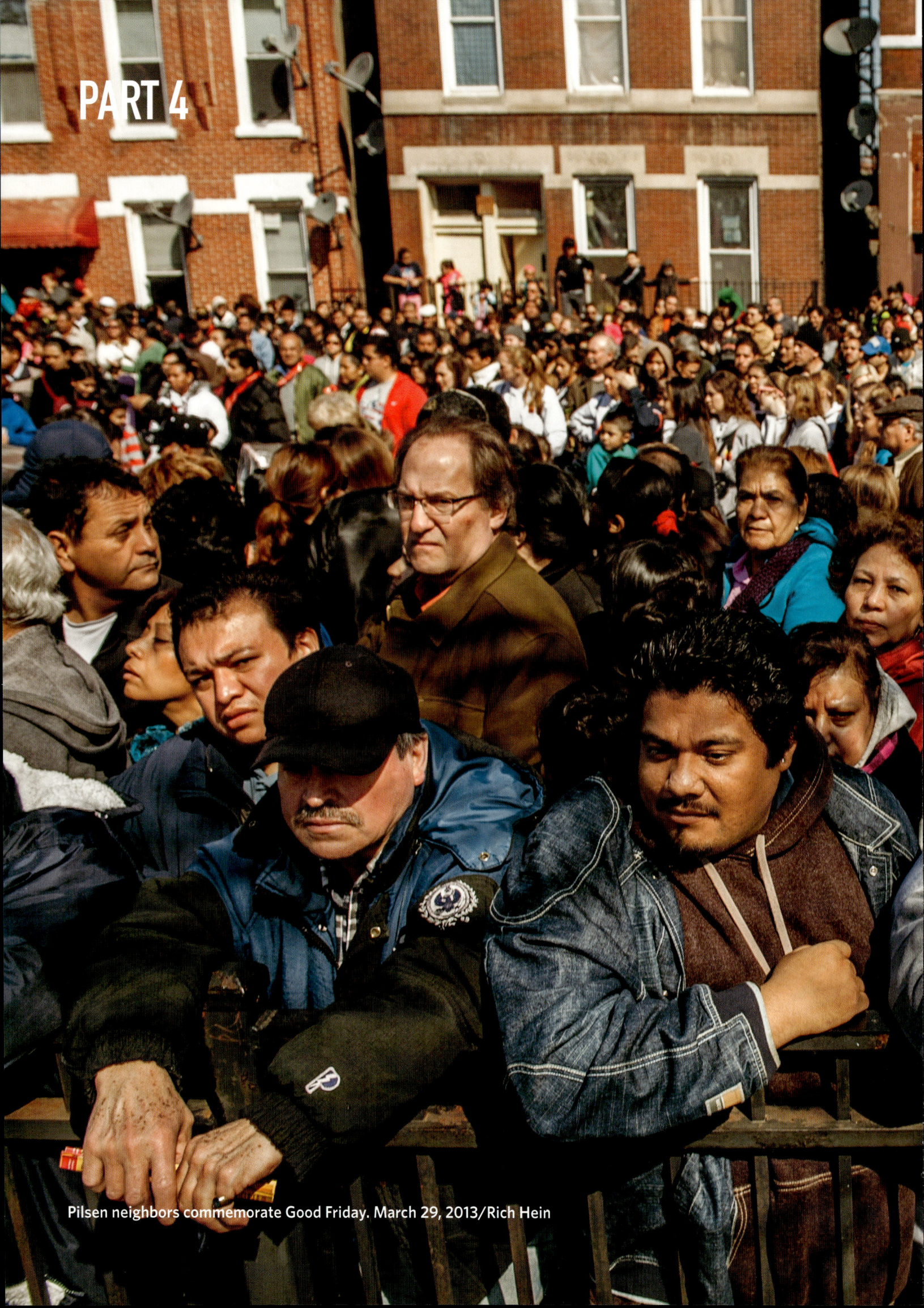

PART 4

Pilsen neighbors commemorate Good Friday. March 29, 2013/Rich Hein

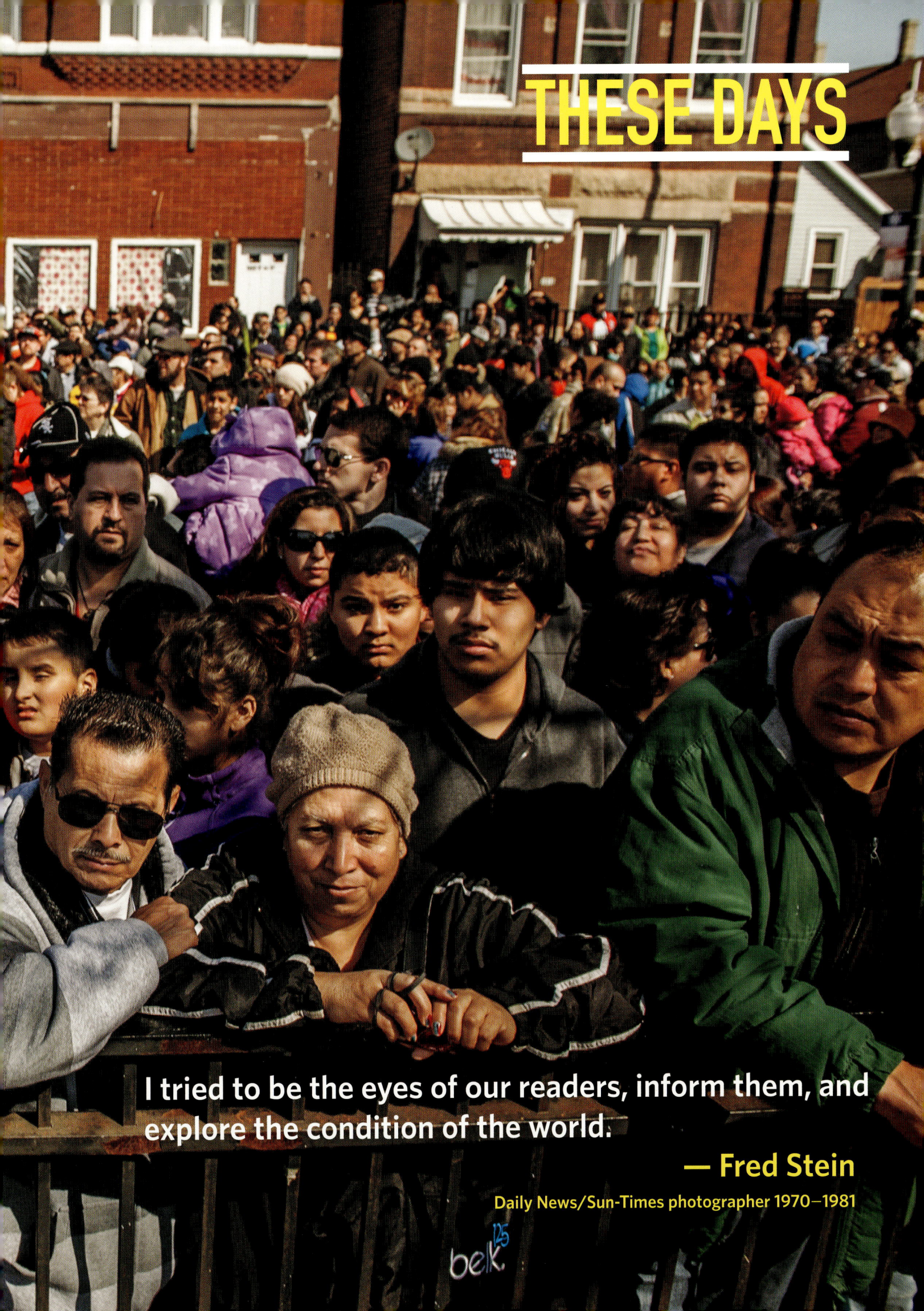

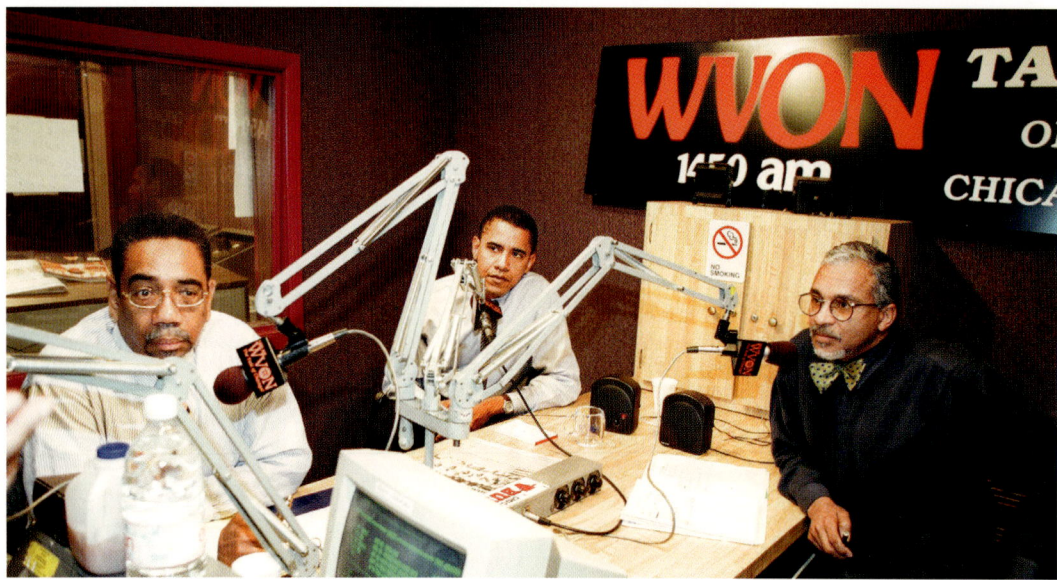

BARACK OBAMA DEBATES BOBBY RUSH (LEFT) IN US HOUSE PRIMARY. FEBRUARY 18, 2000/BRIAN JACKSON

A PLACE WHERE ALL THINGS ARE POSSIBLE

A stage was set up in the south end of the sprawling downtown park that is Chicago's front lawn. In 1968 it had been the scene of bloody rioting during the Democratic National Convention. The searing images of police and protesters battling under clouds of tear gas defined the bitter divisions of the times. On this night, forty years later, the same park had become a moving mosaic of national unity, filled as far as the eye could see with people of all backgrounds.

It was a sea of people with shared hopes but very different stories. Some of the faces were familiar to me. I saw Reverend Jesse Jackson, flag in hand and tears streaming down his cheeks. He could be a shameless hustler and relentless self-promoter, but the reverend also was a trailblazer who had devoted his life to civil rights. He had been there with Dr. King the night he was slain and had, himself, run two symbolic races for the White House. Now the image of the new First Family—a splendid, Black family—introducing themselves to the nation, had the reverend genuinely overcome. I saw Lane Evans, a former congressman from Rock Island, Illinois, whom I had covered back in 1982 when he was an idealistic young legal aid lawyer running a seemingly quixotic race for a House seat owned by the Republicans for decades. A soft-spoken, principled liberal, Lane had been one of the few downstate politicians to stick his neck out and endorse Obama in the 2004 US Senate primary. Now, just four years later, Parkinson's disease had robbed him of his ability to walk, speak intelligibly, or serve in office, but not of his spirit or belief. So there he was in his wheelchair, braving the bedlam to be a part of it. His face was a frozen mask, but as his old friend spoke to the crowd, his cheeks were moist with tears.

"If there is anyone out there who still doubts that America is a place where all things are possible; who still wonders if the dream of our founders is alive in our time; who still questions the power of our democracy, tonight is your answer," Obama proclaimed, in a speech laden with appeals to unity and bipartisanship. "It's been a long time coming, but tonight, because of what we did on this day, in this election, at this defining moment, change has come to America." Though familiar with the words, I truly felt their full weight as I stood in Grant Park and heard America's new leader warn the nation of what lay ahead: "Even as we celebrate tonight, we know the challenges that tomorrow will bring are the greatest of our lifetime."

For us, the end of this extraordinary saga was just the beginning of another—the full demand of which we could not yet fully appreciate as we celebrated into the night.

—David Axelrod was chief strategist for Barack Obama's presidential campaigns and served as a senior advisor. This account is based on his memoir Believer: My Forty Years in Politics.

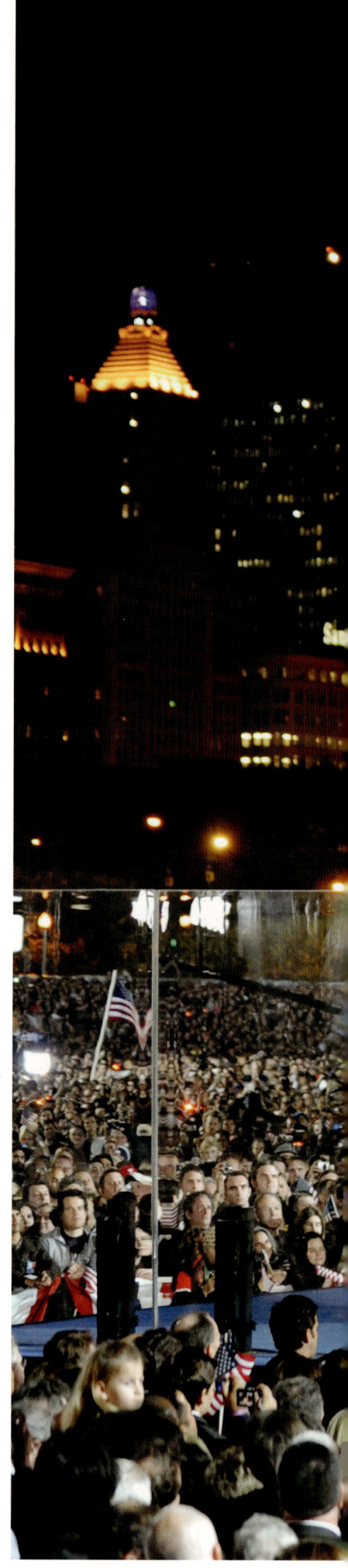

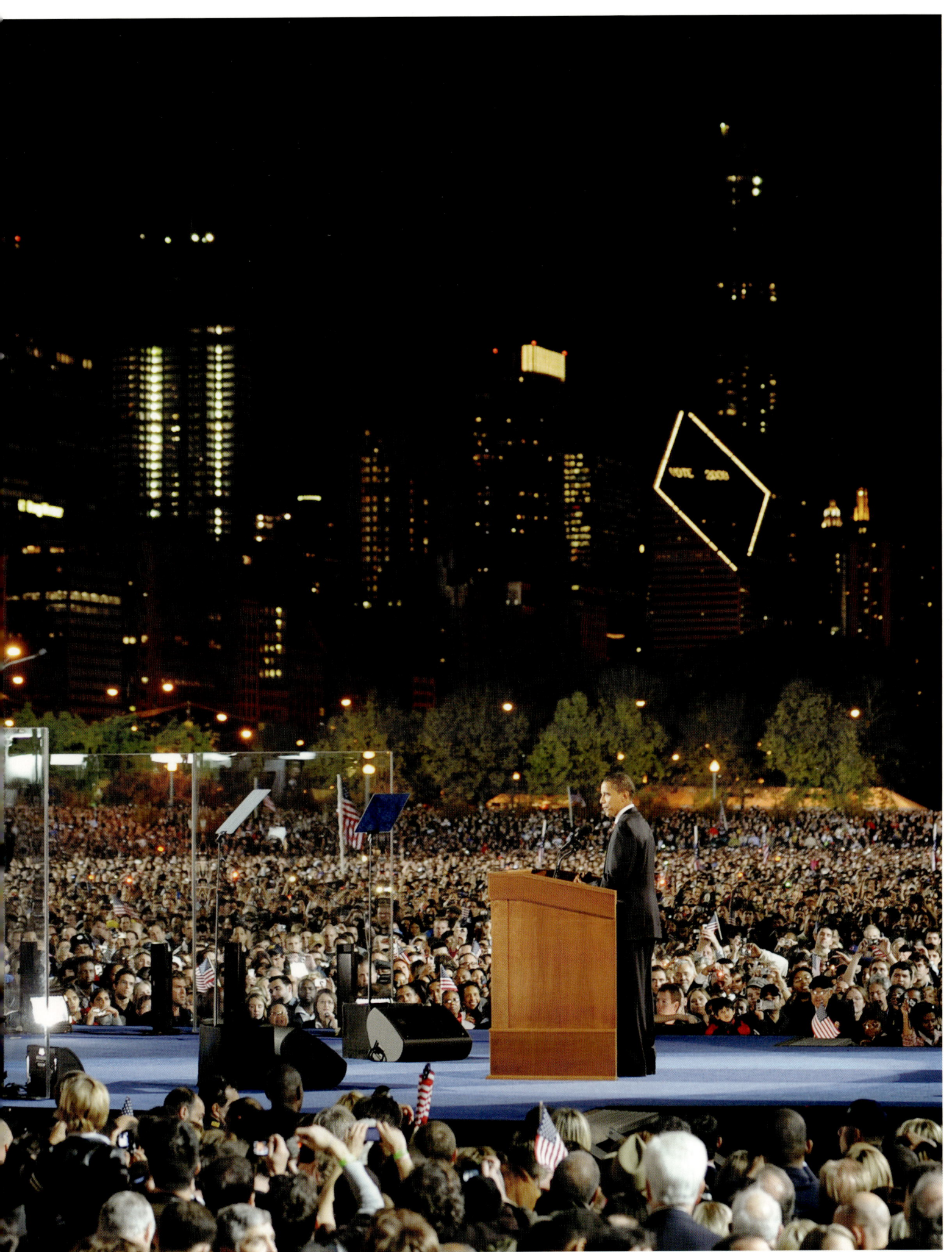

THE NIGHT HE WAS ELECTED PRESIDENT, OBAMA GREETS THOUSANDS IN GRANT PARK: "THIS IS OUR MOMENT," HE SAID. NOVEMBER 4, 2008/JOHN J. KIM

A HOME FOR HOMICIDE

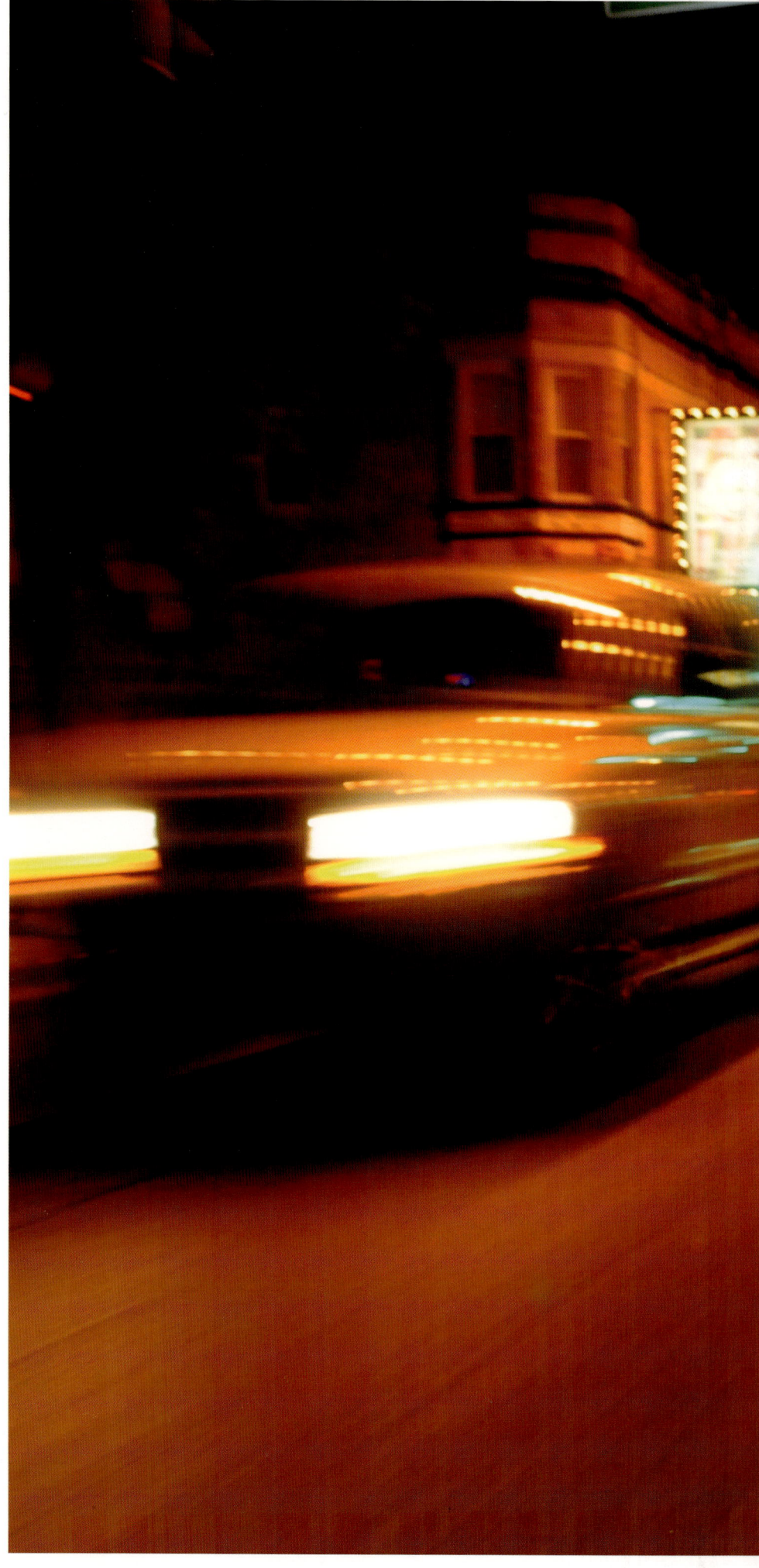

We set out to cover a homicide—from the moment it happened to an indictment. What I learned from spending four or five shifts a week for eight weeks with two Chicago police homicide detectives is that every gun crime has nuance and complications. It's not TV, neatly wrapped up in one hour.

Among many families, we watched the parents of a seventeen-year-old homicide victim describe how their family had moved from one city neighborhood to another, hoping their son would not get entangled with street gangs. Their son, Loreto Miguel, was fatally shot while walking with a friend in the neighborhood of Palmer Square on Chicago's North Side.

They wanted to know why no one had been arrested for his murder.

We watched police lineups as nervous witnesses looked for the person they saw ride up on a bicycle and shoot Miguel in the head. We saw detectives and forensics investigators inspect Miguel's body, which had been covered in a sheet and laid on a hospital bed. We went to his funeral.

I was astonished to witness the many moving parts of a gun-involved homicide case. Investigations often take weeks or months—too slow in the opinion of many of the victims' families. And this process is repeated between 500 to 800 times a year.

More than 2,000 people have been shot in Chicago every year for the past decade. It's a public health crisis, one that should enrage Chicagoans. The resources, in work hours and taxpayer dollars, should inspire action to bolster gun legislation, city budgets, the education system, hospital networks, Cook County courts, and basic life essentials like housing and nutrition.
—*Sun-Times photographer John J. Kim was awarded the 2011 Pulitzer Prize for local reporting, along with Frank Main and Mark Konkol, for their immersive documentation of violence in Chicago.*

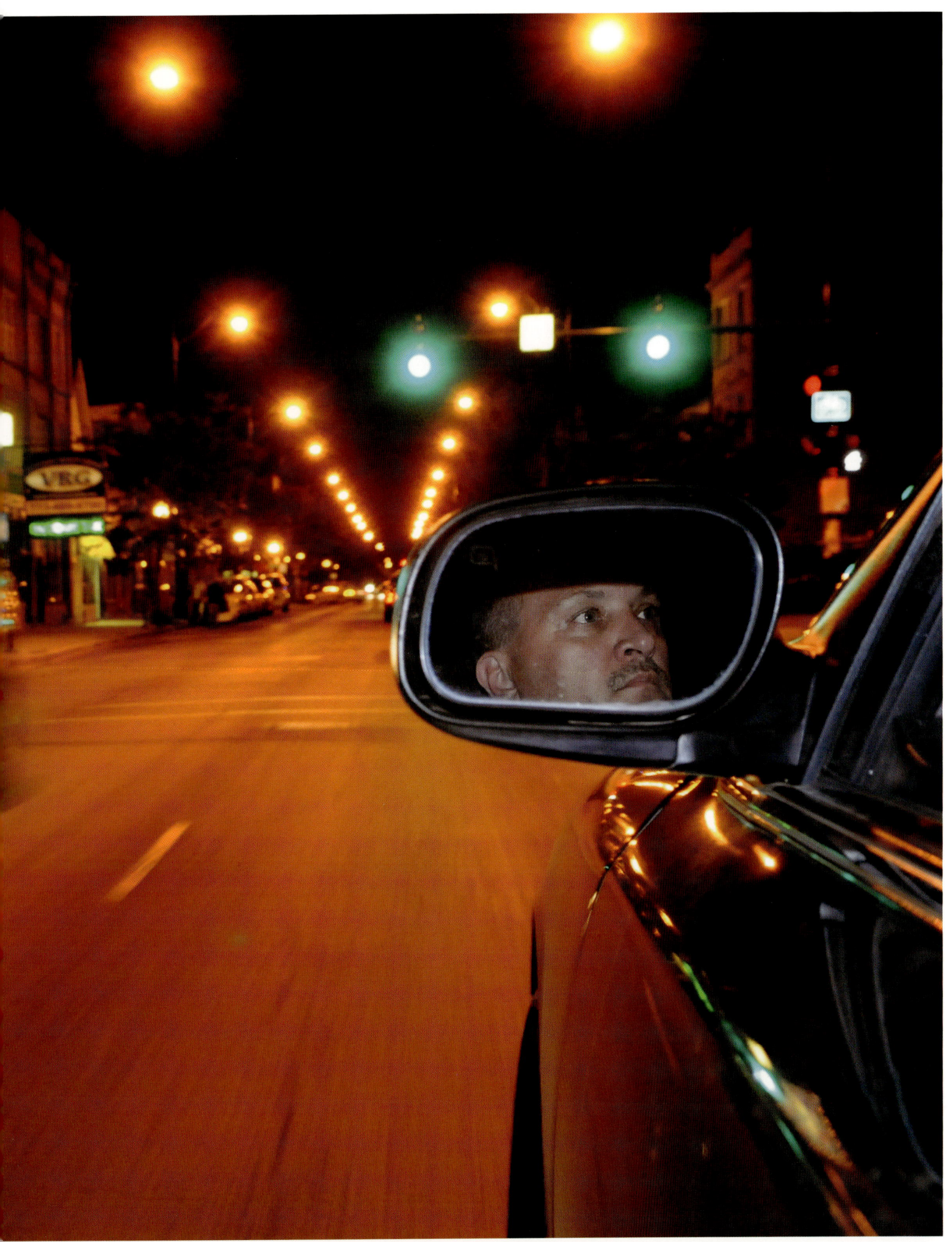

DETECTIVE ANTHONY NORADIN CRUISES THE WEST SIDE. THE PHOTOGRAPH WAS TAKEN FOR THEIR PULITZER PRIZE-WINNING SERIES. JULY 13, 2009/JOHN J. KIM

WHAT THE PROCESSION MEANS

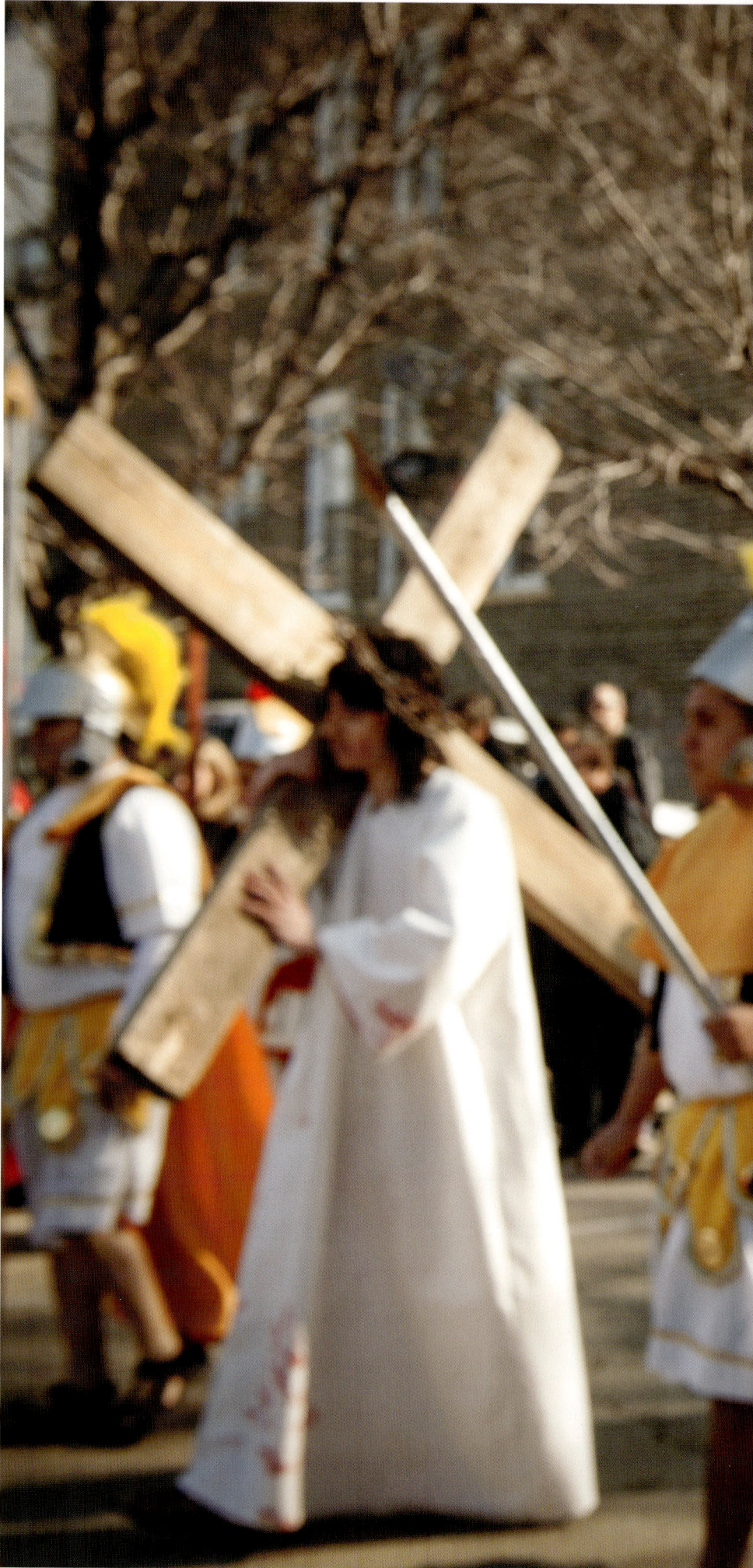

Vía Crucis, Pilsen's Way of the Cross, is so much more than a religious ritual.

The Good Friday procession along 18th Street reenacts an unjust execution and symbolizes the hope for justice in the future. It is a unique expression of spirituality and activism.

It started on the morning of Good Friday 1977, when seven parishes in *la Dieciocho* (The Eighteenth) neighborhood organized a large-scale public passion play. At the time, Pilsen was a hotspot. Residents—especially Mexican-American mothers—organized picket lines and boycotts for better jobs and for worker and immigrant rights. They led protests and hunger strikes to secure a new bilingual high school that respected their culture. That school, now known as Benito Juarez Community Academy, opened that same year.

Pilsen has been a port of entry since 1900. This is where new immigrants learn their rights as citizens and their responsibility to keep government accountable. This is where Mexicans, pushed from their Near West Side homes by the construction of an expressway and university, embraced their Chicano civil rights.

I see the procession as a beautiful, complicated knot—a tangle of liberation theology from South America, activist ideology from Cesar Chavez's California, and the vision of parishioners and lay deacons from Pilsen—that cannot be unwrapped. It is a centuries-old event that originated in Jerusalem, spread to Seville, and then to Mexico City before reaching Chicago.

It has different meanings to different people. Some come because they are hard-core Catholics who relate to the whipped and misunderstood Good Friday Jesus. Some come to pray—for a stop to the violence in Mexico and in Chicago. Some come because it connects them to their Mexican-Latino roots, reminding them of their grandfather or grandmother. And some come simply out of curiosity.
—*Cesáreo Moreno is director of visual arts & chief curator at the National Museum of Mexican Art.*

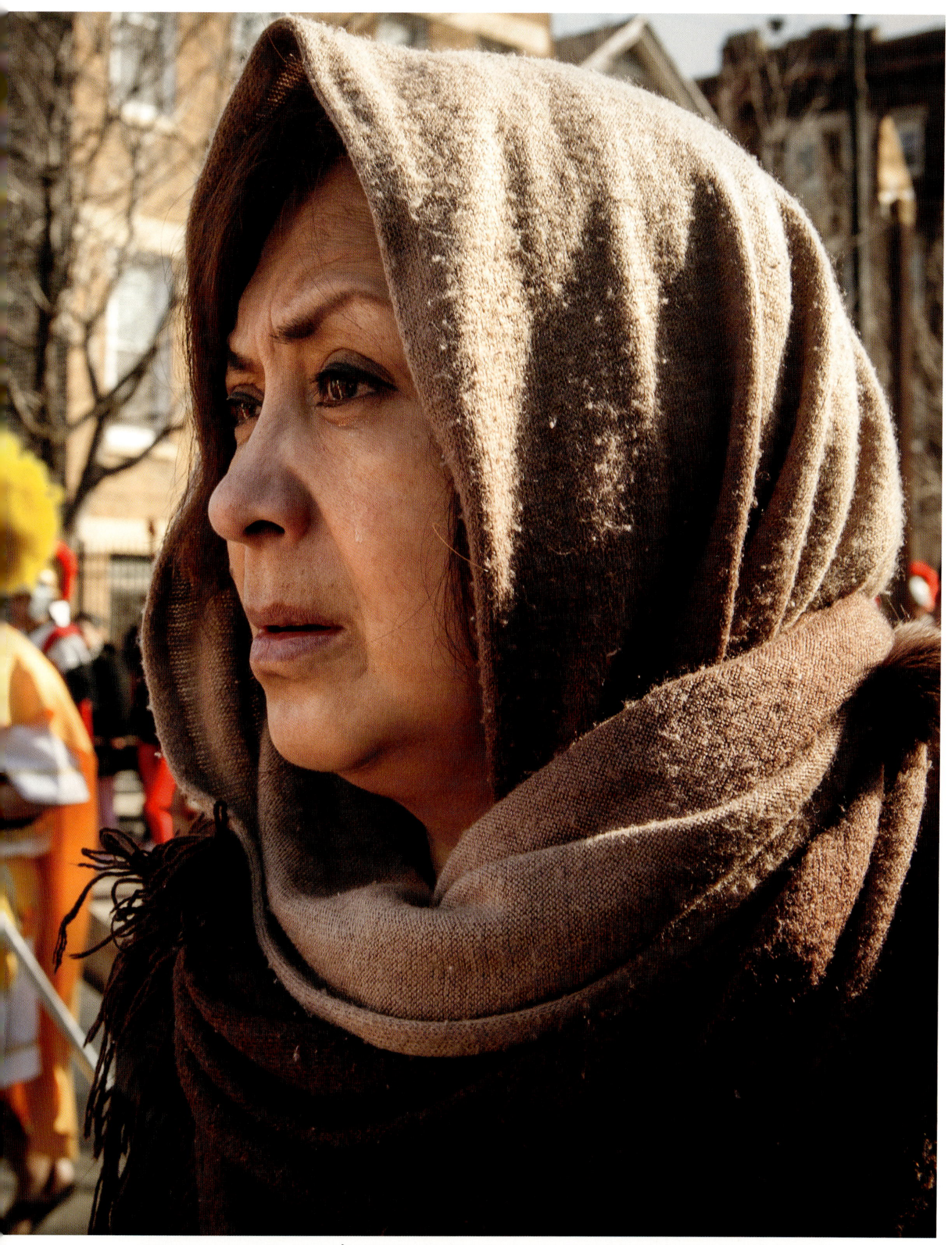

ESPERANZA LOPEZ TAKES PART IN *VÍA CRUCIS*, PILSEN'S WAY OF THE CROSS, ALONG 18TH STREET. MARCH 29, 2013/RICH HEIN

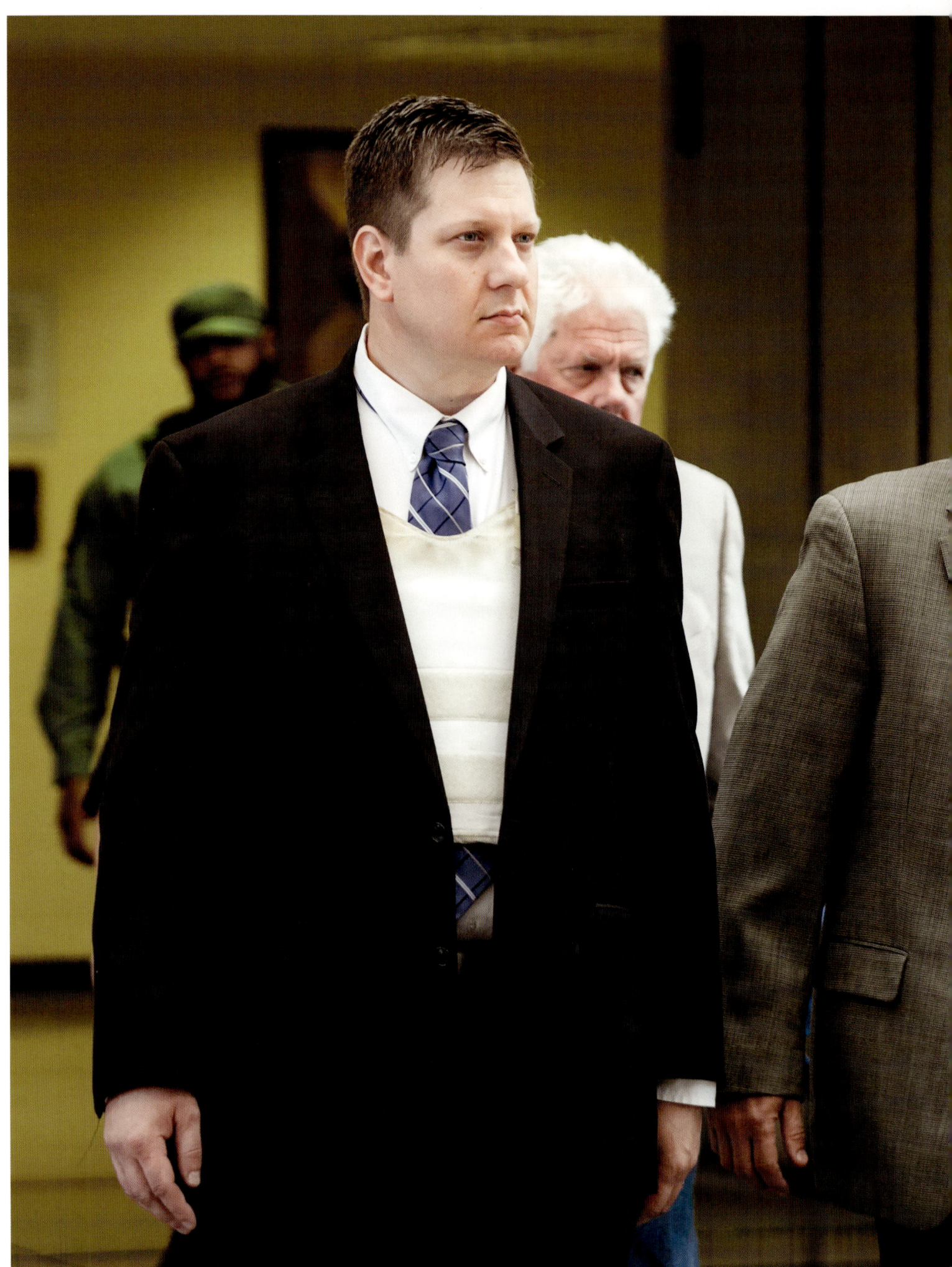

JASON VAN DYKE LEAVES COURT IN BODY ARMOR. HE WAS FOUND GUILTY OF SECOND-DEGREE MURDER. AUGUST 14, 2018/ASHLEE REZIN GARCIA

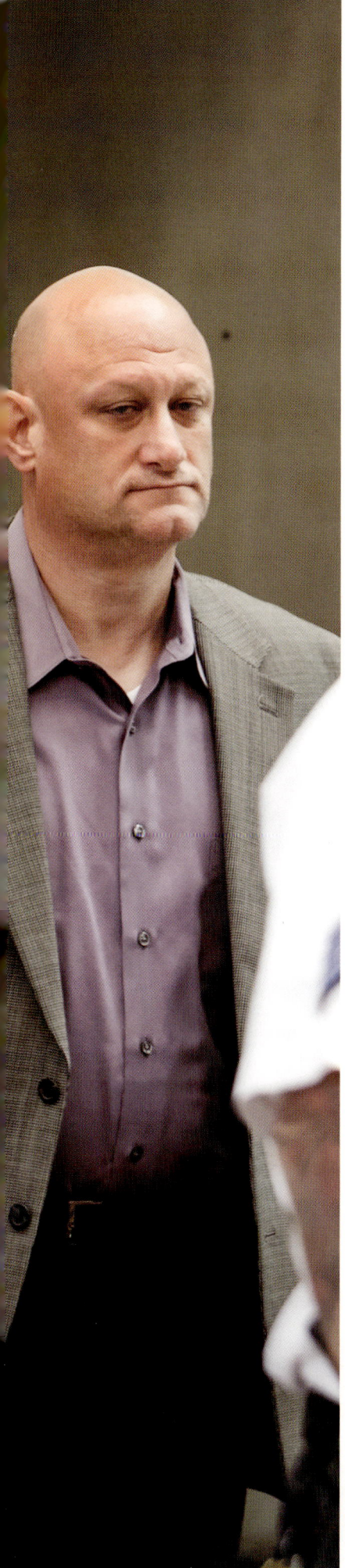

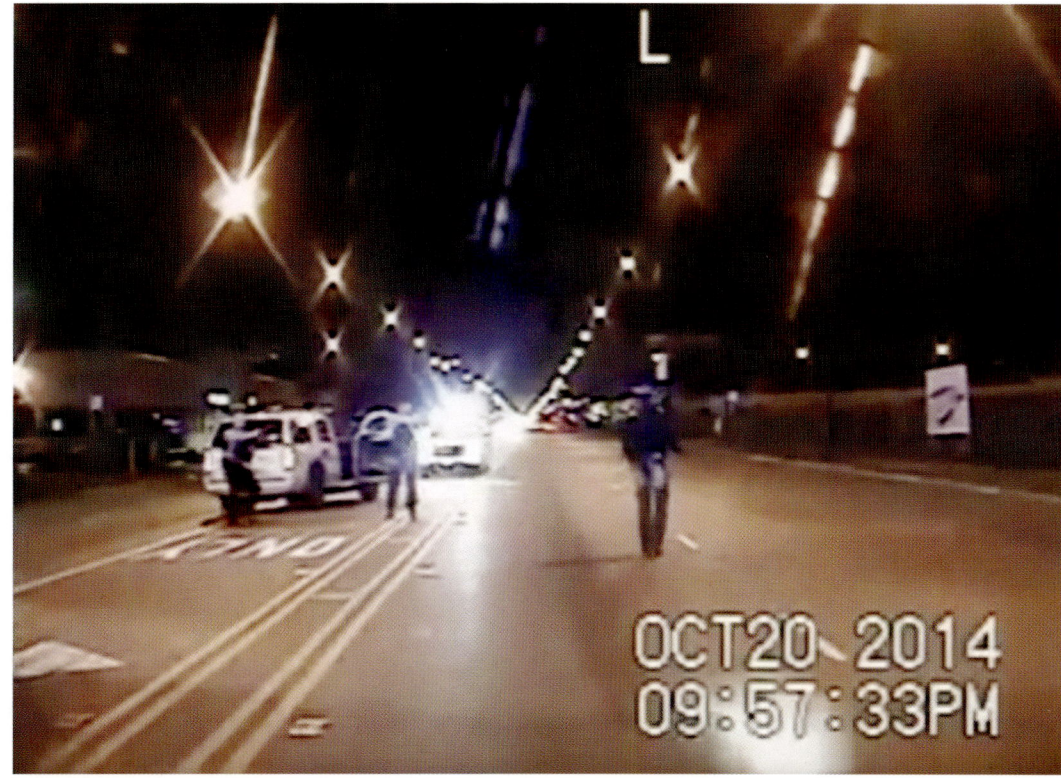

DASHBOARD VIDEO OF LAQUAN MCDONALD POLICE SHOOTING. THREE SECONDS LATER, MCDONALD WAS KILLED.

ACCOUNTABILTY

October 21, 2014. The Chicago Police Department issues a press release—on the superintendent's letterhead—reporting a fatal "police-involved" shooting of a man with a knife "who refused to comply with orders to drop the knife and continued to approach the officers."

One week later, someone in law enforcement tells me that a dashcam video clearly tells another story.

Were it not for that individual, it's unlikely we would know the name of the seventeen-year-old victim: Laquan McDonald. For the city's propaganda machinery is thrown into high gear: evidence destroyed, witnesses intimidated, police reports falsified, public information withheld, and a $5-million settlement paid to McDonald's family. At most every turn, city officials maintain a narrative they knew to be false.

After interviewing an eyewitness and securing the autopsy that contradicts the police account and reveals McDonald had been shot sixteen times, I publish an article in 2015 called "Sixteen Shots" that challenges the city's account and makes known the existence of dashcam video.

Public pressure builds. "Sixteen Shots and a Cover-up" becomes the anthem of a growing protest movement in the streets.

November 24, 2015. The city complies with a judge's order and releases the video. Public outrage at what it depicts— the execution of a teenager—is compounded by outrage that the city knew its contents yet withheld it for more than a year.

A cascade of events: the police superintendent is fired as is the head of the agency that investigates police shootings; the state's attorney is voted from office; the US Justice Department investigates the Chicago Police Department; Mayor Rahm Emanuel decides not to seek reelection; and the officer who shot McDonald is convicted of second-degree murder.

The murder of McDonald has been the framing narrative of a turbulent period in Chicago history. It invites comparison to the lynching of Emmett Till, another child of Chicago, in Mississippi in 1955.

The dashcam video can be seen as the counterpart to the fateful decision of Till's mother to order an open casket at her son's funeral.

It's a portal through which a mutilated Black body illuminates the violence that enforces structures of exclusion and inequality.
—Jamie Kalven is an independent journalist who founded the Invisible Institute, a collective for investigative and documentary reporting.

THE HARDEST YEAR

After seeing images on TV of a diverse crowd of protestors setting a Minneapolis police station ablaze in the wake of George Floyd's death, I figured I had better get to the grocery store.

Floyd, a Black man, died when Derek Chauvin, a White Minneapolis police officer, kneeled on his neck for more than nine minutes.

All hell broke loose. Again.

Although I did not get caught in the chaos of 1968—when a mob of mostly young Black men burned down entire blocks of buildings following the assassination of Dr. Martin Luther King Jr.—I still remember the division the riots caused.

"Keep your ass off the West Side," warned my boyfriend from Vietnam, where Black soldiers were also mourning King's death.

The photos of King on the second-floor balcony of the Lorraine Motel in Memphis moments before a sniper's bullet struck him fueled violent protests across the country. Similarly, the video of Chauvin, with his hands in his pockets nonchalantly kneeling on Floyd's neck, triggered demonstrations, some of them destructive, in more than 1,000 cities across America.

I pulled into the Jewel-Osco parking lot on 75th and Stony Island, and it looked like the entire neighborhood had run out of groceries.

The store was the busiest I'd ever seen. But these weren't shoppers.

People were pushing carts loaded with cases of canned goods. They stuffed their cars with meats and household items. One man was carrying an entire display rack.

I couldn't believe my eyes.

A stream of men and women walked through the broken glass that once was the automatic door as if they were on a regular shopping trip.

But what shocked me most was that these looters were not rowdy.

They were eerily calm.

Those with cars took their time dumping their haul into their trunks. Those without vehicles leisurely pushed the store's overflowing shopping carts down the sidewalk toward home.

The store's security guard stood beside his car with the driver's door wide open, gawking at the spectacle. There wasn't a police officer in sight.

Before I noticed the shattered entrance door, I thought Jewel was sponsoring a food giveaway because everyone was acting so normal.

Unlike the 1968 riots that destroyed property on the South and West sides, this time around local media reported damage to stores on the Magnificent Mile, River North, downtown State Street, as well as at South Side strip malls and in suburban shopping districts. The rioters nearly burned down a neighborhood dollar store.

"A riot is the language of the unheard," King famously said in a speech he gave at Stanford University in 1967.

In this terrible circumstance, the masses heard from the unheard.

I got back in my car and drove off, deciding that whatever was already in my kitchen would have to do.

—*Sun-Times columnist Mary Mitchell began work at the paper in 1990.*

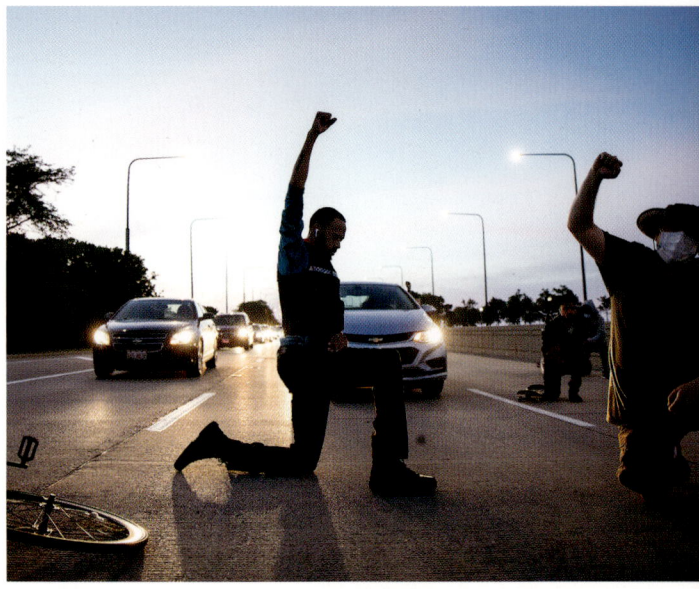

LAKE SHORE DRIVE PROTESTS. MAY 31, 2020/ASHLEE REZIN GARCIA

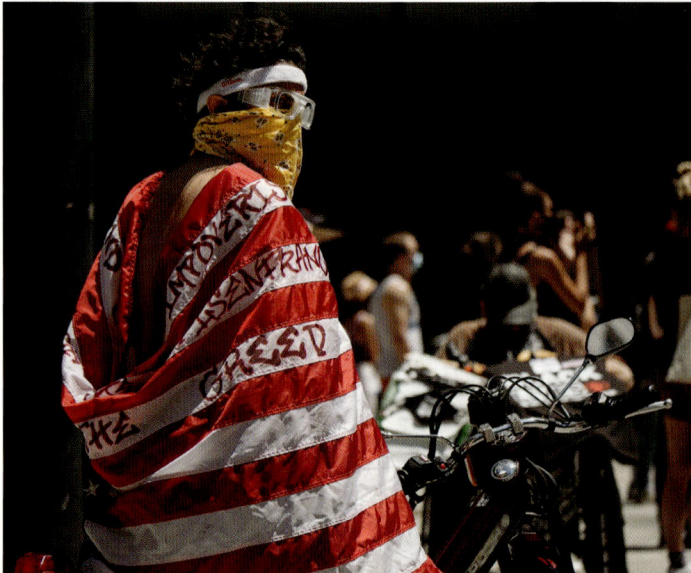

DOWNTOWN BOYCOTT 4TH OF JULY RALLY. JULY 4, 2020/PAT NABONG

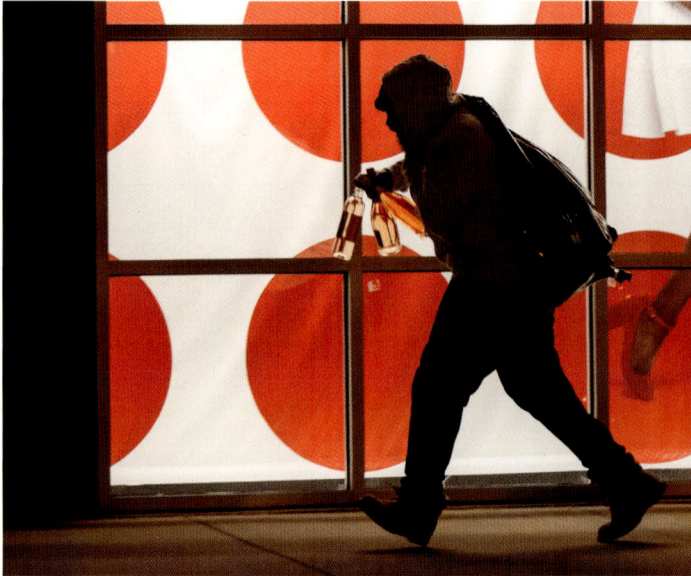

LOOTED WICKER PARK STORE. MAY 31, 2020/ASHLEE REZIN GARCIA

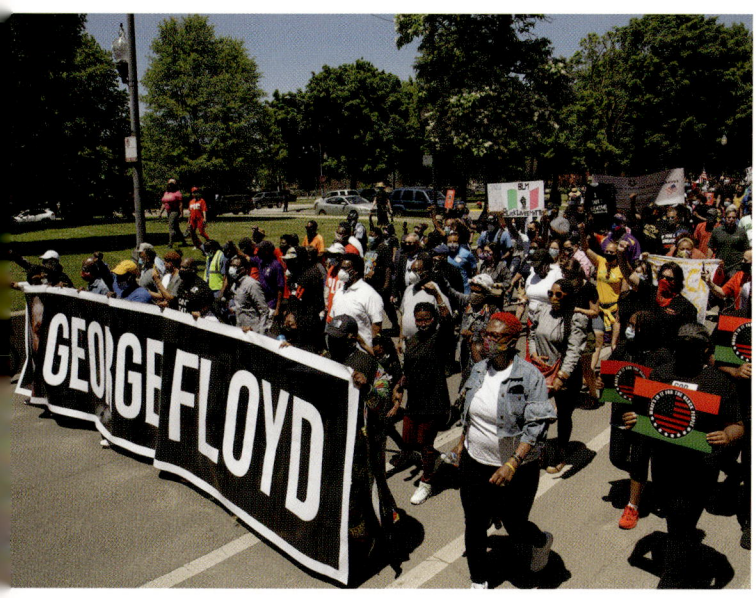
NORTH LAWNDALE MARCH. JUNE 12, 2020/PAT NABONG

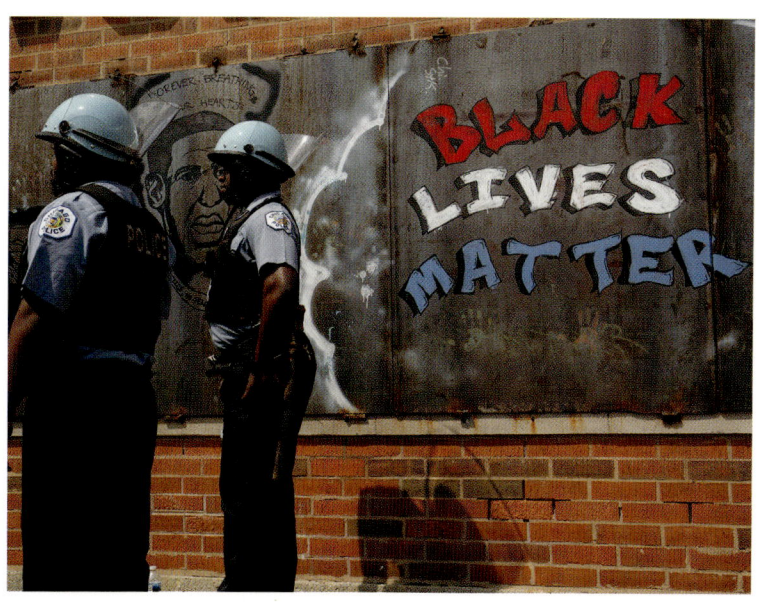
GEORGE FLOYD MURAL BRONZEVILLE. AUGUST 15, 2020/PAT NABONG

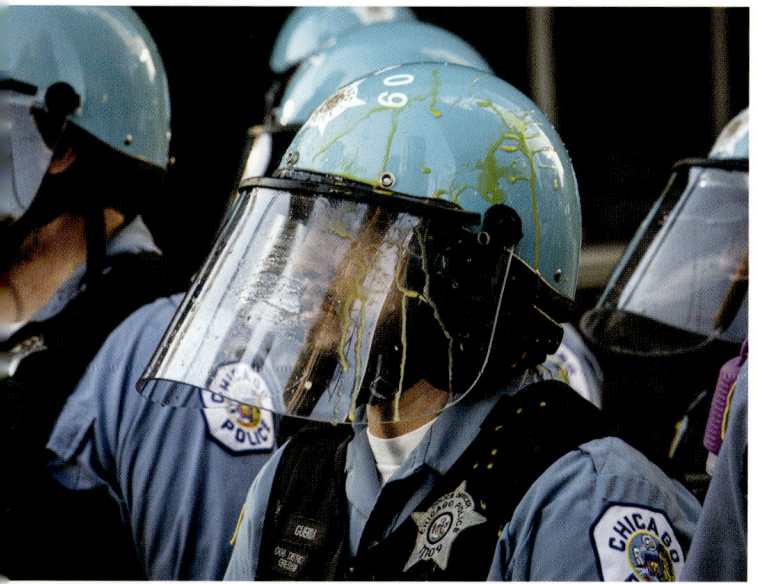
LOOP RALLY TURNS VIOLENT. MAY 30, 2020/ASHLEE REZIN GARCIA

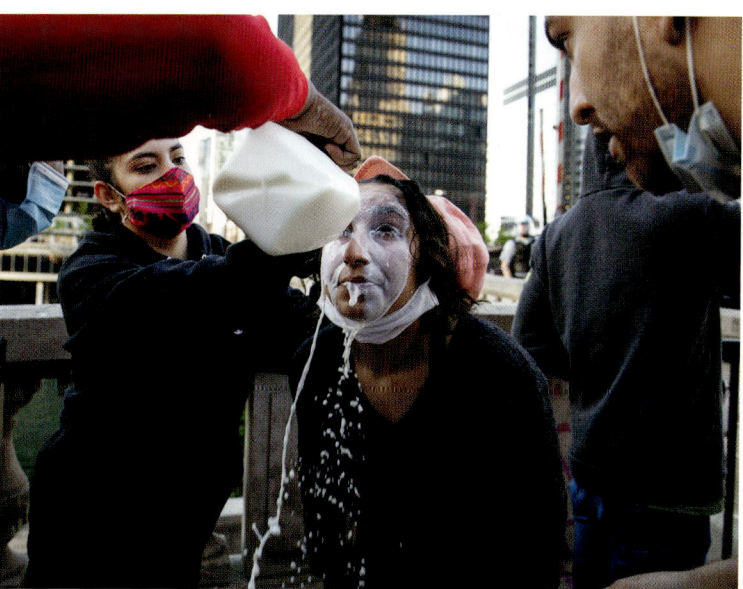
AFTER BEING PEPPER-SPRAYED. MAY 30, 2020/ASHLEE REZIN GARCIA

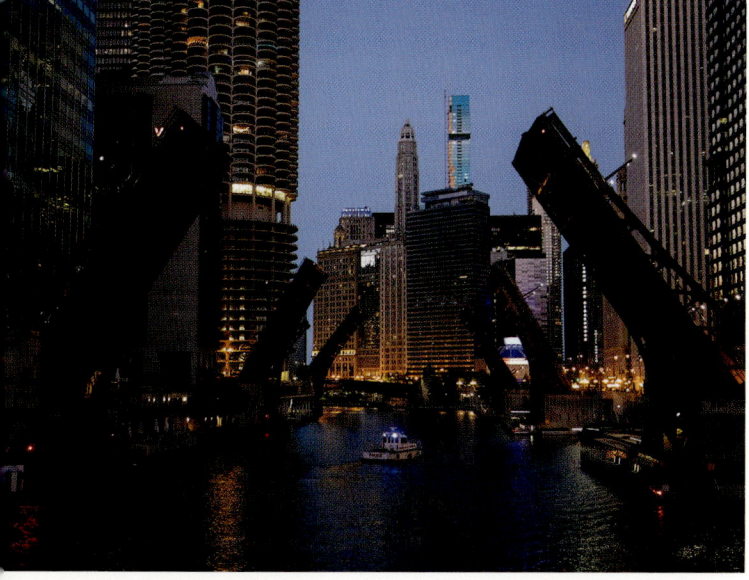
LIFTED CHICAGO RIVER BRIDGES. MAY 30, 2020/ASHLEE REZIN GARCIA

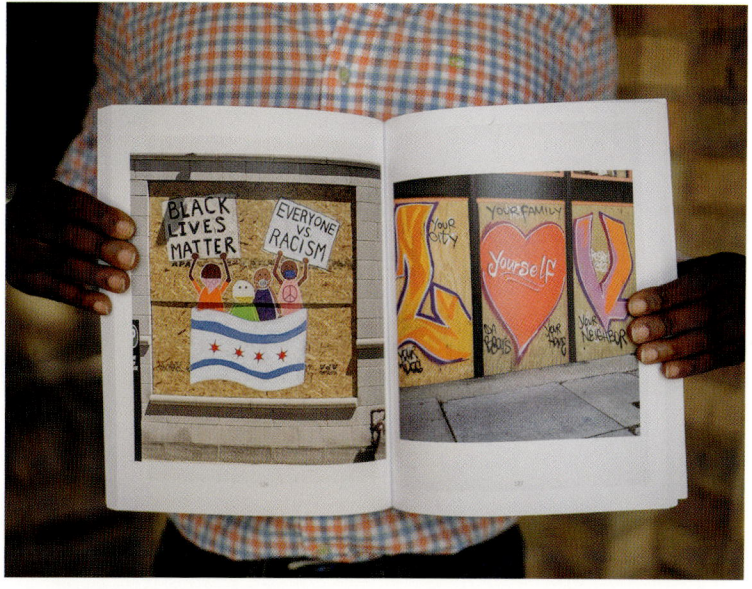
BOOK SHOWS BOARDED-UP STORES. AUGUST 29, 2020/PAT NABONG

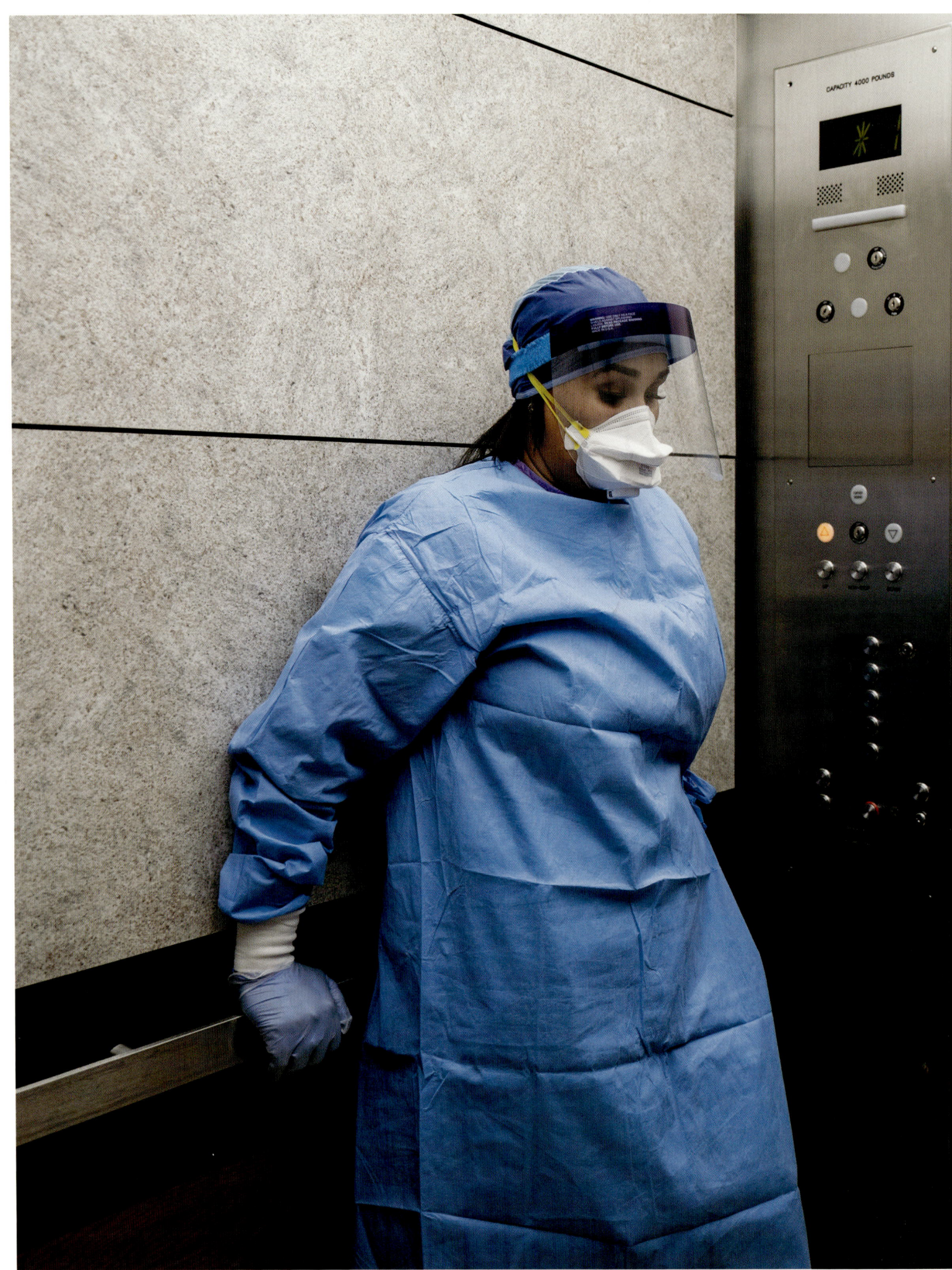

NURSE CAPRI REESE PAUSES AFTER SPENDING THE LAST MOMENTS WITH A PATIENT WHO DIED FROM COVID-19. APRIL 28, 2020/ASHLEE REZIN GARCIA

'OUR WORST DAY'

We didn't say a word to each other.

Nurse practitioner Capri Reese and I had just entered the elevator after watching an 80-year-old man die. He was the third patient with COVID-19 who she saw pass away that day, and her 12-hour shift was only half over.

"It was our worst day," she would later say.

My plan was to shadow a nurse at Roseland Community Hospital so that readers could better appreciate the courage of health care workers during the uncertain times of the coronavirus pandemic.

It was late April, about six weeks after the world had shut down, and we didn't know yet how COVID-19 spread. I had to be very careful. The Far South Side hospital provided me with a gown, face shield, double gloves, and a hairnet. I had my own N95 face mask.

And when my shift ended, I carefully removed all my personal protective equipment and dumped all my clothes into a garbage bag. I wiped down my camera and gear with antibacterial cloths and changed into fresh clothes. My husband left the back door open. I threw the clothes right into the washing machine.

I was amazed at what a difficult process health care workers had to go through every day.

I could have turned this assignment down, but I figured if medical employees could come to the hospital, I could too.

During our day together, Reese responded to five medical emergencies—code blues. In between attending patients, she would rush back to her office to call and plead with coworkers to work the night shift, even on their days off. Roseland was short-staffed because hospital personnel were worn down. I could see why.

Reese ran from room to room; it was hard to keep up with her—except for that moment in the elevator.

I took this assignment for the same reason most photographers take any dangerous job. We understand the power of photography. We recognize that pictures—like words—convey meaning. And we know that pictures help all of us better comprehend events and our world.

Photography is the universal language.
—*Photojournalist Ashlee Rezin Garcia has worked at the Sun-Times since 2013.*

CREDITS

All photographs are from the Chicago Sun-Times Collection, Chicago History Museum, and the Chicago Sun-Times.

PAGE	IMAGE NUMBER	PAGE	IMAGE NUMBER
4-5	ST-17600001	90-91	ST-17501024
6-7	ST-17600002	92	ST-17501044
8	ST-17500928	92-93	ST-17501005
10	ST-17500648	94	ST-17500884
12	ST-14003584-0082	95	ST-17501001
12	ST-14003584-0070	96-97	ST-70004759-0018
12	ST-14003584-0059	96-97	ST-17500795
12	ST-14003584-0177	98-99	ST-17500986
13	ST-50000444-0004	99	STM-003293806
14	ST-17501047	100	ST-17500997
18-19	ST-17501042	100-01	ST-17500988
20-21	ST-17500612	102-03	ST-17501002
22	ST-17501016	104	ST-17501040
23	ST-17501033	104-05	ST-19030975-0004
24	ST-17500588	106-07	ST-17500995
24-25	ST-17500583	108	ST-17500781
26-27	ST-17500945	109	ST-17500784
28-29	ST-17500868	110-11	ST-17500991
30	ST-17600003	112-13	ST-17500890
31	ST-17501034	114-15	ST-17500989
32-33	ST-17501036	115	ST-17500756
34-35	ST-17501041	116-17	ST-17500987
36	ST-17500984	118-19	ST-17500990
37	ST-17501032	120	ST-17500993
38-39	ST-17500914	121	ST-17500795
40-41	ST-17501019	122-23	ST-17500992
42-43	ST-17501039	124-25	ST-17500981
43	ST-17600004	126	ST-17500818
44-45	ST-17600005	127	ST-17500819
45	ST-17600006	128-29	ST-17501003
46	ST-17501007	130	ST-17500994
47	ST-17501022	131	ST-17500982
48-49	ST-17501010	132	ST-17500996
49	ST-17501037	133	ST-17500983
50-51	ST-17500873	134-35	ST-17500790
52-53	ST-17501035	136-37	ST-17500999
54-55	ST-17600007	138-39	ST-17501000
56	ST-17501038	140	ST-17501049
57	ST-17500642	141	ST-17501046
58	ST-17501015	142-43	ST-17500887
59	ST-17501021	144	ST-17500839
60-61	ST-17501026	145	STM-025122269
62-63	ST-17501018	146-47	STM-036326329
63	ST-17501008	148	ST-20002370-0039
64	ST-17501025	148-49	STM-011079877
65	ST-17501027	150-51	STM-018834161
66	ST-17500703	152-53	STM-036326289
67	ST-17500702	154-55	STM-078030023
68	ST-17501014	155	[Public Domain]
68-69	ST-17501030	156-57	STM-091396302
70	ST-17500985	156-57	STM-091396340
71	ST-17500733	156-57	STM-091396372
72	ST-17501004	156-57	STM-091411638
73	ST-17500748	156-57	STM-091412436
74	ST-17501013	156-57	STM-091569825
75	ST-17501045	156-57	STM-091854521
76	ST-17501031	156-57	STM-092487550
76-77	ST-17501020	156-57	STM-092737494
78-79	ST-17501011	158-59	STM-094844722
79	ST-17501012		
80	ST-17501017		
80-81	ST-17501023		
82-83	ST-17501009		
83	ST-17501028		
84-85	ST-17500734		
86	ST-17500881		
87	ST-17500882		
88-89	ST-17500705		

To learn more about the collection, go to: https://images.chicagohistory.org/chicago-sun-times-collection

All images © Sun-Times Media, LLC. All rights reserved.

Note: Captions in the book are followed by the date of a photograph and by the photographer's name when known.

SUN-TIMES PHOTOGRAPHY COLLECTION PHOTOGRAPHERS

Photo files from four Chicago newspapers make up the Sun-Times Photography Collection. This is a partial list of photographers employed by these newspapers. They are listed under the first newspaper where they worked.

Chicago Daily Times
Russell "Bud" Daley, Sol Davis, Art Elwing, George Emme, Mike Fish, Norman E. Grantham, Thomas Howard, Borrie Kanter, George Kotalik, Mel Larson, Dante Mascione, Louis Okmin, Rocco Padulo Jr., William Pauer, Bob Rankin, Mickey Rito, Edward T. Smith, Paul Steger, William A. Vendetta, Al Westelin, Cassie Williams, William Winek.

Chicago Sun
Leonard Bass, William Bender, Anthony Bianco, Louise Clarke, Aldis Darre, Ralph Frost, Charles Gekler, Clyde Hodges, Bill Knefel, Albert Kolin, Joseph Kordick, Felix Kubik, Glenn Malme, Dave Mann, Sid Mautner, John Mendicino, Al Mosse, Harold Norman, John Pagoria, Marjorie Parsons, Carmen Reporto, Al Risser, Bill Sturm, Al Vicker, Doris Wallace, Ralph Walters, Vern Williams.

Chicago Daily News
Mat Anderson, Emmet Barden, Don Bierman, Alden Brown, Clyde T. Brown, Ray Burley, Edward DeLuga, William DeLuga, Richard Derk, Joe Erhardt, Dave Fornell, Henry Herr Gill, Joe Gorg, Keith Hale, Russell V. Hamm, Martha Hartnett, Kevin Horan, John Jaqua, Edmund Jarecki, Luther Joseph, Hartland Klotz, Charles Krejcsi, M. Leon Lopez, Joe Marino, Andrew T. Miller, Russell Ogg, George Peebles, John Puslis, Perry C. Riddle, Elliott Robinson, LaVelda Rowe, LaVona Rowe, Paul Sequeira, Gary Settle, Fred Stein, Robert Stiewe, John Tweedle, John H. White, Joseph Zack.

Chicago Sun-Times
Amanda Alcock, John Arabinko, Ralph Arvidson, Bob Black, Don Burk, Richard A. Chapman, Charles Cherney, André Chung, Annie Costabile, Tom Cruze, Robert A. Davis, Eddie Dean, Louis DeLuca, James DePree, Eliza Davidson, Ellen Domke, Jack Dykinga, Bob Fila, Jim Frost, Ashlee Rezin Garcia, Louis Giampa, Larry Graff, Maria de la Guardia, Duane Hall, Rich Hein, Brian Jackson, Justin Jackson, Barry Jarvinen, John Keating, John J. Kim, Chuck Kirman, Jim Klepitsch, Jessica Koscielniak, Bob Kotalik, Jean Lachat, Bob Langer, Tyler LaRiviere, Randy Leffingwell, Jack Lenahan, Howard Lyon, Bill Mares, Jim Mendenhall, Jim Mescall, Pablo Martínez Monsiváis, Pat Nabong, Dom Najolia, Andrew Nelles, Larry Nocerino, Art Owens, Merrill Palmer, Vaughn Patterson, Gene Pesek, Clarence "Pete" Peters, Al Podgorski, John Rammel, Robert A. Reeder, Kathleen Reeve, Bob Ringham, Bob Rubel, Jon Sall, Michael Schmidt, Al Seib, Howard D. Simmons, Pete Souza, Scott Stewart, Nancy Stuenkel, Anthony Suau, Jerry Tomaselli, Ernie Torres, Anthony Vazquez, Phil Velasquez.

ACKNOWLEDGMENTS

We would like to thank Britta Keller Arendt, Bianca Barcenas, Charles E. Bethea, Karen Burke, Caleb Burroughs, Cate Cahan, Thom Clark, Robin Daughtridge, Allison Davis, Donna Edgar, Edwin Eisendrath, Judy Fidkowski, Emma Florio, Chris Fusco, Chris Galbreath, Rey Garcia, Jeffrey Garrett, Paul Gaynor, Daniel Greene, Dae Hannah, Rich Hein, Kenan Heise, Lucy Hereford, Ginny Holbert, Todd Hochberg, Brittany Hutchinson, Mark Jacob, Caedan Jinks, Julius L. Jones, Bob Langer, Joel Lerner, Katie Levi, Joshua Mabe, Matt Marton, Kayla McCarthy, Colleen McGaughey, Tom McNamee, Gretchen Neidhardt, Liesl Olson, Timothy Paton Jr., Arthur Melville Pearson, Gordon Quinn, Toby Roberts, Jon Rosenblatt, Ike Saunders, Howard D. Simmons, Gerry Souter, Fred Stein, Jennifer Streff, Ernie Torres, Eric Taylor, Carlos Tortolero, Ellen Placey Wadey, Rob Warden, Steven Warmbir, Nykia Wright, and the students and faculty from Lake Forest College and DePaul University who helped process the collection.

PERMISSIONS

Grateful acknowledgment is made to authors and publishers for permission to reprint previous published material:

Axelrod, David. Believer: My Forty Years in Politics. Penguin, 2015.

Black Jr., Timuel D. Sacred Ground: The Chicago Streets of Timuel Black. Northwestern University Press, 2019.

Bray, Rosemary L. Unafraid of the Dark: A Memoir. Anchor, 1999.

Breo, Dennis L., William J. Martin, and Bill Kunkle. The Crime of the Century: Richard Speck and the Murders That Shocked a Nation. Simon and Schuster, 2016.

Coval, Kevin. A People's History of Chicago. Breakbeat Poets, 2017.

Gilpin, Toni. The Long Deep Grudge: A Story of Big Capital, Radical Labor, and Class War in the American Heartland. Haymarket Books, 2020.

McBride, Michele. The Fire That Will Not Die. Etc Publications, 1979.

Moore, Natalie Y. The South Side: A Portrait of Chicago and American Segregation. St. Martin's Press, 2016.

Royko, Mike. "Royko's Tribute: Daley Embodied Chicago." Chicago Daily News. December 21, 1976

Satter, Beryl. Family Properties: Race, Real Estate, and the Exploitation of Black Urban America. Metropolitan Books, 2010.

Simpson, Rosie. "'64 Boycott Raw: Rosie Simpson Interview." Kartemquin Films via Media Burn Archive, 1:37:31. https://mediaburn.org/video/rosie-simpson/

Till-Mobley, Mamie, and Christopher Benson. Death of Innocence: The Story of the Hate Crime That Changed America. Random House, 2011.

Wilbon, Michael. "In Streets and Stands, Chicago Mourns for a Favorite Son." Washington Post. December 3, 1984